T0166991

Praise for *Ballots*

"The history of our nation is a history of racial injustice and the fight to rectify it. In compelling prose, Jim Robenalt's *Ballots and Bullets* does the vital work of shedding light on a pivotal moment in our nation's history, when justice, civil rights, and the unfulfilled promise of America hung in the balance. His intense focus on Cleveland—the first major US city to elect an African American leader to the mayor's office—reminds us how quintessentially American Cleveland's story truly is."

> —**Dan Moulthrop**, CEO, City Club of Cleveland

"This important book recalls some agonizing history, but it is a history we must not forget. With the passage of fifty years, one can ask, as Robenalt does, why has there been so little progress in race relations? Healing starts with honesty and recognition. The pathology of racism continues to stain our land and my enduring concern is whether there is hope for real change."

> —**Walter Beach**, former Cleveland Browns champion and assistant to Cleveland mayor Carl B. Stokes (1967–1968)

"*Ballots and Bullets* is well written, well researched, and accurate. Any reader will be touched both in mind and heart."

> —**Joan Brown Campbell**, general secretary, National Council of Churches, and director of religion, Chautauqua Institution

"A beautiful and moving portrait of a city that explains so much about our racial politics, then and now. Robenalt weaves together the stories of famous and not-so-famous black political leaders to show the consequences of racism and the ways that various leaders have tried to address it. An important topic that everyone would benefit from learning more about."

> —**Michael Smerconish**, CNN host and Sirius XM radio journalist

"With gripping storytelling, James Robenalt recounts and documents the destructive forces of racism and poverty that led to tragedy in Cleveland in 1968. *Bullets and Ballots* is also a tale of leadership—effective and not—that can be instructive as leaders face the challenges that, unfortunately, persist."

—**Nancy H. Rogers**, professor emeritus and former dean, Ohio State University Moritz College of Law, and former Ohio attorney general

BALLOTS AND BULLETS

BLACK POWER POLITICS AND URBAN GUERRILLA WARFARE IN 1968 CLEVELAND

JAMES ROBENALT

Lawrence Hill Books

Chicago

The Library of Congress has cataloged the hardcover edition as follows:
Names: Robenalt, James D., 1956– author.
Title: Ballots and bullets : Black Power politics and urban guerrilla warfare
    in 1968 Cleveland / James Robenalt.
Description: Chicago, Illinois : Lawrence Hill Books, an imprint of Chicago
    Review Press Incorporated, 2018. | Includes bibliographical references and
    index.
Identifiers: LCCN 2017061417 (print) | LCCN 2017051090 (ebook) | ISBN
    9780897337342 (Kindle) | ISBN 9780897337168 (epub) | ISBN 9780897337045
    (Adobe pdf) | ISBN 9780897337038 (cloth)
Subjects: LCSH: Cleveland (Ohio)—Race relations—History—20th century. |
    Black power—Ohio—Cleveland—History—20th century. | Race
    riots—Ohio—Cleveland—History—20th century. | African
    Americans—Ohio—Cleveland—Politics and government—20th century. |
    Police-community relations—Ohio—Cleveland—History—20th century. |
    Cleveland (Ohio)—Politics and government—20th century.
Classification: LCC F499.C69 (print) | LCC F499.C69 N47 2018 (ebook) | DDC
    305.8009771/32—dc23
LC record available at https://lccn.loc.gov/2017061417

Unless otherwise noted, all photos are from the Cleveland Public Library
Collection/Photograph Collection.

Cover design: John Yates at Stealworks
Cover image: Cleveland Public Library Collection/Photograph Collection
Typesetting: Nord Compo
Map illustrator: Chris Erichsen

To Detective Louis G. Garcia, who made it his life's work to remember the awful cost of July 23, 1968. And to Mutawaf Shaheed, who introduced me to the world of the 1968 black nationalists. I could not have written this book without their keen insights, wisdom, and open-mindedness.

Contents

1

"Watch Yourself, Willie"

WHO WAS THIS MAN? PATROLMAN Kenny Gibbons, Badge 285, remembers him like it was yesterday.

When Kenny and his partner, Willard Wolff, lurched to a stop in Car 505—a black-and-white 1964 Ford station wagon marked "Cleveland Police" on both sides with a standard dome on the top—they found themselves in the middle of the intersection of Lakeview Road and Auburndale Avenue in the Glenville neighborhood on the East Side of Cleveland.

That's when Kenny saw the man standing in front of the two-story brick apartment house. He was in plainclothes and tall—at least six feet, four inches—with a blond crew cut, and he held a revolver in his hand. He had a young black man apparently in custody on the ground and he was gesturing vigorously to Kenny and his partner to come over. As Kenny and his partner approached the intersection of Lakeview and Auburndale (Wolff was driving that shift), both had heard two distinct gunshots. Now, Kenny assumed the gunfire was from the plainclothes man—perhaps warning shots to get the black man on the ground.

Sometimes a traumatic event can eradicate memory, and sometimes it leaves an indelible mark. This was an instance of the latter: Kenny has a precise memory of the scene.

The black man was spread-eagled with his face in the dirt and his hands above his head. He did not appear to be injured. An iron fence, not very high, enclosed the small front yard of the apartment house. The black man lay prostrate inside the fenced-in area; the plainclothes man was standing outside it, in a driveway between the apartment building and the Lakeview Tavern, a seedy neighborhood joint that occupied the corner of Auburndale and Lakeview, its front door opening on the Auburndale side.

After pulling Car 505 slightly to the wrong side of Lakeview, Kenny and Willie Wolff jumped out. While they had a 12-gauge shotgun in the car, neither Kenny nor Willie Wolff could release it from its locked rack in between the passenger side and the driver's seat. They were moving too fast and this was a two-man operation. The lock seemed to be jammed. "There is a button which the driver would have to press and the man on the passenger side would then release it," Kenny later testified.[1] Both Kenny and Patrolman Wolff had drawn their pistols, .38 revolvers, as they approached a scene that sizzled with danger, the kind that made their job exciting. Adrenaline highs were a reason to come to work.

"Watch yourself, Willie," Kenny cautioned his partner as they exited the car.

Kenny walked up to the plainclothes man. "We talked for just a second," Kenny would later relate, "and the outcome was that he was going to get a wagon or a car, to take this man that was lying down there."[2]

Then the man trotted away.

Strange, Kenny thought, we have a wagon right here. Why is he running in a different direction?

Kenny turned his attention to the black male on the ground. "I said to this fellow, 'Just relax and everything will be all right,'" Kenny testified. "And he acknowledged."

Just that quickly, Kenny felt a sting in his stomach area. "And the next thing, I felt a slight tap in the stomach and put my hand down and I was covered with blood."

Patrolman Kenneth Gibbons had been shot with a high-powered rifle, an M-2 that had been stolen from a military base some months earlier.

"Then, out of instinct, I started running back for our zone car," he said. Everything became a blur. He could not hear the gunshots, but he was hit multiple times. "There must have been something happened," he said, "because I got shot about six more times."

He was full of holes when he turned the corner around the Lakeview Tavern. He testified he was shot "in the stomach, one in the groin, one through the back, one through the back of the arm, one off the top of my head, and one through the top of my shoulder."

This was not a shotgun, with buckshot pellets, causing the damage. His wounds were from a high-powered rifle. The entrance wounds were small and the exit wounds were "ten times as big as the entrance wounds," he testified. As the prosecutor would later characterize it, the Cleveland Police had squirt guns when compared to the military rifles and armor-piercing ammo they faced. A .38 pistol was no match for a semiautomatic rifle.

Somehow Kenny survived. Several plainclothes detectives who arrived just after Car 505 grabbed Kenny and put him in the back of their car and rushed him to Lakeside Hospital.[3]

Patrolman Wolff was not so fortunate. He was shot with another rifle from inside the apartment house, and the bullet landed right between his eyes. The bullet entered just near the left side of his nose and lodged deep in his brain. He fell dead where he stood, blood spurting from his face.

Willard Wolff was seriously impaired when he was shot. The coroner discovered during the posting of Wolff's body the next day in autopsy that he had a blood alcohol level of 0.25 percent. In Ohio today a blood alcohol content of 0.08 percent is enough to be deemed a drunk driver.

Wolff was five feet, ten inches tall, and weighed 220 pounds. "The average person would need between 14 and 15 ounces of hard liquor, drunk one on top the other, to get to a blood alcohol of 0.25 percent," Dr. Lester Adelson, one of the pathologists, testified about Wolff's state of inebriation at the time of his death.[4] A blood alcohol level of 0.35 to 0.45, Dr. Adelson explained, was considered enough to cause an individual to lapse into a coma.

But all these years later, Kenny Gibbons still wonders: Who was the tall blond plainclothes person holding a black person in custody just before the bullets flew from the apartment? Willard Wolff was not the only police officer killed that night—three were killed, twelve were injured, most with severe wounds from high-velocity missiles fired from rifles or pellets from shotguns. Three black nationalists were known dead and others were suspected to have been injured or killed, many in a house that was set afire and allowed to burn to the ground. The charred remains of the residence were bulldozed by the city of Cleveland days later and no one was ever given a chance to search for human remains.

But obviously a witness who was present at the start of the shoot-out would have been an important source to explain how this gunfire started and then mushroomed out of control on that bloody night of July 23, 1968. Certainly, if he were a member of the Cleveland Police Department, one would think he would be easily identified—tall, military bearing, blond crew cut, on duty that evening.

But Kenny Gibbons testified that no one was ever able to identify this mystery man. Asked during a trial if he had ever seen the man after the incident, Gibbons answered, "No, I haven't."[5]

Yet, after his testimony, Kenny did see the man again. On a break during the trial, Kenny stopped down in the basement of the courthouse to visit a coffee shop run by a man who was blind. And there he was—the tall man with the blond crew cut.

Kenny approached him—happy to see him. "I want to talk with you about what happened that night," he said to the man.

"I don't know anything about it," the man replied, and then, just as he had done that awful night, he wheeled and quickly walked away.[6]

2

"We Will Meet Violence with Violence and Lynching with Lynching"

IF YOU ASKED ROBERT FRANKLIN Williams, the town of Monroe, North Carolina, was never given its due in the firmament of the black power movement in the United States. Williams became the head of the local NAACP chapter in Monroe in the late 1950s. It was in this role that he believed he changed the arc of history for African Americans.

Monroe was a town of ten thousand people, located about twenty miles southeast of Charlotte. It was considered to be a regional headquarters for the Ku Klux Klan and the town's black population was crowded into a section of the city called Newtown. Robert Williams was born in Newtown in 1925. His grandmother had been a slave.[1]

When he was young, he witnessed a Monroe police officer, Jesse Helms Sr., the father of the future US senator, brutalize a black woman in a confrontation where Helms Sr. beat and dragged the woman through the streets of Monroe.

As part of the Second Great Migration, Williams moved to Detroit to find work as a machinist in World War II. He was drafted in 1944 and served a year and a half in the marines (still segregated at the time) before being discharged and later moving back to Monroe.

"I learned more from the Marine Corps than anywhere else," Williams said in an interview, "because of the way they operated, the discipline, the way they dealt in fear—all kinds of things." Williams became the leader of a group of local black war veterans in Monroe and organized them to oppose KKK terrorism. He applied for a charter from the National Rifle Association, falsifying the occupations of his membership in the application, "making them think we were white people," he said. "A cook became a restaurateur; a brick mason became a construction firm owner, and so forth." The NRA charter allowed the men to buy arms, including high-powered rifles, and they practiced shooting in the country, forming a small but disciplined "Black Guard" in Monroe.[2]

The pivotal event for Williams came during the trial of a white man who had been accused of attempting to rape a pregnant black woman. Incensed over the incident, local blacks wanted to take the law into their own hands and at least threaten the white man by spraying his home with bullets from rifles and machine guns. Williams as the head of the local NAACP did not approve.

When the white man was acquitted of the charge before his trial even began, Williams was blamed by black citizens for the failure of the justice system. "All the women in the courtroom turned to me and said, 'If it hadn't been for you, that man would have been punished,'" he remembered. "'Now you've opened the floodgates on us; they feel they can do anything to us with impunity.'"

This rebuke prodded Williams to make a statement on the courthouse steps. He told reporters, "From this day forward, we are going to meet violence with violence, lynchings with lynchings. We are going to become our own judges, our own prosecutors, and our own executioners." A reporter from the United Press International who took down the statement gave Williams a chance to take it back later that night before publishing it. Williams refused and the story appeared in newspapers across the country.

"Next day, it was just like the world was on fire," Williams remembered. "People were calling from everywhere."

Roy Wilkins, the executive secretary of the NAACP in New York City, was one of the callers. He instructed Williams to retract the statement and apologize to white America. Williams said no. "I said, 'Well, if white America is going to apologize to me first for what they've done to us, I will apologize to them.'" The NAACP suspended Williams. "The NAACP does not and has never in its history advocated violence," Wilkins wrote in a statement. According to a *New York Times* article, "Other Negro leaders assailed Mr. Williams's statement."[3]

"This is why you've never heard of Monroe," Williams said decades later, "because there was a conspiracy out there to keep this quiet and not let people know it was effective." His incendiary statements were picked up overseas—in Cuba, in China, and in Africa. "Those people didn't believe in turning the other cheek," Williams said of radicals in these developing nations, "so to them, at last they saw the possibility of some manhood developing among the black struggle in the United States."

According to Williams, a demonstration at a swimming pool in Monroe was the inspiration for his book, *Negroes with Guns*. Williams drove some black high school boys to the all-white community pool, which had been built with federal funds, to demand that blacks be entitled to swim with whites, or at least that blacks have their own separate days set aside for swimming. An angry crowd of whites confronted Williams and the young men, not knowing that they were armed. As the mob closed in on the car, they began to chant, "Kill the niggers, burn the niggers, pour gasoline on the niggers." Williams emerged from his car with a rifle, an Italian carbine. A police officer crept up behind him, hoping to take a shot at Williams from the back, but one of the high school youngsters in the car pulled a pistol and pointed it with trembling hand at the officer, telling him to reholster his gun or he was going to blow his head off. The officer began to retreat, stepped back, and eventually fell into a ditch, causing the crowd to disperse.

Williams saw an old white man who had witnessed this scene, likely drunk Williams thought, begin to weep. "Oh, oh, oh," the old man slowly sobbed, "what has this goddamn country come to? The niggers got guns and the police can't even arrest them."

This was a moment of clarity for Williams. He realized that the old man had been crying because "the gun had been the thing that had always kept them on top—and the police power—and he could see that slipping away," he said.

"This is why I named the book *Negroes with Guns*," Williams later explained, "cause it meant that when we got guns the same as everybody else, we would be treated the same way." Williams said this was not to excuse "guns for the sake of guns" or violence, but it meant "a controlled situation, well-disciplined, well-led." Blacks with guns would lead, he thought, to a sort of balance of power, and this would be to "the advantage of the general public to maintain peaceful relations."

The danger Williams posed was too great not to draw consequences. An event in Monroe in late August 1961 created a pretext to threaten Williams and his family. (He and his wife had two young boys.) Tensions were at a boiling point that summer when reactionary whites blockaded Newtown and drove through Monroe with signs like, "Coon season open," and "Death to all niggers and nigger lovers." Williams's garrisoned home became the center of activity for a group of Freedom Riders—northern civil rights activists, many white college students, who were bused into the South in the summer of 1961. They came south to challenge the continuing segregation of public transportation that had been outlawed as a result of recent Supreme Court cases.

Many of the northerners went into the town to picket at the courthouse on Sunday, August 27, 1961. They were attacked and some were arrested. Thousands of Klansmen poured into the city, threatening to kill Williams. A white couple, not involved in the violence, accidentally drove through the black neighborhood on the way to visit family, and they were stopped by an angry black mob. Williams intervened and allowed the couple to stay in his house for protection and then suggested they leave a few hours later around 9:00 PM when the crowds had diminished. Word spread in Monroe that Williams and some of the Freedom Riders had kidnapped the white couple.

Williams received a menacing phone call that night from an anonymous caller who told him that state troopers were on their way and that he would be lynched that evening in the courthouse square. He gathered his family and left immediately. He made his way to New York City, where he saw that the FBI had issued a wanted poster, as a federal warrant for his arrest had been filed, charging Williams with "unlawful interstate flight to avoid prosecution for kidnapping." The FBI poster warned that Williams "should be considered armed and extremely dangerous."

Williams fled to Canada and from there to Fidel Castro's Cuba, where he was welcomed and given political asylum. Castro himself intervened on behalf of Williams to embarrass the United States. Williams established a radio program in Cuba called "Radio Free Dixie," a play on "Radio Free Europe," the US-funded anti-Communist propaganda broadcasting organization in Europe aimed at the countries behind the so-called Iron Curtain. Robert F. Williams, through his book and his broadcasts, would become an inspiration for the black power movement in the United States and political activists like Huey P. Newton, the founder of the Black Panther Party.

One of the Freedom Riders who was in Williams's home the night of the alleged kidnapping was an African American named Willie Mae Mallory, who preferred to go by Mae. She was the thirty-four-year-old mother of three children from Brooklyn and had come to Monroe to help out with cooking and housekeeping while the Freedom Riders were in residence. Like Williams, she was indicted in Monroe for kidnapping the white couple.

Mae Mallory also escaped, returning to New York City, likely with Robert Williams and his family. She then hitchhiked to Cleveland, where she stayed with friends on the city's East Side. On October 12, 1961, the FBI arrested Mallory under a flight-to-avoid-prosecution warrant. The governor's request from North Carolina for extradition came to the desk of Ohio's Democratic governor, Mike DiSalle, a death penalty opponent who supported John F. Kennedy in Ohio in 1960. Mallory's Ohio lawyers argued that she would be killed if she returned to Monroe, which they claimed had become a lawless city.

Governor DiSalle granted the extradition request in February 1962 and the battle switched to the Ohio courts, with Mallory being incarcerated in the Cuyahoga County jail. The Cleveland *Plain Dealer* was not particularly sympathetic to her plight. "To back up big, portly, bearded Robert F. Williams, a Castro admirer, in that rights fight, Mrs. Mallory rode down from Brooklyn, NY. She got entangled as a headquarters helper for the Freedom Riders," the paper wrote about her in August 1962. "Six months in jail have not made the Brooklyn housewife less plump, less quick tongued, or less militant."[4]

Her case, like that of Robert Williams, received international attention. According to Mallory, when the president and first lady visited Mexico City they were greeted with signs that read, "Libertad para Mae Mallory." She was not sanguine about the prospects of intervention by the Kennedy administration in her case. "I'm afraid the Kennedy administration can save only one Afro-American, and that's Reverend Martin Luther King," she told the *Plain Dealer*. "And they always get HIM out of jail."[5]

Mae Mallory was no great fan of Dr. King. "If the people in Boston Harbor had got on their knees to pray, the way Rev. King and his group are doing in Albany, Georgia, they'd have wound up in the ocean with the tea," she said from her jail cell. Her reading convinced her of one key difference between Gandhi's passive resistance campaign in India and the nonviolence policy of Dr. King in the United States. "One thing Gandhi had going for him we don't have going for us," she said. "The Indians were a majority in their own country. We American Negroes are a minority."

She likened blacks in America to colonial peoples around the world who were engaged in freedom movements. "We are colonials in the country which colonized us," she said. "We were brought here as a labor force. Now automation is here, so we're no longer needed as laborers. Something's got to happen with us. They're going to suggest extermination next."

She knew her status as a political prisoner was being watched, around the country and the world. "Keeping me in jail—all that does is put the spotlight on American justice," she said.

By January 1964, her long legal fight against extradition neared its end. Appeals to the US Supreme Court had produced nothing— the court refused to intervene. Mae Mallory was embittered. She told the news reporters in Cleveland that she expected to be a martyr. When asked to explain what she meant, she said, "It all depends on your definition of martyr. My life is now in the hands of the great white fathers."[6]

On the same day that Mrs. Mallory was losing her extradition battle, the Eighty-Eighth Congress of the United States formally took up a civil rights bill that had been championed by President Kennedy before his assassination in November 1963. The deliberation started when the Chairman of the House Rules Committee ruled that the bill could be brought to the House floor for debate and voting. "The civil-rights battle of the second session of the 88th Congress was, at that moment, launched," a writer from the *Plain Dealer* reported in an article that appeared on the same front page that carried a photo of shackled Mae Mallory in a sheriff's custody being led from the county jail.[7]

Mae Mallory was put on trial with three others before an all-white jury in Monroe, North Carolina.[8] She was quickly convicted—the jury deliberated for just thirty-five minutes—and was sentenced to sixteen to twenty years in prison.[9] The lone white defendant, John C. Lowry, a twenty-three-year-old Freedom Rider from Flushing, New York, was sentenced to three to five years. "The case ended as I expected it to," Mrs. Mallory said, "and I will probably spend the rest of my life in jail because of my color."

Against this backdrop, Dr. Martin Luther King Jr. and Malcolm X, opposing forces in the civil rights movement, each came to Cleveland at decisive moments in their careers. They came to deliver messages of contrasting strategies that they believed would be necessary to change attitudes of white Americans. Both would be invited to the same forum, Cory Methodist Church, an African American church in the Cleveland neighborhood of Glenville, located a mile from where black nationalists would take up arms against Cleveland police in the summer of 1968.

3

"We Will Meet Physical Force with Soul Force"

THE BUILDINGS THAT HOUSE CORY United Methodist Church in Glenville were originally constructed in 1920 as the city's largest synagogue in an area of town that had become a Jewish enclave. More than a place of worship, the complex of buildings became a Jewish Center with a 2,400-seat auditorium, a gymnasium, an indoor pool, and a branch of the Cleveland Hebrew Schools.

But after World War II, the Jewish Center was sold to Cory Methodist Church, one of the oldest African American churches in Cleveland.

In its early days as a village before being annexed by the city, Glenville, situated five miles northeast of the downtown, was considered the "garden spot" of Cuyahoga County. It was "the summer playground of wealthy Clevelanders" who built mansions on the lakefront and in the pastoral surroundings set back from the lake. One of the most famous trotting tracks in the nation was located in Glenville before it was declared illegal in 1908.[1]

Between 1920 and 1930, the surge of Jewish settlers changed the face of Glenville so that by 1939, 65 percent of Glenville families were Jewish. But the Jews who had migrated from the Central district in downtown Cleveland were followed by African Americans from the same area who soon began to outnumber the Jewish residents; the Jews in turn moved farther east to Cleveland Heights. One scholar has suggested that African Americans found areas for residential expansion in Jewish neighborhoods in Cleveland because, in the main, "Jews did not violently resist black influx, in contrast to ethnic Roman Catholics whose more permanent, less 'portable' religious edifices (to mention one factor) made them more prone to territoriality."[2]

By 1961 the *Plain Dealer* wrote of Glenville, "Overcrowding in houses on some of the streets has become a blighting influence. It has come about because the expanding Negro population is confined to certain circumscribed areas and because home purchasers, obliged to pay more than they should, are compelled to take in roomers or share living space with other families to help meet mortgage payments."[3]

In the spring of 1963 at the height of his Birmingham campaign, Dr. Martin Luther King Jr. came to Cory. The African American newspaper in Cleveland, the *Call and Post*, appreciated the symbolism of the visit, noting that King would speak at "a former Jewish temple," ornamented with stars of David and scores of Hebrew sayings and emblems on the walls, as the "dark Moses of today."[4] Another writer in the *Call and Post* called King simply, "America's irreplaceable 20th century Moses."[5]

Dr. King came to Cleveland to raise bail money. In April 1963 he led a nonviolent protest campaign in Birmingham directed at the removal of "white only" and "Negro only" signs in public areas and business establishments; the desegregation of lunch counters, drinking fountains, and restrooms; fair hiring practices by Birmingham businesses; and the reopening of parks and swimming pools on an integrated basis. King labeled Birmingham "the most segregated city in the country."

The campaign was a joint effort by the Southern Christian Leadership Conference (SCLC) and the Alabama Christian Movement for Human Rights, led by a Birmingham clergyman named Fred Shuttlesworth. The activists intended to put pressure on Birmingham merchants during Easter, a major shopping season in Birmingham. Their tactic was to employ nonviolence—sit-ins, marches, and a boycott of local merchants. As King explained, "We don't have to use violence. Our belief in nonviolence weakens [the bigots'] morale, and it works on his conscience. He doesn't know what to do. . . . So put us in jail, and we shall still love you. Burn our homes, beat us, put dogs on us, and we will wear you down."[6]

The operation was launched on April 3, 1963, and over the next weeks hundreds and then thousands were arrested. Money—and a lot of it—was needed to pay bail bonds for the protesters. The city of Birmingham's leaders obtained an injunction preventing further protests on April 10, and King and his SCLC associate, the Reverend Ralph Abernathy, decided to engage in civil disobedience by ignoring the injunction, knowing they would be arrested. On April 12, Good Friday, King and Abernathy were arrested and King was placed in solitary confinement. (President Kennedy had to intervene to insist that King be allowed to talk by phone to his wife, who was home recovering from the birth of their fourth child.) Though they could have scraped together funds for their own bail, King and Abernathy chose to remain in jail, where King wrote his famous "Letter from Birmingham Jail."

Responding to criticisms from moderate white clergymen to the Birmingham protests, King wrote in his letter, "We have waited for more than 340 years for our constitutional and God given rights." He pointed to the liberation movements around the world that were challenging imperialism and overthrowing colonial governments. "The nations of Asia and Africa are moving with jetlike speed toward gaining political independence," King wrote, "but we still creep at horse and buggy pace toward gaining a cup of coffee at a lunch counter."

King wrote that he could not stand by silently as conditions in Birmingham deteriorated. "Injustice anywhere is a threat to justice everywhere," he wrote from jail. "We are caught in an inescapable network of mutuality, tied in a single garment of destiny. Whatever affects one directly, affects all indirectly."

King and Abernathy finally accepted bail and were released on April 20, 1963.

King's problem was that there were not enough adults willing to go to jail in Birmingham, especially as funds for bail had been all but depleted. As a consequence, a local SCLC leader in Birmingham, James Bevel, recommended using teenagers and elementary schoolchildren in demonstrations. While controversial, the move was supported by Dr. King and led to the most searing but effective images from the civil rights movement.

On May 2 one thousand African American students began a march into downtown Birmingham. Multitudes were arrested. The next day, Eugene "Bull" Connor, Birmingham's safety commissioner, ordered his police forces and firemen to blast the children and their teenage and adult companions with high-powered fire hoses, set at a rate of flow that would strip bark from a tree. Police clubbed the protesters and sicced dogs on children and adults alike. The images of the raw police brutality were broadcast across the nation, and they outraged President Kennedy and leaders in Congress.

Businessmen in Birmingham had seen enough—they sought a moratorium on the boycott and protests in return for a promise to negotiate terms with the civil rights leaders. On Friday, May 10, King and Shuttlesworth announced a truce, facilitated in part with the help of Burke Marshall, an assistant attorney general in charge of the Civil Rights Division of the Department of Justice, whom Attorney General Robert F. Kennedy had sent to Birmingham. Later that evening, the hotel where King stayed—and where the peace had been negotiated— was bombed. The following day, King's brother's home in Birmingham was bombed, too.[7] But the tenuous peace held.[8]

Days later, King, Abernathy, and Shuttlesworth were on their way to Cleveland on separate planes (they never traveled together) to speak at Cory Methodist Church to raise funds "for the legal defense and bonds of the more than 3,000 persons who have overflowed Birmingham's penal institutions," the *Call and Post* reported on Saturday, May 11.[9]

The day of King's arrival was like no other in the history of Cleveland's African American community. He came to Cleveland because of the strong connection between its African American citizens and Alabama.

There were two large migrations of African Americans to Cleveland, both associated with the world wars in the twentieth century. Among newcomers from the Deep South to Cleveland, a majority hailed from Alabama.[10] It was not uncommon to refer to Cleveland as "Alabama North." One of the coordinators of special projects for King and SCLC, Carole Hoover, told the *Plain Dealer* that Dr. King's struggles in Birmingham resonated with the black community in Cleveland "because nearly two-thirds of them came from Alabama."[11]

News that the rights leaders were coming to Cleveland was well advertised in the black press and by ministers in African American

churches on Cleveland's East Side on Sunday, May 12, who encouraged
their congregants to turn out for King's speech.[12] When King arrived at
Cleveland Hopkins International Airport on Tuesday he was mobbed
by supporters and reporters.

Thousands began lining up outside Cory Methodist Church early
in the day, though King was not scheduled to speak until 7:30 PM, and
traffic backed up for miles around the church. King spoke briefly at the
mostly white St. Paul's Episcopal Church in Cleveland Heights in the late
afternoon, but the area around Cory Methodist was so congested that
King, Abernathy, and Shuttlesworth were forced to speak to thousands
at three other black churches on the East Side before reaching Cory at
8:45 PM. Cory normally seated 2,800 people, but on that evening nearly
4,000 jammed into church, waiting anxiously for King, singing and praying and speechifying.[13] At least 5,000 more gathered around the church
to listen through loudspeakers.

Dr. Martin Luther King Jr. at Cory Methodist Church, May 14,
1963. He came to Cleveland at the height of the Birmingham
campaign. *Western Reserve Historical Society*

Cleveland police had to clear a path for King to make it to the pulpit to speak. As he entered, the church erupted with applause and cheering. King was overwhelmed with his reception. "I can assure you," he said, "that I have never seen a more aroused response than that I have seen in Cleveland, Ohio, tonight."

He told those assembled of the terrible hatred shown to the Birmingham protesters. "As we face the dogs, the tanks of Bull Connor," he said, "our people are not facing them alone. We must blot out segregation now, henceforth, and forever." He called segregation a cancer, a "new form of slavery." Segregation, he declared, "is the illegitimate child, born of the illicit intercourse between injustice and immorality." One line brought a particularly strong reaction: "There comes a time when people get tired of being trampled by the iron feet of oppression." He was greeted with "thunderous applause."[14]

King was convinced nonviolence was the only answer. "We will meet physical force with soul force," he intoned in his distinctive baritone. "I am committed to nonviolence as a way of life."[15]

Following King, Ralph Abernathy told the audience of a letter he had received from a detractor that suggested that "we get all the Negroes together in America and send them back to Africa." Abernathy replied, "When the Irish go back to Ireland, when the Germans go back to Germany, when the Frenchmen go back to France . . . and when the white man gives this country back to the Indians . . ." He was unable to complete his sentence the cheering grew so loud with each provocation.

Baskets were distributed for collection and over $12,000 was raised in this one night.[16] The "Messiah from Birmingham," as King was labeled, returned to Alabama with a war chest to continue his fight. They sang "We Shall Overcome" in Cleveland.

That year, *Time* magazine would name Dr. King the "Man of the Year," and in 1964 he would win the Nobel Peace Prize for his work in Birmingham. *Time* recognized Dr. King as the representative of African Americans, "for whom 1963 was perhaps the most important year in their history." It declared Birmingham "the main battleground of the Negro Revolution, and Martin Luther King Jr. the leader of the Negroes in Birmingham, became to millions, black and white, in the South and North, the symbol of the revolution—and the Man of the Year."[17]

King was described as having no peer in the movement for black freedom, but he knew that in the North one man had grown up who was becoming his chief rival and a strident critic of nonviolence. Even in his "Letter from Birmingham Jail," King seemed to have sensed this counterforce. He wrote that he found himself standing "in the middle of two opposing forces in the Negro community." One was African Americans who were complacent, so "drained of self-respect and a sense of 'somebodiness' that they have adjusted to segregation." The other force, he wrote, was "one of bitterness and hatred," a group that had come "perilously close to advocating violence." He found this group expressing itself in "various black nationalist groups that are springing up across the nation, the largest and best known being Elijah Muhammad's Muslim movement," he wrote. "Nourished by the Negro's frustration over the continued existence of racial discrimination, this movement is made up of people who have lost faith in America, who have absolutely repudiated Christianity, and who have concluded that the white man is an incorrigible 'devil.'"

Elijah Muhammad was the founder of the Nation of Islam, but by 1963 his leading spokesman, a powerful, mesmerizing orator who had taken the name Malcolm X, was Dr. King's competitor in the North. As one astute scholar, Leonard Moore, noted, "The problems of the black urban poor required a different set of strategies and tactics" than those employed by Dr. King and the SCLC. "Malcolm X became the spokesman for the millions of northern urban lower-income blacks," Moore observed. "They flocked to hear the fiery orator who boldly shouted to the world what many blacks privately thought about white America. Also, his critique of the United States, his relentless emphasis on black self-determination, and his philosophy of self-defense captivated northern audiences. They embraced his indictment of the civil rights movement and its limited agenda."[18]

Many blacks needed no further proof of the empty promise of nonviolence than events in Birmingham following Dr. King's seeming victories in May 1963. Just four months later (after the August 1963 March on Washington and King's iconic "I Have a Dream" speech), the lead paragraph in the *New York Times* told of horrifying events in Birmingham on September 15, 1963: "A bomb severely damaged a Negro church today during Sunday school services, killing four Negro girls and setting off racial rioting and other violence in which two Negro boys were shot to death." The two boys killed were sixteen and thirteen years old, gunned down by police as they ran away after throwing rocks in rioting that followed the explosions at the church. The bombing came three days after the desegregation of three previously all-white schools in Birmingham.[19] Dr. King showed up later that day to assess the damage, powerless to change what had happened or to explain away the apparent triumph of violence over nonviolence.

President Kennedy made a push for a Civil Rights Act after Birmingham. The bombing at the 16th Street Baptist Church in September provoked northern Democrats to add new provisions to strengthen the bill weeks later. On October 29 the House Judiciary Committee finally approved the bill to go to a vote on the House floor. "If enacted, it would be the broadest civil rights legislation ever made law," the *New York Times* reported.[20]

Twenty-four days later, President Kennedy was shot and killed in Dallas, Texas.

Malcolm X, in a highly provocative and indefensible statement, said that the assassination was an example of "the chickens coming home to roost." He accused President Kennedy of "twiddling his thumbs" at the assassination of President Ngo Dinh Diem and his brother in South Vietnam.[21]

These shocking remarks would begin a chain of events that would result in Malcolm X splitting with the Nation of Islam. To explain that break, Malcolm X would come to Cory Methodist Church in Glenville in early April 1964, occupying the same pulpit from which King had spoken a year earlier.

Malcolm X's message, however, was anything but nonviolent.

4

"The Hate That Hate Produced"

MALCOLM X WAS SUSPENDED FROM the Nation of Islam by its leader, Elijah Muhammad, within days of his remarks about chickens coming home to roost. Muhammad said that Malcolm X's statements were not representative of Black Muslim attitudes. "With the rest of the world," Muhammad said, "we are very shocked at the assassination of our President."[1]

Malcolm X expressed his regret, taking his punishment, saying, "I shouldn't have said what I said." He told the press he would abide by Elijah Muhammad's decision and continue to administer the affairs of his mosque in New York City. "I believe absolutely in his wisdom and authority," he confirmed.

But a showdown was already looming. Malcolm X's visibility as the main spokesman for the Black Muslims was causing dissension within the movement. "Many of [Elijah Muhammad's] disciples have been saying recently, in fact, that Malcolm is exerting more influence than Mr. Muhammad himself," the New York Times reported on December 5, 1963.[2]

In May 1925 Malcolm was born in Omaha, Nebraska, but his family soon moved to Lansing, Michigan. His father, Earl Little, a Baptist preacher, and his mother, Louise Norton Little, were ardent followers of Jamaican-born Marcus Garvey, one of the early pioneers of black nationalism and Pan-Africanism, who advocated the return of the "African diaspora" to their ancestral lands. Garvey also founded the Universal Negro Improvement Association (UNIA), an organization dedicated to the "general uplift of the people of African ancestry of the world."

Reverend Earl Little's outspoken support for Garvey, the UNIA, and people of African descent made him a target of a Depression-era white supremacist offshoot of the Klan known as the "Black Legion." The Little home was burned to the ground in Lansing, and a few years later in 1931, when Malcolm was just six, his father was killed when he was run over by a streetcar, the question being whether it was an accident. Malcolm and his family believed, probably correctly, that their father had been murdered by the Black Legion. Malcolm would contend that two of his father's brothers were also killed by white violence. Malcolm's mother was later committed to a mental institution, and he and his siblings were raised in foster homes.

As a teenager, before he had completed junior high school, Malcolm moved to Boston with a close friend to live with an older sister. He ended up in Harlem and became known as the high-living "Detroit Red" (he had a naturally red tint to his hair). He was active in small-time street crime, eventually being arrested for burglary when he had moved back temporarily to the Roxbury neighborhood of Boston. He was sentenced to eight to ten years in a Massachusetts prison in 1946. While in prison Malcolm learned about the Nation of Islam from his siblings—one brother, Reginald, had already converted. Malcolm began to correspond with the Nation's leader, Elijah Muhammad, and decided to convert, too. He dropped the surname a white slave master had given one of his ancestors and began to be known as simply Malcolm X, with X representing the unknown African name of his ancestors. He was paroled in 1952 after being transferred to a Michigan prison.

The orthodoxy of the Nation of Islam was a strange mixture of black separatism, tenets of the Islamic faith, prophesies from the Bible and Koran, and cosmology. Elijah Muhammad, born Elijah Poole in Sandersville, Georgia, in 1897, was a diminutive light-skinned man with almond eyes and a slight lisp. He claimed to have witnessed three lynchings of black men while growing up in Georgia, including one man who had been a boyhood friend. A biographer describes Elijah as a child being approached in town by a neatly dressed white man who smiled at him and held out his hand, only to reveal the severed ear of a black man, a common prize from a lynching.[3]

Elijah was part of the first Great Migration north by many African Americans, moving to Detroit in 1923, just after World War I. There in 1930 he met an enigmatic man named Wallace D. Fard (or Wali D. Farrad or Farrad Muhammad), a speaker on black empowerment and the Islamic faith. Elijah became a follower and changed his surname at Fard's request to a Muslim name, Muhammad. Fard disappeared in 1934 and Elijah Muhammad told his followers that Wallace Fard Muhammad had come to earth as Allah in the flesh—God incarnate. Elijah Muhammad then proclaimed that Fard had revealed core teachings to him and that he was the "final Messenger of Allah." Muhammad eventually settled in Chicago, where he took control of Mosque No. 2 of the Nation of Islam, further consolidated his power, and developed the theology of his faith. He spent four years in prison for failing to register for the draft during World War II.[4]

Elijah Muhammad taught that blacks were the "original man" and that whites were an inferior and devious race, created six thousand years ago by a rogue Islamic scientist named Yakub on the island of Patmos, a eugenicist who fashioned the first whites from the mutated "germs" of blacks. This made whites the opposite of God—a race of devils. Allah placed blacks "on the top" but allowed their subjugation by the white tricksters and archdeceivers for six thousand years as the "so-called Negroes," yet the days of white domination were numbered. "We are the mighty, the wise, the best, but do not know it," Elijah Muhammad wrote. He warned his followers to "give up the white race's names and religion (Christianity)" in order to gain success. A great race war was coming, he foretold. "Do not let anyone fool you," he wrote. "This is the separation and the War of Armageddon."[5]

This apocalyptic war between God and the devil would end the white race. It would come about after great signs in the sun and in the moon and in the stars. Destruction would be delivered from the "Mother Ship" or "Mother of Planes," an indestructible wheel-shaped spacecraft, half a mile wide. "It is a small human planet made for the purpose of destroying the present world of the enemies of Allah," Muhammad wrote. "It is capable of staying in outer space six to twelve months at a time without coming into earth's gravity." The Mother Ship carried in it "fifteen hundred bombing planes with the most deadliest explosives."

The "small circular-made planes called flying saucers, which are so much talked about being seen, could be from this Mother Plane," Muhammad theorized. Blacks would be told where to hide to avoid this great day of reckoning, and whites would be wiped out. Thus, African Americans were to keep entirely separate from white society, creating their own nation. Nation of Islam followers were forbidden from engaging in the American political process.

Elijah Mohammad originally predicted the final race war would take place "sometime around 1970."[6]

Malcolm X, as Elijah Mohammad's most talented and charismatic acolyte, became the national spokesman for the Nation of Islam, or Black Muslims, as they were more frequently called. He helped establish new mosques in Boston and Philadelphia, but his home base was Mosque No. 7 in Harlem. He first came to notice in New York City in 1957 when he dramatically intervened to force police to call an ambulance to take a Nation of Islam member, Johnson Hinton, to the hospital after he had been badly pummeled by police and then jailed without medical aid. Hinton had tried to protect a black man who was being beaten on the street by police, shouting, "You're not in Alabama! This is New York!" The police turned on Hinton. He was found by Malcolm X in the Harlem jail, incoherent and suffering from a brain hemorrhage. Malcolm quickly organized a group of Muslims in protest outside the police station. The police captain, watching Malcolm's control over the crowd, remarked, "No man should have that much power over that many people."[7]

Malcolm X attracted national attention in 1959 when television journalist Mike Wallace (later of *60 Minutes* fame) and Louis Lomax, a pioneering African American writer, created a documentary about the Nation of Islam for a program called *News Beat* on WNTA-TV in New York. The documentary, shown in five half-hour installments in July 1959, was entitled, *The Hate That Hate Produced*. The show was meant to provoke fear and alarm and cast Elijah Muhammad and Malcolm X as menacing hatemongers in charge of a secret organization that was growing like a malignancy under the feet of average Americans.

"While city officials, state agencies, white liberals, and sober-minded Negroes stand idly by," Wallace warned at the start of the documentary, "a group of Negro dissenters has taken to street-corner stepladders, church pulpits, sports arenas, and ballroom platforms across the United States to preach a gospel of hate that would set off a federal investigation if it were preached by Southern whites." Wallace introduced these villains as "a Negro religious group who call themselves 'The Muslims.' They use a good deal of the paraphernalia of the traditional religion of Islam, but they are fervently disavowed by orthodox Muslims." He asserted: "These home-grown Negro American Muslims are the most powerful of the black supremacist groups. They now claim a membership of at least a quarter of a million Negroes." The estimate by Wallace was a huge exaggeration, likely ten-times the actual membership.[8] "Their doctrine is now being taught in fifty cities across the nation. Let no one underestimate the Muslims."

While Wallace showed grainy film of the fez-wearing Elijah Muhammad speaking to black-suited men and white-robed women in a soft, sometimes breaking voice with an almost impenetrable accent, Wallace also spent a good deal of time focused on the assertive, wry, and quick-thinking Malcolm X, "the Muslim's New York leader and ambassador-at-large for the movement." Wallace made sure to emphasize Malcolm X's criminal background, repeating several times in the documentary that he was an ex-convict. "He is a remarkable man," Wallace said at one point, "a man who by his own admission was once a procurer and dope peddler. He spent time for robbery in the Michigan and Massachusetts state penitentiaries. But now he is a changed man—he will not smoke or drink; he will not even eat in a restaurant that houses a tavern. He told *News Beat* that his life changed for him when the Muslim faith taught him to no longer be ashamed of being a black man."[9]

Wallace's coproducer, Louis Lomax, was the person who told Wallace about the Nation of Islam and gained access to Elijah Muhammad and Malcolm X, interviewing both for the program. Born in Georgia in 1922, Lomax pursued graduate studies after college at the American University, where he received a master's degree, and he followed with a

PhD from Yale in 1947. Lomax met Malcolm X in New York City and actually worked with him on early editions of *Muhammad Speaks* (later known as the *Muslim Journal*), a newspaper published by the Nation of Islam. Lomax, however, was a moderate in politics and religion, a keen observer and chronicler of the Black Muslims.[10]

Lomax was able to persuade both Elijah Muhammad and Malcolm X to acknowledge on film that they believed that the white man was a devil, someone incapable of doing right, and that the black man was of God's divine nature. "By nature he is evil," Malcolm said of whites. "He cannot do good?" Lomax asked. "History is best qualified to reward all research," Malcolm replied, "and we don't have any historic example where we have found that they have, collectively, as a people, done good."

It was a frightening portrait, with the Black Muslims predicting the imminent end of the white race and the ascent of black people world-wide. Elijah Muhammad confirmed his belief that the apocalypse for the white race would not come without significant bloodshed. "This is the psychology of the Muslims," Wallace concluded. "They know that the American Negro is angry because he's been cast in an inferior role and they seek to convert him to the Muslim cause by drenching him in a doctrine of black supremacy." Wallace summed it up by saying: "So we learn that a growing segment of the Negro population is losing faith in the American dream. They reject the designation of 'Negro.' They consider themselves, rather, Americans of African descent."

While terrifying to many, including moderate and conservative blacks, Malcolm X became a sort of curiosity for the journalists of the nascent American television news programs. He appeared often to explain a view of black power that was at odds with the pacifist civil rights movement of Dr. Martin Luther King Jr. Whereas Dr. King was a Christian, committed to nonviolence, and in favor of integration, Malcolm X was a Muslim, committed to armed self-defense, and a separatist who espoused black nationalism and a separate state.

Louis Lomax wrote several books attempting to explain Black Muslims, Elijah Muhammad, and especially Malcolm X to white Americans. In the summer of 1963, Lomax published a book entitled *When the Word Is Given*. In it, he was both critical and admiring of the Black

Muslims, but there is no question he venerated Malcolm X. "Malcolm X is the St. Paul of the Black Muslim movement," he wrote. "Not only was he knocked to the ground by the bright light of truth while on an evil journey, but he also rose from the dust stunned, with a new name and a burning zeal to travel in the opposite direction and carry America's twenty million Negroes with him."[11]

"In reality, Western man is on trial in this book," Lomax wrote. "Without the failings of Western society, the Black Muslims could not have come into being; without the continued failings of our society, the Black Muslims cannot endure. Here, then, Western white man, is a bitter pill. Do with it as you see fit."[12]

Sometime in early 1963, disturbing details of Elijah Muhammad's personal life began to emerge, stunning Malcolm X and shaking his belief in the Nation of Islam. In yet another interview with Mike Wallace, this one in 1964, Malcolm X described how slowly it began to dawn on him that many of the very young women who had been secretaries at the Chicago headquarters of the NOI had become pregnant, though they were not married.

"In 1954," he told Wallace, "a teenage sister left Detroit and became one of Mr. Muhammad's personal secretaries, and there in the Chicago office she became pregnant after being there for a year." The same pattern over the succeeding years continued with other young women, but Mr. Muhammad's followers concluded that because a father was never brought forward in these circumstances that it must have been a non-Muslim.

"I knew nothing about it," Malcolm claimed in the interview, "until 1963, when Mr. Muhammad's son, who had been in prison, came out, and he began to hear these rumors around Chicago, so he went to one of the sisters [who had had a child] and the sister admitted to him that the rumor was true. And it was he who first told me about it."

Malcolm X wrote to Elijah Muhammad confronting him about his infidelities. Elijah Muhammad admitted his adulteries, but told Malcolm that he would explain it all within the context of religious prophecy. (Biblical prophets had many wives, he would later say.) Some around Elijah Muhammad began to fear that Malcolm, who was growing increasingly uncomfortable with Muhammad's behavior, might bring the scandal into the public light. "And it was at that time that they used the statement that I made against President Kennedy *as a pretext* to cut my authority and some other things happened that finally forced the split," Malcolm told Wallace.[13]

One of the secret followers of the Nation of Islam who would become entangled in the falling-out between Malcolm X and Elijah Muhammad was a young boxer from Louisville named Cassius Clay.

Clay had won the light heavyweight gold medal in Rome in 1960. A new biography suggests that Clay began flirting with Black Muslimism in Miami when he was training to turn professional. The worldview of the Black Muslims fit with Clay's father's admonition to trust no white man.[14] In June 1962 Clay met Malcolm X in Detroit when he attended a Nation of Islam rally and heard Elijah Muhammad speak for the first time in person. "My first impression of Malcolm X," Clay would later say, "was how could a black man talk about the government and white people and act so bold and not be shot at? How could he say these things? Only God must be protecting him."[15]

By the end of 1963, Clay was set to fight the heavyweight champion Sonny Liston in Miami the following February. Liston, an eight-to-one favorite, was a brutal fighter with underworld connections. Few bet on Clay save friends like Malcolm X. Elijah Muhammad kept his distance, believing that boxing was a white man's game in which African Americans were exploited. Malcolm saw the public relations coup of having a heavyweight champion as a member of the Nation. He was also hedging his bets and realized that Clay could be an asset for him if he was expelled from the Nation.

The break between Malcolm X and the Nation was becoming more and more certain. February 26, a high holy day for the Nation of Islam (known as Saviours' Day in recognition of W. D. Fard's birthday), was usually a day when Malcolm X took a leading role in the movement's national convention. In 1964, he was not invited. "The conflict between Malcolm and the Chicago headquarters, according to an increasing number of reports, not only involves personalities but also a sharp difference of opinion about the role the Muslims should play in this election year," the *Times* reported.[16]

As things deteriorated between Malcolm and Elijah Muhammad, Malcolm found support and solace in being close to Cassius Clay. He took his family to Miami in January to vacation as Clay trained for the Liston fight. When the promoter of the fight found out that Malcolm was among Clay's entourage, he threatened to cancel the fight. Malcolm left Florida, but quietly came back for the fight on February 25, sitting in the seventh row near Clay's corner. "I shocked the world, I shocked the world!" Clay yelled from the ring when the fight was called in the seventh round because Liston refused to come out of his corner, claiming a tear in one of his biceps left him unable to fight.

That night, Clay spent time with Malcolm X and the next day at a press conference the subdued twenty-two-year-old champion told the press, "I'm free to be who I want." While not declaring that he was a member of the Nation of Islam, he spoke glowingly of the Black Muslims. "I go to a Black Muslim meeting and what do I see?" he asked. "I see that there's no drinking and their women wear dresses down to the floor. And then I come out on the street and you tell me I shouldn't go in there. Well, there must be something in there if you don't want me to go in there."[17]

A reporter for the *New York Times* was put off by Clay's show of antagonism towards the press; he noted that Clay "refused to play the mild and socially uninvolved sports-hero stereotype."

The *Times* reporter elaborated, "Clay put down the civil rights movement ('I'm a citizen already'), defended Malcolm X, the Black Muslim leader ('If he's so bad why don't they put him in jail?'), and questioned those who attacked his leanings ('I catch so much hell, why? Why me when I don't try to bust into schools and march around or throw bricks?')."[18]

One person who was taking an increasing interest in Malcolm X was an African American in Cleveland named Fred Evans. Evans was a Korean War army veteran who resembled Malcolm X in build—he was tall and thin, about six feet, four inches in height. Evans had been a champion boxer in the army, and he considered Malcolm X to be the "father of Black Nationalism in the United States."[19] Over time, he would change his name to Ahmed, telling Cleveland reporters that Malcolm X was his "enthusiasm."[20]

In 1964, when Malcolm X came to Cleveland to speak, Louis Lomax accompanied him. And Fred Ahmed Evans would be in the audience.[21]

5

"You Little Nigger Pickaninnies, Stay Out of Our Schools, This Is Our Neighborhood!"

THE CRISIS THAT BROUGHT MALCOLM X and Louis Lomax to Cleveland arose from the continuing segregation of Cleveland's public schools—a full decade after the US Supreme Court ruled in *Brown v. Board of Education* that segregation of students in public schools violated the Equal Protection Clause of the Fourteenth Amendment of the US Constitution. "Segregation of white and colored children in public schools has a detrimental effect upon the colored children," the Supreme Court found in 1954. "The effect is greater when it has the sanction of the law, for the policy of separating the races is usually interpreted as denoting the inferiority of the Negro group. A sense of inferiority affects the motivation of a child to learn."

In the South, Dr. King was dealing with Jim Crow laws that still enforced segregation. In the North, cities like Cleveland engaged in segregation not as a matter of law but de facto. Students attended schools in their neighborhoods, and because the neighborhoods were rigidly racially divided, the schools were almost entirely racially segregated. And as the African American neighborhoods were overcrowded, the schools in these neighborhoods became overfull as well.

Glenville was ground zero in the fight to desegregate Cleveland's public schools. In a 1964 study, the Cleveland City Planning Commission stated the obvious: "Glenville is a community with problems."[1] The problems were both physical in nature (such as aging housing stock) and social and economic. The latter did not "have their roots in the community itself," the Planning Commission wrote. "They are the resultants of exterior forces that pre-condition and overshadow total community life. They will take longer to correct, and are beyond the scope and general control of physical city planning." In short, no amount of city planning was going to solve these social or economic difficulties—they required intense political intervention, something that proved well beyond the city's leadership.

The statistics of Glenville in 1964 were grim. In 1940, blacks made up 2 percent of Glenville's total population of 61,614 residents. By 1950 that number had jumped to 40 percent, and by 1960, of the 67,509 residents in the neighborhood, a full 96 percent were classified as "Negroes." The planning commission recognized this sweeping turnover posed serious challenges: "Of the many kinds of urban population changes involving people of differing nationalities or cultural backgrounds, complete racial change appears to leave the deepest and most permanent scars on the community affected."[2]

In Cleveland, the African American migrants from the South generated a huge demand for housing. While whites out-migrated to leafy suburbs like Shaker Heights, blacks were ghettoized because of discriminatory and predatory lending practices of local banks and property owners, race-based deed restrictions, and the general hostility of white residents who often resorted to violence against any black pioneers who dared to buy into an area considered white only.

A succession of Cleveland mayors made this cruel situation worse. Mayor Anthony Celebrezze oversaw "urban renewal" programs designed to clean out the slums near the downtown area. This clearing process meant the demolition of a swath of black homes and the creation of

Cleveland's first public housing projects. The projects were poorly planned, part private, part public, built on or near garbage dumps, with rents that were astronomical. They failed wretchedly, with rent strikes and evictions commonplace occurrences.

Celebrezze, an otherwise progressive mayor, had a tin ear when it came to the impact his programs were having on the African American poor who were displaced. In creating the Erieview downtown business district, he celebrated the destruction of one flophouse neighborhood as "Cleveland's chance to wipe away the wrinkles of age."[3] When President Kennedy named Celebrezze his secretary of health, education, and welfare in the summer of 1962, his replacement, a Romanian-born lawyer and law director named Ralph S. Locher, was clueless. Mayor Locher had a similar penchant for favoring downtown business development over the creation of decent housing for Cleveland's black citizens who were left without homes. So eager was he to pursue urban renewal, Mayor Locher actually came up with the idea of home-burning parties to lower the cost of demolition. "I never thought I'd stand by and watch a place burn," he told reporters, "but this is a beautiful sight. It has such a cleansing effect."[4] Locher's critics called it "dislocation without relocation."[5] Eventually, the federal government pulled its funding for all urban renewal programs in Cleveland when the whole mess spiraled into recklessness.

In Glenville the result was that African Americans were crammed into an area where the average building was over fifty years old and badly in need of repair and maintenance. The lack of construction of new housing during this time of black influx meant that one-family homes were converted in large numbers to multifamily units. The overcrowding and physical deterioration were exacerbated by buildings constructed in an age of horse and buggy—they were too close together, leaving residents with poor light and ventilation.[6]

There was a sharp spike in poverty indicators in Glenville between 1950 and 1960: city and county general relief cases increased by 251 percent; juvenile court neglect cases rose by 300 percent; aid to dependent children applications jumped by 589 percent. The workforce became "unskilled" and unemployment became the norm.[7]

What really concerned city planners was an expected "population explosion." They wrote that "this is inherent in the age, sex, and mortality characteristics of the present population. Assuming that these and other characteristics, such as, mobility, birth, and fertility rates do not vary too greatly from what they are today, commencing in 1967 Glenville's population will begin to out-distance any in its previous history." The fear was that the community would be "faced with the basic problems of how to adequately feed, house, clothe, educate, employ and, otherwise, to produce productive citizens of the future exploding population."[8]

School overcrowding in Glenville became the catastrophe that energized a large protest movement. The Cleveland Board of Education failed to foresee that the population increases in Hough and Glenville would warrant new school construction. When overloading made the situation untenable, the Cleveland Board of Education instituted what became known as "relay classes" in Hough and Glenville, effectively running two half-day sessions at the schools. Complaints from black parents' groups resulted in plans to bus children from the black neighborhoods to nearby white neighborhoods where there were vacant classrooms available, beginning in January 1962. The hitch was that when white parents predictably grumbled, the school board responded with assurances that the black students would not mix with their white counterparts. There would be no sharing of bathrooms, cafeteria, or gym facilities. Even the Hough and Glenville teachers were bused with the students to ensure complete segregation.[9]

These conditions and other civil rights problems in Cleveland, including discriminatory employment practices, gave rise to the creation in 1963 of the United Freedom Movement (UFM), a large conglomeration of thirty-four participating organizations, including church-based groups; the local chapters of the NAACP and the Congress of Racial Equality (CORE); and grassroots startups like the Freedom Fighters, the Defenders of Human Rights, and the Afro-American Cultural Institute.[10]

Picketing by UFM and negotiations with the Cleveland School Board in the fall of 1963 produced an agreement to expedite "the total and voluntary integration" of the pupils bused to white schools by September 1964, but in fact the board of education quietly began to draw up aggressive plans to build new schools in Glenville, so that bused students could be returned to their fully segregated neighborhood schools.[11] These actions should not have been surprising. The school board was run by an Irish-Catholic from the West Side of Cleveland, thirty-six-year-old Ralph McAllister, who sent his children to parochial schools and who declared publicly that African American children were "educationally inferior" to white students.[12] A black civil rights attorney who called for McAllister's removal said of his remarks: "In essence, McAllister, as president of our school board, told the people of Cleveland that Negro pupils in effect were a bunch of morons and would degrade any class to which they were admitted."[13]

When the pace of reforms was not as promised by January 1964, African Americans and the UFM, including many white ministers and clergymen, decided to protest by picketing outside the white schools to which the black children of Glenville had been bused. In white enclaves like Collinwood and Murray Hill the new black students had been physically threatened and spat upon by white parents when their buses pulled into the schools. "You little nigger pickaninnies, stay out of our schools, this is our neighborhood," one white mother shouted at the terrified schoolchildren.[14] Now a showdown loomed.

Picket lines were set up outside Brett Memorial Elementary School in Collinwood on January 29, 1964, where protesters wearing placards "Separation Is Not Equal" were crowded and jostled by angry whites, many of them mothers, who confronted and heckled, but there was no serious outbreak of violence.[15] The crisis came when the newspaper announced that the UFM planned to picket Murray Hill School in an area known as Little Italy the next day. At the time, Murray Hill received nine classes from Hazelwood Elementary in Glenville.[16] The people of Little Italy were prepared the next day to respond to what they considered an affront to their community.

Little Italy was a microcosm of Cleveland in the 1960s. Many of Cleveland's neighborhoods were still reserves for different ethnic groups, mainly from southern and eastern Europe. "Immigrants from Italy's south, lured by the great dream that America represented, flocked to [Murray Hill], built frame houses with balconies and made their living in the little shops on the slope," the Cleveland *Plain Dealer* wrote.[17] Each year, Holy Rosary Catholic Church celebrated the Feast of the Assumption with an elaborate summer fair and street parade, including a statue of Mary carried aloft, dollar bills stuffed by revelers into the crevices of the figurine.[18]

The calm of this picturesque but insular neighborhood had been shaken by the busing. "We were told two years ago it was on a temporary basis," one resident, Sam Fratantonio, told the paper, blaming the priests of Holy Rosary who "talked them into" letting the transfer students come to the neighborhood school. "[Fratantonio] said the transfer system worked out well until the current demands of civil rights groups came up to obtain 'total integration.'"[19] These angry residents were not about to let outsiders picket in their neighborhood for integration without a fight.

The next day, chaos erupted. The newspaper described the violence: "A crowd of whites that at one time numbered about 1,500—mostly young men—roamed the neighborhood, beat up several Negroes and a number of news photographers, smashed half a dozen automobiles and hurled eggs, fruit, rocks, bricks, and bottles at policeman, news men, Negro passersby, and even some priests." At one point, a black couple that had accompanied their child were backed against a wall in a side alley where a press photographer nearby had just been jumped and kicked in the groin, his camera smashed. A white woman began screaming "No! No! Not when they've got the kid with them."[20]

A wider disaster was only avoided when ministers of the UFM decided early in the morning, after reports of violence reached them, to call off the main contingent of protesters. One group of Catholic priests who tried to disperse the white mobs finally went to black parents to urge them, "as a matter of life and death, not to carry out their demonstrations."[21]

But despite the widespread violence and rioting, only two white young men were arrested—and then only after they vandalized a car. Many of the police stood by watching. Blacks took note that the police would do little to enforce the riot laws against the whites. As Lewis Robinson, one of the Freedom Fighters, wrote: "Complaints were filed with the Police Department, the Cleveland Community Relations Board, the NAACP, and even the US Justice Department, yet nothing was done about white hoodlumism of Murray Hill, then or now."[22]

Cleveland's incompetent and skittish mayor, Ralph Locher, predictably took a hands-off approach to the school crisis. "Intervention by a public official in a situation where he lacks legal authority will most likely prove futile unless both sides to the dispute request his consideration of the matter," he lamely declared.[23]

If it were only police indifference, that would have been one thing. But the deeper problem was a long history of police brutality that had been visited upon Cleveland's African American community. Just days after the Murray Hill disturbances, UFM protesters picketed the Cleveland Board of Education at its downtown location, staging a sit-in. Men and women were forcibly removed by police, some being dragged by their feet and hair down three flights of stairs. "After the stick wielding, cursing police officers waded through the demonstrators and carted them like cattle off to the jails," the *Call and Post* wrote, "several heads were smashed and two Negro women were hospitalized." One woman arrested was made to strip while male policemen watched. Five of the protesters were charged with obstructing justice and other crimes, while none of the police faced disciplinary proceedings. "Cleveland's police department should be on trial, not these five demonstrators," one of the UFM attorneys said.[24]

Among the lawyers on the legal team of the UFM was a young African American named Louis Stokes, whose younger brother Carl was moving up the political ladder. In 1963 Carl became the first African American to be elected to the Ohio House of Representatives as a Democrat. By 1964, Carl began to dream of a run for the mayor's office.[25]

"Police brutality had been a problem for Cleveland's black community for decades prior to the 1960s," scholar David Swiderski has recently written, "with accounts of the more sensational episodes frequently drawing concern and detailed coverage in the *Call and Post*." But with the dawning of the black freedom struggle of the 1950s and 1960s, police oppression amplified. "Police brutality . . . was less a problem of individual misdeeds by particular officers than a manifest expression of naked state power that operated without restraint to compel compliance with and submission to the prevailing system of racial oppression among black Clevelanders," Swiderski observed. The targets of a nearly all-white Cleveland police force became a segment of the black community that "demonstrated the greatest potential for rebellion: young boys and young men," Swiderski wrote.[26]

There was no better example of the everyday police cruelty faced by young African American boys and men than an incident in the summer of 1963. James Long, a seventeen-year-old Glenville High School student, took his two sisters to a playground. Long ran off to a baseball game nearby while his sisters played. One of his sisters got into a verbal fight with another girl and police showed up. Patrolman Thomas Horgan and his partner, Dennis Kehn, tried to figure out the origin of the dispute when James Long walked back from the baseball game to check on his sisters. Long was hard of hearing, having had three operations on his ears. When police began to question him and he only smiled in response, Horgan and Kehn became enraged, thinking the young man was being disrespectful. They began to viciously slap and punch him in the face and then one of them savagely pistol whipped him.

James Long was hurt so badly that doctors feared he would lose his hearing entirely, yet he was charged with assaulting an officer. A woman who witnessed the entire encounter told the *Call and Post*: "It was a pity the way cops beat that boy."[27] This woman and fourteen other witnesses who appeared in juvenile court testified that the police attack was unprovoked. James Long was cleared, but neither of the officers faced any charges.[28] Mayor Locher initially refused to meet with outraged citizens from Glenville until they staged a sit-in and he relented.

These sorts of encounters had a cumulative impact on the black community in Cleveland. Mutawaf Shaheed, an original members of the Muntu poets, a group that became one of the chief artistic voices of the black nationalist movement in Cleveland during the late 1960s, said that African Americans "hated police from the bottoms of their hearts." It was not any one person or any specific incident, but the police as a part of a system and the entire power structure they represented. The police, to Cleveland's African Americans, were the face of white oppression. "You can't understand how deeply black Clevelanders hated the police."[29]

To make things worse, black citizens felt that the entire system of justice supported the police and their abuse of blacks. From judges to prosecutors, to grand jurors, to ordinary jurors, no one would call police on their tactics. And blacks knew that the police understood this lack of accountability left them inoculated from any consequences for the brutality they unleashed on black citizens. Further, with a police force that was almost entirely white (2,200 whites to 150 or 160 black patrolmen), even black cops had to toe the line or face retribution from their fellow white officers. Black police regularly found lockers or personal cars vandalized. They were subject to malicious name-calling and physical attacks but dared not complain lest they lose their jobs.

In the same issue of the *Call and Post* that reported on the beating of James Long, an article told of "15 Negroes" who were among the fifty-nine candidates for positions on the Cleveland Browns. Among the hopefuls to join a team that featured star running back Jim Brown was Walter Beach, an air force veteran who had gone to Central Michigan University. "The sleeper of the Negro rookie backs is Beach," Bill Jackson of the *Call and Post* wrote, "a 6-0, 185 pounder, who was wearing number '49,' Bobby Mitchell's number [a future Hall of Fame halfback and flanker]."

Beach's NFL career started with the Giants who cut him and he was picked up by the Boston Patriots. Prior to the 1962 season, a workout coach for the Patriots posted the separate itineraries for black and white players in training camp. Beach noticed that white players were assigned to hotel quarters while black were assigned to accommodations in out-of-the-way places. When the team was to play an exhibition game in New Orleans, Beach and other black players were to stay with local black families while the white players lodged in a luxury hotel. Beach objected, saying he would fly down the day of the game.

"As a result of my advocacy [for racial equality], I earned a one-way ticket out of the league and was released by the Patriots the very next day," Beach wrote. He was twenty-nine years old at the time. The next summer he was invited to the Browns training camp. He would play on the 1964 championship team, but not without some major drama.[30]

In the summer of 1968, Beach, along with a young councilman named George Forbes, would be the last outsiders to see Ahmed Evans before the shoot-out.

But that was four years away, and in early 1964, the table had been set in Cleveland for the appearance of Malcolm X.

6

"The Ballot or the Bullet"

"MR. MODERATOR, BROTHER LOMAX, BROTHERS and sisters, friends and enemies," Malcolm X began his remarks at Cory Methodist Church in Glenville on Friday night, April 3, 1964. "I just can't believe everyone here is a friend," he quipped, "and I don't want to leave anybody out."[1] This line, one that was a standard of Malcolm X speeches, brought warm laughter and a scattering of applause from the standing-room-only crowd that had come to a Congress of Racial Equality (CORE) rally, after which attendees were invited to a participate in a torchlight protest march with the Glenville parents' association to the sites where new schools were being constructed.[2]

Just after the Murray Hill riots, there was a small article buried in the Cleveland *Plain Dealer* announcing an acceleration of construction of new schools in Glenville by the board of education. "As a step toward solving the school integration crisis, largely triggered by the need to transport pupils from overcrowded schools to others, the board of education has ordered a speedup in the schools that will end the need for transportation classes," the article read.[3] The plan was to have three new schools in Glenville open by the fall of 1964.

Integration problem solved—by sending the African American students back to their segregated schools.

The move provoked an even larger protest movement in Cleveland. "Continuous building is a waste of money when there is empty space for 12,000 pupils throughout the city," the president of the Hazelwood

Parents Association told the newspaper.[4] The parents and national education experts who spoke at Cleveland's City Club suggested construction of educational parks, discontinuing neighborhood schools that only preserved segregation. The UFM handed the board of education an ultimatum at the end of February seeking an immediate moratorium on any new construction. "We charge all three schools as being both separate and unequal in violation of the 1954 Supreme Court ruling," the UFM statement read.[5] CORE invited Malcolm X and Louis Lomax to come to Glenville as part of this expanded protest drive.

The visit to Cleveland allowed Malcolm X to explain his split with the Nation of Islam and to lay out his new views on political involvement and black unity. The term that kept coming back to him was "the ballot or the bullet."

After the Liston fight, it was clear that Malcolm X and Elijah Muhammad would not reconcile. The battle over Cassius Clay became something of proxy war between the two opposing forces. Initially Malcolm X appeared to have the upper hand. On Sunday, March 1, Clay unobtrusively checked into the Hotel Theresa in Harlem, a place where Malcolm X rented offices. (Fidel Castro had been Malcolm X's guest there in 1960 when he came to address the United Nations.) Clay went to see films of his victory over Liston at the Trans-Lux theater the next night, attracting a large crowd.[6]

A few days later, Clay visited the United Nations and declared his intention to visit African and Asian countries. "I am the champion of the whole world," he told journalists, "and I want to meet the people I am champion of." The *Times* reported, "Among those accompanying the champion were his brother, Rudolph, Archie Robinson, his personal secretary, and Malcolm X, the New York spokesman for the Black Muslims."[7] Clay told reporters he had changed his name to Cassius X Clay. "X is what slave masters used to be called," he artlessly responded when asked what it meant.[8]

The standard protocol for joining the Nation of Islam included the mailing of a form letter to Mr. W. F. Muhammad in care of the Nation's Chicago headquarters. "Savior Allah, Our Deliverer," it began, with the following confession of faith: "I have been attending the teachings of Islam by one of your Ministers, two or three times. I believe in it, and I bear witness that there is no God but Thee, and that Muhammad is Thy Servant and Apostle. I desire to reclaim my Own. Please give me my Original name. My slave name is as follows: [to be added by the applicant]."[9]

What Cassius Clay meant to say was that his slave name was "Clay" and that he wanted to replace it with an X, representing his lost African name and heritage. This naming convention was widely followed. In a Nation of Islam Temple, for example, if there were two men with the name John, one would be John X, another John 2X.[10] Louis Lomax explained: "The 'X' is the Black Muslim's way of saying that his own origins—before the white man—and name are a mystery; it is also the Muslim's shout that he is an 'ex,' and 'no longer what I was when the white man had me deaf, blind, and dumb.'"[11]

It was then up to Elijah Muhammad to decide if he would confer a new, more divine Arabic name. For the time being, though, Cassius Clay would go by Cassius X.

While at the United Nations, Clay was asked about a report from the Louisville *Courier-Journal* that he had flunked an army predraft psychological test taken a few weeks before the Liston fight. He had not heard anything of it. When Malcolm X was asked if he was exercising undue influence over the champ, he responded, "He's got a mind of his own."[12]

Malcolm X used this moment of positive publicity with the heavyweight champion to make his break with Elijah Muhammad. On the following Sunday, March 8, Malcolm announced that he was going to organize a black nationalist party. "I have reached the conclusion," he said, "that I can best spread Mr. Muhammad's message by staying out of the Nation of Islam and continuing to work on my own among America's 22 million non-Muslim Negroes." He said he would remain a Muslim, "but the main emphasis of the new movement will be black nationalism as a political concept and form of social action against the oppressors."[13]

Malcolm X had decided that total segregation taught by Elijah Muhammad, including an uncompromising ban on voting and political activity, was too constrictive, narrowly sectarian, and counterproductive. In this sense, Malcolm X was moving toward Dr. King. "I am prepared," he said, "to cooperate in local civil rights actions in the South and elsewhere and shall do so because every campaign for specific objectives can only heighten the political consciousness of the Negroes and intensify their identification against white society."

This did not mean he bought into King's integrationist philosophy. "There is no use deceiving ourselves," he declared. "Good education, housing, and jobs are imperatives for the Negroes, and I shall support them in their fight to win these objectives, but I shall tell the Negroes that while these are necessary, they cannot solve the main Negro problem."

He still was convinced that Dr. King and others with him were leading African Americans down the wrong path. "I shall also tell them that what has been called the 'Negro revolution' in the United States is a deception practiced upon them, because they have only to examine the failure of this so-called revolution to produce any positive results in the past year." The murder of the young girls in Birmingham after Dr. King's nonviolent direct action campaign there was much on the minds of black Americans.

What was clear is that Malcolm X, released from the burdens of deferring to Elijah Muhammad and the Nation of Islam, felt liberated, and he was ready to jump into the political fray. "It's going to be different now," he said, "I'm going to join in the fight wherever Negroes ask for my help, and I suspect my activities will be on a greater and more intensive scale than in the past."

Malcolm X intended to reach out to black Americans who were dissatisfied with the progress of the civil rights movement but were uncomfortable with Islam. "The white power structure is hopeful that the civil rights leaders will channel the demands and the bitterness of the Negroes into a token painless compromise," he said. "They are mistaken. The white leaders don't realize the extent to which the civil rights leaders have deceived them about the true feelings of the Negroes."[14]

Thus, in these first tentative steps (he prudently pointed out that he was not trying to split the Black Muslims, nor take followers of Elijah Muhammad), Malcolm emphasized the power of the ballot; he would come later to the bullet.

By the middle of March his rhetoric was turning incendiary. "There will be more violence than ever this year," he predicted at a press conference at the Park Sheraton Hotel in New York on March 12. "White people will be shocked when they discover the passive little Negro they had known turns out to be a roaring lion. The whites had better understand this while there is time. The Negroes at the mass level are ready to act."

Echoing Robert F. Williams, he urged blacks to abandon the doctrine of nonviolence. "It is criminal to teach a man not to defend himself when he is the constant victim of brutal attacks. It is legal and lawful to own a shotgun or a rifle. We believe in obeying the law."

He pointed out that the government had failed in its duty to protect black citizens, especially when they exercised their right to picket or protest injustice. "We should form rifle clubs that can be used to defend our lives and our property in times of emergency, such as happened last year in Birmingham."[15]

Toward the end of the month, Elijah Muhammad tugged back on Cassius Clay, bestowing upon him the name Muhammad Ali. "Don't call me Cassius Clay," Clay admonished several newsmen on March 20. "I am Muhammad Ali, heavyweight champion of the whole world. That is a beautiful Arabic name. That's my name now." The comments came during an interview where Ali was asked about the fact that the army had declared him not qualified to be inducted because of low test scores. "I just said I'm the greatest," Ali joked. "I never said I was the smartest."

The press picked up on the implication of the name change. "Clay also has called himself Cassius X, but that was before Malcolm X split with the national leadership of the sect," a reporter for the *New York Times* wrote.[16] Ali would soon have to declare his allegiance.

In his first public rally after the split with the NOI on March 22, Malcolm X announced the formation of his new Muslim Mosque, Inc., which would hold religious services at the Theresa Hotel on 7th Avenue and 125th Street. In this speech, Malcolm first played with the ballot or bullet concept, but he was yet to flesh out its full elucidation. He told one thousand "enthusiastic Negroes" in Harlem that "it's time for you and me to let the government know it's ballots—or bullets."[17]

Twelve days later on Friday, April 3, three thousand people packed into Cory Methodist Church in Glenville, on a cool but seasonable spring night, for the debate between Malcolm X and Louis Lomax. Lomax went first, giving a commendable talk, but then the person they had all come to see took over.[18] "The question tonight, as I understand it, is 'The Negro Revolt and Where Do We Go from Here?' or 'What's Next?'" Malcolm said.[19]

Malcolm X at Cory Methodist Church, April 3, 1964, delivering his "Ballots or Bullets" speech. *Western Reserve Historical Society*

He started with his general answer: "In my little humble way of understanding it," he said, "it points toward either the ballot or the bullet."

The crowd was immediately taken off guard, mystified and electrified.

Then he turned to the fact that religion had been the cause for fractionalization among blacks in the civil rights struggle. He assured his audience he remained a Muslim and that his religion was still Islam. But he wanted to set religion aside and talk about what unified African Americans. "Although I'm still a Muslim," he said, "I'm not here tonight to discuss my religion. I'm not here to try to change your religion. I'm not here to argue or discuss anything that we differ about, because it's time for us to submerge our differences and realize that it is best for us to first see that we have the same problem—a common problem— a problem that will make you catch hell whether you're a Baptist, or a Methodist, or a Muslim, or a nationalist."

"Whether you're educated or illiterate, whether you live on the boulevard or the alley, you're going to catch hell just like me," he continued.

"We're all in the same boat and we all are going to catch the same hell from the same man. He just happens to be a white man."

He said this didn't mean he was antiwhite, but it did mean that he was antiexploitation, antidegradation, antioppression. "And if the white man doesn't want us to be anti-him, let him stop oppressing and exploiting and degrading us."

He spoke of 1964 being "a political year." He said, "If we don't do something real soon, I think you'll agree that we're going to be forced either to use the ballot or the bullet. It's one or the other in 1964. It isn't that time is running out—time has run out!"

Malcolm X said he wasn't a Republican, or a Democrat, "and I don't even consider myself an American." He said, "If you and I were Americans, there'd be no problem. Those Honkies that just got off the boat, they're already Americans. Polacks are already Americans; the Italian refugees are already Americans. Everything that came out of Europe, every blue-eyed thing, is already American. And as long as you and I have been over here, we aren't Americans yet."

He had a hooting Cleveland audience and they even liked it when he attacked them. "It was the black man's vote that put the present administration in Washington, DC. Your vote—your dumb vote, your ignorant vote, your wasted vote put in an administration in Washington, DC, that has seen fit to pass every kind of legislation imaginable, saving you until last, then filibustering on top of that."

He pointed to LBJ's extraordinary majorities in Congress. Two-thirds of the House members were Democrats, as were sixty-seven senators. "Why," he pointed out, "the Democrats have got the government sewed up, and you're the one who sewed it up for them. And what have they given you?"

"So it's time in 1964 to wake up," he said in his beautiful baritone. "And when you see them coming up with that kind of conspiracy, let them know your eyes are open. And let them know—it's the ballot or the bullet. If you're afraid to use an expression like that, you should get on out of the country; you should get back in the cotton patch; you should get back in the alley."

Democracy had failed the Negro; the white man had failed the Negro.

"So where do we go from here?" he asked. "First, we need some friends. We need some new allies. The entire civil rights struggle needs a new interpretation, a broader interpretation." He said the old interpretation excluded black nationalists. It was time for collaboration, inclusion, and unity.

But more, Malcolm X wanted to reframe the question as not just a civil rights struggle but a *human rights* struggle. And this, he argued, would bring the issue before the whole world as an international problem. "Civil rights means you're asking Uncle Sam to treat you right. Human rights are something you are born with. Human rights are your God-given rights. Human rights are the rights that are recognized by all nations on the earth."

He pointed approvingly to "some rice eaters" in Korea who had battled the United States to a standoff. "That's a loss," he said. And because the risks of using nuclear weapons were incalculable, the weapons remained in their silos and the United States, with all its "machinery for warfare," had shown that it could not win a contest against peasants who engaged in guerilla warfare.

"It takes heart to be a guerilla warrior," he said, "because you are on your own."

In detail, Malcolm X explained his view of black nationalism. "The political philosophy of black nationalism means that the black man should control the politics and the politicians in his own community; no more." He urged blacks to use their ballots wisely. "A ballot is like a bullet," he said. "You don't throw your ballots until you see a target, and if the target is not within your reach, keep the ballot in your pocket."

"The economic philosophy of black nationalism is pure and simple," he added. "It only means that we should control the economy of our community. Why should white people be running all the stores in our community? Why should white people be running all the banks in our community? Why should the economy of our community be in the hands of the white man?"

Malcolm X told his Cleveland audience that he would work with them on school boycotts. "We will work with anybody, anywhere, at any time, who is genuinely interested in tackling the problem head-on, nonviolently as long as the enemy is nonviolent, but violent when the enemy gets violent."

He said he didn't believe in integration but that he didn't worry much about it "because I know you're not going to get it anyway." The reason: "You're not going to get it because you're afraid to die; you've got to be ready to die if you try and force yourself on the white man, because he'll get just as violent as those crackers in Mississippi, right here in Cleveland."

Nevertheless, he said, he would work to defeat segregated school systems because such schools were inferior and produced students with crippled minds. "But this does not mean that a school is segregated because it's all black," he pointed out. "A segregated school means a school that is controlled by people who have no real interest in it whatsoever." White schools were never referred to as segregated. "The white man controls his own school, his own bank, his own economy, his own politics, his own everything, his own community; but he also controls yours."

"When you're under someone else's control, you're segregated," he argued with piercing logic. "They'll always give you the lowest or the worst that there is to offer."

At last, he came to the topic that was guaranteed to raise the most controversy: Negroes with guns.

"I must say this concerning the great controversy over rifles and shotguns. The only thing that I've ever said is that in areas where the government has proven itself either unwilling or unable to defend the lives and property of Negroes, it's time for Negroes to defend themselves." He was not advocating violence—"Don't go out shooting people," he said, "but any time, brothers and sisters—especially the men in this audience; some of you wearing Congressional Medals of Honor, with shoulders this wide, chests this big, muscles that big—any time you and I sit around and read where they bomb a church and murder in cold blood, not some grownups, but four little girls while they are praying to the same God the white man taught them to pray to, and you and I see the government go down and can't find out who did it."

"No," he said, "if you never see me another time in your life, if I die in the morning, I'll die saying one thing: the ballot or the bullet, the ballot or the bullet."

The audience was spellbound. They had never heard such direct talk, such an unflinching view of black power and armed self-defense. Scholars would rate the speech as one of the most influential speeches of the twentieth century.[20]

Fred Evans was in the audience, but so was a man who was about to cause an immediate sensation. His name was Lewis G. Robinson. He was busy handing out a typed press release to newsmen at the end of Malcolm X's talk. It read: "A meeting will be held on April 7 at 8:00 PM at the home of Lewis G. Robinson, 1402 East 120th Street, to discuss the formation of a rifle club to protect civil rights demonstrators and black students if the police department is unable or unwilling to protect all citizens equally."

Lewis Robinson, as Malcolm X would say, was about to catch hell.

7

"There's No Room for a Rifle Club Named After Medgar Evers"

THE THOUGHT OF AFRICAN AMERICANS with rifles or shotguns injected a bolt of terror into the nervous system of Cleveland. A banner headline in the Sunday paper two days after Malcolm X spoke at Cory Methodist warned of the formation of a rifle club by Lewis G. Robinson, the leader of a "militant civil rights group here," and described Mayor Ralph Locher as "alarmed." Locher promised an intense police investigation.[1] No mention was made of the Second Amendment, or the National Rifle Association, or of the many rifle clubs operated by whites across greater Cleveland. That African Americans wanted to bear arms was justification in itself for police action.

On the other hand, Lewis Robinson could not have been more provocative in his statements to the press. "We expect whites to be shocked by this because Negroes have been so passive in the past," he told the *Plain Dealer*. "We hope the American people will wake up. We want them to know how serious the civil rights issue is." Robinson ominously described how his club members would wear army fatigues, helmets, heavy boots, and carry two-way radios. His group was looking for sites

Lewis G. Robinson, civil rights activist, derisively referred to in the *Plain Dealer* as the "Cleveland Rifleman." *Cleveland Public Library Collection/Photograph Collection*

in the country to use as a practice range. He said the impetus for his club came from recent statements by Malcolm X.

Robinson also pointed to the Murray Hill disturbance as a basis for the club, charging that the Cleveland police failed to protect protesters. "We will not go into another Murray Hill situation without police protection," he said. "Any time the police fail to protect us we will be prepared to protect ourselves."[2]

Mayor Locher responded that "vigilante groups are in direct opposition to law and order on which our democracy is based." His safety director, John N. McCormick, said that the club was "contrary to every standard of decency."[3] It was learned that the Cleveland Police Department's Subversives Unit, headed by a veteran Communist fighter named Sergeant John Ungvary, had already opened a file on Robinson, but the police would not confirm or deny reports of an expedited shipment of rifles.

Robinson said that he planned to name the rifle club after the assassinated civil rights leader Medgar Evers, who had been gunned down in his driveway by a white supremacist in June 1963, a month after Dr. King's visit to Cory Methodist. Evers was a World War II veteran who fought in the Battle of Normandy as part of the D-day operation. Back home, he worked tirelessly to end segregation in the public schools and at the University of Mississippi. He was ambushed by a man with a rifle the day after President Kennedy spoke to the nation in a televised address on civil rights (speaking to yet another Alabama crisis—this one an impasse with Governor George Wallace, who stood in the way of two black students registering for classes at the University of Alabama). "The fires of frustration and discord are burning in every city, North and South," President Kennedy cautioned. "Where legal remedies are not at hand, redress is sought in the streets, in demonstrations, parades, and protests, which create tensions and threaten violence and threaten lives. We face therefore a moral crisis as a country and a people. It cannot be met by repressive police action."

A major editorial in the *Cleveland Press* that weekend stated: "There's no room in Cleveland, or in the United States, for a rifle club named after Medgar Evers." The *Press* conceded that there was reason to honor Evers, but found the name used in connection with a rifle club menacing. "Certainly there is reason to commemorate the slain Negro leader. But no matter what the announced purpose of a rifle club, it is difficult not to connect it with some sort of violent retaliation for the death of Evers in Mississippi."[4]

Lewis Robinson was an Alabaman who came north to Cleveland. He grew up on a farm in Decatur, Alabama, left home at fifteen, and moved in with relatives living at East 71st Street and Euclid Avenue in Cleveland. He worked part-time jobs as a porter and busboy to pay rent to his relatives and cover his high school education expenses. In 1946, still seventeen, he volunteered for duty in the army and served in Japan. He returned to Cleveland in 1947 and worked at Republic Steel. He used GI Bill funds to complete college and law school at a small school in Boston. With a law degree in hand he returned to Cleveland, but no legal jobs were open for him, so he returned to the steel mill. In 1959 he applied to become a housing inspector for the city of Cleveland.[5]

Robinson formed the Freedom Fighters, which became a leading militant group in Cleveland, and he began to organize picketing campaigns against local businesses like Central Cadillac for discriminatory employment practices.

He met his second wife, Beth Wolland, on the picket line. She was white and from upscale Shaker Heights but had taken a job for an obscure African American weekly in order to follow and publicize the efforts of the Freedom Fighters. They were married on January 10, 1964, the day Mae Mallory was extradited from Cleveland to North Carolina. Robinson said the couple spent their weekend honeymoon "worrying about Mae."

"Mae Mallory brought to Cleveland the word 'black' instead of Negro and the natural 'Afro' hair style," Robinson wrote in his autobiography. "Kinky hair became *good* hair and black became beautiful."[6]

It was during a belated wedding party that Robinson and fifty guests began to discuss Murray Hill and the need for "a black man's peace patrol." Robinson wrote of that night: "One father who had three kids being bused to the white neighborhoods said, 'Look, Malcolm X is saying it has got to be the "ballot or the bullet" in 1964 for the black people. The black man has been playing the white man's political game for the last hundred years and what has it got us? More segregation, more oppression. We're going from the wolf to the fox, from the Democrats to the Republicans.'"[7]

Robinson contacted "some brothers in Detroit and Chicago" to tell them of their tentative plans. "We all agreed," he wrote, "that the impact would be a greater propaganda coup if a Cleveland announcement were followed up by one in Detroit and Chicago. This would represent two million blacks in these three cities."[8]

Robinson and his new wife endured sleepless nights in the days after his announcement of the rifle club. But a tragedy was about to overshadow his announcement and Malcolm X's fiery rhetoric. CORE had scheduled demonstrations the week following Malcolm X's speech at the sites of the schools being constructed in Glenville. School board president Ralph McAllister was belligerent, refusing to meet with an interfaith group of religious leaders who insisted on a moratorium on construction: "I cannot develop much enthusiasm for meeting with an organization when one of its leaders whom I have never met, was allowed to castigate me publicly."[9] McAllister said the construction would continue "if we can depend on vigorous and prompt law enforcement."[10]

Monday, April 6, protesters gathered at one of the Glenville schools without incident, though many picketers were arrested. Tuesday was a different story. That morning, Rev. Bruce Klunder, a white Presbyterian minister associated with the Church of the Covenant on the campus of Western Reserve University and Case Institute of Technology and the director of the Student Christian Union, told his wife that he had made up his mind that he would protest at the Lakeview Road site of a new school in Glenville. He understood the risk of being arrested and sent to jail was great.

Klunder was raised in Oregon and completed his undergraduate education there, but moved to Cleveland in 1962 after attending Yale Divinity School. He and his wife Joanne became founding members of the local chapter of the Congress of Racial Equality. He was twenty-seven and the couple had two young children, six and three years of age.

Klunder struggled with his decision to join the demonstration. He had a trip planned to Peru that summer to work in a YMCA Building for Brotherhood program and he worried that a trial might prevent him from leaving the country. "We talked about it for several days," Joanne Klunder wrote, "and Bruce made his decision only a few hours before the demonstration was to begin. He came to the nursery school where I teach and told me he *had* to go to the school construction site." He told her he had to "stick all the way" with the struggle. "I understood," she wrote, "and I agreed. He told me to keep my promise to the children that I would take them to the zoo that afternoon. Then we said goodbye, and he left."[11]

A large assembly of protesters gathered at the construction site for the new Stephen E. Howe Elementary School. Some decided to stage a "lie-in" to stop the construction equipment from moving. At the time, the construction company was under a deadline to complete the school by November 1 or face stiff delay penalties. Several African Americans lay down in front of a bulldozer being operated by a man named John

White. White's front loader was raised and he could not lower it without hurting the people lying in front of the bulldozer. According to White, he did not notice that Bruce Klunder had thrown himself behind the earth mover to prevent it from backing up. When White put the bulldozer in reverse to avoid hurting the people in front of him, he ran over Klunder and did not stop until he had passed over Klunder's body entirely. Klunder was immediately crushed to death.

News of Klunder's death sparked a flash of violence in the neighborhood. The bulldozer driver was attacked and saved only by police intervention. A small riot broke out, cars were vandalized, some stores were looted, and throngs of young men battled with police. "Police, in steel helmets, were forced to use tear gas bombs to scatter crowds that would not clear out of the neighborhood."[12]

"I knew something had happened the instant I heard my name was called over the loudspeaker at the zoo," Joanne Klunder wrote about that terrible day. She was told at the zoo of the accident, that her husband was dead. "When I saw Bruce again, he was at the Cuyahoga County Morgue," she remembered. "His crushed body still bore the awful marks the bulldozer treads had made."[13]

Reaction in the white community was sharp. The Cleveland *Plain Dealer* published a rare editorial on its front page blaming the protesters. "The accidental death of the Rev. Bruce Klunder was the direct result of a lawless use of force initiated by civil rights groups attempting to stop construction of a school building the location of which they opposed."[14] In emergency negotiations between the board of education and CORE, a common pleas judge, John V. Corrigan, issued a court order barring picketing and halting construction. Judge Corrigan said, "Everything we have results from our system of government. If we destroy it, what have we left?"

The board president, Ralph McAllister, walked out on negotiations before the judge had brokered a deal. "This is a victory of anarchy," he bitterly told the press later that night. The *Plain Dealer* wrote that McAllister had thin skin about any criticism leveled against him or the board. "He follows carefully everything that is written or said about himself and the board," the paper observed. "He sometimes appears

Reverend Bruce Klunder, crushed in protest over building new segregated schools in Glenville, April 6, 1964, days after Malcolm X's "Ballots or Bullets" speech. *Western Reserve Historical Society*

sensitive to criticism and especially to any suggestion of disagreement among board members."[15]

Nationally, Klunder became a martyr in the civil rights firmament. CORE's national director, James Farmer, came to Cleveland, as did John Lewis, veteran of the demonstrations in the South and chairman of the Student Nonviolent Coordinating Committee (SNCC).[16]

Klunder was cremated and his ashes were interred in the columbarium of the Church of the Covenant.

Within days of Klunder's memorial service, school construction in Glenville resumed.[17]

Meanwhile, Lewis Robinson came under intense scrutiny. His boss at the Cleveland Housing Department was told to fire him. Letters to the editor demanded swift and decisive action against the formation of a Negro rifle club. "The people of this city expect that Malcolm X and his band of insurrectionists will be kept under strict surveillance," one reader wrote. "If the situation so much as gets one hair out of line, these men in public office [Mayor Locher, his safety director, and the chief of police] must be held accountable."[18]

A particularly rancorous editorial from Louis Seltzer, the irascible editor of the *Cleveland Press*, set Lewis Robinson off. "There may be some devious purpose behind this movement to form 'rifle clubs,' some effort by those who profit from a divided American people," Seltzer wrote. "One can also imagine a Machiavellian plot by civil rights opponents; the reaction of most Americans to armed agitators will benefit segregationists more than integrationists." Robinson took this as the editorial jargon of Communism. "What the hell does Communism got to do with black Americans enjoying their God-given rights of citizenship?" he wrote.[19]

Days later, Seltzer was at it again, claiming an informant at the first meeting of the Medgar Evers Rifle Club told the *Press* that "violence was discussed." The unnamed informant also supposedly said, "It was all very formal, like a cell meeting."

The article was false. Believing the *Press* was out to destroy him, Lewis Robinson filed a $250,000 libel suit against Seltzer and the *Press*, a decision that would come to haunt him in the coming years.[20] By Monday, April 13, ten days after Malcolm X's speech at Cory Methodist, Lewis Robinson was terminated from his employment with the city of Cleveland.[21]

The day before Robinson's firing, Malcolm X delivered his "Ballot or Bullet" speech at the King Solomon Baptist Church in Detroit, Michigan. Walter Beach, the Cleveland Browns defensive back, was in attendance. Beach was raised in Pontiac, a suburb of Detroit, and had grown up two doors down from a civil rights lawyer named Milton Henry and his family. Milton Henry, though a Christian, was a proponent of Malcolm X and his emerging philosophy of black nationalism and the separation of the races. In Detroit he cofounded an organization called the Group on Advanced Leadership and the Michigan Freedom Now Party. He became a leading spokesman for black Christian nationalism.

Beach attended Malcolm X's speech at King Solomon Baptist Church and afterward went to Henry's house in Pontiac, where Beach said he "sat at the feet" of Malcolm X, who had come to a gathering in his honor. The encounter left an indelible impression.

Milton Henry was a remarkable figure in his own right. Born in Philadelphia in 1919, he became a member of the all-black Tuskegee Airmen (along with future Detroit mayor Coleman A. Young) during World War II. After the war, he attended Lincoln University in Pennsylvania and then Yale Law School, graduating in 1950, and moved with his family to Pontiac where he set up a law practice.

A councilman in Pontiac from 1954 to 1960, he grew disillusioned with the meager progress that was possible on a local political level. He quit council in 1960 and traveled to Africa to visit an acquaintance he had met through Lincoln University, Kwame Nkrumah, who led the West African nation of Ghana to independence from Great Britain in 1957 and became its first prime minister and president. During this extended trip, Henry likely first encountered Malcolm X, who happened to be in Africa touring with Elijah Mohammad. Returning to the United States, Henry was perplexed by the appeal of Martin Luther King Jr. and his tactics of nonviolence. "Everything hadn't dawned on me completely," he wrote. "It was a transitional thing. But I knew there was something wrong with people on the street getting their butt beat."[22]

He and friend Rev. Albert Cleage invited Malcolm X to deliver the keynote address on November 10, 1963, to the Northern Negro Grass Roots Leadership Conference (also at King Solomon Baptist Church in Detroit), where Malcolm delivered a talk entitled "Message to the Grass Roots."

The day after his "Ballot or Bullet" speech in Detroit, Malcolm X boarded a plane and flew to Jeddah, Saudi Arabia, to perform the ritual of hajj, a pilgrimage to Mecca, continuing his transformational journey toward conversion to the traditional Sunni faith.

In Cleveland that summer, Walter Beach joined the Browns in training camp. He was viewed with suspicion by owner Art Modell because of his "troublemaking" while with the Boston Patriots. "You're a race man, aren't you?" Modell privately asked Beach in one encounter. "I am," Beach responded. "Well, I've done more for the Negroes than they have ever done for themselves," Modell declared. "Art, I doubt it," Beach drolly replied. To Beach, Modell's attitude fit a pattern. In his life he had met many white men in power who suffered from what he called "a God complex"—a paternalistic view of African Americans that came with little to no self-awareness. While Walter Beach was not confrontational, he knew how to stand his ground—and he did several times with Art Modell.

Now in training camp at Hiram College, Beach once again had a "race" target on his back. Sometime in July, Beach was visited by a linebackers' coach, nicknamed the "Turk" because his appearance at the threshold of a player's room meant that the player was about to be let go. "Walt," the Turk said to Beach late in training camp, "Coach Blanton [Collier] wants to see you."

Walter Beach knew what it meant when he was told to bring his playbook with him. When he entered the dorm room where the coaches were meeting, Art Modell was present. None of the coaches would make eye contact with Walter Beach. Someone, Beach cannot recall who, said, "We're sorry. We're not going to go with you. We have a couple of other guys we are looking at."

Back in his dorm room, Beach began to pack his things. Jim Brown, the legendary running back, poked his head into Beach's room on the way to the afternoon practice.

"What's up man?" Brown inquired. "Let's go to practice."

"I can't. They just put me on waivers, Jim."

According to Beach, Brown's countenance changed—he took on a look of determination and strength and left to speak with the owner and the coaches. When he returned fifty minutes later, Brown merely said, "Let's go to practice."

Not another word was said to Beach by the coaches or Art Modell about being cut.[23]

That year, 1964, the Cleveland Browns would win the NFL Championship thanks to the critical play of Walter Beach, who was a shutdown corner, stifling the powerful passing offense of the Baltimore Colts, led by future Hall of Famer Johnny Unitas and his all-star receivers, Raymond Berry and John Mackey.

The Browns blanked the Colts twenty-seven to zero.

In Cleveland, Lewis Robinson, fired by the city of Cleveland for daring to start a "rights" rifle club, bought his first guns. "Until May 15, 1964," he wrote, "I had never owned any kind of firearms. I went downtown to Adler's Army and Navy Store at East 6th and Prospect Avenue and purchased a German Mauser rifle for myself and several rifles for the brothers." He set up a practice range in Ashtabula County, east of Cleveland.[24]

A few weeks later, two young African American students who worked nights in maintenance at the downtown Greyhound Bus Station were arrested "on suspicion" by the Cleveland Police. Taken into custody, the young men were beaten, forced to get on their knees, and ordered to "Bark like a dog, nigger." One of the victims wrote in a statement: "When they got us upstairs on the fourth floor, this policeman, badge 343, who arrested us, took off his gun, his coat, laid down his night stick, rolled up his sleeves, then just started to beat me, calling me a black animal, and a black dog." Attorney Stanley Tolliver called for an immediate federal investigation to find out "the truth behind this incredible example of police sadism and terrorism within the confines of our halls of justice."[25]

None of the policemen involved were disciplined.[26]

8

"I Am on the Outside"

MALCOLM X TOOK AN IMPORTANT step back from the Nation of Islam's antiwhite bigotry during his extraordinary hajj in April and May 1964. "Never have I witnessed such sincere hospitality and overwhelming spirit of true brotherhood as is practiced by people of all colors and races here in this ancient Holy Land, the home of Abraham, Muhammad and all the other Prophets of the Holy Scripture," he wrote from Mecca. "There were tens of thousands of pilgrims," he described in wonderment, "from all over the world. They were of all colors, from blue-eyed blonds to black-skinned Africans."

Malcolm X's split with Elijah Muhammad also caused the final rupture with Muhammad Ali. The two men ran into each other in Ghana when Malcolm was on his slow return from his pilgrimage and Ali was making the first stop on his African tour. "He was wearing the traditional Muslim white robes," Ali wrote later, "further signifying his break with Elijah Muhammad. He walked with a cane that looked like a prophet's stick and wore a beard. I thought he had gone too far." Ali snubbed Malcolm X when he approached him. "Brother Malcolm," Ali brusquely said, "you shouldn't have crossed the Honorable Elijah Muhammad." For the rest of his life, Ali regretted this moment.[1]

In an interview with *Ebony*, reporter Hans Massaquoi asked Malcolm X if it was correct that since his pilgrimage to Mecca he no longer held the view that all whites are evil. "True," Malcolm responded, "my trip to Mecca has opened my eyes. I no longer subscribe to racism. I have adjusted my thinking to the point where I believe whites are human beings—as long as this is borne out by their humane attitude toward Negroes."[2]

But this did not translate into his welcoming a mixing of the races—he was still for separation and continued to support the idea of establishing a separate African nation within the United States. Back in New York from his trip abroad, he founded the Organization of Afro-American Unity (OAAU) on June 28, 1964, modeled on the Organization of African Unity (OAU), a Pan-Africanist association of thirty-two African countries established a year earlier and dedicated to the eradication of European colonialism and white minority rule in Africa.[3] The purpose of Malcolm X's American version of the OAU was to restore links with Africa, to unify and educate American blacks about their African heritage, and to encourage black control in every aspect of the African American community in the United States.

When asked whether he would accept whites into his new organization, Malcolm replied, "Definitely not." He paused, and then qualified: "If John Brown were still alive, we might accept him. But I'm definitely not interested in nonviolent whites or nonviolent blacks. If you show me a nonviolent Negro, I'll show you a Negro whose reflexes don't work or one who needs psychiatric care."

He was unrelenting in his belief in armed self-defense. "We don't advocate violence, but nonviolent tactics based solely on morality can only succeed when you are dealing with a basically moral people," he said in his *Ebony* interview. "A man who oppresses another man because of his color is not moral. It is the duty of every Afro-American to protect himself against mass murderers, bombers, lynchers, floggers, brutalizers, and exploiters. If the government is unable or unwilling to protect us, we reserve the right as citizens to defend ourselves by any means necessary. A man with a rifle or a club can only be stopped by a person with a rifle or a club."

But Malcolm X's most important goal in creating his new organization was to elevate the plight of the American Negro to a higher plane than simply that of an American problem. He was recasting the American civil rights struggle as a global human rights struggle, part of worldwide self-determination by people of color against imperialists. He told the *Ebony* reporter that his new organization was a "non-religious

and non-sectarian group organized to unite Afro-Americans for a constructive attainment of human rights." In announcing the founding of
the OAAU, Malcolm X first uttered the phrase for which he would
become best known: "We declare our right on this earth to be a man,
to be a human being, to be respected as a human being, to be given the
rights of a human being in this society, on this earth, in this day, which
we intend to bring into existence *by any means necessary*."

Later in the summer of 1964, Milton Henry traveled with Malcolm
to Africa, this time to attend the Second Organization of African Unity
Conference in Cairo. Malcolm attended as an observer and distributed a memo from the OAAU on behalf of twenty-two million African
Americans "whose human rights are being violated daily by the racism
of American imperialists." Henry filmed and interviewed Malcolm X
through his Afro-American Broadcasting Corporation.[4]

In doing all this, Malcolm X was tapping into the worldwide liberation movements of his time, especially in Africa, but elsewhere, too.
This produced a peculiar mixing of black nationalism with Socialism
and Communism. In Detroit, for example, Milton Henry attended a
Christian church pastored by his friend Albert Cleage that also attracted
Marxists and members of the Socialist Workers Party. As one author
noted, "Few saw any ideological or political incongruities in moving
from a SWP forum, to attending a talk by Cleage, to traveling to or
otherwise supporting the Southern branch of the struggle. Rather, it was
a fertile social and political space in which younger activists and older
radicals were striving to make connections: between an 'old left' and a
'new left' one, between national and international struggles for justice."[5]

In Cleveland, a junior high school teacher named Don Freeman helped
to found the Revolutionary Action Movement (RAM) with a Philadelphia
black nationalist and revolutionary named Max Stanford. Freeman and
Stanford met in 1961 while college students (Freeman attended Western
Reserve and Stanford was enrolled in Central State in Wilberforce, Ohio)
at a conference sponsored by the National Student Association in Madison, Wisconsin. In April 1962 Freeman was introduced to Malcolm X in
New York through a friend Freeman had known since childhood, a young
man who had grown up with him in the Outhwaite Homes projects in

Cleveland. Freeman's friend, a musician drawn to New York, had joined the Nation of Islam and Malcolm X's Mosque No. 7, abandoned his music career, and became the mosque's secretary. This encounter began a working relationship between Freeman and Malcolm that would grow over the next three years, though Freeman did not become a Black Muslim.[6] Both men shared the stage at the Grass Roots Conference in Detroit in November 1963, and Freeman was invited by Malcolm X to speak at the Audubon Ballroom in New York on Easter weekend in 1964 (just before Malcolm X came to Cleveland to give his "Ballot or Bullet" speech).

Stanford and Freeman were intrigued with the idea that African Americans were the subjects of "domestic colonialism" and that their predicament was aligned with the nationalist revolutionary movements in Africa, Cuba (Castro), and China (Mao). Thus, the answer for black Americans lay not in nonviolent protests or sit-ins but in the Leninist idea of fomenting conflict (here race struggle, as opposed to class struggle) through the formation of a revolutionary vanguard—a clandestine, paramilitary, tight-knit group—that would build political consciousness and spread revolution through the avocation of mass protests and armed rebellion.[7]

The paradigm of domestic colonialism rang true to young Don Freeman. A 1962 article written by black essayist Harold Cruse entitled "Revolutionary Nationalism and the Afro-American" had much influence over Freeman. Cruse explained his idea of domestic colonialism thus: "From the beginning, the American Negro has existed as a colonial being. His enslavement coincided with the colonial expansion of European powers and was nothing more or less than a condition of domestic colonialism. Instead of the United States establishing a colonial empire in Africa, it brought the colonial system home and installed it in the Southern states."[8]

Freeman founded the Afro-American Institute in October 1962 in Cleveland as its first RAM outpost.

"In the spring of 1964," Max Stanford wrote, "a revolutionary black nationalist organization named the Revolutionary Action Movement (RAM) began to work with Malcolm X. . . . RAM as an organization advocated urban guerilla warfare, mass rebellions, and national black strikes as forms of struggle for the black nationalist movement. Its goal was to create an independent black republic through a socialist revolution."[9]

Robert F. Williams, in exile in Cuba, was a muse for Stanford and
Freeman. "Williams was the forerunner of the revolutionary nationalist
movement," Stanford wrote.[10] In the February 1964 issue of a newsletter
Williams published from Cuba called *The Crusader*, he wrote of the kind
of urban guerilla warfare in the United States that would line up with the
black liberation movements and third world fights with colonial powers.
"The new concept of revolution defies military science and tactics," he
theorized. "The new concept is lightning campaigns conducted in highly
sensitive urban communities with the paralysis reaching the small communities and spreading to farm areas." These sorts of guerilla tactics in an
urban setting, Williams argued, would neutralize the US government and
its "modern and fierce weapons," which would be of little use in heavily
populated areas.[11] The US military would be vulnerable to an internal
war, and so would the police. The guerilla tactics would create "a state of
confusion," with wholesale destruction of property, massive sniping and
organized rebellion against the symbol of the white oppressors: the police.

Robert Williams was named president-in-exile of RAM by Max Stanford, who was smuggled into Cuba in 1964 along with other radical
students from Detroit and California, including Ernest Allen who came
from the University of California at Berkeley. Allen met Don Freeman
at the JFK Airport upon his return to the United States and traveled to
Cleveland and Detroit before taking Freeman's RAM ideology back
to California, where it inspired his inner circle, including Bobby Seale,
one of the cofounders of the Black Panther Party.[12]

In the summer of 1964, Lewis Robinson and members of his rifle
club decided to organize a nationalist center for young people. They
secured a storefront on the northern border of Hough, 8801 Superior
Avenue, and began to clean it up. The plan was to open in the evenings
to present culture and history talks and offer recreational activities for
neighborhood kids to help "curb juvenile delinquency." Two organizers
with Robinson were Harllel Jones, a city sewer department laborer, and
Albert Ware, a disabled Korean War veteran. They named the center
the JFK House, not in honor of the fallen president, but in homage to
Jomo "Freedom" Kenyatta, the anticolonial fighter and the first prime
minister of Kenya.

Robinson's leaflets describing the JFK House proclaimed it would "promote family togetherness and family unity." Children would be urged to obtain high school diplomas and even attend college. Lectures would focus on budgeting and money management, legal rights, sewing classes, birth control, and child care.[13] Don Freeman spoke on African history and culture.

But Robinson's controversial past cast a shadow over his new venture. Even the *Call and Post* referred to the center as the "Rifleman's youth center." In an article in December 1964, a reporter wrote, "There were many eyebrows raised a few months back when Lewis Robinson, labeled the city's rifleman, opened a center for young people in the Superior-Wade Park area."[14] Yet police from the Sixth District, according to the article, inspected the center and gave it a tentative seal of approval.

One of the first guest speakers to present at an evening event at the JFK House was the attorney Carl Stokes.[15] Stokes had been elected to the Ohio House of Representatives in the fall of 1962 as the first black Democrat in the Ohio legislature. By the end of 1964, though, Stokes was already tiring of the tedium and conservatism of the state legislature (When he joined, Republicans outnumbered Democrats 5 to 2 and whites outnumbered blacks 184 to 2.)

Stokes was a kid who grew up in true poverty. Like Don Freeman, he lived in Outhwaite Homes, the first federally funded housing project in Cleveland, constructed as part of Franklin Roosevelt's Public Works Administration. Outhwaite was a paradise compared to the ramshackle home in which he had lived. When Carl was two, his father, a laundry worker, died. He and his older brother, Louis, lived with their mother on the first floor of a "rickety old two-family home" on East 69th Street. There was no central heating. Rats infested the home. ("We covered the rat holes with the tops of tin cans," Carl remembered.) Carl, Louis, and their mother shared one bed. Their mother worked as a domestic in the homes of white people. "She worked hard and made so little that she had to accept welfare to scrape enough for us to live," Stokes wrote.[16]

Though his mother was a person of service, she had a deep-seated pride in her work and her two boys. "Louis and I saw in her an example of how our people are forced into not merely the labor but the style of servitude, with its superficial deceits," Carl wrote in his autobiography. "We all know that servility is an act, something we do with our faces and voices when we have to. . . . But after a time the habit of the servant wrenches a man at the roots of his being. . . . It takes a deeply felt and abiding personal integrity to survive as a whole person. Fortunately for Louis and me, our mother is such a person."[17]

While Carl did well in elementary school, he became something of a street tough and hustler once he hit adolescence. His hostility toward the white students at East Technical High School was intense. "I remember spending a good deal of my time in the afternoon beating up white kids," he wrote. "My motivation and rationale for this were as illogical and senseless then as were unprovoked attacks on black boys who dared to venture into white neighborhoods. It is impossible for me to recall now what was going on in my mind then, what I was trying to accomplish."[18]

Stokes took up boxing and hit the pool halls. He dropped out of high school and enlisted in the army in July 1945. "This was no moral decision," he said. "The war was over. I just wanted to get the hell out of a world I had had enough of." The army sent him to Fort McClellan in Alabama, "where I learned a clean-edged unadulterated hatred of whites," he wrote. After basic training Stokes was shipped off to postwar Europe where contact with "educated black men in the army" made him rethink the value in furthering his education.

After the service, he took advantage of the GI Bill to finish high school and attend Western Reserve University and then began working for a black man who was a chauffeur and had important contacts in Ohio politics. Stokes soon landed a job with the Ohio Department of Liquor.

Inwardly, though, Carl Stokes was haunted by his upbringing, his poverty, and his second-class citizenship. He was born in a nation and in a city where he was hated simply because of the color of his skin. One of his recurring nightmares provides a searing searchlight into the damage racism caused his soul. "I am walking in front of a house," he recalled. "It is cold outside, and I can feel the wind cutting through my thin jacket. I look into the house through the big picture window and I see a white family in the living room. The father throws his baby into the air to make it laugh. A fireplace is going, the family is warm, happy, and alive. There is a fence in the front of the house. I am outside."[19]

9

"The Black Stalin"

DON FREEMAN WAS LIVING A double life. He was a mild-mannered, popular, and respected social studies teacher at Kennard Junior High School by day but a revolutionary in any spare time he could find. He was constantly traveling during school breaks and weekends to other cities, visiting college campuses to find "like-minded" African Americans who believed in the idea of black nationalism and revolution. Eventually, he came to the notice of the FBI.

A month after Malcolm X delivered his "Ballot or Bullet" speeches in Cleveland and Detroit, Freeman, Stanford, and some RAM students at Fisk University in Nashville, a historically black university, held a conference to discuss unity with African, Asian, and Latin American revolutions and to try to find financial backing for RAM from abroad. A black newspaper reporter from Baltimore named William Worthy wrote about the Fisk University meeting in the October 1964 edition of *Esquire* magazine in an article entitled "The Red Chinese American Negro." Worthy himself famously traveled to China and Cuba in defiance of State Department bans.[1] His take on the Fisk confab: "Radical Negro militants are turning to Mao Tse-tung for support in overthrowing the US Government." He called it "the most frightening news story of 1964."[2]

Worthy noted that about seventy-five students attended the Fisk conference. He identified RAM as a galvanizing group that grew out of the frustration on Negro campuses that followed Dr. King's nonviolence campaigns in the summer of 1963, for the very reason that those demonstrations bore so little fruit and in fact produced catastrophe in Birmingham with the killing of four young black girls. "For months," he observed, "one such group known as RAM—the Revolutionary Action Movement—moved several roving organizers into the South, recruiting the dissidents in CORE and the Student Nonviolent Coordinating Committee and preparing for the conference of radicals that took place in Nashville."

This meeting represented a dynamic fusion of northern militants with the mostly southern-based SNCC, which was then being led by John Lewis, a proponent of nonviolence and integration. According to Freeman, Lewis attended the Fisk meeting and while he did not buy into the RAM agenda of revolution and violence, he did not discourage his organization from further contacts with RAM. When his successor, Stokely Carmichael, became SNCC's chairman in 1966, the seeds planted at Fisk took root—Carmichael did espouse a militant response to American racism.

"How do the Negro revolutionaries expect to win?" Worthy asked in the *Esquire* article. "Those who have studied events in China and Vietnam believe that, as state power is used to repress upheavals and rioting in ghettos, Negroes in the armed forces will defect to protect their homes, taking with them their own guns and stolen weapons as well."

Worthy profiled Robert F. Williams at length and keyed in on the worldwide anti-imperialist forces that were propelling RAM and its adherents, writing, "The widespread psychological defections from a government that tolerates violence against its citizens have been accompanied by a growing acceptance of a concept that the U.S. is really composed of two nations, one the colonizer, the other the colonized, that Negroes are engaged in what Joseph Alsop has called a colonial war at home, that 20,000,000 black Americans are part of an international colored majority, and that victory here will come only when the world revolution against colonialism and neocolonialism finally triumphs."

With uncanny foreshadowing, Worthy cited writings of Robert Williams that predicted the nature of the urban uprisings that were about to hit the United States. "The weapons of defense employed by Afro-American freedom fighters must consist of a poor man's arsenal," Williams had written in *The Crusader.* "Gasoline fire bombs (Molotov cocktails), lye or acid bombs can be used extensively. During the night hours such weapons, thrown from rooftops, will make the streets impossible for racist cops to patrol."

Chillingly, Williams also predicted the kind of warfare that would come to Cleveland in the summer of 1968. "High-powered sniper rifles are readily available," he wrote. "Armor-piercing bullets will penetrate oil storage tanks from a distance."

Worthy noted that the RAM leaders did not intend to convert RAM into a mass organization known to the general public. Instead, he said its "dedicated and well-read leaders see themselves as a vanguard group that will disseminate revolutionary ideas and will remain in communication with revolutionary forces everywhere."

All this landed Freeman and Stanford on the FBI's list of subversives to follow. The local FBI office in Cleveland in turn partnered with the Cleveland Police Department, in particular the Subversives Unit headed up by Sergeant John J. Ungvary. Ungvary was a throwback to the days when Eliot Ness was Cleveland's safety director, and he built his reputation hunting Communists during the heyday of the McCarthy era. But in the 1960s his inquiring eye turned to the trouble brewing in Cleveland's African American community.

Don Freeman intended to stay underground, but he made the mistake of writing an article for the 1964 fall issue of RAM's publication *Black America*, distributed out of Detroit.[3] He reported on the Fisk University conference with an almost academic detachment, writing about "bourgeois reformism" and enhanced "potentialities for the emergence of a viable Nationalist Youth Movement." But his association with Max Stanford, who wrote of violent revolution and of "war with White America" in *Black America*, painted Freeman in the same threatening light.

According to an FBI counterintelligence memo, a document entitled "The Revolutionary Action Movement Manifesto" was handed over to the FBI by an informant on November 3, 1964. "This document stated, in part," the memo recited, "that RAM was officially organized in the

Winter of 1963, by Afro-Americans who support the revolutionary objectives of Robert F. Williams, then residing in Cuba, and his concept of organized violence to achieve the liberation of the Afro-American people in the United States."[4]

Don Freeman was specifically called out in the FBI file as a threat to national security. "On November 16, 1964," the memo stated, "a second source advised he learned recently from a RAM member that the organization began in Detroit, Michigan, largely under the impetus of Don Freeman, described as the 'Father' of RAM and referred to as RAM's 'Black Stalin.' Freeman served as RAM Chairman, with Maxwell Stanford (now of Philadelphia, Pennsylvania) serving as RAM Field Chairman."

This is the way the FBI worked. The infamous COINTELPRO (counterintelligence program) which was launched in the 1950s to sow discord in Communist-inspired groups, turned its attention to black nationalist "hate groups" beginning in the early 1960s. An FBI memo from 1967 described its purpose and tactics: "The purpose of this new counterintelligence endeavor is to expose, disrupt, misdirect, discredit, or otherwise neutralize the activities of black nationalists, hate-type organizations and groupings, their leadership, spokesmen, membership, and supporters, and to counter their propensity for violence and disorder."[5]

To spread dissension, the FBI relied upon paid informants who infiltrated the targeted organizations. Their purpose was not just to gain inside information but to leave members of the group in a state of paranoia, constantly wondering if someone—anyone—might be "police," or a paid Judas. The suspicion itself was intended to exacerbate any already-existing internal tensions or frictions that might exist among the group's members, which in turn would tear at the group's sense of cohesiveness with the ultimate goal of collapsing the group from the inside.

Don Freeman was one of the earliest victims of the FBI's program to expose and discredit black nationalist leaders. He would be very publicly fired from his job as a Cleveland schoolteacher in February 1965, but Freeman saw his firing not as isolated retribution against him for secretly advocating revolutionary acts but as part and parcel of a series of events all linked and directed, he believed, at RAM and emerging militant black nationalism.

The first was the arrest on February 16, 1965, of four individuals in New York City who were alleged to have plotted to blow up the Statue of Liberty, the Liberty Bell, and the Washington Monument. The "small group of Negro extremists" consisted of three young black men who were part of the "Black Liberation Front," along with a white woman from Canada who smuggled dynamite from Montreal to New York. She was a French Canadian nationalist. The group had been infiltrated by an undercover New York City patrolman.[6]

The leader of the black extremists was an employee of the New York Public Library who was described as "pro-Castro" and "pro-Chinese." He had traveled to Cuba the year before on the same trip with the RAM activists. Freeman said this group in New York was actually a RAM cell.

Meanwhile, Malcolm X, who was a RAM supporter, had been on the run since breaking with Elijah Muhammad, and he told many reporters, including Mike Wallace, that he was a "dead man," facing constant death threats from the Nation of Islam. He spent eighteen weeks out of the country in the summer and fall of 1964, in part to get away from daily perils and attempts on his life. When he returned to the United States on November 24, 1964, he continued his rapprochement with the civil rights movement, despite the grave risks that his apostasy from the Nation of Islam had created.[7] Evan Muhammad Ali, once a Malcolm X acolyte, made ominous statements about Malcolm, saying, "Malcolm X and anybody else who attacks or talks about attacking Elijah Muhammad will die."[8]

Malcolm began restlessly roaming the country as if he knew he was running out of time. On February 3, 1965, he lectured at the Tuskegee Institute in Alabama and then detoured to Selma to show solidarity with a voting rights protest that Dr. King and the Southern Christian Leadership Conference had organized. At the time of Malcolm's appearance in Selma, Dr. King had been arrested and was in jail. (Because of literacy tests and other barriers to voting, there were 9,543 whites compared to 335 blacks registered to vote in Dallas County, where Selma was located. Presented with this evidence, a federal court issued an order requiring the county to register more Negroes with all due speed.[9] Bloody Sunday, March 7, 1965, and the march across Edmund Pettus Bridge was just a month away.)

Malcolm X was invited by SNCC students, surprised by his appearance, to speak at a rally at Brown Chapel AME Church where he told his audience that the "white man should thank God that Dr. King is holding his people in check, because there are other ways to obtain their ends."[10] While he did not have the time to visit King in jail because of the request to speak and his need to get back to New York to prepare for a scheduled trip to attend a conference in Europe, Malcolm did take a moment to speak privately with Coretta Scott King, explaining his thinking about coming to Selma. "I thought if the white people understood what the alternative was that they would be more inclined to listen to your husband," he told her. "And so that's why I came."[11]

That weekend, Malcolm X flew to London to attend the first Congress of the Council of African Organizations. When he traveled to Paris a few days later to speak, he was barred at the airport from entry by French security officials who branded him a troublemaker.[12] He returned briefly to the United Kingdom, and then back to the United States late on Friday night, February 12.

Saturday night he and his family went to bed in their small brick home in Queens only to be awakened by three bottles of gasoline with fuses being hurled through the windows. Malcolm rushed his four small children and his wife outside into the twenty-degree cold. "The house has been the subject of a prolonged controversy between Malcolm X and the Chicago-based Black Muslim movement, of which he is a former representative," the *Times* reported. "The Black Muslims hold title to the house. They demanded Malcolm vacate it when he broke with them to found his own organization."[13]

Despite a night of terror, Malcolm flew to Detroit the next morning, Sunday, February 14, to give a speech to a group assembled by attorney Milton Henry. "I was in a house last night that was bombed," he told the crowd. "It isn't something that made me lose confidence in what I am doing," he explained, "because my wife understands and I have children from this size down, and even in their young age they understand. I think they would rather have a father or brother or whatever the situation may be who will take a stand in the face of any kind of reaction from narrow-minded people rather than to compromise and later on have to grow up in shame and in disgrace."

In the face of physical exhaustion, Malcolm spoke at length in Detroit. "Brothers and sisters," he said at one point, "if you and I would just realize that once we learn to talk the language that they understand, they will then get the point. You can't reach a man if you don't speak his language. If a man speaks the language of brute force, you can't come to him with peace. Why, good night! He'll break you in two, as he has been doing all along."

He concluded his remarks by praising Milton Henry "and the brothers here in Detroit who are very progressive young men." He urged others to follow their lead and to unite in a common human rights struggle.[14]

Back in New York, he ramped up his attack on Black Muslims at a meeting in the Audubon Ballroom on Monday, February 15, accusing them of firebombing his house and cowardly attacking sleeping babies. To further disparage Elijah Muhammad, he told the group that he had once worked with him to make peace with the Ku Klux Klan in the South so Muhammad could buy land there and live in segregated peace. But now, surveying the bleak landscape following his break with Muhammad, he said he only regretted "that two black groups have to fight and kill each other."[15]

By week's end, assassins had gathered and made their plans. One of Malcolm X's bodyguards was an undercover cop, and he alerted his superiors that violence seemed imminent.[16] Yet on Sunday, February 21, security outside the Audubon Ballroom was unusually lax, while across the street at Columbia-Presbyterian Medical Center twenty officers were assigned in what otherwise would have been a slow Sunday.

Malcolm told his friends that he did not feel right about being at the Audubon Ballroom that day and many urged him to go home and rest. He insisted he needed to speak. His wife and daughters were in the audience. When he was finally brought on stage around 3:00 PM, he barely uttered words of greeting when five men created a diversion with a smoke bomb in the crowd and then approached him to unleash a murderous barrage of shotgun blasts and pistol shots. Chaos ensued. No doctor from the Medical Center would come over to offer medical assistance and police gathered up Malcolm's body on a stretcher to walk him across the street. Not long afterward, a hospital spokesman said, "Gentlemen, the man you know as Malcolm X is dead. He apparently was in a death-like condition when brought to the hospital."[17]

He was thirty-nine.

In Cleveland, six days later, on February 27, 1965, the *Cleveland Plain Dealer* ran the banner headline "TEACHER TIED TO NEGRO REBELS." Don Freeman was the subject of a blistering exposé aimed at taking down RAM in Cleveland and Freeman in particular. It is not clear who tipped the newspaper, but it had the earmarks of an FBI COINTELPRO planted story. In what was clearly fabricated news, the *Plain Dealer* repeated what the *New York Daily News* had reported in a February 24 story: "Top New York police and federal investigators believe RAM members plotted the death of Malcolm X last Sunday in New York City."[18]

Don Freeman believed this false assertion was the result of a COINTELPRO disinformation campaign. He also believed that while the gunman who cut down Malcolm X came from the Nation of Islam, the FBI facilitated or at least collaborated in the assassination. The arrest of the New York bombers, Malcolm X's killing, and his exposure in quick succession, in Freeman's thought, show that these events were all linked—that the FBI was trying to destroy the militant black nationalist movement in its infancy in the United States.[19]

For Don Freeman, the *Plain Dealer* coverage was devastating. His picture was on the front page of the paper under alarming headlines. "Donald Freeman, a social studies teacher at Kennard Junior High School, 2510 E. 46th Street, is a contributing author to a fiery nationalist publication advocating a Negro revolution against 'the white American ruling class,'" the article began. Freeman was said to have used his East Cleveland home (where he lived with his mother and father) as the subscription headquarters for *Black America*, "the official organ of RAM, an organization that describes itself as the Black Liberation Front of the U.S.A." The article described the Fisk University meeting and Freeman's writing about it.

The article stressed RAM's association with the dangerous Robert F. Williams, "the branch official repudiated by the NAACP in Monroe, N.C., now in Havana, Cuba, headquarters of his monthly newsletter, *The Crusader.*" It was pointed out that Williams had fled the country because of kidnapping charges and that he wrote, "It is better for oppressed people to be fanatics for freedom and justice rather than to cow timidly and submit to the evils of dehumanization and slavery." The article also connected a dot to "Mrs. Willie Mae Mallory," reminding readers that she was also involved in the kidnapping case and had been returned to North Carolina from Cleveland where she was tried and found guilty.

Again quoting from the likely FBI-inspired *New York Daily News* article that claimed RAM had been involved in Malcolm X's assassination, the *Plain Dealer* ominously reported, "The *Daily News* said RAM is composed of 'hard-core young hot-heads from both the prophet's and Malcolm's organizations, who dream of a global black revolution.'" The description of RAM militancy and extremism could not have been more dramatic. RAM was "master-minded" by Robert F. Williams and was "strong in Detroit, Chicago, and Cleveland, and became active in New York City six months ago when police became aware of 'guns and ammunition' pouring into Harlem."

Freeman spoke with a reporter and was clearly thrown on the defensive. Admitting he was "associated with RAM," he denied he was a leader of the organization. When pressed about RAM's call for black revolution and violence, Freeman replied, "My position is that such a thing is not in the offing. From reading the magazine, some people may have that impression, but I am not concerned." In a move that probably pleased the local FBI office, Freeman fingered Max Stanford as the "young militant" who was running RAM out of New York. Freeman portrayed himself as more of a political tactician or theoretician.

The newspaper pointed out that as a Cleveland school teacher, Freeman was required to sign a loyalty oath that provided that he would "support and defend the Constitution of the United States against all

enemies, foreign and domestic." Freeman said he had likely signed such
an oath and that he "had no objection to signing it."

By no happenstance the *Plain Dealer* carried an article in the same
edition entitled, "Most Negroes Oppose Own Extremism." Citing a
recent poll conducted by Louis Harris, the newspaper stated that the
pollster found that "94% of the Negroes support the Rev. Martin Luther
King Jr., and 92% back the National Association for the Advancement
of Colored People," whereas a mere 8 percent supported "Malcolm X
and Black Muslims." Don Freeman, the article noted, was part of an
extremist organization that "the vast majority of Negroes oppose."

Freeman, isolated, naively pled for the public's discretion. "Freeman
said he preferred no publicity about his RAM activities because 'after
all, I have to eat,'" he told *Plain Dealer* reporters. "He also asked that
his parents be 'kept out of this.'"[20]

But the paper was not about to comply with Freeman's request for
his family's privacy. The next day, in an article entitled "Teacher's Family
Unaware of His RAM Ties," Don Freeman's mother was quoted as saying, "I have no control over what my son says or does, and it is extremely
upsetting to wake up to a nightmare like this." The *Plain Dealer* coverage
had provoked threatening phone calls to his parents and just to make
sure the public had all the relevant information, it printed a correction
on its front page, giving the home address where the Freeman family
lived, having erroneously provided the wrong address the day before.
"The *Plain Dealer* regrets the typographical error," the editors wrote.[21]

Freeman protested that his parents "had no relationship to this
whatsoever," and the local CORE chapter issued a statement accusing
the *Plain Dealer* of engaging in McCarthyism and First Amendment
violations. "Mr. Freeman is an excellent teacher," CORE wrote. "His
private life should be his own business and needs no investigation by
the school board, nor should there be any threat to his job status if he
is performing adequately in the classroom."[22]

But the board of education member (and previous president) Ralph
McAllister—the man whose actions and comments helped instigate the
Murray Hill violence a year earlier—had found a cause célèbre, and
he pushed the school superintendent, Paul W. Briggs, to institute an

aggressive probe into whether Freeman had violated his loyalty oath through his support of RAM. "We must consider the rights of the students," one official said. Don Freeman was now in full reverse, telling the *Plain Dealer* that he had just been a writer and that he no longer had any "concrete connection" with RAM. Lewis Robinson expressed his support. "Donald Freeman at age 26 is one of Cleveland's finest and most respected teachers at Kennard Junior High," Robinson told the *Plain Dealer*. "We need more like him."[23]

On the weekend that Don Freeman faced the avalanche of negative publicity, Malcolm X was laid to rest in New York. Across the country mainstream newspapers reviled him as a violent man who met a violent death.[24] But to many he was a hero. According to the *New York Times*, "Ossie Davis, the Negro actor and playwright, who delivered the eulogy, said, 'Malcolm was our manhood, our living black manhood. In honoring him we honor the best within us.'" Attorney Milton Henry from Pontiac, Michigan, was one of the pallbearers.

Two days after the *Plain Dealer* stories appeared, Don Freeman was suspended from his duties as a teacher; by March 16 he was fired by the board of education for "conduct unbecoming a teacher." Stanley Tolliver, a rising African American rights attorney who took Freeman's case, asked for a public hearing before the entire board. "To be fired because his views are different from what someone thinks they should be is an infringement of freedom of speech," Tolliver said. "He is not a person who advocates the violent overthrow of the government, nor is he a subversive."[25]

Not satisfied with the firing, Ralph McAllister continued his attack on Freeman by insisting perjury charges be filed against him for lying before the full board of education about being in Nashville for the Fisk Conference on May 1. Freemen testified he was not in Nashville when he took sick leave that day—which McAllister said was a lie.[26] Records presented to a grand jury showed that Freeman registered at the Nashville YMCA that day. The perjury case would take two years to prosecute and Freeman would eventually be found not guilty, but McAllister had accomplished his purpose in harassing Freeman.[27]

The "Black Stalin" had been neutralized; Malcolm X was dead.

10

"Whatever You Fear
Is What You Worship"

ONE OF THE PEOPLE CLOSELY following the rise of the militant black nationalist movement in Cleveland was Fred Evans. He was in the audience when Malcolm X delivered his "Ballot or Bullet" speech at Cory Methodist Church in Glenville; he called Malcolm X his "enthusiasm"; he mourned his violent death; he ridiculed the integrationist efforts by Martin Luther King Jr.; and he befriended nationalists in Cleveland like Don Freeman, Lewis Robinson, and Harllel Jones. Some have suggested he secretly became the leader of a loosely organized RAM cell in Cleveland.[1]

Fred Allen Evans was born in Greenville, South Carolina, on April 23, 1928.[2] His large family (he was one of twelve children) migrated to the Cedar-Central neighborhood in Cleveland when he was young and he attended Washington Irving and Bolton grade schools and Rawlings Junior High.[3] He said various things about his formal education—one time that he made it through fifth grade, another that he finished eighth grade.[4] FBI files recorded that Evans had "an 11th grade high school education."[5] Whatever the case, his formal education was bleak, though he considered himself self-taught in areas that interested him as an adult. Evans told one interviewer that he was teased relentlessly by classmates who called him "the Big Dumb" because of his gangling size and his learning difficulties.[6]

On April 14, 1948, Evans joined the US Army. He successfully navigated basic training at Fort Dix, New Jersey, where he was taught about the use and maintenance of firearms, hand-to-hand combat, judo, and other self-defense techniques. He was tall, rangy, and strong, becoming a boxing champion. He was selected to join the Eighty-Second Airborne and underwent further training at Fort Bragg, North Carolina, to become an army ranger. Evans claimed that the white orientation officer told his segregated parachute unit, "You are all niggers, not white, and will be treated as such."[7]

Evans was stationed in Guam, Manila, and Okinawa. Though he claimed to have been a participant in a race riot in Guam, that incident (the Agana race riot, where white marines and black marines fought for two days) occurred in 1944 during World War II. The riot was probably important lore still circulating among black troops when Evans joined the army. Journalist Dick Peery wrote that Evans, like Carl Stokes when he served in postwar Germany, found his time away from the United States liberating. In Japan, Evans experienced "the best treatment of his life," according to Peery. The bonds of American racism seemed a distant thing when he lived overseas. "They didn't see me as anything but a man," Evans said of the Japanese. "It was the only time in my life I was accepted, understood, treated well. If I could have got back there, I would still be there."

When the Korean War broke out, Evans was transferred to the Seventy-Third Combat Engineers Battalion in support of the Third Marine Division, arriving in Korea on September 15, 1950. "We were back-up troops for the 3rd Marine Division," Evans testified. "We supplied them with bridges and roads, laid land mine fields, what-have-you."[8] He was in Korea for eleven months, receiving silver and bronze stars for participating in five major battles.[9] He was a squad leader and promoted to the rank of staff sergeant.

Evans witnessed war atrocities by the Americans during the time he was in Korea. Peery wrote, "But his experience in the Korean War made a deep impression on him. 'I saw a regiment of North Koreans gassed by the Americans. Bodies were stacked like cordwood. I saw how cheap life is.' Authorities may deny that this happened, but Ahmed is convinced it did."[10]

An accident while in Korea seemed to have left him with some sort of lingering brain or nerve damage. He was injured while erecting a fifty-ton bridge used to support the transport of Pershing tanks. "Something went afoul while I was under the bridge," Evans recalled, "and parts of it collapsed, and I fell with the wreckage." He was confined to a hospital for six weeks.[11]

On April 2, 1952, Evans was honorably discharged from the army when his term expired. He returned to Cleveland and worked as a bus driver for the Cleveland Transit System, but had a hard time adjusting to civilian life and pace. Police records show an arrest on December 4, 1953, for a home break-in, but he was released on December 8 without a conviction. He reenlisted in the army on February 5, 1954, yet something wasn't right with him. "I had enlisted in the army for the purpose of going back to the Far East, Japan," he said, "and I had been shipped to Texas, and I stayed there with another engineer battalion. I had some symptoms of battle fatigue." He got into a fight with a white officer. "In fact," he admitted, "there were quite a few people I assaulted at one time." He claimed he blacked out at the start of the fight and that he was told it took nine to ten people to restrain him.

Evans later explained that part of his reason for wanting to go back to the Far East was to make amends for "undue things" that had been visited on the Korean people by Americans during the war. "I wanted to go back, and if there was anything I could have done to have helped the people of Korea, I had intended to spend the rest of my life there."

His FBI files recite the following from his military records: "He was tried and convicted by a general court-martial January 28, 1955, for striking his superior officer. He was sentenced to a dishonorable discharge (remitted to undesirable), forfeiture of all pay and allowances, and confinement at hard labor for two years (remitted to one year and six months). He also received 10 days restriction on July 5, 1955, as Unit Punishment for missing bed check."[12]

Evans described what he thought was the reason for the remission of his sentence. "This was due to the fact that I spent 11 months and 19 days in the combat zone in Korea," he testified some years later, "and

I was there when I began—the going got pretty rough. It does something to a man. It is called being shell-shocked, I believe it is called, or something of that nature, and I experienced this to that extent, I did."

Medical records suggest something more than shell shock. Evans testified in a proceeding in early 1968, "I have a record at Crile Hospital [now an army veterans' hospital in Cleveland named for the surgeon who founded the Cleveland Clinic] that states that during this time, when I had had this accident during the construction of the bridge, that certain nerves along the right side of my head had been damaged and that I had incurred several other accidents, that is, one to the back and one to the right knee. And they were at this time in a very bad condition, and I had spent time in and out of the hospitals, for this reason or that trouble, with my right eye or some type of paralysis along my right side, up and down the right side of my body."

Evans said that his injuries meant he had to "give up my boxing career which had started out with all victories." The damage to his brain, he claimed, continued to manifest in strange symptoms and behavior into his adult life. "I was very young at the time," he said, "and as I grew older and went into different fields of life, this took on some peculiar aspects that I had dizzy spells for a while. For a spell I did. And I was unable to work on certain jobs, do certain—perform certain tasks."[13]

On April 13, 1955, Evans was examined by an army psychiatrist at Fort Crowder Disciplinary Barracks, who wrote the following in a report:

> He is extremely polite and aloof. He is pedantic and guarded in his behavior. Otherwise, he is cooperative. This man has much hostility which he ordinarily controls but under stress it breaks forth with aggressive behavior. He also has some paranoid tendencies and this adds to his aggressiveness and resentment. It is believed that this man will probably have severe difficulty in the future in controlling his behavior. He resents demands imposed upon him and has some grandiose ideas about himself and his abilities. These are symptomatic of a paranoid type of personality. Generally, however, his behavior is that of a passive-aggressive personality. . . . Clinically, there is no evidence of insanity and he is well oriented in all spheres. It is possible for this man

to become gradually more severe and develop psychotic-like behavior under stress. Diagnosis: Passive-Aggressive Reaction, Chronic (with paranoid tendencies).[14]

A month later, another army psychiatrist added the diagnosis of "Epilepsy, Psychomotor." Given the precarious state of his mental health, the idea that Evans could navigate a smooth transition back into society in Cleveland seemed not only remote but all the more dangerous given the lack of support veterans experienced after returning from the war.

Yet back to Cleveland Fred Evans was sent after being discharged from the army on October 28, 1955. Unsurprisingly, he was arrested for assault and battery on October 3, 1956, but did not spend time in jail.[15] He found a low-wage job as a laborer on the Pennsylvania Railroad, working as a track man, general laborer, and machine operator. He lived from paycheck to paycheck but was employed on and off with the railroad for the next ten years. One friend from the time, William Russell Jr., said that Evans had an overweening pride in his military service and his rank as a sergeant. "He was the All-American Negro," Russell said of Evans during this time.[16]

But something remained amiss. Evans began living with a woman named Laura Van Hoose in 1952 after his first discharge from the army and they had three children together over the next turbulent years: Fred Jr. and two daughters, Patricia and Pamela.[17] When Evans came back from his second discharge, the family moved frequently, as did many African American families like them who had trouble keeping up with rent payments. The relationship with Laura was troubled. Bill Russell tells of Evans frequently arguing and fighting with Laura, sometimes publicly, and coming to stay with him during long periods of estrangement, usually without sharing in Russell's rent. "He got paid every two weeks," Russell remembered, "and he took it over to Laura. He didn't have two plug nickels."

Evans looked for escape in music, playing saxophone in a popular jazz and funk band Harvey & the Phenomenals.[18] Harvey Hall described the tireless nightclub schedule the band kept up during the time Evans was a member. "We'd play the Cougar Lounge every Saturday until 2 AM," Hall said. "Then we'd go to a breakfast party at Robert's Steakhouse from 4 to 8 AM. Then we'd go someplace else. We wouldn't go to bed, it was fun! They were the best days of my life."[19] Perhaps, but with Evans holding down his day job at the railroad, this relentless gigging left little time for his young family.

Then in 1962, Evans claimed he saw a flying saucer and that it changed his life. "I saw a UFO at Seventy-ninth and Kinsman," Evans said. "It hovered for a while and disappeared." Though strikingly similar to a tenet of the Nation of Islam and the idea of a mother ship coming to destroy the white man, Evans did not take this message from his experience, nor did he join the Nation. Instead, he created his own strange orthodoxy centered on astrology and numerology. "That started me thinking about the stars and God," he said of that night, "and I thought that I was thirty-three and Jesus had died at thirty-three and I hadn't even got started yet. So I moved off by myself to study the science of astrology and philosophy. I wanted to put things in perspective, to know the whereabouts of things, the history of the matter. The position I occupied in life definitely was not suitable to me and I wanted to know why. In astrology I found a never-failing relationship of cause and effect which teaches one lesson: that which ye sow ye also reap."[20]

Struggling to find his identity, Evans was ripe for the teachings of black nationalism, a political philosophy of realism that was starting to reach large numbers of African Americans who saw the civil rights movement's passive resistance tactics—with dogs attacking defenseless children and men and woman being beaten senseless—as demeaning and ineffective. These African Americans wanted to find unity and strength in the idea of black power, at the ballot box, or in the streets, or as Mao preached, "out of the barrel of a gun." Separateness of the races, not integration, would establish this power.

"I heard of a group of people who were in the process of forming a sort of unity among members of the community," he said. "At this point it wasn't known as Black Nationalism. It was just a group of young people. We met whenever the situation occurred. It might occur in a park. It might occur in my house. Or it might occur in someone else's house. We had no permanent place."

He was tired of being a Negro. He envisioned himself as a warrior from his experiences in the army and Korea—and he had grown weary of living in constant fear. "The principles of Black Nationalism is to believe in God, to know God, to understand I was afraid of everything—the grave, everything else," he testified. "I was just a body of fear. I mean I was afraid of being hungry, afraid of being ridiculed, afraid of society, afraid to live, you know. And that is what it means to be a Negro."

He didn't think whites would ever understand his meaning. "You have to know what it means to be afraid of everything," he said to one white interrogator. "You have to be a coward in every respect. I mean, you have to be able to endure, you know."

He encapsulated his thinking in an oft-repeated phrase: "I have come to learn that fear is worship; whatever you fear is what you worship."[21] It was time for Fred Evans, in his own self-preserving way, to transition to another level of being—he no longer wanted to worship fear. It was a choice. "I do not fear anything anymore," he declared.

His homegrown philosophy had pronounced echoes from what Elijah Muhammad and Malcolm X taught about "so-called Negroes."

"I don't mean to say that to be a Negro is a despicable thing," Evans said. "It is definitely not. I mean, there is a reason why black people are Negroes now. Black people were not always Negroes, to begin with. There were black people before the pyramids were built, before the ancient cities of Egypt were built. There were black people before white people or any other people."

To explain the state of historical imbalance among the races, Evans adopted generously from Elijah Muhammad. "It was necessary that black people become Negroes," he asserted in testimony he later gave, "not the way you may think, because they were stupid or because they were inferior in any way; this isn't true. They became Negroes because of the exclusive will of God, and that is why they are Negroes now, and they will remain Negroes as long as God wants them to be Negroes."[22]

In 1964, Fred Evans went to New York and returned a black nationalist, visiting with members of Malcolm X's Organization of

Afro-American Unity in Harlem. "I was a slave until 1964 when I became a Black Nationalist," Evans recalled. "By this time I had become Ahmed," he said. "I wasn't Fred Evans anymore."

This was the time when Evans became involved in Lewis Robinson and Harllel Jones's JFK House. He began teaching young people about astrology and African culture and history. "The kids who hung out there began asking me for advice," he said. "I began making astrological predictions and to have faith in myself."[23]

A year later, Fred "Ahmed" Evans had reason to be optimistic. In February 1965, black political activists began to promote Carl Stokes for mayor of Cleveland. Stokes sensed his opportunity. "By 1965," he wrote, "it was becoming clear to me that the ethnic machine that had run Cleveland for more than a generation was running out of steam."[24] Mayor Ralph Locher was indecisive and showed little empathy for African American citizens who were quickly becoming the dominant political bloc in Cleveland politics.

The numbers suggested what had seemed impossible: Stokes could win. In the nation's eighth largest city, African Americans made up more than 300,000 of Cleveland's 850,000 population. In fact, through careful study of voter rolls and figures from legislative races, Stokes and his political strategists "figured out that although blacks made up only thirty-five percent of the actual population, they comprised thirty-nine percent of the vote."[25]

This was exactly the type of voting bloc that Malcolm X had in mind in his "Ballot or Bullet" speech a year earlier. "What does this mean?" Malcolm asked when discussing the 1964 presidential election. "It means that when white people are evenly divided, and Black people have a bloc of votes on their own, it is left up to them to determine who's going to sit in the White House and who's going to be in the dog house."

The stars seemed to be aligning for Stokes. County auditor Ralph Perk, a vote-getting Republican, joined the race on June 22. (The newspaper said Perk was "especially strong in the nationality neighborhoods and among elderly voters.")[26] And Ralph McAllister, the hero to nervous whites in the school battles, filed nominating petitions with Stokes on July 1, both to run as independents (though both were registered

Democrats) because they did not want to face the sitting Democratic mayor in the primary. Stokes had what he wanted: Perk, Locher, and McAllister would split the white vote and he would corner the black vote. "Our thirty-nine percent loomed large," Stokes wrote.

If there was a symbol of police hostility to African Americans, it had to be Mayor Ralph Locher's chief of police, a man named Richard R. Wagner. Wagner was a "policeman's policeman." He joined the force in 1937 when Eliot Ness was safety director. He rose steadily through the ranks as a sergeant, captain, deputy inspector and inspector in charge of the detective bureau. "A husky man with a whitish crew cut, Wagner has a reputation for knowing every hoodlum in town who needs watching," the *Plain Dealer* admiringly wrote of him. Wagner replaced the seventy-one-year-old Frank Story as chief of police at the beginning of 1963, when Mayor Locher asked Story to step down. At fifty, Wagner was seen as an ace administrator who would modernize the force and "keep his men on their toes."[27]

Wagner's appointment came as the Cleveland Police Department faced a sticky internal scandal. In December 1962, it was discovered that police were running a burglary ring out of one of its West Side districts, and it had gone on for years. The leader of the group, William Marlowe, pled guilty and was sentenced from three to fifty years. Policemen who knew about the ring, but who were not participants, were paid money "to keep their mouths shut."[28] Chief Story's firing came within weeks of the revelation.[29] The story was buried deep in the newspaper. Seven of the officers arrested were quietly let go by the grand jury. Only three would stand trial.

Wagner, while an upright teetotaler, was an odd man to lead a two-thousand-person police force. He was a loner who was fascinated with guns. One article described him as a "rugged, square-jawed, Dick Tracy type of policeman, with a direct look that tells you nothing, few if any friends—even within the official police family. He is a man who eats alone, and thinks to himself."[30]

And he had a staggering racial animus toward blacks. In May 1965 Chief Wagner appeared before the Ohio House of Representatives Judiciary Committee, which at the time was considering the abolition of the death penalty for murder (except in cases of the murder of a president, governor, prison guard, or policeman).

Wagner told the committee he opposed the abolishment of the death penalty because it was needed in Cleveland to cow black nationalists.[31] Specifically, Wagner pointed to RAM and Don Freeman. The *Plain Dealer* richly embellished the story by running a huge front-page headline: "POLICE RAP RACIST PLOT HERE." The first paragraph of the lead article, written by a normally reserved political reporter, James M. Naughton (who later wrote for the *New York Times*), was meant to arouse deep fear in the white community: "Police Chief Richard R. Wagner charged yesterday that a black nationalist group in Cleveland is part of a plot to 'overthrow the government of the United States and, incidentally, shoot all Caucasians.'"

The newspaper repeated many of the stories that circulated when Don Freeman was fired: that a RAM group, also known as the Black Liberation Front, was responsible for the bomb threats against the Statue of Liberty, the Liberty Bell, and the Washington Monument. This time, the paper wrote that the bomb plot "linked the conspirators with RAM organizations in Cleveland and Philadelphia."[32]

Wagner testified that if the death penalty were abolished, it would provide aid and comfort to revolutionary black nationalist groups like RAM. He said eliminating capital punishment would allow RAM to "tell its agents, as a recruiting argument: 'If you are sent to prison [for murder], we will release you when we take over.'"

The remarks provoked a firestorm back in Cleveland. Two black city councilmen demanded an immediate explanation from Mayor Locher. Did RAM exist and if so what were its activities? Did the mayor agree with the remarks of his police chief? The African American newspaper *Call and Post* attacked both Wagner for "inflaming racial feelings in the community" and the *Plain Dealer* for reporting on the story in a way that was calculated to create "racial hysteria in Cleveland."

The black weekly wrote that Wagner's testimony was "one of the most irresponsible public statements ever to be uttered by a high-ranking Cleveland official."[33] The question was, Why were blacks singled out by Wagner in a discussion about the death penalty? Rights leaders, per the *Call and Post*, "have asked for Chief Wagner's reasons for using the existence of a Negro group, none of whose members have ever been accused of murder, as one of his arguments in favor of capital punishment while leaving unmentioned the Ku Klux Klan, whose members are accused of killing several civil rights workers."

The letters to the editor of the *Plain Dealer* were equally stinging. "The United States government has armed strength that could stagger any foe yet Police Chief Richard Wagner has the absurd idea that a small organized group such as the Revolutionary Action Movement can overthrow the government and kill all the whites," one reader wrote. "This one-sided thinking and action causes the formation of such militant Negro groups," she continued. "Society has many organized enemies that have menaced the people for years, but Chief Wagner overlooked them all and picked as his example for keeping the death penalty this small Negro group that so far has done little more than talk. I'm not for or against the death penalty, but if we must keep it—make it equal."[34]

Lewis Robinson and his Freedom Fighters issued a statement calling for the immediate resignation of Wagner. Addressing the mayor, they wrote, "You have the responsibility to the community to have law enforcement officials who command respect. How can any fair-minded person, white or black, respect Wagner? How can anyone have confidence in a police official who contributes toward fomenting racial discord?"

"Pity our frightened Police Chief," the editors of the *Call and Post* wrote in a piece dripping with sarcasm that questioned whether the Cleveland Police Department was only interested in protecting the lives of "Caucasians." The editorial concluded that "Negroes of Cleveland will do well to see that the capital punishment remains a part of Ohio statutes" because "they may need its threat to safeguard themselves against the mass violence from scared white folks such charges are calculated to incite."[35]

Anger built when Mayor Locher refused to meet with members of the United Freedom Movement, saying they should talk to Wagner or the safety director first. "No one is going to coerce me," the mayor defiantly declared.[36] The UFM staged a "wait-in" at City Hall for several weeks, insisting the mayor distance himself from Wagner. Instead, Locher eventually agreed with his police chief's remarks. The "wait-in" ended in mid-June when a group of whites calling themselves the National Association for the Advancement of White People showed up at city hall "to support Mayor Locher in not giving an audience to the UFM."[37]

Carl Stokes was relatively quiet about the whole imbroglio, always walking the tightrope between not alienating white voters versus solidifying his base. When the Freedom Fighters met at the JFK House in June 1965 to join the effort to get Stokes's name on the ballot, they wanted to see more backbone on this issue. The group "urged Stokes to publicly declare himself for a Citizens Police Review Board in Cleveland to begin to meet the problems of police abuse more effectively."[38] Stokes did not take up the suggestion.

On June 9, 1965, the *Plain Dealer* carried two headlines on its front page. The first was "House Kills Vote on Electric Chair," reporting that the Ohio House "eloquently debated and then killed yesterday a resolution calling for a statewide vote on the issue in November."

The second was "Freeman Indicted on Perjury Counts."

That summer, a traffic stop in Watts would mark the start of a prolonged period of some of the worst racial violence in American history, almost all in urban areas. Cleveland would know its share.

11

"Their Fight Is for Dignity and Work"

A MONTH AFTER MALCOLM X visited Selma, peaceful marchers there hoping to cross the Edmund Pettus Bridge—named for a Confederate brigadier general and Grand Dragon of the Alabama Ku Klux Klan—were met with severe violence from state troopers and local vigilantes, many on horseback, on March 7, 1965. The day became known in the civil rights' lore as "Bloody Sunday."

The protesters were beaten with nightsticks and whips and choked by tear gas, all to enforce an order by Governor George Wallace to prevent their "unlawful assembly." Fifty-seven were injured and at least seventeen hospitalized with serious injuries. John Lewis, chairman of the Student Nonviolent Coordinating Committee, was admitted to a hospital with a possible skull fracture after being clubbed with a nightstick. "I thought I saw death," he later recalled. The scene that day was terrifying. "Some 200 troopers and possemen with riot guns, pistols, tear gas bombs, and nightsticks later chased all the Negro residents of the Browns Chapel Methodist Church area into their apartments and houses," the New York Times reported.[1]

The protest was meant to dramatize the voter registration drive by the Southern Christian Leadership Conference and Dr. King in Alabama. Congressional pressure for a new federal voting rights law now mounted, "as members of both parties expressed anger and disgust at Alabama's violent repression of the Negro marchers in Selma, Alabama," the *Times* reported.[2] President Johnson delivered a speech a week later, on March 15, recommending immediate passage of a voting rights act. It was perhaps Johnson's most memorable speech (crafted by speechwriter Richard Goodwin). "I speak tonight for the dignity of man and the destiny of Democracy," the president started his speech. "At times, history and fate meet in a single time in a single place to shape a turning point in man's unending search for Freedom. So it was at Lexington and Concord. So it was a century ago at Appomattox. So it was last week in Selma, Alabama."

President Johnson said that the cause of blacks in Alabama must be the cause of all Americans. "Their cause must be our cause, too," he said. "Because it's not just Negroes, but really it's all of us, who must overcome the crippling legacy of bigotry and injustice. And we shall overcome."

The *New York Times* wrote that "no other American President has so completely identified himself with the cause of the Negro. No other President had made the issue of equality for Negroes so frankly a moral cause for himself and all Americans." Martin Luther King Jr. wept as he watched Johnson's speech on television in a home in Selma.[3]

The Voting Rights Act of 1965 passed and was signed into law in the rotunda of the Capitol on August 6, 1965. Five days later, the Watts riots in Los Angeles erupted.

The coincidence seemed a puzzle to most white Americans. Yet it should not have. A writer in the *Negro Digest* explained why the passage of the Voting Rights Act of 1965 held little significance for African Americans in urban areas like Watts. "How meaningless to the rioters are all the federal laws attempting to enfranchise the Southern Negro," an instructor from Ohio University wrote at the time. "In the North and West, the Negro has enjoyed the right to vote, to patronize most restaurants, air terminals and hotels. Recently these have not been the goals of the Northern Negro."[4]

To many, Watts seemed like the least likely of the African American ghettos to explode in rebellion. Located in sunny Southern California, in neighborhoods that were not filled with burned-out high-rise housing units, and with a burgeoning black middle class, Watts appeared stable. But that was only on the surface. The same troubling issues that vexed most northern cities were extant in Watts: overcrowding, segregation, poor schools, low employment, especially for young African American males, and, most significant, severe police hostility.

A writer for the *Negro Digest* captured it succinctly: "The rioters vented a despair with our democratic process as they have come to know it," he observed. "For them it is a way of life that has frustrated and aborted their dreams of a better life."

And it cannot be overstated how much the police became the symbol of oppression, the focal point of a war by northern blacks to avenge the wrongs of a society that alternatively ignored them or attacked them, without recourse. If a cop wrongfully arrested, injured, or even murdered a black man or woman, no one did anything about it.

A more recent study by a scholar from UCLA looked back at the urban uprisings from the 1960s and concluded the decisive factor in sparking the upheavals was police brutality. "Although inadequate housing, unemployment, poor city services, poor schools, and a lack of black-owned businesses exacerbated conditions in the ghettos, the catalyst for most of these rebellions was an act of police misconduct," Robin D. G. Kelley wrote in 2002 in *Freedom Dreams: The Black Radical Imagination*. "Between 1964 and 1972," Kelley summarized, "riots erupted in some 300 cities, involving close to a half-million African Americans and resulting in 250 deaths, about 10,000 serious injuries, and millions of dollars in property damage. Police and the National Guard turned black neighborhoods into war zones, arresting at least 60,000 people and employing tanks, machine guns, and tear gas to pacify the community."[5]

The Watts rebellion began innocently enough. A routine stop of a young black driver for suspicion of driving under the influence of alcohol on a very hot day somehow mushroomed into mad fits of violence and destruction over a forty-six-square-mile area. The young man driving the car was Marquette Frye. He had been born in Oklahoma, grew up in Wyoming, and moved with his family to Los Angeles when he was in junior high school. He had studied with mostly white classmates in Wyoming and, according to his mother, had difficulty adjusting to all-black schools. In Watts he was frequently suspended for fighting and had a minor arrest record.

When he was pulled over by police with his stepbrother in their mother's 1955 Buick, he was twenty-one years old. Field sobriety tests administered on the scene showed he was probably intoxicated. The arresting officer claimed that Marquette put up no resistance and even joked with the officer as he was being taken into custody.

Meanwhile, Marquette's mother who was at home just blocks away learned of the police stop. Despite the closeness to her home, the police insisted that they were going to tow her car (which meant the family would lose the car because, as it turned out, the towing fines and penalties made it too expensive to recover). The mother, Rena Price, who had raced to the corner of 116th Street and South Avalon Boulevard, at first began arguing with her son for driving while drunk. "You're not acting normal," she said. "You're not acting right. Get away from me!"

But then the young man with a short temper began to trade punches with police and his mother jumped on the back of one of the cops and ripped his shirt. A general scuffle broke out. "Everything was going fine with the arrest until the mama got there," Officer Lee Minikus recalled in an interview years later. A crowd of onlookers had gathered, and they turned ugly when Marquette's mother was put in handcuffs and placed in custody. Another woman in the crowd was also arrested.

Someone spit on one of the policemen. Word spread that cops had roughed up two pregnant women (neither was in fact pregnant). This incident started six days of violence, looting, and burning in which thirty-four people were killed, more than one thousand wounded, and property damage approached $100 million. Nearly four thousand people were arrested.[6]

A commission headed by former CIA chief John McCone, a Californian, was assembled by Governor Edmund G. Brown to investigate the causes of the rioting. The report, delivered in December 1965, recommended emergency literacy programs and job training measures, but assigned little blame to the Los Angeles police force for years of misconduct.[7] The commission warned that if racial problems were not addressed nationally, Watts would be a mere "curtain-raiser."[8]

There was something else profound afoot. Civil rights—voting, public accommodations, public transportation—were not the galvanizing forces in the North as they had been in the South. Jobs, housing, safety, especially from police abuse—issues of basic human dignity—drove the unrest and fueled the rise of black nationalism. It was a time when the civil rights movement began to ebb and the focus shifted. Radical voices like those of Stokely Carmichael, Huey P. Newton, H. Rap Brown, Bobby Seale, and Eldridge Cleaver gained credibility, moving them into the forefront of the public debate on racial injustice.

Dr. Martin Luther King Jr. flew to Los Angeles the day after the Watts rebellion began to subside. King and the Southern Christian Leadership Conference had already decided that summer to launch a "People to People" tour of northern cities, including Chicago, Philadelphia, Detroit, and Cleveland. On July 27 and 28 King spent two busy days in Cleveland emphasizing the power of the ballot and encouraging voter registration. "Dr. King is expected to cry about the shameful disinterest of citizenship participation in the Special Voter Registration and Education's campaign to register 60,000 un-registered Clevelanders," the *Call and Post* wrote. "He will contrast the ease with which Cleveland Negroes may register with the terror that is wrought upon the Negroes of the South as they attempt to obtain the right to vote."[9]

King's trip to Watts three weeks later, though, marked the real start of King's own dramatic mission shift out of the South. "What we are witnessing here," King wrote in a statement he delivered to the press in Los Angeles on August 20, "is the beginning of the stirring of those people in our society who have been passed by the progress of the past decade. For this reason, I would minimize the racial significance and point to the fact that these were the rumblings of discontent from the 'have nots' within the midst of an affluent society."[10]

He explained that the backlash of black citizens in the lower economic strata included anger at some African Americans who enjoyed a modest degree of participation in the nation's growing wealth. "There is also a growing disillusionment and resentment toward the Negro middle-class and the leadership which it has produced," King added. "This ever-widening breach is a serious factor which leads to the feeling that they are alone in their struggle and must resort to any method to gain attention to their plight. The non-violent movement of the South has meant little to them since we have been fighting for rights which theoretically are already theirs."

"Their fight is for dignity and work," King said. "This is the reason that the issue of police brutality looms so high. The slightest discourtesy on the part of an officer of the law is a deprivation of the dignity which most of the residents of Watts came North seeking. But the main issue is economic."

Dr. King's statement contained a grave warning. "I must confess that this is not only a crisis for Los Angeles and the northern cities of our nation," he cautioned. "It is a crisis for the non-violent movement. I a[m] trying desperately to maintain a non-violent atmosphere in which our nation can undergo the tremendous period of social change which confronts us, but this is dependent on progress and victories if those of us who counsel reason and love are to maintain our leadership."[11]

In Cleveland, Carl Stokes made a run of it. In the four-way race, the three Ralphs (Locher, McAllister, and Perk) divided the "nationality" neighborhoods and Stokes took the black vote and then some. In a blustering debate at the City Club just before the elections, fireworks erupted over the turmoil in race relations in Cleveland that had reached a boiling point during the last two years under Mayor Locher's leadership. The mayor was again confronted with the question of why he refused to meet with UFM members over Police Chief Wagner's death penalty remarks. Locher, red-faced with anger, pounded the rostrum saying no mayor "worth his salt" would bow to such pressure. Stokes, smooth in debate, responded that the "question is how best, with those pressures, to do what is in the best interest of all the people. A hard-nosed, podium-pounding attitude isn't helping any."

Ralph McAllister was asked if his election "would put Negroes and whites on a collision course." He was bellicose in reply. "Bloodshed occurred at [the school site on] Lakeview," McAllister said, "because the police department was restrained from carrying out its duty until too late." Stokes turned his fire on Locher, as he knew that McAllister had little chance of winning, charging that the mayor had told police not to arrest white demonstrators during the Murray Hill troubles. "Police must arrest anyone who violates the law," Stokes insisted. Locher denied the charge.[12]

Despite his obvious shortcomings, both of the daily newspapers endorsed Ralph Locher.

On election day, drama built, and as the vote began to be counted that night, it turned into a very close two-way race. Locher's early lead began to evaporate around midnight when the returns from black wards started streaming in and Stokes gained by leaps and bounds. In the end, Locher won by a mere 2,431 votes. Locher received 87,661; Stokes 85,230. Perk posted around 40,000 votes and McAllister ran a very poor fourth with just 22,000 votes. A recount was ordered but did not change the result.[13]

There was a sense of relief in Cleveland's white community that they had avoided electing a black mayor, though the "squeak-through victory" of Locher was too close a call for most whites. The *Plain Dealer* was satisfied with its prosaic mayor. "In an era of razzle-dazzle politics," one editor wrote, "Ralph Sidney Locher stands out because he has shunned the razzle and avoided the dazzle."[14]

The floodgates, however, would not hold for long. It wasn't just Watts and race flare-ups that bedeviled the country—something dark let loose by the Kennedy assassination seemed to be crawling over the entire nation. Lyndon Johnson's grave mistake in escalating America's involvement in the Vietnam War starting in August 1964 after the Gulf of Tonkin incident was already causing a revolution of its own among the younger generation, whose males were subject to the draft.

On the day that Locher won reelection in November 1965, the *Plain Dealer* carried the grisly story of a thirty-two-year-old Quaker father of three who committed suicide by burning himself to death in front of the Pentagon. He was upset over the administration's policy in Vietnam. "The suicide victim had with him a blond, blue-eyed, year-old girl," the paper reported. "According to witnesses, he placed the baby about 15 feet away before dousing himself with gasoline or kerosene that he had in a gallon jar. Then he set himself ablaze."[15]

A brutish violence was sparking up everywhere. The president increased US troop presence in Vietnam to nearly two hundred thousand by the end of 1965.

America's involvement in Vietnam provided grist for the anti-imperialist mills of those around the world seeking liberty from colonial oppression and black nationalists within the United States seeking freedom from racial discrimination. Robert F. Williams in Cuba continued to foment black revolution and urban guerilla warfare in the United States through his monthly newsletter, radio program, and RAM connections. Williams traveled to Hanoi in November 1965 to address the International Conference for Solidarity with the People of Vietnam Against US Imperialistic Aggression for the Defense of Peace.

Calling himself the "Chairman-in-Exile" of the Revolutionary Action Movement, Williams said, "Yes, the US government has sunken to the level of devil of the world. The same racist savages whose bombs blow the heads off black babies in Birmingham, USA, who viciously club pregnant Afroamerican women into insensibility on the streets of America, are the same beasts who murder, torture, and maim the patriots of Vietnam."

He proclaimed that he and RAM believed in the right of armed struggle. "We believe in the people's right to defend themselves in Vietnam as well as in Harlem, New York, or Jackson, Mississippi, USA." He promised to intensify that struggle in the United States. "We shall take the torch of freedom and justice into the streets of America and we shall set the last great stronghold of Yankee imperialism ablaze with our battle cry of freedom!"[16]

Williams was always more closely aligned with Che Guevara than Fidel Castro in Cuba. Williams sparred with Castro over the lack of black leadership in his revolutionary government. Castro, as other Soviet-based Communists, contended that class struggle, not race struggle, needed to be paramount. If revolution happened in the United States based on class struggle, Castro argued, the race struggle would solve itself. Racism was a capitalist sickness; remove capitalism and racism would also disappear. Williams, to say the least, was skeptical. A biographer wrote:

When one black radical wrote to Williams seeking to make ties
with revolutionary Cuba, Williams pushed indigenous African
American insurgency instead: "I think it should be more Nat
Turner than whitey's Marxism-Leninism." To Mae Mallory, who
had once had her own problems with Communists in Harlem
and was now serving a prison sentence on the kidnapping charges
that Williams had fled, the exile wrote, "I am not going to become
another [hypocrite] and put a new set of crackers on top who are
using Marxism to maintain world-wide white supremacy."[17]

When a serious philosophical and political split developed between
Castro and Guevara over Castro's ties to the Soviet Union, Williams
decided it was time to leave Cuba. Guevara favored third-world solidarity—more China focused—and charged that the USSR was a "tacit
accomplice of imperialism" at the Organization of Afro-Asian Solidarity
in Algiers in February 1965. Williams agreed with Guevara and eventually left for Vietnam and then Beijing in late 1965.[18]

In Cleveland some of Fred "Ahmed" Evans's friends began to change
their names—not to African or Arabic names, but rather names like Ho
Chi Minh. Though Evans did not consider himself a Communist or agree
with the Communist philosophy, he and his cohorts read with delight
every issue of *The Crusader* produced by Williams, which were shipped to
bookstores in Detroit and Cleveland that carried underground magazines.[19]

In his speech in Vietnam in November 1965, Williams predicted
trouble in the summer in 1966 in the United States. "The coming summer is going to be hot in more ways than one," he told his audience in
Hanoi. "Those who thought the so-called Civil Rights Bill opened up a
new epoch of first class citizenship for darkies are sadly mistaken. The
vast majority of the US whites are infected with a form of racist neurosis
that will require more than legal writs and therapeutic couches to cure."

Williams saw a showdown coming. "Massive violence is in the offing," he said. "Afro-Americans must organize and prepare to defend
themselves and their communities collectively. Arms and ammunition
must be secured in great quantities."

Martin Luther King Jr.'s greatest fear was about to become reality
in Cleveland.

12

"A Daily Battle Against Depression and Hopelessness"

"THAT MONTH OF JANUARY 1966 was hell," Lewis Robinson wrote in his autobiography. Ostracized as Cleveland's "rifleman," he had been unable to find work at a decent wage. His youth center, the JFK House, struggled to stay open owing to lack of funding.[1] And a skirmish between black teenagers from Hough or Glenville and whites from the adjoining mainly white Sowinski neighborhood gave Cleveland police an excuse they were looking for to arrest and harass Robinson.

On Wednesday, January 20, two white teenagers and their fifty-two-year-old father, a janitor at St. Thomas Aquinas School named Chester Satola, were attacked by a gang of blacks at East 87th Street and Superior Avenue, a racial borderline. It started when two white teenagers, fifteen and thirteen, phoned their mother from a drugstore on their way home from their part-time jobs to report that they were being bothered by a gang of blacks who were wielding bats and pipes, demanding fifty cents "protection" money. As the Satola boys tried to get home, they were encircled. The boys' father arrived and was viciously knocked to the ground but defended himself with a tear-gas pen that he fired into the face of one of the attackers. One of the Satola boys and the father were hospitalized, both with fractured skulls. Police began a massive search for the perpetrators, making dozens of arrests that day.

Two nights later, two juvenile officers, both black, turned up at the JFK House and began to intimidate and rough up some of the kids in further search for the culprits in the attack. Word came to Lewis Robinson, who drove over to find out what was going on. Officer John Smith, a black man who had been Robinson's coworker at Republic Steel years earlier, walked up to Robinson.

"Smitty," Robinson claimed he said to his old friend in front of a gathering of parents and children, "for two days you and your boys have been rounding up our kids like you're a sheriff in Dodge City out West someplace. You're denying our kids their rights."[2]

Officer Smith was in a tough spot—he had been publicly called out by another black man. He and his partner, Charles McWhorter, were two of only 133 black members on the Cleveland Police rolls; at the time the entire force numbered 2,100. In 1966 only two of these blacks were sergeants; the rest were patrolmen.[3] The black Cleveland policemen therefore had to walk a delicate line—knowing that they had to appear to be even tougher with African Americans than their white counterparts to gain the trust and acceptance of their fellow officers.

Officer Smith shot back at Robinson, "Are you trying to tell me how to do my job?"

"No, man," Robinson replied, "but you wouldn't go to Murray Hill rounding up white kids. In fact, in the first place your boss wouldn't send you up there, and if they did, the white folks would run you out."

Smith pulled Robinson aside, taking him inside the JFK House. "Robbie," he said, "what are you trying to do? Make me look bad?"

"No, man, you know I am telling the truth," Robinson replied. "Don't run over our kids just because two white kids have been beaten up. Hell, you never see the white policemen arrest white kids when black kids are beaten. It's just another nigger to them."

Smith had heard enough. "I'm going to have to take you in," he said to an astonished Robinson. "What for?" Robinson asked. "We'll think of something," Smith responded, and called for the paddy wagon. Robinson spent the night in jail and was let go the next morning. His car was towed. The next afternoon, police showed up at his house to arrest him again, this time with a warrant for reckless driving and disorderly conduct.

The *Plain Dealer* carried an article blaming the JFK House for the beatings of the Satolas. Under a headline "Gang Traced to JFK House," the newspaper reported that Cleveland detectives "found that a gang of youths at the house were 'nothing but troublemakers.'" The police charged that the gang had been "terrorizing the neighborhood, pushing women off the sidewalks and taking groceries and money from kids."[4]

The same cold weekend that Lewis Robinson was arrested, Dr. King announced that he had put a deposit down on an apartment in a Chicago tenement with the plan to move in with his family later in the week. "The president of the Atlanta-based Southern Christian Leadership Conference plans to live in the dingy third-floor walk-up while conducting the civil rights organization's first 'movement' against racial discrimination in the North," the *Times* reported on January 21.[5] King came to Chicago as the next proving ground for his nonviolence strategy. This new campaign would come to be called the Chicago Freedom Movement. It would fail spectacularly.

Since Watts, King had been writing and speaking about the reasons that African Americans in the North had turned so suddenly hostile and even militant. "The disillusion of the Negro in the North is an enigma only to the insensitive or uniformed," he wrote in one editorial. "Embittered with his lot in a South, which has sought to suppress the Negro sense of 'somebodiness,' . . . the Negro migrated North. By the thousands and the hundreds of thousands, he made the pilgrimage to Washington, to Detroit, Chicago, New York, Los Angeles, and San Francisco and Philadelphia and New Jersey," King explained. "He was seeking the Promised Land. But the Negro soon learned that the North is not the Promised Land; that the subtle nuances of de facto segregation in the North are as humiliating psychologically as the more obvious segregation of the South."

Exacerbating the situation, King wrote, was the fact that while the South had "slowly, reluctantly begun to turn to face her destiny," the opposite was true in the North. If anything, "the rigidities of Northern discrimination and segregation have stiffened."[6]

King recognized that the blacks in northern ghettos presented an entirely new situation and an incredibly complex challenge. Chicago alone had over a million blacks, crammed into teeming slums. He knew that if he was to touch the northern Negro, he would have to reach out to what he called the "grassroots," people like Lewis Robinson and Fred "Ahmed" Evans in Cleveland. King put it this way in an autobiography, talking about his Chicago experience:

> During 1966 I lived and worked in Chicago. The civil rights movement had too often been middle-class oriented and had not moved to the grassroots levels of our communities. So I thought the great challenge facing the civil rights movement was to move into these areas to organize and gain identity with ghetto dwellers and young people in the ghetto. This was one of the reasons why I felt that in moving to Chicago I would live in the very heart of the ghetto. I would not only experience what my brothers and sisters experience in living conditions, but I would be able to live with them.
>
> In a big city like Chicago it is hard to do it overnight, but I thought that all of the civil rights organizations had to work more to organize the grassroots levels of our communities. There, the problems of poverty and despair were more than an academic exercise. The phone rang daily with stories of the most drastic forms of man's inhumanity to man and I found myself fighting a daily battle against the depression and hopelessness which the heart of our cities pumps into the spiritual bloodstream of our lives. The problems of poverty and despair were graphically illustrated. I remember a baby attacked by rats in a Chicago slum. I remember a young Negro murdered by a gang in Cicero, where he was looking for a job.[7]

In Cleveland, the Satola beatings set off a sporadic race war in and around the border between Hough and Glenville to the south and east and the Sowinski and St. Clair-Superior neighborhoods to the north— Superior Avenue being a sort of Mason-Dixon Line in eastern Cleveland. Teenagers painted swastikas on structures in Sowinski Park and messages like "Niggers keep out!" Fights between white and black gangs began to intensify.[8]

Spring brought its own trouble. As it happened, from April 1 to 7, the US Civil Rights Commission held hearings in Cleveland to take testimony on the state of civil rights in the inner city. The Ohio State Advisory Committee prepared a report to the commission entitled *Cleveland's Unfinished Business in Its Inner City*. The findings were more an indictment of local and state government than anything else, especially under the leadership of Ohio's governor Jim Rhodes and Cleveland's Mayor Ralph Locher. "MONEY," the report started, "is the common theme of many of the recommendations in this Report. Public funds, existing tax monies, are not adequate today to pay for the services needed to keep citizens in health and decency." The report accused Ohio and Cleveland of neglecting essential services to the poor, running, as they put it, government "on the cheap."

The US Commission on Civil Rights was created by Congress as part of the watered-down Civil Rights Act of 1957, passed during the Eisenhower administration. Its mission was to act as an independent, bipartisan, fact-finding federal agency and to inform the development of the national civil rights policy. Whenever the commission decided to focus on a community, it sent an advance staff to gather statistics and information to use in the hearings and reports. "The hearing [in Cleveland] is the commission's first northern city hearing in two years," the *Plain Dealer* reported. "There were hearings in Newark, N. J. in 1962, and in Indianapolis in 1963. Its last hearing was in Jackson, Miss., in 1965."[9]

In 1966, the commissioners were mainly academics, all white males except for one black female. Father Theodore Hesburgh of Notre Dame was one of the commissioners, as were Michigan State University president John Hannah, Erwin Griswold of the Harvard Law School, and Duke political scientist Robert Rankin.

The commission accurately identified most of Cleveland's pressing problems. In the area of education, statistics showed that 91 percent of Cleveland's public schools were either 80 percent white or 80 percent black. De facto segregation was guaranteed to continue and get worse if the Cleveland School Board found no alternative to the seemingly benign concept of neighborhood schools. In housing, blacks lived exclusively in areas on the East Side of town. "85 percent [of Negroes] live in Census tracts with at least 70 percent Negro population and 50 percent live in tracts with a 95 percent Negro population," the commission found. The federal urban renewal programs were so poorly administered and so counterproductive (tearing down houses without replacing them) that the commission actually recommended that the "Federal Government withhold or withdraw funds for local projects as a means of ensuring contract commitments made by the city."

Employment figures showed that blacks had great difficulty being hired by trade unions. "There are 17 Negroes among 1,038 apprentices in 22 building trades," the report noted. "There are only 4,976 Negroes among 38,631 journeymen members in the same trade unions." Unemployment in the inner city was widespread. "Negroes constitute 17 percent of the labor force in Cleveland, but 38 percent of the population."

On police-community relations, the report concluded that the police had "lost the respect of Negro residents in the Inner City." Blacks were regularly arrested and detained without probable cause. "Unlawfully detained persons are not charged with a violation of law," the report stated, "but, before being released, are told to sign a waiver. This waiver is a police department form on which the signer admits to a charge, usually that of being a 'Suspicious Person,' and waives his rights to sue the city for unlawful arrest and detention." As disturbing was the fact that citizen complaints about police abuse were handled by police commanders of the officers against whom the complaints were filed. No citizen board of oversight existed.

Infant mortality and premature births were 50 percent greater for blacks than whites. There was an acute shortage of neighborhood-based family health centers in Hough and Glenville. Welfare assistance, especially Aid to Dependent Children, provided only 70 percent of the minimum requirements for health and decency established by the state.

Deficient municipal services posed nothing short of a health threat. Garbage pick-up was spotty, as was street cleaning; investigations of sanitary code violations were woefully insufficient. "Cleveland," the report stated, "is one of the most heavily rodent-infested large urban communities in the Nation, according to the United States Public Health Service."[10]

A *Plain Dealer* reporter, Doris O'Donnell, blithely summed up what she expected from the commission's report of its time in Cleveland. "It can be safely predicted," she wrote, "that the six-member blue-ribbon commission will be highly critical of the Cleveland administration of federal programs for the poor. But the strongest criticism will be aimed at the city's handling of millions of dollars in urban renewal funds and failure to create new housing." She cheerfully concluded her article with a positive quote from a resident of Hough. "At least someone listened to us," she wrote of one African American's reaction to the hearings.

Doris O'Donnell, however, was more of an apologist for the white power structure in Cleveland than an objective newspaper reporter. Two weeks after penning her article about the US Civil Rights Commission, O'Donnell lashed out at Lewis Robinson and the JFK House. Robinson had been trying to reopen the youth recreation center since a lack of funds forced it to close in February. He proposed programs to encourage kids to help elderly people in the neighborhood: "They would mow their lawns, clean their basements and attics, clean and paint their homes, clean the streets. They would be building that kibbutz unity that is what I mean by black nationalism."[11]

Robinson was supported by a white Presbyterian minister, Rev. Charles W. Rawlings, who was the executive director of the Metropolitan Affairs Commission of the Council of Churches of Christ of Greater Cleveland. Rawlings and other ministers strongly believed Robinson, Harllel Jones, and Albert Ware-Bey were performing work that was essential to bridge the "communication gap" between blacks and whites in greater Cleveland.[12]

O'Donnell was not a believer. She wrote that "Robinson has been closely identified with civil rights movements. His youth club has received unfavorable publicity because of complaints of rowdy activities." She again tied the Satola beatings to the JFK House, though no evidence ever surfaced to support the assertion. It was all innuendo and slur. "Police rounded up about ten youths and adults in connection with it," she alleged. "Some of the youths were picked up by Cleveland police at the JFK House. At the time Robinson was also arrested. He allegedly used abusive language to police who were making the arrest."[13]

The next day, the *Plain Dealer* carried an editorial, "JFK House Should Stay Closed." The paper labeled the effort to reopen it as reckless.

"The fund drive to reopen JFK House with Lewis G. Robinson as its head is an example of irresponsible interference by those who ought to know better," the editors scolded. They painted the center as "a hangout and hideaway for juveniles in trouble and a place of disorder requiring almost constant police surveillance."[14]

Doris O'Donnell stepped up her attack two days later with a front-page article that emphasized criticism from a conservative black Cleveland city councilman, Leo Jackson (someone the nationalists considered to be a "Tom"). "My reaction to news that a group is going to sponsor the reopening of the place was first incredulity and then amazement," Jackson told O'Donnell. Jackson unambiguously charged that Robinson's leadership was conducive to the unruliness O'Donnell had deplored. He recommended that young blacks participate in the Police Athletic League. "This kind of recreation provides discipline and responsibility," he said.

The ministers who supported Robinson responded to the criticism. The recommendation to fund the JFK House, they wrote in a cutting letter to the editor, had come after a careful investigation and many conferences and "dialogues" with Robinson, his supervisors, and some of the kids served by the JFK House. "We are greatly disturbed by the personal attack on the Rev. Charles W. Rawlings of the Council of Churches," the group wrote. "The citizens of Cleveland should be apprised that a sizable segment of responsible society is beginning to be concerned about the consequences of the problems of the ghetto and has commenced to do something about it."[15]

One angry reader was especially annoyed by Councilman Jackson's comments and observed: "The fact that you suggest that these youngsters might 'engage in wholesome activities with policemen at police athletic centers and develop friendly relations with them' betrays your abysmal ignorance of the jungle we call the inner city. . . . I'm afraid it is too late in the game to ask these kids to become one big happy family with their friendly policeman (whom they have learned to despise and hate)."[16]

Even the *Call and Post*, published by William O. Walker, another conservative black Republican who at the time was serving as the director of the Ohio Department of Industrial Relations in the Rhodes administration, took on Robinson and the JFK House. The paper strongly disapproved of white ministers interfering in the black community and acting as "saviors of the Negro."[17] They said Robinson was "a zealous, determined, entirely sincere young Negro, whose immaturity led him into the ill-advised proposal that a gun-club was the end answer to Cleveland's mounting racial tensions."

As might be expected, this stirring of the racial pot only increased tensions. Beginning in late May, gangs of whites and blacks fought. From the perspective of the African Americans, none of the white perpetrators were arrested but blacks were regularly rounded up. A particular trouble spot continued to be Sowinski Park through which blacks had to walk or bike to get to Lake Erie for summer fishing. On June 16, ten black youths, ages nine to twelve, were attacked in the park. That same night when fighting broke out at East 79th Street and St. Clair Avenue, a white cop allegedly told the white youths, "Don't beat them up here. Do it in the park so I can't see it." Lewis Robinson warned neighbors, white and black, near the JFK House that police were not protecting children in the area.

On Wednesday, June 22, several black youths were beaten at East 79th Street and Superior Avenue. A crowd gathered. Kids began throwing rocks and bricks and Molotov cocktails. The next evening, two white men in a car drove down Superior and shot into a crowd of black youths who had been hurling stones and bricks at passing cars, hitting nine-year-old Stephen Griffin in his groin.[18] Lewis Robinson wrote that "a couple of ghetto guns opened up and returned the fire." He and others from the JFK House walked the streets that night to try to keep things calm, though some looting and sniping broke out. There was a heavy police presence—upward of two hundred patrolmen—that weekend. One policeman said: "It's like sitting on a steam kettle. We've got it under control, but, man, you can feel the steam under you."[19]

"All the anger and hatred of the police for their indifference to the many beatings blacks had suffered in the Sowinski area and the memory of the Satola case where the police had acted—quickly, harshly, and brutally—because whites were involved, all this was spilling out," Robinson recalled.[20]

The week after the June 23 Superior Avenue fracas, Mayor Locher agreed to meet secretly with Lewis Robinson, Harllel Jones, and others from the JFK House. They presented a nine-point list of demands for the city's assistance with the JFK House and more vigorous, even-handed law enforcement. This private meeting received no publicity and Locher committed only to "do what I can."[21]

A week later, the mayor met with a group of more conservative black leaders, including William O. Walker. At this meeting, the black leaders presented an eight-point plan to address racial tension and what was clearly a growing rift between the white power structure and militant blacks in the ghetto. However, most of the requests from this black delegation dealt with rooting out "the source of the leadership initiating the troubles in the community and distributing incendiary race hate literature." The Stephen Griffin shooting remained unsolved, yet it seemed that conservative blacks were more concerned with suppression of people within their community whom they considered troublemakers, like Lewis Robinson and Harllel Jones. Walker explained: "The people who live in the community have a stake here in businesses and in homes and they realize that Negroes will be the losers [in any race violence]. More Negroes [will be] killed, more property destroyed, more slums—it is up to us, our responsibility . . . to ferret out the people who are trying to ferment [sic] racial unrest."[22]

Thus, the rift between the white power structure and the militant, "grassroots" blacks extended in Cleveland to a fissure between conservative, middle-class blacks and their poverty-stricken, desperate neighbors. People like Lewis Robinson felt isolated and abandoned, even by his own people; he saw leaders like William O. Walker as an open collaborator with whites.

A similar dynamic was at play in Chicago where Dr. King was at wits' end, sounding the alarm of an imminent split between the nonviolent civil rights leaders and militants like SNCC and CORE who espoused defensive violence and black power. "Dr. King attributed the rise of black power sentiment to the failure of public officials and the 'power structure' to create meaningful changes in the lives of Negroes," the *New York Times* reported. King saw his own influence waning. "Again and again, in more than two hours of conversation," the *Times* wrote, "he talked of public officials and what he said was a failure to respond to conventional methods of nonviolent protest." Dr. King warned, "When they drain the steam out of the nonviolent movement and give no concessions, they are planting the seeds of a Watts-like situation."[23]

His fears were realized three days later when rioting broke out in Chicago. On July 12 police in a Near West Side neighborhood turned off water hydrants that were being used by black children to "cool off during near-100-degree afternoon temperatures." Fights erupted between police and youths as they battled over reopening the hydrants. Over the next three days, black gangs fought with police and rioting, looting, and burning ensued. "Windows were broken, rocks were thrown, and Molotov cocktails were hurled from a public housing project," the newspapers reported.[24] Two blacks were killed, and six policemen were wounded by sniper fire. Fifty-one were injured. By Friday, July 15, 1,400 national guardsmen, armed with rifles and bayonets, arrived to quell what remained of the rioting and looting.[25]

Martin Luther King Jr. was powerless to control the situation. He had fought in vain with Chicago's mayor, Richard J. Daley, who refused to meet demands for sweeping action. (Daley only reluctantly agreed after the rioting to add sprinklers to some fire hydrants in the ghetto.) King was being openly mocked by black youths who walked out on him in public meetings he called to try to relieve community tension.[26]

For his part, Mayor Daley charged that the riots had been "spurred by outsiders," though he declined to release his evidence.[27]

William O. Walker of the *Call and Post* figuratively wagged his finger at militants in his community who condoned the Chicago violence. He acknowledged that "most Cleveland Negroes find themselves hemmed in by walls of prejudice," and that the "average Cleveland Negro lives in a ghetto, not because he likes the ghetto, but because powerful forces, including those in elective office, have long conspired to keep him there." Yet, he worried that militancy would only make things worse. He encouraged his black readers to remember how close African Americans had come to winning city hall in 1965. "Don't get mad, get smart!" he wrote. "No sane man tears his house down around his head because the roof is leaking."

"In the hot summer days ahead," Walker questioned, "Cleveland Negroes must make a choice. Shall it be ballots or bayonets?"[28]

On Monday, July 18, the day Walker's editorial published, he would receive an emphatic answer to his rhetorical question.

13

Hough

THE UGLINESS STARTED ON MONDAY, July 18, in a dingy bar called the Seventy-Niner's Café at the corner of East 79th Street and Hough Avenue that was run by two white brothers, Abe and Dave Feigenbaum. Their clientele was almost entirely black. "It has 20 stools," a *Plain Dealer* article described, "a couple of booths, and a cigarette machine that would stick, and when it did, someone would pound on it to get his change back. Sometimes he would pound so hard that he would get everyone else's change and all the cigarettes too."

The previous Saturday evening, a hopeless young woman named Mary Sullivan died of a heart attack, leaving three children. Mary Sullivan was a prostitute and had been arrested dozens of times for soliciting sex. She had a first child at sixteen and two more before she suddenly died at twenty-six. A friend, identified by the press only as Louise, left a greasy cigar box in the Seventy-Niner's on Sunday, July 17, with a sign asking for contributions for Mary Sullivan's funeral expenses and her orphaned children. When she returned to retrieve the box around 5:00 PM on Monday, July 18, Dave Feigenbaum began fuming. He and his older brother considered Sullivan and Louise to be "undesirable characters" and had banned them from entering the bar in the past. After a rough exchange of "vulgarities and cursing and other things," Dave Feigenbaum "bodily ejected" Louise. Some say Louise left a sign on the bar about Negroes not being served there.[1]

The Feigenbaums were reviled in the neighborhood. Abe was thirty, Dave twenty-four. Their tough manner and excitable temperament left many irate customers. On a night in the previous January, a patron attempted to set one of their cars on fire.

Violence seemed linked to the bar. Benjamin Feigenbaum, the uncle of the brothers, told reporters in 1964 that he was growing concerned about "robberies and muggings, the narcotics addicts, prostitutes, and panderers in the Hough area" and claimed that businessmen were not receiving enough police protection.[2] His business partner and brother-in-law, William Maltz, shot and killed a customer in May 1964 who was menacing other customers in the bar with a broken bottle. Police ruled it a "justifiable homicide."[3] Then in September 1965 Benjamin Feigenbaum himself was brutally murdered, shot nine times in the head and chest as he sat behind the wheel of his car parked not far from the bar.[4]

A second incident on the night of July 18, 1966, though, was likely the spark for the Hough rebellion. A black man came into the bar and purchased a pint of cheap wine to go. While sitting at the bar, he asked for a glass of ice water. One of the Feigenbaums instructed a bartender (a black woman) "not to give no nigger a drink of water." The man left, livid. He came back shortly thereafter and taped a sign on the bar: "No Water for Niggers." Some remember it as "This Place Will Not Serve Coloreds."[5]

The Feigenbaums later had an explanation for what happened. They argued that the law required that wine purchased to carry out cannot be consumed on the premises, but that it was not uncommon for someone to drink it in the bar by asking for a glass of water. "The wine heads dump the water and pour the wine into the glass," Dave Feigenbaum told a reporter. "It's cheaper than buying a straight glass of wine."

News about the sign spread quickly and a sizable crowd began to gather outside the bar. The brothers had gone home (where they lived with their mother) but came back to find the situation spinning out of control. They appeared in front of the bar with guns. Abe, a former marine, held a .44-caliber Ruger rifle; Dave, a pistol. They were soon chased back into the bar when people began throwing bricks and rocks.

The brothers claimed it was lack of decisive action by police and firefighters that allowed the situation to tip into a full-scale riot. When they initially called the police (they claimed four calls), they received no response. They then called television stations and the fire department. When the firemen arrived, one asked, "What's the problem?" Abe responded, "We have a riot out there." The fireman responded, "We don't have a riot; you have a riot," and left. By the time several police units did arrive, the scene was teetering on the brink of chaos. The police formed a circle in the street, facing outward, like an old-fashioned circling of the wagons. The tense standoff grew worse as rocks and other missiles were thrown at the police, who were not in riot gear. Then, things turned deadly when sniping began, mostly from shadows on rooftops.[6]

What happened next is still a matter of speculation. Some claim that the police efforts to disperse the crowd drove the crowd to other targets, shattering storefront windows with rocks and bricks and unsystematic looting. Others saw an organized response.

One eyewitness account from that night was provided by a black female reporter for the *Call and Post*. Daisy Craggett heard about the developing riot on radio and television and decided to find out for herself what was transpiring. "As a woman reporter, I could easily have escaped this duty—in fact, I was told to stay out of the dangers involved, but Hough people are my people, and I felt that no matter what peril I encountered, some friend I had made down there would bail me out." She was not prepared for what she found. She was "shocked beyond description over the senseless lawlessness and the avid lust for loot I witnessed between the hours of 9 PM and 3 AM."[7]

Daisy Craggett noticed that the mob that formed outside the Seventy-Niner's Café was composed of "mostly young adults and teenagers." The shrill sound of police sirens, she thought, was like a "call to action." Her description of the response supports the view that there was some shaping effort behind the rioting:

> It seemed to me that there were two different factions operating during the outburst of violence. One segment of it operated under some kind of leadership and apparently following some set plan. This group set out to strike at specific targets, which

like the offending Seventy-Niner's Café, had given Negroes cause for anger and indignation. Stores with a reputation for exorbitant prices or flagrant discourtesy to Negro customers, especially those on relief, provided most of the targets. Behind the would-be "avengers" followed a disorganized and fragmented army of hoodlums bent on looting. The pattern soon became familiar, hit and loot, then come back and destroy.[8]

Years later, Max Stanford, the Philadelphia native who started the Revolutionary Action Movement with Don Freeman, wrote a thesis paper in support of his master's degree at Atlanta University in which he claimed that Hough resulted from special tactics and strategies of urban rebellion that had been developed and taught by RAM. More, he identified Fred "Ahmed" Evans as one of the leaders of RAM in Cleveland. Quoting from a source he identified only as "Brother E," Stanford wrote:

> Ahmed Evans and Ali Kahn ... were section leaders of RAM in Cleveland. Ahmed, Ali, and others met during the spring of 1966 and decided to create another "Watts." They decided it was time to test urban guerilla warfare. Military units were trained and the city was divided into areas, with each unit having its own territory and commander. The units were named the Black Nationalist Army.[9]

Lewis Robinson described Monday, July 18, as an ordinary day at the JFK House. "There were about twenty kids in the main hall of the center," Robinson recalled. "About half of them were playing ping pong while others were dancing, listening to records, and just horsing around."[10] He was spending time that evening refereeing boxing matches in the basement of the center.

But then a young woman came and said to him: "Mr. Robinson, Mr. [Harllel] Jones is looking for you. A boy from Hough is upstairs telling him that a colored woman has been shot on a bus on 79th Street." Robinson remembered his first reaction was that some "stupid ass white kids" had started something again, like the Superior Avenue shooting.

Harllel Jones followed the young woman downstairs and reported that kids on the street were saying that two white men at a bar at Hough and 79th Street were "holding guns on black people and refusing to give a black man a drink of water in the bar."

Robinson warned the kids at the JFK to stay out of it, but that was impossible given the level of excitement. Robinson drove about a mile south from JFK House on Superior, deep into Hough, and got out of his car. He began to wander toward the Seventy-Niner's Café from East 86th Street. Night had fallen. As he walked toward the cafe, he noticed that several businesses had already been hit along Hough Avenue. But the pattern was clearly established that businesses owned by blacks or friendly whites were left alone. Close to midnight a light rain began to fall, which turned into a heavy rain. Robinson returned to his home for the night, believing the rain would tamp down the excitement. "While I slept," he wrote, "the rain stopped and Hough began to burn itself down in earnest."[11]

When police finally showed up in enough strength that night, they began to react forcefully to the rioting and especially what they perceived was sniping from darkened windows or rooftops. Chief of Police Richard R. Wagner, who testified a year earlier in favor of the death penalty in Ohio, personally patrolled the streets, bringing with him his favorite hunting rifle.[12] Three blocks west of the Seventy-Niner's Café, police shot out the streetlights as they battled with what they thought were snipers near 75th and Hough. Twenty-six-year-old Joyce Arnett, the mother of three, was walking on Hough Avenue with her cousin and his wife back toward her house at 1882 East 81st Street (a block on the other side of East 79th), when they encountered police who were dealing with crowds and snipers. A policeman pushed Arnett and her cousins into an apartment building at East 73rd and Hough Avenue, where they made their way to the second floor.[13]

Arnett, who lived just blocks away, began to panic about the well-being of her children as gunfire outside increased. She stuck her head out of a second-story window and began screaming, "I want to go home. My God! I want to go home to my kids." At that moment, she was hit by three bullets, two entering the right side of her head and one in her chest. She fell back inside, mortally wounded. She was pronounced dead at Mt. Sinai Hospital at 1:40 AM.[14]

In a nearby apartment complex at 7310–14 Hough Avenue, police rampaged to find snipers. "It was like a nightmare," one resident said. "All the tenants wanted to know," the *Call and Post* reported, "why policemen kicked in doors, broke up furniture, and chased defenseless women and children from the safe confines of their home into the streets to face bricks, bottles, bullets, and pouring rain." One elderly grandmother said she was kicked down a flight of stairs by a policeman. The men were all taken into custody and jailed for the night, many of them without proper clothing. One man was arrested with a ten-month-old baby.

"A seven-year-old boy showed how police, with guns pointed at him, made him march out of the apartment house with his arms behind his head," the black newspaper reported. The tenants said the police used "epithets" in speaking to them.

"This is my home, I worked hard all my life to maintain this home for my family," one woman cried that night. "Now I don't know what I will do."[15]

There were other shootings as nervous cops tried to find snipers. Five blocks east of the Seventy-Niner's Café, Wallace Kelly and his sister were visiting friends who lived in an apartment on Hough Avenue. The group had decided to leave the area and to find safety at Kelly's apartment some three miles away. But as Kelly was walking toward a screen door to exit the building with the others, a policeman outside leveled a shotgun and shot through the screen, hitting Kelly in the chin and neck. He was taken to Mt. Sinai Hospital where he would spend the next four weeks recovering.

While police were certain that there were many snipers that first night, one scholar is skeptical. No policeman was hit by gunfire, though many were injured by rocks or bricks. No snipers were ever found. And none of the persons arrested on the first night were armed.[16] This skepticism was shared by many blacks. An article in the *Call and Post* asked the question of whether the police were the snipers who killed blacks during the riot.[17]

One person who had no doubts about the snipers was Chief Wagner. In the wee hours during the rioting, Chief Wagner met with reporters in his office of the Central Police Station. He was dressed in a green T-shirt and gabardine trousers and leaned heavily on his hunting rifle. He was confident, he said, that his 2,100 men could control Hough. "This situation will not get out of hand because I've got my men there to see that it won't," he told reporters.

The chief described his own exploits in trying to bag a sniper. He climbed the roof of one building to get "a bead on a sniper" on a nearby rooftop, he said, but the slope of the roof and the rain combined to prevent him from gaining a solid footing. So he went to another building and made his way to the fifth floor where he could peer out a window, but he was unable to locate "the hidden sniper."

He said he was convinced that his men had not killed Joyce Arnett, insinuating that she had been deliberately killed by blacks. "There was a similar occurrence in the Chicago riot," he told newsmen. "They sacrifice one person and then blame it on police brutality."[18]

Tuesday, July 19, found some of the people of Hough in a mood that was almost jubilance, despite the widespread destruction. They felt unity in retaliating against predatory businesses in their community and experienced gratification in witnessing police officers dance with fear when they were pelted with rocks and bricks the night before. As one elderly woman expressed it, "I think these young folks have proved something to Mr. Charlie tonight. We ain't scared no more!"[19]

Lewis Robinson had two primary reactions. He saw black men in particular walking with a sense of pride. He thought few whites could understand this reaction. "A survivor of a concentration camp will understand," he wrote, "but not the majority of whites who will perhaps never know the meaning of true freedom—a freeing of the mind as well as cutting the physical restraints that bind you."[20]

His second reaction is that he and the JFK House would be blamed for the uprising. "It is easy to predict what would happen after the shock had worn off," he wrote. "It happened in cities across the country. The demonstration would not be explained as the predicted revolt of people who had nothing to lose but their rat-infested streets, their high-rent hovels, but as the result of the hoodlum elements stirred by outside subversive elements—a few radicals and communist agitators."[21]

About four in the afternoon, Robinson wrote, "the brothers returned to the streets." Despite Chief Wagner's confidence that his men could contain the riots, Mayor Locher asked Governor Rhodes to call up the National Guard. Units would arrive around midnight. Locher called it a "tragic day in the life of our city."[22]

Lewis Robinson tried to keep his JFK kids off the streets and drove around picking them up to take them home later that night. Around 11:00 PM, he was stopped by police with three boys in his car. "Lieutenant," Robinson said, "You know I'm Robinson. I'm trying to keep our kids out of Hough." The lieutenant responded, "I know who you are, get out of that damned car, all of you."

Robinson and the three boys were lined up against the wall of Gale Super Valu Market with feet spread and arms high above their heads. They were roughly searched as some police tore up Robinson's car to try to find weapons or contraband. At one point, one of the cops kicked the legs out from all of them, causing them to fall on their faces. "You guys keep cool and don't say a damned thing," Robinson warned the boys. The police threatened to kill them. "To reinforce the threat," Robinson wrote, "one of the cops took out his leaded riot stick and swung at my mouth. I ducked and he hit me across the bridge of my nose smashing the left lens of my glasses." Finally, the police let them go and drove off laughing, according to Robinson.[23]

That same night, a thirty-six-year-old man named Percy Giles was shot in the back of the head and killed at Hough and East 86th. Police claimed he was caught in a cross fire; blacks believe police shot into a crowd and killed Giles in response to bottles thrown at the police. An eyewitness said Giles was fleeing the police shooting when he was hit in the back of the head. "I witnessed the shooting and it wasn't a sniper," the eyewitness later told a panel. Giles, he said, was in the area to help a friend board up his business.[24]

Hough suffered two more days of rioting and two more blacks were killed by white vigilantes. One, Benoris Toney, was shot in the face by a white man from the Little Italy area of Murray Hill.[25] The shooter claimed self-defense and was acquitted by an all-white jury. His lawyer compared "the vigilante actions of the Little Italy area to American pioneers protecting kith and kin."[26] The defendant, twenty-nine-year-old Warren LaRiche, said after a first trial and hung jury that he was "going to celebrate by eating a spaghetti dinner at the home of his parents."[27] In a retrial, he was acquitted by another all-white jury.[28]

A particularly disturbing display of police force involved the Townes family. Caught in their home near a building that was on fire on Thursday morning, Henry Townes and his wife loaded their two boys, one twelve and the other seven months, and a three-year-old nephew into the family's 1957 Ford convertible. The driveway was blocked by a police vehicle and, after the officer steadfastly refused to move it, Townes drove across a neighbor's lawn to escape the nearby inferno. Three white officers approached the car and began to grab and strike Henry Townes with clubs. His wife, Diana, wrapped her arms around him to keep him in the car, pulling him away from the punches of the police. The tussle caused Henry to slip to the floor of the car, which in turn triggered the car to "lurch forward." At this point the police opened fire, striking every member of the family in the car. Ten bullet holes pocked the door nearest Diana, and she was shot in the head and the arm. Diana lost her right eye and suffered brain damage; her nephew was also shot in the head.[29]

Tellingly, the National Guard stationed nearby did not fire a shot. In fact, where the Cleveland Police used up vast amounts of ammunition during the four days of rioting, the National Guard, according to its official report, shot "very few rounds of ammunition."[30] Lewis Robinson bitterly remarked, "The police, knowing they had reinforcements, went 'nigger hunting.'"[31]

Robinson correctly predicted who would be blamed. The city administration's neglect and police misconduct, so carefully cataloged by the US Civil Rights Commission just months earlier, would not be pointed to as causing factors responsible for the seething anger and frustration that let loose in Hough. Scapegoats were needed, and scapegoats would be found.

Even as the rioting was still under way, Cleveland's safety director, John N. McCormick, began to push the conspiracy theory. "We are worried about outside influences from other parts of the country that may be playing a role in this disturbance," he said in a press conference on Wednesday, July 20. He had to admit, though, that he had no evidence for his theory. "It is being investigated," he said. "I have no evidence here now to support it. But I do believe this catastrophe has attracted undesirables from out of town."[32]

Mayor Locher joined the cacophony to give the conspiracy a Communist-inspired hue. The same day that McCormick spoke, Locher also held a press conference and said, "I certainly do not deny the possibility, as the president states, that individuals who do not favor our form of democratic government may be playing a part in the disturbances which have swept the country in recent weeks. I also know that the great majority of our Negro community is not a part of the lawlessness."[33]

President Johnson in a televised news conference from the East Room in the White House earlier in the day had warned blacks that violence might set back the recent gains in civil rights. "The president pointed out that Negroes constituted a 10 percent minority in the United States," the New York Times wrote. "He said that while he believed that most of the 90 percent white majority supported racial equality and justice, they wanted these to be achieved without violence."

When asked specifically about the emergence of "black power" movements in Chicago and Cleveland, Johnson said he was not interested in black power or white power but was concerned with democratic power with a small d. A reporter then inquired if Johnson thought the big city riots were the work of "professional agitators." He responded: "Where there is trouble there are always individuals that suspicion is attached to, but I would not want to say that the protests and the demonstrations are inspired by foreign powers." He added, qualifiedly, that he could not say that "people who do not approve of our system" sometimes did contribute to racial violence.

That day, Johnson's attorney general, Nicholas Katzenbach, specifically denied that the riots were "masterminded" by anyone. He told the House Un-American Activities Committee that he "discounted a report in *Life* magazine that an organization known as RAM ... had inspired recent disturbances in this country." He pointed out that RAM and Robert F. Williams, still in Cuba, were being investigated, "but I wouldn't want to create the impression that the activities of these juvenile gangs have been masterminded by Williams out of Cuba."[34]

The white backlash and campaign to find culprits in Cleveland ratcheted up as more force was brought to bear in Hough and the rioting began to burn itself out, literally and figuratively. The leading reactionary stoking the racial hatred was Doris O'Donnell of the *Plain Dealer*. On Friday morning, July 22, the banner headline above O'Donnell's article— the lead on page one—shouted, "Rioters Follow Pattern: Burn, Run." Her article began with these inciting words: "A 'hate whitey' revolution, plotted and predicted for many months in Cleveland, has finally hit the community with fire and gunshot." She made a case that would stick, one that the city administration could fully embrace and hide behind:

> Rioting in the Hough area came as predicted weeks ago by a small band of extremists. At first the stunned city tried to accept the blazing buildings and looted stores as the work of roving, unorganized gangs, a spontaneous outburst of racial unrest.
>
> But no longer are thoughtful officials accepting the view that the sporadic fires and the hit-and-run tactics of faceless arsonists are based on the impulsive urges of wild, free-wheeling bands of Negro youths.
>
> The city administration has been reluctant to point accusatory fingers at the groups or individuals.
>
> But Police Chief Richard B. Wagner has finally said publicly what he believed privately.
>
> The false fire and police alarms all over the Glenville and Hough areas "seem to indicate there was some form of organization behind them," he told a reporter.[35]

O'Donnell's spew of hatred against African Americans fed into all the worst stereotypes that had already found favor among many in Cleveland's white community. She asked rhetorically, Why? Her first and primary answer was welfare. Quoting an unnamed black man, she said that the Aid to Dependent Children check "captured" the African American and reduced the community to desperation and dependency. O'Donnell drew her own conclusions from this alleged interview. "The 'CHECK'—called 'the thing'—supports the matriarchal structure of the ghetto Negro family," she wrote. "It pays the rent for a woman and her brood, which in many cases is illegitimate. It makes a weakling of the Negro male, who eats and sleeps off his woman's ADC check but rarely bothers with matrimony or employment."[36]

There was a complete disconnect between Cleveland's white power structure and the people rioting in Hough. Lewis Robinson said that the people of Hough were practicing their own version of urban renewal by burning down homes and structures that were abandoned and rat infested. They were retaliating against predatory merchants who did not live in the neighborhood and who overcharged and disrespected people who had limited means of transportation and faced systemic discrimination in hiring and employment. They were responding to police abuse by hurling rocks and bottles and bricks.

On the second evening of rioting a group of over five hundred adults and children gathered outside the Stephen E. Howe Elementary School in Glenville—where Bruce Klunder had been run over by a bulldozer—and began throwing Molotov cocktails and other incendiary bombs on its roof to burn it down. Only a massive show of force saved the structure. "About 100 police and guardsmen, walking in squads of four, formed a protective ring around the Stephen E. Howell Elementary School, 1000 Lakeview Road, N.E., where a crowd had gathered," the newspaper reported.[37]

Some, like Vice President Hubert Humphrey, showed some understanding of the root of the violence. He said that if he had to live in a ghetto with rats nibbling at his children's toes, he might "lead a mighty good revolt" himself. When Republicans criticized his remarks, Humphrey stood his ground. "Intolerable slum conditions are a seedbed for trouble," he responded, "and every responsible American public official should be aware of this fact."[38] The *New York Times* published an article entitled "Hating Police Is a Way of Life in the Hough Area of Cleveland."[39]

Yet in Cleveland, the leading newspaper carried a special front-page editorial at the end of the momentous week with a headline that said it all: "Crack Down Harder." In a separate story on page one, Doris O'Donnell singled out the JFK House for responsibility. "Police believe fire bombs used to set off fires in the Hough area were manufactured by youths with ties to the controversial JFK House," she wrote. The principal accuser, as might be expected, was the chief of police, Richard R. Wagner.[40]

Lewis Robinson denied the reports that JFK was a bomb-making factory and his wife pointed out that the center had been raided multiple times without anyone finding a "drop of gasoline." Yet there is no question that lessons of the futility of civil discourse and negotiation were being learned. Robinson told a reporter from the *New York Times*, "These people are getting guerrilla experience. We're going to take it right to the Charlie's [the white man's] front door." He pointed to Washington and Jefferson as inspirational American revolutionaries and said, "The great American experiment, that's what we are, the great American experiment."[41]

Exactly one month after Hough, Don Freeman sat in the living room of his home in Glenville with Fred "Ahmed" Evans. The two men had become friends. That night, Freeman's wife went into labor with their second child. As Freeman and his wife packed to go off to the hospital, Evans wished them well and left.

Before exiting, though, Evans turned back and said to the couple, "I hope it's a warrior."[42]

14

"Reliability and Discretion Assured"

AL ROBY IN CHICAGO, LIKE Don Freeman in Cleveland, was a public school teacher. He was one of the people who asked the Southern Christian Leadership Conference and Dr. King to join the Chicago Coordinating Council of Community Organizations in its freedom campaign in Chicago during the summer of 1966. The conflict over school integration in Chicago was ultimately a fight about ending discriminatory housing practices. "No longer could we afford to isolate a major segment of our society in a ghetto prison and expect its spiritually crippled wards to accept the advanced social responsibilities of the world's leading nation," King wrote. Open housing became a goal of the Chicago campaign.[1]

But breaking down Chicago's "infamous wall of segregation" would prove to be more complicated and frustrating than the attack on Jim Crow laws in the South. It's one thing to create laws to protect against discrimination in areas of voting and public accommodations; it is altogether different to force people to integrate schools and housing. Violence was a certain reaction.

Five miles southwest from the loop in Chicago is a group of neighborhoods known as the Gage Park, Chicago Lawn, Marquette Park area. The *New York Times* described it as a giant white enclave in Chicago: "It has approximately 100,000 residents, all but seven of them white, according to the 1960 census. About a third of the residents are listed by census takers as being of 'foreign stock,' mostly Poles, Lithuanians, Germans, and Italians." Some six hundred civil rights workers planned to march for open housing through this area on Saturday, August 6, 1966, two weeks after the Hough riots in Cleveland. The mood was already sour in Chicago from rioting that had taken place over the fire hydrants. Now the situation was about to become even more explosive.[2]

The protesters began to assemble in a staging area in Marquette Park, a huge grassy, open recreational area with a golf course and a large lagoon. The marchers were late, arriving around 4:00 PM. Already an angry crowd was there to meet them, described as "hundreds of teenagers, many waving Confederate flags and banners saying 'Elect George Wallace—the Governor from Alabama—President.'" As the afternoon had worn on, more and more young adults and well-dressed parents joined the white crowd, as it surged to over four thousand people. There were large numbers wearing Nazi-style helmets; Confederate and swastika flags were flying everywhere. They chanted: "Two, four, six, eight, we don't want to integrate." Almost a thousand Chicago police were on hand to try to keep the peace.

Knowing Dr. King was expected, many yelled, "We want Martin Luther Coon—Kill those niggers—Send them home." To the police, they jeered, "Look at those nigger-loving cops." Other signs read, "King would look good with a knife in his back," and, "Go home, Communists, go home."

When King arrived around 5:00 PM, he was surrounded by twenty-five policemen as he made his way from his car to the staging area. Rocks and empty glass soda bottles began to shower down. One volley flew over the heads of Dr. King and his protective police escort, but a second round resulted in direct hits. Martin Luther King Jr. was hit on the right side of his head, just above the ear, by a massive rock that knocked him to his knees. He was stunned but slowly got back up and insisted on continuing the march.

The marchers wound their way through the heated mob for almost three miles before being taken from the scene in buses the police had arranged. Rocks and bottles continue to rain down and even the retreating buses were attacked, with windows smashed. "God I hate niggers and nigger-lovers," one gray-haired woman swore at the parade. Another older man said, "I worked all my life for a house out here and no nigger is going to get it!"[3]

Martin Luther King could hardly believe the ferocity of the whites in Chicago who fought the protesters and the police (twenty-eight whites went to hospitals with wounds; almost fifty were arrested). "I've never seen anything like it in my life," he told reporters. "I think the people of Mississippi ought to come to Chicago to learn how to hate."[4]

Beaten but not bowed, King left for Atlanta the next day but promised to return to continue to march for fair housing in twenty nearly all-white neighborhoods. Behind the scenes, however, he was beginning to lose his grip on his northern leadership.[5]

In Cleveland following Hough, the expected came to pass—the administration, the press, the courts, and the police "cracked down harder." Lewis Robinson and his wife Beth were arrested late at night on suspicion and released. The JFK House was shut down owing to "sanitary violations" on July 27, and a grand jury was empaneled by the Court of Common Pleas of Cuyahoga County to investigate the causes of the Hough riots.[6] On July 28, the embers of the fires in Hough barely cool, Robinson and his wife appeared at the same time to testify before the grand jury. It is highly unusual—actually unheard of—for two people to testify before a grand jury at the same time. Obviously prosecutors wanted to show a black man and white woman as a married couple to inflame the prejudices of the grand jurors.[7] The grand jury was composed of fifteen members and two alternates. Only two of the members were black.[8]

What Lewis Robinson had to notice was that the grand jury foreman was Louis B. Seltzer, the flamboyant and powerful editor of the *Cleveland Press*, Cleveland's high-circulation afternoon paper. Seltzer was in his final year as editor of the *Press*, but his career had been long and controversial. His resume included the *Press*'s sensationalistic and one-sided coverage of the Sam Sheppard trial—Seltzer relentlessly attacked the Bay Village doctor who was accused of killing his wife. The *Press* coverage made a "carnival atmosphere" of the pretrial and trial proceedings, contributing to the reversal of Sheppard's conviction by the US Supreme Court.

Robinson had sued Seltzer and the *Press* in April 1965 for $250,000 in connection with a 1964 article that falsely described one of the first meetings of the Medgar Evers Rifle Club.[9] The suit was still pending at the time the grand jury met in the summer of 1966.[10]

The other target of the grand jury was Harllel Jones, a cofounder of the JFK House. Jones was younger than Lewis Robinson but had become a darling to liberals on Cleveland's East Side because of his good looks (he was tall and athletic) and his charismatic speaking style. He was often invited to speak before white audiences at churches and in private homes in Cleveland Heights and Shaker Heights as part of "dialogues" between whites and blacks.

Jones was born into a large Hough family with a strict father who worked two jobs to support twelve children. "My father was a very moral man," Jones wrote. "I think in my early childhood I had more Christian philosophy than anyone in the neighborhood. At the age of three, we were put in Bible school every summer and we had to go each and every day and on Sunday we had to go to church."[11] His father had difficulty conceiving of Harllel's radicalization. "After I became a Black man," Harllel wrote, "he couldn't understand what had happened to his poor little son," he remembered. "He used to tell me, 'I don't know what the hell is wrong with you. You went crazy or something? Why you talking all that stuff?'"

Harllel was smart and did well in school but became a delinquent as he entered his teenage years. "After I left high school," he wrote, "I was taken over to the old Kinsman area and over there the cats was rough. The cats from Quincy was hard core." He was arrested at least ten times, he admitted, and was in and out of jail and juvenile detention centers. His older brothers thought he was "just a little hoodlum," he wrote.

Then he started studying black nationalism. He dabbled a bit in the Nation of Islam but ended up a follower of Malcolm X and his brand of nationalism. He once told reporters that Malcolm X had offered him a scholarship to attend a university in Cairo, Egypt. "If I had nationalism when I was young, I probably never would have went to no penal institution, see, but I didn't have this," he recalled. "There wasn't no black talk then but the youth today really have something to cling to. They don't have to smoke marijuana. What they can do is something useful for their people. They will have self-satisfaction in that alone."[12]

Jones told his white audiences that it was during the heyday of the civil rights movement in the South that he turned to black nationalism. "Every day you turned on the television and saw a bunch of white folks beating blacks, women and children, while the so-called Negro man was fighting for integration," he said. "I think at that time I came to an awareness that the majority of the people in this country were not really for integration. The whites were ready to kill black folks, to lynch and burn black folks. So at that time the only thing black folks could do was to get themselves together and instead of using the white man's toilet, get your own toilet."[13]

Harllel Jones was subpoenaed to appear before the Seltzer-led grand jury after the Hough riots. He was a city sewer department employee at the time, but he was about to lose that job. A fiery article, "Harllel Jones: His Hatred Is White Hot," appeared the day before he testified in the *Plain Dealer* just below the article summarizing Lewis and Beth Robinson's testimony before the grand jury. He was identified as Robinson's lieutenant at the JFK House and the article cited a previously unreleased lengthy interview with a local TV news station and an alleged interview with Doris O'Donnell in which Jones predicted a "long hot summer" in 1966. He also supposedly told the news station that he saw "no way but all-out warfare and barricading the ghetto to get black control of the Negro community."

What O'Donnell and the *Plain Dealer* failed to advise their readership was that O'Donnell was being used by the FBI in its COINTELPRO campaign of disinformation and disruption against black nationalists. FBI files only recently uncovered show that the FBI considered her to be a cooperative and trustworthy reporter to spread information and half-truths about the JFK House, Lewis Robinson, and Harllel Jones. In April 1966, for example, the FBI field office in Cleveland urgently requested permission to leak information privately to Doris O'Donnell, as they had done in the past:

Bureau authority requested to furnish lead information re forego-
ing to Doris O'Donnell, feature writer, *Cleveland Plain Dealer*,
daily and Sunday morning newspaper, who has been used in
counterintelligence programs in the past and whose reliability
and discretion [are] assured.[14]

Segments of this FBI memo made its way into multiple articles
penned by O'Donnell and others at the *Plain Dealer* over the next few
months. The exposé on Harllel Jones just before his grand jury testimony
on July 28 is sprinkled with information from the memo. For example,
the FBI memo referred to a "WYW taped interview [of Jones], not yet
released," in which Jones "predicted riots in Cleveland in 1966," and
said "the first ones to suffer will be the 'Uncle Tom' Negroes." The
Plain Dealer exposé took these nuggets and embellished them: "In this
report [referring to the TV interview], never used fully, Jones predicted
a 'long hot summer' and said that policemen who had offended the
Negro community would be targets of violence. He said they had even
been selected by badge number."[15]

The bottom line on Harllel Jones, per the *Plain Dealer* article, was
that he was blindly motivated by hatred of whites. The article was deliberately provocative. Despite his dialogues with white church leaders and
liberals on Cleveland's East Side, the paper claimed that Jones maintained, "But I still hate the white man."[16]

In the same paper, on the same front page, Doris O'Donnell carried the byline under an article entitled "City Offers Married Poor Free
Birth Control." The program was aimed at women too poor to afford
children, those women Doris O'Donnell had identified as Hough's welfare queens.[17]

The verdict from the grand jury investigating the causes of Hough
was swift and expected. After taking just seven days of testimony, the
grand jury released a seventeen-page report on the evening of August
9. "Jury Blames Hough Riots on Professionals, Reds," the *Plain Dealer*
headline read. "A small but hard-core cadre of professional troublemakers, including some members of the Communist party, was responsible for the harrowing Hough riots, the Cuyahoga Grand Jury said last
night," the paper reported. Who were the lead culprits? "They are Lewis

G. Robinson, a former city housing inspector fired for his activities connected with a rifle club, and Harllel Jones, city sewer department employee," the grand jurors found.[18] Harllel Jones was described as an "outright exponent of violence, a black power apostle with a bitter hatred for all whites." RAM was given honorable mention. Robinson, the jury report said, "has been affiliated with the Freedom Fighters of Ohio, the Medgar Evers Rifle Club (which he helped found), the JFK House, of which he is the ultimate head, the Deacons for Defense, and the Revolutionary Action Movement."[19]

Despite all this, no indictments were handed down. Robinson, Jones, and Albert Ware-Bey (another cofounder of the JFK House) were all named, yet none of them was arrested or ever charged with a crime. The grand jury report offered a lame excuse for the lack of indictments, referencing the lack of antirioting laws on the books. But the fact remains there was no evidence to support their charges. No less than the Cleveland Police Department's head of its Subversive Unit, John Ungvary, reported to the FBI privately: "There was no evidence that members of the JFK House or their leaders planned, instigated, or executed any disturbances in the Hough riot."[20]

Most Clevelanders accepted the result, happy to find a scapegoat other than government malfeasance. The Communists named (also not indicted) were perplexed as to how they got mixed up in the grand jury findings. The two mentioned in the report, a couple from Cleveland Heights, called it a "total fabric of lies." They were nowhere near Hough during the rioting.[21] The grand jurors, however, found it convincing that J. Edgar Hoover had named an organization they belonged to—the W. E. B. Dubois Club—as a "Communist-sponsored youth organization." That was enough proof.

Thinking Clevelanders, however, found it terribly suspicious that people who had encouraged and organized the worst rioting in Cleveland's history were not indicted. One such Clevelander was Harvey L. Pekar, the legendary underground comic book writer best known for his autobiographical work *American Splendor*, which was eventually adapted into a highly awarded film, starring Paul Giamatti.[22] Pekar's letter to the editor of the *Plain Dealer* slashed at the grand jury report:

It has been said that if the American people had the choice of
retaining or repealing the Bill of Rights in a referendum they
would repeal it. This seems almost plausible when considering
the favorable reaction of newspapers and a large segment of the
public to the Grand Jury report on the Hough riots.

Louis B. Seltzer served as foreman of the jury although he
is now being sued by Lewis Robinson. Obviously Seltzer should
not have been permitted to maintain such a position.

The policemen who did undercover work and testified before
the grand jury claimed that they had not heard members of the
groups they infiltrated planning the riots; nevertheless, the jury
accused these organizations of starting them, though it did not
indict the people it had labeled agitators.

Added to this, the FBI, which has been observing the racial
conflict in Cleveland, has not seen fit to make any arrests. The
Grand Jury report seems to me an effort to exonerate the Cleveland power structure for its indifference to the slum conditions
which caused the riots. The newspapers, which are part of the
power structure, have, by applauding this effort, demonstrated
cynicism and a disgusting lack of courage.[23]

Pekar's reaction, however, was far from the norm. The more common response of Clevelanders was reflected in a letter from a man from
Willoughby, who wrote, "For my part, I will take the word of [Common
Pleas] Judge Thomas J. Parrino, Louis B Seltzer and other Grand Jury
people and the record of testimony given while they were in session."[24]

Lewis Robinson was furious, reminding Clevelanders that he was
suing Louis Seltzer for $250,000. He charged that Mayor Locher and
Chief of Police Wagner should have been indicted. His reaction to the
report was that it "sounds like a comic strip from someone smoking
pot. I believe once the people find out the facts about this Red smear
the people are intelligent enough to sift the lies from the truth."[25]

So exasperated were black citizens with the grand jury findings that
a citizens' committee was formed to conduct its own hearings into the
causes of the Hough riot. The committee held hearings and took the testimony of more than fifty witnesses. The committee, headed by Baxter

Hill, Cleveland's CORE chairman, hired lawyers Stanley Tolliver and Louis Stokes to examine witnesses.[26]

In Chicago, Martin Luther King Jr. negotiated an agreement on August 26 with Mayor Daley on housing and called for a halt to further marches through white neighborhoods. The ten-point plan, according to the *New York Times*, provided "for better implementation and enforcement of fair housing laws, along with increased educational and moral pressure by religious, civic, and union leaders."[27] Dr. King hailed the accord as "the most significant program ever conceived to make open housing a reality in the metropolitan area."

But the plan had no teeth. There was no enforcement mechanism, no force of law. It was simply a group of promises that could be, and would be, broken by the city of Chicago, lending institutions, and residential brokers. Some of King's supporters were bitter. They believed that his great test in the North in Chicago had suffered an ignominious collapse.

Despite King's call for a moratorium on all open-housing marches after the pact with Mayor Daley, the leaders of CORE in Chicago and other dissident groups moved forward with a march in the all-white Cicero area of Chicago.[28] Cicero had no blacks and had suffered a horrendous race riot fifteen years earlier when a black family attempted to move into an apartment in the area. The march on September 4 turned violent, and members of the Illinois National Guard actually bayoneted some of the white hecklers. As in Marquette Park, the marchers were harassed by whites who screamed epithets and threw bottles and rocks.[29]

Days later in Chicago, twenty-five-year-old Stokely Carmichael, national chairman of the SNCC, told the newsmen that he was touring the country to explain and define the meaning of "black power" and that he would welcome a black unity conference. He declared "his organization would 'join hands' with the Black Muslim leader, Elijah Muhammad, and with the Revolutionary Action Movement." He also said he intended to meet with Dr. King.

"Black power means that black people have to politically get together to organize themselves so that they can speak from a position of power and strength rather than a position of weakness." When he was asked about the looting and firebombing in Cleveland, Carmichael said, "I'm not opposed to violence."[30] Martin Luther King had clearly lost control of his movement in the North.

Harllel Jones was suspended from his job with the city of Cleveland sewer department. The official reason cited was "excessive absenteeism."[31] He would be hounded by the police and Doris O'Donnell. Through a church group, he found a job with Head Start as a janitor in late October, but a grand jury indicted him and several others on November 15 on charges that were meant to imply that he had finally been arrested for the Hough rioting, but the events were unrelated.[32] The "rampage" he was indicted for was the defacing of property in Cleveland's Cultural Gardens, where black power slogans were spray-painted on monuments on September 7, six weeks after the Hough riots.[33] He was also indicted for an attempt to burn down a grocery store in Hough in June, a month before the riot. And he was indicted for alleged felonious assault of a fifteen-year-old girl in the basement of the JFK House.

None of this precluded the *Plain Dealer* from attempting to link the indictments to Hough rioting. Its story began, "Harllel B. Jones, former city sewer department employee and self-proclaimed black nationalist, was one of eight men secretly indicted for destruction and violence on Cleveland's East Side."[34] Anyone who did not read farther than the lead paragraph would have assumed Jones had been charged for the Hough riots.

Sergeant John Ungvary of the Subversives Unit of the Cleveland Police Department kept up the pressure. He raided several apartments in Hough and Glenville and claimed that he uncovered evidence of the formation of a group called the United Black Brotherhood (UBB) in one apartment on Superior Avenue. The police told the press that they discovered minutes of a meeting of the UBB showing it was formed on August 18, 1966. Harllel Jones was listed as an officer, as was Albert Ware-Bey. Later in the year, the police raided another apartment in Glenville on Lakeview Road where they purportedly found Molotov cocktails, empty bottles, rags, and oil to make more. They also discovered menacing UBB signs, a manual telling how to make gunpowder, and some "completed products."[35]

A cleric on the West Side came to Harllel Jones's defense, asserting that he was being persecuted by the Cleveland police. "Jones has come to symbolize all reaction," the minister said. "He still has all his black nationalism or black power, not as a warrior, but as a man who had a voice for the people he knows. He is not a warrior or hate man."[36]

Against all this tumult, the problem was not just that Dr. King had lost his footing in Chicago. The violence and the rioting were creating a significant backlash in the white community, even among liberals. Pollster Louis Harris recognized a trend in the fall of 1966. In a nationally televised program, "Black Power—White Backlash," Harris demonstrated statistically that the division caused by the racial violence was going to "tear the Democratic Party apart at the seams in the North where, traditionally, low income whites and low income Negroes must be on the same side."

"Today," Harris said, "they're not on the same side over civil rights. This could cost the Democrats and cost them heavily."[37]

Martin Luther King Jr. and his wife withdrew to Jamaica during the first two months of 1967 to vacation, meditate, and consider his next steps. Jamaica and its people had had a profound influence on him since his visit in 1965. Its national motto, "Out of Many, One People," held tremendous meaning and appeal to him. In early 1967 he rented an isolated house near Ocho Rios, on the island's picturesque north coast, where he worked in his pajamas and sometimes failed to shave.

He took the time in Jamaica to write his book *Where Do We Go from Here: Chaos or Community?* Vietnam and the question of peace were becoming the focus of his soul.

Richard Nixon and George Wallace were paying close attention to the white backlash that was being stirred up by the civil rights movement. What would become Nixon's "New Majority" was beginning to take shape in the South—and now in the North. It was being propelled mainly by race but would be amplified by the storm of protest gathering over the escalation of the Vietnam War.

15

"Blood Will Flow in the Streets"

IN JANUARY 1967 A JURY acquitted Don Freeman of the perjury charges brought against him in connection with his firing in the spring of 1965. He was definitely out of the revolution business, his life in tatters. But his original partner in RAM, Max Stanford of Philadelphia, continued to plot and plan, if the police and FBI are to be believed.

In New York City, a RAM cell was infiltrated by several undercover detectives starting in July 1965, five months after Malcolm X was assassinated. One of the detectives became so deeply embedded that he was appointed the vice president of the group. These undercover detectives would testify to a grand jury later in 1967 that the RAM members in Queens were in conspiracy with Max Stanford in Philadelphia. They claimed that the group was planning and training for guerrilla warfare in New York City during the summer of 1967.[1]

Bill Russell, with whom Fred Evans lived during periods of estrangement from his wife, remembered traveling with Evans and others by car twice to New York City around this time. His memory is that Albert Ware-Bey, one of the cofounders of the JFK House, went with them. On one trip, Russell said, they stopped in the Catskills where a woman named Audley Moore, better known as Queen Mother Moore, was holding a black nationalist rally of some sort. Russell said they then went to New York City and stayed at the YMCA in Harlem, where they met with Max Stanford and other nationalists.[2]

Russell had a specific recollection of Ware-Bey and Stanford in Moore Park (today, Moore Playground) in Harlem discussing the idea of training in guerrilla warfare tactics somewhere in the rural South. He recalls Fred Evans being uninterested. Evans sarcastically responded to Stanford, "Why don't you go South and do the training?"

At some point in 1966 or 1967, Evans lost his job with the Pennsylvania Railroad. Evans claimed his dismissal was the result of the railroad discovering that he was a black nationalist.[3] According to FBI files, Evans became a member of the United Black Brotherhood—the group formed just after the Hough riots and the closing of the JFK House. Sergeant Ungvary told the FBI that on March 1, 1967, Evans "decided to break off from this organization [the UBB] and start his own Black Nationalist group with headquarters located in a store front astrology shop, 11105 Superior Avenue, Cleveland, Ohio."[4] Ungvary later testified before the Senate Subcommittee on Internal Security that "several black nationalist groups in Cleveland had merged to form the Harlem People's Parliament, headed by a 'prime minister' named Fred Allen Evans, also known as Ahmed."[5]

The police were not happy about the opening of Evans's astrology shop on Superior in Glenville, twenty-six blocks east from the closed JFK House. A week after the astrology shop opened, several Cleveland Police officers were dispatched to harass Evans and some of the teenagers who had started to follow him. One of the officers, a black traffic policeman named William Payne, came with a sledgehammer.

On Wednesday evening, March 8, Payne stopped three black teenagers who were driving Evans's car. Though they had broken no traffic laws, Payne took the youths to Evans's astrology shop, which was being refurbished as a bookstore. Evans and a twenty-six-year-old African American named Johnny Sileen Walker, along with others, were at the astrology shop. Walker had been drinking and was likely intoxicated.

Evans and Payne got into an argument over what Evans considered police harassment of the young men who were driving his car with his permission. Evans said that Payne threatened to kill him twice. Payne finally asked him to step outside.

Evans would later say that he could have killed Officer Payne with his own hands, as he was a combat veteran, a champion boxer, and had learned judo during his six years in the army. Payne, according to Evans, threatened him with the sledgehammer. "I simply grabbed the sledge hammer he threatened me with," Evans would testify, "exerting the proper pressure, then exerted proper pressure again, leading [Payne] to the ground, where he attempted to draw his gun from his left side." When police reinforcements arrived they found Evans on top of Payne, holding him down.[6]

Evans and Walker were both taken into custody. Evans was charged with aggravated assault, a felony. Walker was charged with intoxication and aggravated assault.

Furious, Officer Payne took his sledgehammer and began to break all the windows in the astrology shop and then destroyed equipment inside the store. Photos in the *Call and Post* a week later documented the damage.[7] The white policeman stood by and watched. The *Call and Post* reported, "Ahmed said Payne was so incensed at the undignified position his fellow officers found him in—with Ahmed a-straddle him—that he got up and deliberately smashed the windows of the astrology shop."

Once they were taken downtown, police began to brutally beat Walker in his cell. "At the police station," Evans told the newspapers, "they took Walker into one cell and about eight white policemen left their desks and came into his cell and began to beat him." Walker still had bruises to show the press a week later. "I asked two Negro policemen in the station to look at them beating Walker," Evans elaborated, "but they refused; they turned their heads." He said these same black cops had slapped him on the head when he was first brought into the station. Several officers, including sergeants, lieutenants, captains, in brass braid, "walked to our cells and spit on Walker and me," Evans alleged. "Walker spat back at them."[8]

What happened next made Ahmed Evans famous in Cleveland and even around the country. Sergeant Ungvary came to visit Evans in his jail cell a couple of days after he was arrested. He asked the purpose of the astrology shop. Evans told him that he intended to teach astrology and black culture to young people. He also said he was going to "manufacture skull caps with astrological signs and Islamic cult gowns [not unlike, it should be noted, Elijah Muhammad]." He told Ungvary that he turned to astrology several years earlier after seeing "flying saucers" buzzing around East 79th and Kinsman Road (two miles due south of where the Hough riots started).

Then things got even weirder. Evans said that his review of astrological forecasts led him to believe that there would be a partial eclipse of the sun, visible early in the morning on May 9, 1967. This he took as the sign that a race war would break out on that day, not just in Cleveland, but worldwide. "When the eclipse comes, it will be the end of an era," Evans told Ungvary. "I'm afraid to say what will happen. Hostilities will begin between China and the United States."

"Blood will flow in the streets," Evans predicted. He was for a total separation of the races, he said. He wanted to "turn the white markets out" of the ghetto and allow blacks to experience economic self-sufficiency.

Anyone steeped in race history in the United States perhaps would have heard the echo Evans likely meant to Nat Turner and his bloody slave insurrection in Virginia in 1831. Turner, like Ahmed Evans, gave a confession while in jail of the reasons behind his deadly rampage. A spirit appeared to him, Turner supposedly relayed to a southern lawyer named Thomas Gray, telling him signs in the heavens would make known to him "when he should commence his great work." Turner told his confessor, "And on the appearance of the sign (the eclipse of the sun last February) I should arise and prepare myself, and slay my enemies with their own weapons."[9]

Ungvary leaked this bizarre interview to friendly reporters at the *Plain Dealer* who filed a story deep in the paper on page 43. "Astrologer Charged in Policeman's Beating," read the headline on Saturday, March 11. The paper wrote about Evans being "interviewed in the city jail," but failed to disclose the source was Ungvary. The paper also noted that Harllel Jones and others, "affiliated with black nationalist groups," picketed outside the jail, seeking Ahmed Evans's release.

The paper further revealed that Evans said he was receiving money from the Cleveland Browns football star Jim Brown through his Negro Industrial and Economic Union (NIEU), though he said Brown didn't know the loan was for a black nationalist group. A spokesman for NIEU later denied any involvement.[10]

This sleepy back-page story went national days later, on Tuesday, March 14, when two enterprising reporters for the *Wall Street Journal* put Ahmed Evans on the front page of their paper. The headline read, "Racial Powder Keg: Negro-White Hostility Mounting in Cleveland as City's Efforts Fail." Fred Ahmed Evans was the star in the article's lead paragraphs:

> To Ahmed, the high priest of Negro militancy here, the white man is a "beast" to be overcome. He predicts May 9 will be the "terrible day" that the anger of this city's black ghetto erupts into violence—partly because, by his calculations, that will be the day when an eclipse of the sun darkens the sky.
>
> Ahmed is dismissed by many white Clevelanders who doubt that astrology has any value. Besides, Ahmed, whose real name is Fred Evans, was arrested last week on charges of assaulting a police officer; he has been released on $5,000 bond.
>
> Nevertheless, Ahmed's warnings that "blood must flow" and "some must die" are gospel to a small but growing number of followers, who gather every other Thursday night to hear him or other Negro radicals conduct what they call "dialogues in black." And though these sessions may be a muddle of mysticism and menace, they are all too symptomatic of the tensions that make this city one of the nation's leading radical trouble spots. Even to some city officials, Cleveland's inability to make a significant start toward coping with racial discontent seems to foreshadow a sequel, when the weather warms, to last summer's five-day "riot" in the "tough Hough" slum that left four dead.[11]

It was a banner day for Fred Ahmed Evans; it was a disaster for Mayor Ralph Locher. Locher was already under intense pressure politically because the Johnson administration had cut off funding for his urban renewal programs. Now Locher looked bad to the businessmen and bankers who met at the old-line Union Club, where many of the city's power brokers gathered for lunch or afternoon drinks. Locher was making a fool out of Cleveland nationally.

The mayor's trouble with the Department of Housing and Urban Development (HUD) began after the Hough riots. He agreed to a sixteen-point plan to improve the Hough neighborhoods with HUD money, but little had been accomplished by the end of the year. On January 16, 1967, the city and its government were knocked off their feet by a letter from HUD Secretary Robert C. Weaver, who pulled HUD funding—tens of millions of dollars. "HUD Axes City Renewal Funds" ran the headline greeting Clevelanders on Thursday morning, January 19, 1967. Despite some desperate efforts to ameliorate the problem, HUD stood firm and said it would not provide any further funding until the city of Cleveland got its act together. Projects had stalled for years. HUD described the management of urban renewal in Cleveland as "chaotic."[12] The *Plain Dealer* editorial board wrote that the "massive blow dealt Cleveland's urban renewal program is a direct result of the city's failure to act." They noted that Cleveland's urban renewal programs have been "virtually on dead center for years."[13]

The *Wall Street Journal* played up the failures of the Locher administration. They called on the chairman of the US Civil Rights Commission to weigh in. John Hannah, president of Michigan State University, said, "The accounting of (Cleveland's) accomplishments is very short, and the agenda of its unfinished business is very long." The national business paper highlighted the problems Locher was having with HUD, saying city hall and the federal government "are at odds." It pointed out that Cleveland drew up plans for urban renewal in dozens of projects, yet by 1967 it had only closed the books on one.

The paper ticked off one example after another where the community and its government were "at odds": city hall and the Cleveland business community, city hall and responsible Negro leadership, and the Negro community and the police. They quoted Harllel Jones as saying that the cause of the explosive mood in the ghetto came down to one thing: "police brutality." Police Chief Robert Wagner responded cynically, "We have no critics west of the Cuyahoga; we cannot appease those east of the Cuyahoga." The *Journal* translated Wagner's referenced geographic divide for the national audience: "Most whites live on the west side of the Cuyahoga River, which runs through the middle of Cleveland; most Negroes live on the east side."

The *Journal* even devoted a paragraph to Lewis Robinson. "Lewis Robinson, identified by a grand jury as a leader in last summer's riots but never indicted, and now a participant in the 'dialogues,' says of them, 'We've had factionalism. Now we want to pull all these things together.' He views rioting as 'productive and good, a warning that drastic measures must be taken.'"

On the other side, the *Journal* pointed to the growing white reaction. One man, Robert Annable, was profiled as the chairman of the Cleveland-based National Christian Conservative Society and the head of the North American Alliance of White People. He told the *Journal* that he believed "Negroes are culturally and intellectually inferior" and promised to hold rallies starting in May. Whites were reportedly arming themselves in Murray Hill, Collinwood, and Sowinski on the East Side of Cleveland and all across the West Side. Members of one rifle club called the White Chain Gang told the *Journal* reporters that they were practicing with guns in the basement of a member's house and "shooting at targets they call 'niggers.'"

The *Journal* wrote that Dr. Martin Luther King Jr. expected to visit Cleveland in the near future "to help prepare for simultaneous demonstrations this summer here and in other cities." CORE said it was narrowing its search for a "demonstration city," and Cleveland was "quite possible." White nationalist groups warned of counter-demonstrations should the black protests come to pass. The Ku Klux Klan and the American Nazi Party also threatened to organize in Cleveland.

Even Mayor Locher's black director of human relations had a pessimistic outlook for the coming summer. "I suspect that it won't be confined to the Negro community," Bertram Gardner told the *Journal* of a potential outbreak of racial violence. "I'm afraid it will extend to the white communities and downtown—not a massive movement but guerrilla warfare."[14]

It was a propitious time for Carl Stokes to start thinking about running for mayor again. He had been reelected to the Ohio House of Representatives in the fall of 1966 and was a leading candidate to replace Locher in 1967. Stokes blamed Cleveland's many problems on official neglect and a willful failure to see and address the problems of urban blight. Stokes wrote in his autobiography,

> Over the years the newspapers, the business community, and the electorate, comprised mainly of lower-middle-income blue-collar whites, had successfully resisted taxes and spending in vital areas to the basic health of the city. After World War II, when the deterioration of our cities became apparent, there was a complete failure to respond. City government was praised when it could show itself to be frugal. Nobody cared that it wasn't providing health services, wasn't enforcing housing and building codes, wasn't adequately collecting garbage and rubbish or building recreational areas. . . . And these same attitudes toward money were causing the collapse of our school system.[15]

On March 19, a study group funded by a Cleveland foundation issued a report that put a spotlight on housing problems faced in Cleveland. "The report said that more than 200,000 residents of Cuyahoga County lived in substandard housing and that one out of four families lived in a rat-infested dwelling," the *Times* reported. It was a foreboding assessment that warned that the price of delay in addressing urgent needs would be the "sacrifice of human dignity."[16] A dangerous despair was creeping in.

Meanwhile, poor blacks and poor whites in the city began to arm themselves. By the end of March 1967 white and black hate groups began to terrorize Cleveland neighborhoods in outbreaks of violence. A black city councilman found a common problem that whites and blacks faced. "At the root of the present scattered racial violence," the *Times* quoted Councilman Leo Jackson as saying, "is lack of communication between poor Negroes and poor whites who are struggling for social survival in the face of automation and deteriorating job prospects for the unskilled." Jackson elaborated: "They have been left alone in the inner city, the poor Negroes and the white national groups, Poles, Hungarians, Italians. They are afraid of losing their jobs and they view one another as competitors and don't realize they share the same economic fate. The Anglo-Saxon middle class has long moved to the suburbs."[17]

Regardless of its causes, by the end of March 1967, everyone in Cleveland was bracing for another outbreak of racial violence that summer. Cleveland elites and government officials continued to worry, without proof, that violence in Cleveland was being sponsored by outside money and instigated by outside agitators.

At just this moment, one event would change the trajectory of things. On April 4, 1967 (exactly one year to the day before his assassination) Dr. Martin Luther King Jr. publicly denounced the war in Vietnam, causing a severe personal rift with President Johnson and moving King to the outer fringes of the power structure. It was an especially agonizing decision for King given that President Johnson had provided such powerful support for King and his movement and had, through dint of extraordinary parliamentarianism, brought about groundbreaking civil rights legislation.

But King in good conscience could no longer remain silent. Taylor Branch, a King biographer, noted the viciousness of the war at this time: "Weekly U.S. casualties reached 1,200 by January 1967 and exceeded 2,000 before the end of March with carnage tenfold higher for the Vietnamese."[18] Dr. King began his remarks in New York's Riverside Church on the Upper West Side to crowd of more than 3,000 people by saying, "A time comes when silence is betrayal."

King understood that the diversion of federal money and attention to the war in Vietnam was causing the civil rights movement and the Great Society's war on poverty to stall. He also knew that blacks were fighting and dying in Vietnam at twice their proportionate numbers relative to the rest of the population in the United States.

War, poverty, racism all had become interrelated. They arose from a sickness of the American mind, a pathology that King connected to racism, the aggregation of wealth, imperialism, and colonialism, at home and abroad. "The war in Vietnam is but a symptom of a far deeper malady within the American spirit," he said. America had become the greatest purveyor of violence in the world and if the sickness King spoke of went untreated, America was sure to be "dragged down the long, dark, and shameful corridors of time reserved for those who possess power without compassion, might without morality, and strength without sight."

He saw the normalizing of state-sponsored violence as encouraging violence in the ghettos. "As I walked among the desperate, rejected, and angry young men, I have told them that Molotov cocktails and rifles would not solve their problems," he said. "I have tried to offer them my deepest compassion while maintaining my conviction that social change comes most meaningfully through nonviolent action. But they asked, and rightly so, 'What about Vietnam?' They asked if our own nation wasn't using massive doses of violence to solve its problems, to bring about the changes it wanted?"

He called for blacks and "all white people of goodwill" to boycott the war by becoming conscientious objectors to military service and encouraged ministers to give up ministerial exemptions in order to become conscientious objectors.

He proclaimed, "Somehow this madness must cease." He quoted John F. Kennedy, who had predicted five years earlier, "Those who make peaceful revolution impossible will make violent revolution inevitable."

There was no turning back. "We still have a choice today: nonviolent coexistence or violent co-annihilation," he concluded.[19]

King's course was leaning to the radical. Though he decried Stokely Carmichael's slogan of "black power" in Mississippi in 1966 because it could be misconstrued as an endorsement of violence and reverse racism, he now found himself on Carmichael's side in opposing the war, embracing those who wanted a systematic and even revolutionary change of values in America. Like Malcolm X, King was moving to a higher plane during the final year of his life. "It was a speech for America," Congressman John Lewis would later say, "but the speech he delivered in New York, on April 4, 1967, was a speech for all humanity—for the world community."[20]

King underestimated the backlash that would follow, from friend and foe alike. The war still enjoyed broad support in the United States. The NAACP denounced King's mixing of the peace movement with the civil rights movement, calling it "a serious tactical mistake." Whitney Young, director of the National Urban League, said the civil rights movement and the peace movement had different goals and it would be inappropriate to merge them.[21] A writer for the *New York Times* forecast that King's speech "dampened his prospects for becoming the Negro leader who might be able to get the nation 'moving again' on civil rights."

The *Times* writer opined that when he attacked the war, "Dr. King automatically aligned himself with the black power wing of the civil rights movement, which had long preached against the war, and cut himself adrift from the moderate wing of the movement."[22]

But there was something more sinister at play than simple disagreement with Dr. King's newly declared stand against the war. The FBI, always suspicious of King, amped its plans to undercut his authority and destroy his reputation. Secret FBI memos show that the FBI sought out friendly reporters to ask King embarrassing questions that would point out his political reorientation and nefariously link him to the Communist Party. The memos also claim that King's voter registration drive in Chicago "failed miserably" and that he was "sensitive about allegations that his personal appeal to the ghetto Negro is waning."[23]

The storm of criticism stung. "It was a low point in my life," he wrote. "I could hardly open a newspaper."[24] He had not advocated the merger of the peace movement and the civil rights movement—it was a myth. He continued to focus his efforts in the South and in Chicago—but Cleveland offered a dynamic opportunity for redemption of a sort. King knew that Carl Stokes had a good chance of being the first elected black mayor of a major American city. So he came to Cleveland.

But when he came to Cleveland, he would not only have to deal with Carl Stokes, he would need to reach out to black nationalists—and there was no one more militant and more prominent in the nationalist community, now with his *Wall Street Journal* exposure, than Fred Ahmed Evans.

16

"Life for Me Ain't Been No Crystal Stair"

Two days after Dr. King delivered his Vietnam speech in New York City, the *Plain Dealer* began a three-part series on racial tensions in Cleveland, written by one of its few black reporters, Robert McGruder. It was an ominous piece of writing. "Even very rational, very hopeful men and women believe that Cleveland will be on fire this summer," McGruder began his first of three articles. No one, he wrote, knew what to do.

McGruder interviewed several black nationalists, who "call themselves the only real spokesmen for the poor and the oppressed in the ghetto." The nationalists referred to their tormentors as "beasts," meaning white oppressors, mainly police. "Black people are tired of that beast (the white man) coming out here beating our men and insulting our women," one nationalist told McGruder. "We are tired of rats and roaches crawling over our children. We are tired of the garbage in the streets, the landlords, the police, the men who take the money out of the ghetto, and the white men who come in at night for our women and go back out to the Heights after some racist cop arrests the woman."

The mood in Cleveland was explosive. "We have been mistreated. There has to be retribution," an anonymous nationalist warned. Asked if there was a plan for rioting in the summer—McGruder pointed out that those in the ghetto called it a rebellion, not a riot—the nationalist replied, "You don't need a plan. Just let one of these cops start beating on a brother."

McGruder reported that unemployment in the slum area of Cleveland was near 16 percent, according to the US Department of Labor, the "highest in the nation." Cleveland's overall unemployment was near 4 percent. He also stressed what the US Civil Rights Commission had found in the spring of 1966, before the Hough rebellion, that the "police had lost the respect of the residents of the inner city."

Mayor Locher's response to it all: "We must accentuate the positive."[1]

The next day, McGruder's series profiled Harllel Jones and Fred Ahmed Evans. "The Black Nationalist," McGruder wrote generically, "claims that he is the new leader of the ghetto." Harllel Jones spent much of his time in his interview defending himself against the lingering charges from the grand jury the summer before that found that he was one of the leaders of the Hough uprising and that the JFK House was a school for teaching how to make Molotov cocktails. "Anybody can make a fire bomb," Jones said. "*Life* magazine showed people how to do it. You don't have to go to school for it."

Jones said that nationalists were not the propagators of violence. It originated with others. "We are not interested in violence," he told McGruder. "We will protect ourselves. We won't take any stuff from Hitler's babies if they come into the ghetto. But you won't find me or any other Nationalists going into another neighborhood to start trouble," he said. "You find people coming from Murray Hill [to the ghetto] to shoot people, but we don't do things like that. And they call us violent." He said that blacks just wanted to be left alone. "I would say that 95% of the white people don't want Negroes around them. So why should I try to force myself on them? I will live in my ghetto and try to make it better."

Evans was described as an eccentric astrologer. "His star rose very suddenly recently," McGruder punned, perhaps unintentionally, "when he was proclaimed high priest of Black Nationalism in Cleveland. The title was given to him by whites in the *Wall Street Journal*, not by nationalists." McGruder took note of Evans's prediction of racial violence on May 9, 1967, only a month away:

For Ahmed the truth about man, especially the black man, is written in the stars. He gets a mystical look in his eyes and says all he wants to do is pass along those truths to his brothers. One of these truths is a May 9 racial confrontation.

Ahmed says he never uses the word hate. "I believe in the universal laws of justice. I believe that men should get along. Hate begets hate and peace begets peace."

One of the universal laws of justice is that a beating Ahmed alleges he received from the police must be avenged. In fact all the injustices of the world must be avenged.

"Retribution," he says, "is a universal law of justice."

The article concluded with the observation of Bertram Gardner, Mayor Locher's black director of the community relations board, saying that 99 percent of the black community rejected the leadership and tactics of the black nationalists but nevertheless excused them because these were black men acting on behalf of their community. Bertram said that the same was true in the white community, where vigilante groups were organizing to protect their homes and families. "Even law-abiding whites tolerate these people because they secretly believe in what these groups are doing," Gardner reasoned.[2]

All the newspaper attention paid to Ahmed Evans landed him once again under the intense surveillance of Cleveland Police Subversives Unit. Police wanted to find a way to get him off the streets ahead of May 9 so he could not lead the rebellion he predicted. They found a pretext a week after the McGruder series ran in the *Plain Dealer*, during the third weekend of April.

Trouble began on Saturday night, April 15. A street carnival at East 75th and Superior Avenue attracted a band of marauding teenagers who ran through the makeshift fair attempting to grab prizes and money. A fight between a black man and a white man triggered additional violence.[3] The chaos then spread along Superior Avenue into Glenville, a hundred blocks east from where the carnival was situated. Looting and rock throwing broke out on Superior and Euclid Avenues. Dozens of youths were arrested, most between the ages of fifteen and seventeen. Nearly two miles from where the disorder started, Ahmed Evans and several of his followers were arrested in the early hours of Sunday, April 16, for allegedly encouraging a gang of juveniles to loot a menswear store in the middle of Glenville at 1040 East 105th Street. "Police said Ahmed and others were noisy and profanely threatened the managers of Hatlo's store, uttering cries of 'Get whitey' as police attempted to restore order following the break-in and looting," the *Call and Post* reported.[4]

The next day, without the benefit of a lawyer, a municipal judge found Evans guilty of disorderly conduct and creating a disturbance and sentenced him to thirty days in the Cleveland Workhouse. Perhaps under pressure from police, Evans and his compatriots pleaded "no contest" before being sentenced (the *Call and Post* called it a "surprise move"). The *Plain Dealer* noted that as a result of the sentence "Ahmed will miss the disorders he has predicted for May 9."[5] The next night, Glenville suffered another night of looting. Police Chief Wagner said the Monday-night disturbances were "in retaliation for the arrests of certain persons," referring to Evans and his friends.

Evans, interviewed by the black newspaper in the workhouse, admitted he pleaded no contest "but, actually, was not guilty of the charges, and that he would seek to reopen the case when he obtained a lawyer."[6]

At week's end, Ahmed's astrology shop was closed down by the police sanitation unit for alleged housing violations. The police said that the store was "used as a public gathering place but failed to provide two rest rooms" and that "poor ventilation and general squalor made the place 'unfit for human habitation.'"[7]

Cleveland was in the mood for a crackdown. A *New York Times* article on April 24 declared that few leaders, black or white, objected to mayoral commands to the police to end recent vandalism and arson. Mayor Locher, the day after Evans and his friends were sentenced, ordered Police Chief Wagner to get tough. "Fill every jail in Cleveland if necessary," Locher said. For his part, Wagner proposed to arm city firemen with shotguns to ward off barrages of rocks and bottles that greeted them when responding to fires set in the ghetto. One city councilman said, "If the police have to break a few skulls, what will be the reaction of the people in this area? Riots? Or will they rise to the occasion and support the police? Let's find out."

Cleveland's safety director, former FBI agent John McCormick, went on television to say that he expected police brutality charges to flow from the crackdown. But he was indifferent: "I don't care." One fearful black city councilman asked Locher to request Ohio's governor to summon the National Guard, now. Another West Side councilman recommended that the police "shoot 'em dead." He said, "The only good hoodlum is a dead hoodlum."[8]

Bertram Gardner said he was advising fellow blacks to "forget this police brutality business, and if the cops have to use a little force look up at the stars, look away."

The New York Times reported that Ohio governor Rhodes ordered Ohio Highway Patrol helicopters to fly over Cleveland's ghetto to take photos of areas suspected of being firebomb factories. "Many of the nearly nightly fires in Hough, Superior, and Glenville sections have been set by homemade Molotov cocktail firebombs—fused, gasoline-filled bottles," the Times wrote.

Rev. Charles Rawlings, the thirty-six-year-old white minister who supported Lewis Robinson, Harllel Jones, and the JFK House, was one of the few voices of dissent. He called the suppression of Negroes by the Locher administration a "deliberate escalation of, and public invitation to, violence and vengeance." He said that the violence in the ghetto was not organized; it was chaos. "It is not organized militancy," Rawlings declared. "The people have learned black pride and this poison has come because they are still trapped in the white system with no way out." He predicted that if the city pursued its plans, "they will need stockades to hold all the people by this summer."[9]

Ahmed Evans and his friends finally retained an attorney—the ever-present Stanley Tolliver—who filed a motion seeking a new trial on the basis that the men did not have lawyers and did not know their constitutional rights when they pled no contest. The judge reluctantly granted the request on Tuesday, April 25, and ordered a jury trial, set for mid-June. So after spending ten days in the workhouse, Ahmed Evans was released on bail. That afternoon back in his astrology shop (apparently reopened), Evans gave an exclusive interview to a Call and Post reporter, Bob Williams, in which he repeated his prediction of race disturbances on May 9.

"I predict that May 9th will mark an eclipse of the Sun and the Moon, and that there is a great possibility that racial violence will erupt—and of difficulty between Red China and this country," he told Williams.

When Bob Williams pointed out to Evans that his predictions were getting him into hot water, causing stepped-up police activity and public alarm, Evans deflected, "I'd be a fool to say that I would start an uprising in this country." Yet he maintained the stars were always right. "The causes above are responsible for the effects below," he explained. "These are conditions that are entirely out of the reach of mankind."

A few hours later, an airplane carrying Dr. Martin Luther King Jr. touched down at Cleveland-Hopkins International Airport, where King held an impromptu press conference. Earlier in the day, Mayor Locher had labeled King an "extremist" whom he refused to meet with (lumping him with Alabama governor George Wallace and Floyd McKissick, the head of the Congress of Racial Equality). "I don't intend to have any discussion with these three extremists," Locher explained. King responded that he was "very sad" that Locher took this view. The paper pointed out that King, the winner of the Nobel Peace Prize, could only say, "I have been and will continue to be a peacemaker, not a peace-breaker."

King said that he came to Cleveland to meet with black leaders to learn what could be done to solve the problems of "poverty and degradation." He declared that he would not be a "peace candidate" for president in 1968, and though he spoke briefly about Vietnam and the sustained criticism he was suffering, he noted that his Cleveland appearances would be "strictly on civil rights." King was scheduled to visit three East Side schools the next day, including Glenville High School, which was in the neighborhood where Ahmed Evans's astrology shop was located.[10]

The next day, Dr. King appeared before some eight thousand students at three different schools. In his talk at Glenville, where he knew there was great disaffection and alienation among the students, King was personal and inspirational, but he also had a cautionary tale for the teenagers who might be behind some of the recent waves of violence and firebombing in Hough and Glenville.

He started with a homespun joke that loosened some of the tension in the room. After a flattering introduction by a teacher, King said he didn't deserve all the praise and adulation. "As she was introducing me, I felt something like the old maid who had never been married," he quipped. "And one day she went to work and the lady for whom she worked said, 'Ann, I hear you're getting married.' She said, 'No, I'm not getting married, but thank God for the rumor.'"

King said that "all the wonderful things that were said about me can't be true, but thank God for the rumor."

King then began his remarks in earnest by speaking to the students in a very personal way—they must, he said, develop "a sense of some-bodiness." What he meant was that others should not define what they thought of themselves—"Don't let anybody make you feel that you are nobody," he preached. He recalled growing up in Atlanta where he had to take public transportation to the black school on the other side of town. He rode segregated buses where Negroes were required to sit in the back of the bus, sometimes standing over empty seats because seats up front were reserved for whites only.

But his parents, he maintained, had instilled in him "from the very beginning that I was somebody." Thus, while a young King always rode a segregated bus, he had a desegregated mind. "I started getting on that bus going across town," he recalled, "and every time I got on the bus, even though I found myself having to take my body to the back of the bus, I always left my mind on the front seat." This brought a warm ovation.

Toward the end of his twenty-minute address, Dr. King delivered a "warning signal." He agreed that freedom was never voluntarily given to the oppressed by the oppressor—it had to be demanded. But he counseled that in this passion to obtain first-class citizenship, young activists should never resort to "second-class methods." He talked straight to the kids who were attracted to the black national-ists and those who might have participated in the latest arson and looting.

"Our power does not lie in Molotov cocktails," he said. "Our power does not lie in bricks and stones. Our power does not lie in bottles."

He continued, now making reference to the Hough rebellion, still fresh in his listeners' minds:

> Our power lies in our ability to unite around concrete programs. Our power lies in our ability to say nonviolently that we aren't going to take it any longer. You see the chief problem with a riot is that it can always be halted by a superior force. But I know another weapon that the National Guard can't stop.
>
> They tried to stop it in Mississippi, they tried to stop it in Alabama, but we had a power that Bull Connor's fire hoses couldn't put out. It was a fire within. And I say that we can have that same kind of fire all over the United States of America. And we can transform dark yesterdays into bright tomorrows through this method. And so I come to you today and urge you to work in the civil rights movement, to join the civil rights organizations, to give of your time and your activity, when you have spare time, in community action.

King then got to the underlying reason for his most immediate interest in Cleveland. "One of the things we need in every city is political power," he said with a nod to Stokely Carmichael's black power slogan and a resonance to Malcolm X's speech in Cleveland two years earlier. "Cleveland, Ohio, is a city that can be the first city of major size in the United States to have a black mayor and you should participate in making that a possibility," King said. "This is an opportunity for you." He encouraged each student to create "a committee of one" to work on parents to encourage them to register to vote.

He wrapped up with a poem entitled "Mother to Son," written by Langston Hughes, the celebrated Harlem poet who attended high school in Cleveland, where he first started composing his works. Of Hughes's poem, King said, "with ungrammatical profundity that mother says": "Well, son, I'll tell you / Life for me ain't been no crystal stair."

Dr. King told the Glenville students that "life for none of us has been a crystal stair, but we must keep moving. We must keep going. And so, if you can't fly, run. If you can't run, walk. If you can't walk, crawl. But by all means, keep moving."[11]

In the meantime, a terrified Cleveland business community privately began to back Carl Stokes for mayor. The tide ran so much in Stokes's favor that he started to consider entering the primary as a Democrat to directly challenge Locher and the machine behind him. "Slowly the movement built," Stokes wrote of his courtship with big business, "and when I formally threw my hat into the ring I had two leading business executives playing major roles in the campaign."[12]

A week after Dr. King left town, Sergeant John Ungvary of the Cleveland Subversives Unit was called to Washington to testify before the Senate Subcommittee on Internal Security, a branch of the Judiciary Committee, which had begun public hearings on whether subversives had influenced rioting in the United States and whether federal antiriot-ing legislation might be of assistance to law enforcement in the various states. The grand jury that looked into Hough in Cleveland specifi-cally complained that there was no adequate state law that would have allowed police to go after those who advocated or instigated the rioting. Senator James Eastland of Mississippi and Senator Strom Thurmond of South Carolina led the charge in bringing Ungvary to Washington to act as the subcommittee's first witness.

To law and order advocates, an antiriot law was long overdue; to those concerned about civil rights, the law posed a threat to civil liber-ties as it could be used to punish advocacy or to repress political speech and legitimate dissent.

Ungvary told the Senate subcommittee that the Hough riot was "planned and started by black nationalists whose leaders had Communist connections." As his first order of proof of the Communist connection, he pointed to Don Freeman (who had not even been named by the Hough grand jury). The *Times* reported it this way: "He said a school teacher in Cleveland involved in the black Nationalist Movement there had attended a convention of the Afro-American Student Movement in Nashville, but reported to the school board that he was absent from work because of illness."

That none of this had anything to do with the Hough riots, didn't stop Ungvary from complaining about the inability to prosecute Freeman. "We had nothing to charge him with," Ungvary testified, "so we had to charge him with perjury. The result was the charge was dismissed and he was released."

The subcommittee, uncertain what to do with this non sequitur testimony, led Sergeant Ungvary back to the actual grand jury findings. "Much of Mr. Ungvary's testimony," the *New York Times* reported, "was a repeat of the grand jury report made in Cleveland last summer after the riot. He said black nationalist groups held schools in violence, taught teenagers how to shoot and make Molotov cocktails."

When it came to discussing Lewis Robinson and the Medgar Evers Rifle Club, Ungvary seemed far more interested in providing titillating testimony that Robinson was "married to a white woman" who "had once taught school in Cuba and toured the country as a member of the Fair Play for Cuba Committee, an organization Eastland's committee has investigated over the years."

He summed up this vague mix of assertions: "We have to conclude there is Communist influence there."

But in trying to tie the Hough riots to Communist agitators, Ungvary inadvertently gave more press to Fred Ahmed Evans. He repeated Evans's prediction of the May 9 race riots and a war that would break out between China and the United States. "Mr. Ungvary said Ahmed reasoned that the National Guard would then be drawn into national service [in the war with China], 'leaving them to have a rebellion [in the United States],'" the *Times* wrote.

Ungvary assured the senators that his unit had checked with the science editor of the *Plain Dealer* to confirm that there would be an eclipse on May 9, but found out it would be only a partial eclipse. "Therefore, Mr. Ungvary reasoned, the black nationalists may use the lack of a full eclipse as a 'face saving' device and not stage a riot after all."[13]

Ungvary told what had to be a perplexed subcommittee that he wanted Congress to pass a law that allowed police officers to "take action before an overt act is committed." He also said he hoped for legislation that would "enable him to arrest all black nationalists because they have all pledged to destroy the US government and set up a Negro state." Thinking about the sweep of the statement, he hedged. "But we are not interested in throwing hundreds into jail," he said. "We don't want to throw the kids into jail."[14]

Upon his return to Cleveland, Ungvary had some explaining to do. "As a result of his testimony," the *Plain Dealer* reported, "news stories have spread throughout the country that a police officer had predicted a planned black power rebellion here for May 9." Ungvary said "nothing could be further from the truth," and clarified that he had not had much time to prepare his remarks.[15]

The letters to the editor from more progressive Clevelanders were ugly. A representative of the ACLU wrote that there already were laws on the books that would allow prosecution of riotous activity.[16] Several readers wondered why the police were only interested in arresting adult black nationalists "but not the George Rockwells [of the American Nazi Party]?" Or how about the KKK, "whose members have been carrying out bloody revolution for the past century?" "Could skin color be the qualifying factor?" another rhetorically asked. The First Amendment implications were obvious to some. "Would it mean that a Negro would either give up his rights of freedom to think and speak, or else face the prospect of going to jail?"[17]

The fateful day—May 9—came with its partial eclipse but without any race riots or world conflagration. Police took no chances. Having shut down Evans's astrology shop after he was arrested for disorderly conduct in mid-April, they shut it down again on Friday, May 5. Nonetheless, Evans and about eighteen people were found in the shop on the night of Tuesday, May 9. Those assembled included a New Yorker, Lincoln Lynch, who was the associate director of the Congress of Racial Equality, and Marjorie Hirsh, an NBC researcher, looking for a story on the day of the eclipse. All were charged with intoxication and inhabiting an uninhabitable building. Lynch was aghast at the raw police treatment. "The cops are unenlightened here," he said. "They came in with loaded shotguns. They were harassing us. Not physically but mentally."

Of the nonevent of May 9, Evans simply declared, "I never said that stuff about May 9. I got misquoted."[18]

17

"He Speaks My Views"

THE DAY AFTER MAY 9, Lewis Robinson was in Washington testifying in front of the same Eastland subcommittee on internal security before which Sergeant Ungvary had appeared a week earlier. The committee had paid his expenses to Washington to answer the charges Ungvary made against him and the JFK House.

Robinson was interrogated for three and a half hours. He said that Sergeant Ungvary suffered from a "persecution complex" and that the Cleveland Police Department, the city administration, and the newspapers were in a "conspiracy against militant Negroes." He characterized the JFK House as a place that fostered black pride and freedom and that it was not "a hotbed of insurrection." He said his intent was to build a bridge between whites and blacks. "We took our kids in do-rags to white churches to talk to white kids to show how they live and what hopes they have," he explained. Likewise, "We wanted to show our kids that all white men are not seeking Negro prostitutes; that some whites are interested in our well-being not as Negroes but Americans."

The *Plain Dealer* dismissed his testimony as "rambling."[1]

In the following week, Martin Luther King Jr. returned to Cleveland to announce his intention to begin a Chicago-like "creative nonviolent" campaign to organize the ghettos in Cleveland starting June 1. Though he listed familiar goals of open housing, boycotting businesses that did not hire blacks (known as Operation Breadbasket) and working on establishing respectful relations between blacks and "persons of authority in this community," it was obvious that his concentration in Cleveland was going to be on registering blacks in massive numbers to vote for Carl Stokes for mayor.

King said that he intended to spend at least every other week in Cleveland "to help step up Negro political power, organize buying power, set up collective bargaining units for Negro tenants, press for open housing, and develop a full-service bank for the Negro community."[2]

Sitting next to Dr. King in the press conference at Olivet Institutional Baptist Church were ministers from the United Pastors Association dressed in business suits—and Fred Ahmed Evans, adorned with his traditional African skullcap, dashiki, and sunglasses. "Before the lights and cameras with King sat Ahmed and the pastors [of the United Pastors' Association], which has engaged in continuous dialogue on racial tensions for the past several months," the Call and Post reported. "Now, Cleveland has called

Dr. Martin Luther King Jr. with Rev. Henry Payden, Rev. Jonathan Ealy—United Pastors' Association, and Fred "Ahmed" Evans, May 16, 1967. Cleveland Public Library Collection/Photograph Collection

upon us for assistance in their struggle against the evils of racial injustice and economic exploitation Northern style," King announced.

"Like many of our nation's cities," he continued, "we find Cleveland a teeming cauldron of hostility. The citizens of the Negro community reflect the alienation of the total community, which has constantly ignored the cries for justice and opportunity and responded to their joblessness, poor housing, and economic exploitation with crude methods of police repression rather than compassion and creative programming."[3]

At the conclusion of the press conference, one newspaperman asked Ahmed Evans, arms folded defensively and reclining in his chair, if he supported King's agenda and programming. His reply was terse: "He speaks my views."[4]

The announcement that Dr. King and the SCLC meant to make Cleveland a target city for nonviolent direct action did little to calm the fears of an already skittish Cleveland populace. Blacks and whites alike questioned the wisdom of a potentially aggravating campaign that could stimulate simmering hostilities. "We need no sermons," a middle-aged black woman told a reporter from the *New York Times*. "If Mr. King brings jobs for our men and something to do for our kids—okay. If it's all talk, talk, talk, there'll be trouble again, and we sure don't need more of that, mister."[5]

The reaction from whites, especially on Cleveland's West Side, was predictable and strident. Robert Annable, the head of the North American Alliance of White People, said, "Dr. King is an agitator, a trouble-maker nigger—go ahead and print this," he told the *Times* reporter. "He talks nonviolence but wherever he goes violence follows." Annable, who denied he was a member of the Ku Klux Klan (but "had no quarrel with them"), was busy organizing "anti-Negro" rallies across Cleveland.

Even the mild-mannered Rev. Charles Rawlings said that it remained to be seen whether Dr. King's program held the potential to salve deep racial wounds, "since the Negro people of this city and others like it are in very grave danger, perhaps the greatest danger since Reconstruction."

Lewis Robinson declared that "if the city doesn't do its part, there'll be trouble and unrest. The whole Negro community will unite behind Dr. King, but the question is, what will the white community do?"[6]

The next day, J. Edgar Hoover testified before a House subcommittee on appropriations that Stokely Carmichael, the leading advocate of black power and recently elected chairman of the Student Nonviolent Coordinating Committee, was linked with "leftists seeking the overthrow of the government." He took direct aim at RAM, headed by Max Stanford, who he said was associated with Carmichael.

"In espousing his philosophy of black power," Hoover testified, "Carmichael has been in frequent contact with Max Stanford, field chairman of the Revolutionary Action Movement, a highly secret all-Negro, Marxist-Leninist, Chinese Communist-oriented organization which advocates guerilla warfare to obtain its goals."

Hoover said that RAM was "dedicated to the overthrow of the Capitalist system in the United States," and that it had a "total membership of about 50 and had organized units in several of the larger cities." He further warned that various leaders of RAM "have participated in activities organized by the more militant civil rights leaders in order to expand influence in racially tense areas."[7]

Hoover's spotlight on Max Stanford would soon bear fruit and likely influenced events in Cleveland in the summer of 1967.

Mayor Ralph Locher came under increasing attack in Cleveland because of the racial animus that had built up in the city. "Civic leaders and influential members of the Mayor's own Democratic Party are seeking a change in City Hall to ease racial strains here and improve relations with Washington," the *New York Times* reported on May 24. Locher was not seen as a mean-spirited bigot, a Bull Connor–type character—he was just an incompetent mayor, unable to communicate in any meaningful way with over a third of his citizens.

"Mr. Locher," the *Times* wrote in profile, "a 51-year-old amiable Rumanian-born lawyer, is not a man who evokes violent feelings. Most of his adversaries concede that he is well-meaning and honorable, though they contend he is inept." The *Times* noted that a leading contender for the mayor's job was state representative Carl Stokes, though he had not yet announced his plans. The paper described the

support Stokes had in the Johnson administration—seen as critical in
light of Cleveland's loss of HUD funding. "It is widely believed that
Vice President Humphrey would like to see Mr. Stokes elected," the
Times reported.

On the Republican side the *New York Times* predicted that the likely
candidate for mayor was going to be Seth Taft, "a grandson of President Taft and nephew of the late Senator Robert Taft."[8] If the matchup
between Stokes and Taft came to pass, the great-grandson of a slave and
the grandson of a president would square off for the job.

Probably the cruelest cut from Locher's viewpoint was criticism
from the conservative and powerful Cleveland Bar Association, which
condemned him for not meeting with Dr. Martin Luther King Jr. "I
think the mayor is playing a very dangerous game of brinksmanship,"
the president of the bar said. "In order to represent what he thinks is
the majority view of the white people of Cleveland he is building a stone
wall against the Negro population in Cleveland." Locher considered himself a lawyer's lawyer, having come to the mayor's job from the city law
director position. The loss of faith of his peers had to sting.[9]

As if the racial pot needed any more stirring, Muhammad Ali came
to Cleveland in the first week of June to talk with recognized black
athletes about his recent decision to become a conscientious objector
to the Vietnam War. The whole affair was organized by Jim Brown,
considered perhaps the greatest running back in NFL history, who
invited several prominent black athletes to meet privately with Ali to
determine if they could publicly support Ali's refusal to be inducted
into the US Army.

Brown shocked the football world when he abruptly retired from
football in the summer of 1966 (just four days before the Hough riots
began). When he was pressed by Browns owner Art Modell with an ultimatum to return for the start of training camp in July 1966 from a film
shoot Brown was working on in London (the movie *The Dirty Dozen*),
Brown decided it was time to retire, after only nine years in the NFL.[10]
His friend Walter Beach continued with the Browns in the 1966 season,
but he was at risk with the loss of Brown's protection. Walter Beach also
spoke out after Hough, much to the displeasure of Art Modell.

Beach had begun to work with Carl Stokes in 1967, supporting his candidacy—which probably didn't help when it came time for decisions to be made later that summer in the Browns training camp. Beach in fact would be waived before camp even started.[11] He later sued the NFL and the Browns for racial discrimination in a federal suit over the way he was let go.[12]

Jim Brown had started an organization called the Negro Industrial and Economic Union (NIEU) in 1966 with three Browns players— himself, guard John Wooten, and Walter Beach. Carl Stokes acted as national legal counsel and was on the board of directors. The purpose of the organization was to provide technical skills and business training to African Americans.[13] Ahmed Evans, for one, claimed to have received a loan from NIEU to help fund his astrology shop.

Brown asked John Wooten, who was acting as the executive director of NIEU, to call black athletes who could meet with Ali in Cleveland to talk about his resistance to the draft and the Vietnam War. Wooten said every person he called showed up. No one declined the invitation, though Ali's position was highly controversial. Some within Ali's camp, including Elijah Muhammad's son Herbert Muhammad (who had become Ali's manager), wanted Ali to reconsider and hoped these black athletes might talk him into rethinking his decision.

Jim Brown and Walter Beach had both served in the military (Brown was ROTC at Syracuse), as did others in the group. In addition to Brown, Beach, and Wooten, the stars assembled that day in Cleveland included Bill Russell of the Boston Celtics; Lew Alcindor (later Kareem Abdul-Jabbar), then a sophomore at UCLA; Bobby Mitchell of the Washington Redskins; Sid Williams of the Cleveland Browns; Curtis McClinton of the Kansas City Chiefs; Willie Davis of the Green Bay Packers; and Jim Shorter, a former Brown.[14]

The athletes sequestered themselves with Ali at Brown's NIEU offices on Euclid Avenue near University Circle. They met for several hours in a back room while curious supporters of Ali peered through the glass windows of the converted storefront. The *Plain Dealer* continued to refer to Ali as Cassius Clay two years after he had changed his name ("Cassius Still Won't Go," read its headline). According to reports, the meeting got heated.

Muhammad Ali meets in Cleveland with Jim Brown, Bill Russell, Lew Alcindor, and other black athletes, June 1967. *Western Reserve Historical Society*

"There was a serious debate for over two hours," Walter Beach recalled. "We grilled him and some tried to change his mind. In the end, though, it was clear that his reasoning was based on his religious beliefs and he deserved the same respect that any white man would receive in claiming conscientious objector status."[15] At a press conference after the private meeting, Jim Brown told a gaggle of reporters and cameramen assembled, "After two and a half hours of friendly discussion we decided that he is sincere in his religious beliefs. He convinced us that his stand is based on that."[16]

In what has become an iconic photo of the "Ali Summit," Carl Stokes and Walter Beach stand next to each other in the back row. Stokes was the only one in the photo who was not a professional athlete. He was weeks away from announcing his candidacy for mayor.

On June 16, Stokes, forty years old, finally made it official and joined the race. Stokes made it clear he had one winning theme to play and he would play it hard: he alone could quench the racial fires that were burning in Cleveland. "State Rep. Carl B. Stokes predicted yesterday that his campaign for mayor will help Cleveland avoid racial turmoil this summer," the lead story in the *Plain Dealer* read. "It will be the same as 1965, he said, when 'we had a quiet summer because the people who react to the frustrations and despair of unmet needs became constructively involved in our campaign, an effect that promised them some hope.'"[17]

Though the election would be all about the issue of race, Stokes knew he had to carry some whites, so while he said he was the solution, he softened it by declaring, "I am proud of my Negro heritage, but I am not running as the candidate of the Negro community or any other special group."[18] He also talked tough, saying he would not tolerate violence in the street, "but would work to eliminate the causes."

Locher stubbornly refused to leave the office and three days before Stokes he declared his candidacy for reelection. Locher's statement was, true to his personality, a lackluster and succinct announcement. "My reelection will be based on the record of this administration," he wrote in a prepared statement. "I pride myself on being honest." Unpromisingly for a sitting mayor, the head of the local Democratic Party shrugged, saying, "At this point there is no candidate who has the endorsement of the Democratic Party."[19]

Over that weekend, the FBI and local law enforcement officials in New York City and Philadelphia prepared for what would be a series of dramatic predawn raids the following week. On Tuesday morning, June 21, more than 150 police officers swarmed quiet residential neighborhoods in Queens and Manhattan and arrested fifteen men and women on charges of advocating anarchy. All were tied to the Revolutionary Action Movement. Two of their number, including Herman Ferguson, a popular assistant principal of Public School 40 in the Jamaica neighborhood of Queens, were also charged with plotting to kill moderate black leaders Roy Wilkins of the NAACP and Whitney Young, executive director of the Urban League. (Coincidentally or not, they had recently excoriated Dr. King for his antiwar speech.)

In Philadelphia the police finally nabbed Max Stanford in the lone raid in that town. The *New York Times* wrote that the FBI described Stanford as "the national leader of the revolutionary group."[20]

The police seized ten rifles, a machine gun, a shotgun, three carbines, four knives, three metal arrows, and more than a thousand rounds of ammunition from assistant principal Herman Ferguson's home in Queens. The police and FBI had infiltrated the group and gave affidavits in support of the indictments telling that "all the defendants were members of the Revolutionary Action Movement, also called RAM. The FBI has described the group as pro–Red China and openly committed to the overthrow of governments by violence and assassination."

The *Times* took the opportunity to remind readers that Robert F. Williams, "a Negro now living in Communist China," had been "reported to have been the first leader of RAM." Williams had in fact moved to China in 1966 at the invitation of Mao Tse-tung after a falling out with Fidel Castro, becoming somewhat of a celebrity in China, appearing at Mao's side during several public events at the height of the Cultural Revolution.[21]

When police arrested Max Stanford in Philadelphia they discovered a portrait of Mao on a bedroom wall, a .30-caliber carbine, a .32-caliber revolver, and 150 rounds of ammunition. The *Plain Dealer* seized the moment to congratulate itself for being "one of the first newspapers in the country to reveal the existence of RAM," citing the good work of Doris O'Donnell, and again blasting Don Freeman.[22]

As details emerged, it became clear that all the information in the indictments came from law enforcement plants who first infiltrated the RAM cell beginning in the summer of 1965. The affidavits signed by the undercover law enforcement agents told a frightening saga. Over time, they alleged, RAM agents had taught and practiced urban guerrilla tactics. The newspapers reported that material collected from search warrants "was also said to have included instructions on how to pull down high-tension wires, how to make Molotov cocktails and how to use a hatchet to kill [a] man."[23]

The White House even got involved, asking the FBI for further detail on the assassination plots and who else might have been marked for murder.

Similar to the allegations against Lewis Robinson in Cleveland, the indictments in New York charged that the defendants had formed the Jamaica Rifle and Pistol Club in December 1966, "as a cover and front for legal possession of weapons." Further, it was alleged that two of the members intended to commit arson at gasoline stations, a subway station, and a lumber yard.

The undercover cops in New York provided sworn statements that a "test run" of street violence had been conducted on the night of June 16. Two of the defendants supposedly raced through the Jamaica section of Queens "firing shots from a car into store windows." As the district attorney would later put it, "Their plans were made; their timetable set; weapons had been distributed—they were ready to go."[24]

Aside from the specific charges on the assassinations and the arson, most of the defendants were rounded up under New York's criminal anarchy law, which would prove to be troublesome for prosecutors. The law made it a criminal felony to advocate, advise or teach "the doctrine that organized government should be overthrown by force, violence, or any unlawful means."[25] This placed the law in potential conflict with the right of free speech guaranteed under the First Amendment of the US Constitution. As Justice William O. Douglas wrote about New York's anti-anarchy law, citing Oliver Wendell Homes, "Every idea is an incitement."

Here, it was not clear that the defendants not implicated in the so-called assassination plot or the arson charges did anything beyond possessing guns and possibly advocating revolution. As a consequence, the lawyers representing these defendants, including Max Stanford, would tie up the criminal proceedings for years, at one point filing a separate federal action to challenge the constitutionality of the New York anarchy law.

But thirty-three-year-old Max Stanford, as a result of his arrest in late June 1967, was out of commission, for the short term at least. His bond was set at $100,000, significantly higher than the bail set for the New York defendants, including those arrested on the assassination plot (the New York bails were set between $2,500 and $40,000). Clearly, Stanford was seen as the leader of the movement and law enforcement authorities wanted to sit on him during the dangerous summer of 1967.

The possibility exists that this clampdown on RAM and Max Stanford had implications in Cleveland that summer. It will be recalled that Stanford published a dissertation in 1986 that claimed that Ahmed Evans was a "section leader of RAM" in Cleveland. True or not, Stanford elaborated on what happened in 1966 and 1967 with details that track and tie into Hough and Evans's story. Stanford quoted from a purported interview with "Brother A" from Cleveland, telling of RAM's surreptitious actions in the city:

> During the rebellions in the summer of '66, the Black Nationalist Army went down into action. They fought police sometimes door to door in neighborhoods. Some sections of the inner city rose up in complete support of the nationalists as we battled police. During 1967, units of the army couldn't utilize the situation because a major commander was underground and several key members of the units had been imprisoned as a result of their activity in the 1966 rebellions, and subsequently, there was a division between the sectional commanders. Finally in 1968, the army regrouped. Ahmed was constantly being harassed by the police.[26]

Is the elusive reference to a "major commander" who had gone "underground" an allusion to Max Stanford himself? Or Ahmed Evans? Both men were under indictment in the summer of 1967 and had to maintain low profiles. Or was it possible that RAM leadership was decimated by persons jailed after the Hough riot?[27] Many arrests were made during the Hough uprising and many went to jail or juvenile detention centers for crimes like arson.

Perhaps Carl Stokes's theory was correct. Maybe with Stokes in a winnable race for mayor, tensions did ease with African Americans seeing the real potential for a political solution to Cleveland's racial unrest.

From China, Robert F. Williams reacted to the New York and Philadelphia arrests by writing a stinging article in the July 1967 issue of his newsletter, *The Crusader*. He suggested that indeed there was a retreat of some RAM actors in different cities in the United States during that summer. "This vicious plot against RAM and other black militants was supposed to serve as a brake on America's headlong plunge into the long hot summer," Williams declared. "RAM had been informed months ago by sympathetic police sources that a frame-up was in the making. This is why some brothers moved out of the New York area. This is why they had become deliberately inactive."[28]

Nevertheless, some of the deadliest rioting did break out that summer in Detroit and Newark. The Detroit riot began on July 23, 1967, and lasted five days. Governor Romney called in the National Guard and President Johnson sent US Army troops to stamp out the rebellion. The toll was horrific: 43 dead, 1,189 injured, and 7,200 arrests. More than two thousand buildings were burned and destroyed. It was the worst riot in American history save the 1863 draft riots in New York during the Civil War (and later the LA riots in 1992). There was heavy sniping.

In Newark rioting between July 12 and 17, 1967, left twenty-six dead and hundreds wounded. The inciting incidents for both uprisings were acts of police brutality during arrests. H. Rap Brown, a special director of the Student Nonviolent Coordinating Committee, stood outside a municipal courthouse in Newark where thirteen youths arrested for looting were being arraigned and told a crowd of a hundred blacks that it was time to "wage guerrilla war on the honkie white man."[29] He threatened, "If they don't let them out, we're going to burn this courthouse down."

Despite the relative calm in Cleveland and the rosy outlook for Carl Stokes in the coming election, Stokes found himself in the summer of 1967 suddenly faced with a threat to all his plans from the most unlikely source.

18

"He Desperately Needed a Victory"

THE LAST PERSON CARL STOKES wanted to see in Cleveland in the summer of 1967 was Dr. Martin Luther King Jr.

King had become a lightning rod now for two different reasons: race and patriotism. His stance against the war was wreaking havoc in the civil rights movement and muddying his campaigns in northern cities like Chicago and Cleveland, where there was already a palpable racial hatred at work.

In Chicago, for example, one black pastor asked Dr. King to "get the hell out of town" in late April. Chicago had had its fill of the violence and bitterness created by King's marches. "The marches don't represent the masses of the Negro people," he said, "who prefer to live in their community." King, the clergyman asserted, "created hate" wherever he went.[1]

In Cleveland the *Plain Dealer* criticized him for his position on Vietnam, labeling it "Martin Luther King's Mistake" in a lead editorial. The editors said King dealt a blow to the civil rights movement, which had only recently been "rent asunder by last year's 'black power' issue." They placed the harm King had done by his antiwar announcement as "somewhere between awful and disastrous." The conclusion of these newspapermen was that Dr. King had "abdicated" his responsibility to the civil rights struggle.[2]

Of more immediate concern was the political fallout from war criticism. In late May, Louis Harris reported the polling consequences of Dr. King's call for an immediate peace accord. "Today," Harris wrote in a nationally syndicated column, "73% of the American people disagree with Dr. Martin Luther King Jr. in his denunciation of the war in Vietnam and 60% believe his position will hurt the civil rights movement." Harris wrote that while blacks were somewhat more supportive of King as a group, he would likely only be able to line up a third to half of black voters behind any candidate he endorsed for president. (By contrast, LBJ had taken 95 percent of the black vote in 1964.) At the time, King was telling people he supported Bobby Kennedy or Illinois Republican Charles Percy.[3]

To compound the problem, King seemed to be floundering on almost every front. He couldn't solve Watts or Chicago or Cleveland. He faced stiff internal resistance at the Southern Christian Leadership Conference, which was near bankruptcy. He was at cross swords with Stokely Carmichael, the new head of the Student Nonviolent Coordinating Committee, and black nationalists in general. He was openly feuding with Lyndon Johnson, his former patron, the president of the United States. And on June 12, as if to punctuate his agony, the US Supreme Court upheld King's criminal conviction of violating a state court injunction when he marched in Birmingham, Alabama, in the spring of 1963.

Birmingham had been a crowning achievement—not only leading to the Civil Rights Act of 1964, but also playing a major role in his receiving the Nobel Peace Prize in 1964 (at thirty-five, the youngest recipient ever). King authored his famous "Letter from Birmingham Jail" while imprisoned for eleven days for violating the injunction but was released on bond before serving his entire term.

Now, four years later, King would suffer the ignominy of being sent back to the Birmingham jail to serve an additional five days for criminal contempt. The Supreme Court was sharply divided, 5–4, but the majority found that King was not at liberty to ignore a court injunction, even where the underlying law, the permit, and the injunction may have been found legally and constitutionally defective. According to the court,

Dr. King and his lawyers had to at least seek to dissolve the injunction before engaging in the protest. "No man can be the judge in his own case . . . no matter how righteous his motives," Justice Stewart wrote for the court. The dissenters, including Chief Justice Earl Warren, found the parade ordinance was "patently unconstitutional on its face" and that King and others with him had the right to march despite the injunction.[4]

The *New York Times* agreed with the court's "respect for the law" ruling but admitted that it was "profoundly embarrassing" to have one of the nation's foremost religious leaders and a Nobel Prize laureate thrown in jail.[5]

King continued to fight, asking the court to reconsider, but eventually gave up and served his time in the Birmingham jail in late October, just before election day in Cleveland.[6]

What Dr. King began to envision out of this jumble of gloominess was that it was time for African Americans to concentrate on attaining political power. He wrote a long article in the *New York Times* on June 12, defining "black power" as he saw it. "We must frankly acknowledge that in the past years our creativity and imagination were not employed in learning how to develop power," he wrote. "This is where the civil rights movement stands today. Now we must take the next major step of examining the levers of power which Negroes must grasp to influence the course of events."[7]

What better place than Cleveland, Ohio? King had looked over the horizon and seen the "fast-gathering Negro majorities in the large cities." And the large cities in the North, he reasoned, substantially determined the "political destiny of the state." States in turn helped determine presidents. Cleveland, therefore, seemed the perfect political laboratory to study black political power—and to share in what probably would be its coming glory.

The problem is Carl Stokes was terrified that Martin Luther King Jr. could ruin everything. "How could I have ever dreamed," Stokes wrote in his autobiography, "that suddenly a threat to all my plans, my attempt to put black people in power in the eighth largest city in the country, would appear in the form of Dr. Martin Luther King Jr., the most honored black leader in America?"

Stokes felt his African American base was intact from the 1965 run for mayor. So he carefully calculated how he would fare with white voters. He elaborated on his plan in his autobiography: "The principles were elegantly simple. I had on paper what was out there, where the votes were, both for and against us. And I had in my head the things I knew had to be done to protect the votes for me and neutralize the votes against me. The delicacy of the structure lay in the proportion of my base vote; or, taken the other way, I had to keep the sixty-two percent of the white vote from using its strength against me."

King threatened that delicate balance. He could assist in registering black voters—which he did—but the key was to keep him from alienating or turning off white voters.

Stokes perceived that Dr. King was "at a low point" after his Chicago experience. "He had just come out of Cicero, Illinois, with great disappointment," Stokes wrote, "discovering just how profound are the white man's hatred and prejudice. He desperately needed a victory."[8] Stokes wrote that when it began to look like he was going to win, "Dr. King let us know he wanted to come."

But Stokes didn't need Dr. King. "We already had the black community organized, mobilized, and energized," he wrote. His worry was the counterreaction: black pride could prod white fears.

Stokes turned to his campaign chairman, Dr. Kenneth B. Clement, a clinical practitioner and professor of surgery, to try to talk to some of Dr. King's aides. He told them that "Dr. King's coming would only release the haters and the persons looking for an issue to excite racist reaction to what we were doing." The entreaty did not work.

When King came to town, the publisher of the *Call and Post*, William O. Walker, arranged for a private meeting between Stokes and King. Stokes painstakingly explained his concerns to King, that there was so much at stake, and that he could ill afford to aggravate the white voter. "Martin," Stokes said, "if you come in here with these marches and what not, you can just see what the reaction will be. You saw it in Cicero and other Northern towns. We have got to win a political victory here. This is our chance to take over a power that is just unprecedented among black people. . . . I would rather you not stay."

Dr. King listened but would not relent. He told Stokes he understood his concern, but he had made a pledge to the United Pastors. Stokes found the reason unconvincing. "The United Pastors was a group of about a dozen ministers who were in an internal struggle with other ministers and were bidding to establish their own community leadership," he cynically observed.

Stokes finally recognized his arguments were futile. "He needed to stay on the scene of a victory," he wrote.

Dr. King did agree to tone it down. "I will have to stay," he told Stokes, "but I promise you there will be nothing inflammatory."[9]

King mainly kept his word. On June 6 he came to Cleveland for a three-day retreat to plan his Cleveland campaign with leaders of the United Pastors Association, but the meeting was purposely held at an undisclosed location. "The location is being kept secret so that participants can map strategy for Dr. King's campaign for Cleveland in privacy," the newspaper reported. A week later he returned to meet with over two hundred white and black clergymen of all faiths at St. Timothy Baptist Church just south of the Hough border on Carnegie Avenue. King reported on his plans, but the event was low-key and garnered little public notice.[10] King focused attention on Operation Breadbasket whose aim was to boycott businesses that did not employ sufficient blacks in good positions. The goal was to force changes in how businesses, especially those who sold into black communities, hired and promoted African Americans.

The first targets were bread companies in Cleveland. "We will start negotiations tomorrow with bread companies to get new and better jobs and increase the income and buying power for Negroes," Dr. King said on June 15.[11] While the bread companies were no doubt perturbed, this sort of economic direct action did not evoke the level of emotional response that marching through neighborhoods to promote open housing did—the thing that caused King so much trouble in Chicago. No one paraded through all-white Parma or Little Italy to end housing discrimination.

The bread companies were defensive, to be sure, saying they hadn't hired or promoted African Americans because they could find no "qualified candidates." To prove his goodwill, one executive told an interviewer: "I don't see any problem here. Why, just now a Negro guard walked by and gave me a friendly wave."[12]

Even Mayor Locher yielded and said that he would consider meeting with Dr. King. King responded, "I'm happy he's changed his mind. If we are to solve problems there has to be a dialogue. I am anxious to be at the meeting."[13]

In the following week, another organizing event was scheduled, this one at Emmanuel Baptist Church, a mile south of where the Hough rioting originated. This time a broad audience was invited, not just clergy. The notice went out to "religious, civic, fair housing, political action, anti-poverty, fraternal, and neighborhood groups."[14] The affair was to organize a "general assembly" to help plan Dr. King's and the United Pastors Association's programs for Cleveland.

And this time, the FBI was monitoring the situation and had an informant in attendance. This meeting provided one of the earliest references to the FBI surveillance of Fred Ahmed Evans. His celebrity brought increased, unwanted scrutiny.

An informant, known in FBI memos as simply CV T-3 (CV stands for Cleveland Field Office; T-3 indicates an informant or telephone wiretap), advised that on June 22, 1967, "a meeting was held at Emanuel Baptist Church, East 79th and Quincy Avenue, Cleveland. The featured speaker was Reverend MARTIN LUTHER KING. Approximately 350 people were in attendance, including FRED EVANS and approximately 15 of his followers, who wore Afro-robes."[15]

Dr. King gave a fiery oration on what he called the "invisible wall" behind which blacks lived "in a triple ghetto of race, poverty, and human misery." The *Plain Dealer*, counting over five hundred people in attendance, wrote that King charged that the wall is kept standing by "white moderates who believe in order and not justice, and say 'wait'; white politicians more concerned with political power than with people they represent; white ministers of the gospel who remain behind the security of their stained glass windows."

King received his greatest sustained applause when he attacked "an administration more concerned with winning an ill-considered and unjust war than winning a war on poverty."

But consistent with his pledge to Carl Stokes to stay away from
more inflammatory acts or rhetoric, Dr. King's agenda for the programs in Cleveland was announced as limited to four areas: "tenant
unions, voter registration, formation of an African American bank,
and Operation Breadbasket." Open housing was conspicuous in its
absence.[16]

A different sort of event was scheduled for the following week to
highlight landlord predation. "A SCLC worker announced that next week
there will be a 'mock trial' of a ghetto landlord. The landlord, and perhaps
the city, will be tried for criminal neglect which allows children to be bit-
ten by rats and to be lead poisoned from eating the paint that peels from
apartment walls," Robert McGruder of the *Plain Dealer* wrote.

Ahmed Evans was asked to participate as a mock juror panel-
ist alongside Dr. King. King would come to Cleveland for the fourth
straight week.

The mock jury was held on Wednesday evening, June 28, at the
Greater Avery African Methodist Episcopal Church on Wade Park, seven

Dr. Martin Luther King Jr., Fred Ahmed Evans, and Lewis
Robinson at the Ghetto Grand Jury, Greater Avery A.M.E.
Church, July 28, 1967. *Cleveland Public Library Collection/Photograph
Collection*

blocks north from the heart of where the Hough rebellion started.[17] The church, established in 1918, was of moderate size and was filled to capacity on the night of the mock trial, with 350 sitting and 150 standing in every corner.

Dr. King, guarded by two county deputy sheriffs, was an hour late, flying in from Chicago. "The city of Cleveland and many landlords in the city are guilty of trampling over the dignity and worth of human personality," King said. "While in Mississippi, Negroes are being physically murdered, the Northern cities are murdering the Negro spiritually and psychologically. The Negro is robbed of education, adequate housing, adequate health facilities, and job opportunities."

Lewis Robinson, having served as a former Cleveland housing inspector, came to discuss lead poisoning. A woman whose two-year-old was hospitalized after ingesting paint chips testified that her landlord steadfastly refused to correct the problem. Dr. King offered to personally pay for the woman's expenses and the repainting of her apartment.

Police brutality was underscored by testimony from the friend of a man who alleged he was beaten by police in custody. "The man appeared, unable to talk, with a swollen jaw," the *Call and Post* reported. The black newspaper had only recently carried a lengthy story of an African American man who was beaten while in handcuffs following a traffic stop witnessed by several people. Concerned onlookers tried to intervene and when it didn't stop, called the police, saying, "These two policemen out here seem to be going crazy," as they battered the defenseless man.[18] "The cop is sick," a witness said of the policeman who was most aggressive.

Ahmed Evans spoke. "Although King drew a standing ovation when he arrived," the paper noted, "the biggest applause went to Fred (Ahmed) Evans, one of the jurists, when he said, 'The beast (the white man) is spending trillions of bucks trying to get to the moon and he can't even see Hough.'"[19] Evans continued to demand a full separation of the races and economic self-sufficiency for African Americans. An informant for the FBI noted that Evans was a "leading participant" in the proceedings.[20]

A follower of Ahmed Evans named Amir Rashidd (formerly James Taylor) read a poem he entitled "The Beast." Rashidd was part of an avant-garde group calling itself the Muntu Poets, young nationalists who created a poetry workshop at the urging of Russell Atkins, a rising poet and editor of the literary magazine *Free Lance*. Atkins had been a protégé of Langston Hughes. The Muntu Poets played jazz, listened to John Coltrane, and wrote raw, stinging poetry as voices of black awakening and dissent on Cleveland's East Side. "They felt that everyone else was putting honey and perfume on shit," Mutawaf Shaheed (born Clyde Shy), a Muntu founder and musician, said of their work.

Rashidd's militant poem "The Beast" became an anthem of sorts for black nationalists in Hough and Glenville, often recited at dialogues-in-black (rap sessions held in all-black areas) and gatherings like the mock jury proceeding with Dr. King. Rashidd delivered it on this night:

> Beneath the tall and shadowy trees
> My brother black danced with ease
> And yet the morning brought disaster
> The beast is coming faster, faster.
> . . .
> War with the beast, it must be won
> The task of fate has now begun
> We must strike with such great pain
> So that the beast will never rise again.
> Brothers black all free men cry
> We've won our life through endless plights
> Brothers black walk without sigh
> The beast is dead, hear freedom cry.[21]

After three hours of testimony, the eight-member mock grand jury, including King and Evans, retired to deliberate for five minutes before returning with a verdict of guilty against the city of Cleveland for criminal neglect of its black citizens.

In July after a long public argument, Mayor Locher agreed to approve a parade permit for the Hough Memorial Parade to honor the "innocent victims" of the Hough riot on the first anniversary of the uprising. The original permit had been turned down because police were afraid the march itself would provoke renewed rioting. The parade permit finally was issued by the city to (of all people) Lewis Robinson, the march coordinator. The paper noted that "Fred (Ahmed) Evans will be in charge of a 'peace patrol' to accompany the marchers."[22]

The parade down Hough Avenue took place on the night of July 20. (The original march date was set for July 18—the anniversary of the start of the conflict—but it was postponed due to rain.) A thousand people, many children, peacefully marched. They were met by another four thousand awaiting them in a playfield provisionally named after Joyce Arnett, the woman killed in the first day of the rioting.[23] Speakers included Lewis Robinson, Ahmed Evans, and Harllel Jones. Planners of the event said they intended to make the parade an annual event. Robinson said as the line of procession passed 79th and Hough, "This is as great as a Selma march."[24]

There is no record that Carl Stokes joined in the memorial.

Three days later, the Detroit riot started. President Johnson appointed a national commission to study the causes of the urban riots racking the nation, asking Democratic Illinois governor Otto Kerner to act as the chair.[25] Johnson was now in free fall. In a little over a month, his ratings dropped nineteen points to an all-time low of 39 percent, attributable, Louis Harris found, to the twin scourges of rioting in the major cities and the country's feeling that the war in Vietnam was "not going well."[26]

Dr. King visited Cleveland at the end of July to speak at the annual progress banquet of the Olivet Baptist Church. He said that at the rate the United States was going, "it will not achieve the Kingdom of Heaven."[27] Dr. King told his audience, "I have preached it, and even when I was a child I read that if you are not concerned with the least of these, you will not enter the Kingdom of Heaven." He pointed to the fact that the United States with all its wealth spent little on the eradication of poverty. He said that "the people who have no stake in society—these are the people who will riot, these are the people who will throw Molotov cocktails."

Nationally, commentators noticed Dr. King's decided shift in emphasis. Jack Nelson of the *Los Angeles Times* wrote that "to win the allegiance of Negroes being wooed by the growing black power movement, Dr. Martin Luther King has adopted a more militant stance and embraced some precepts of the movement."[28]

And indeed, the black power leaders were leaning into extremism in their frustration over the lack of meaningful social and economic progress achieved by the civil rights movement. Stokely Carmichael traveled to Cuba to address the Organization of Latin American Solidarity, attacking the United States and pledging support for "Latin Red revolution." He told a Cuban news agency that "American Negroes were organizing urban guerrillas for 'a fight to the death.'"[29] He added that "it is the young blood that contains the hatred mentioned by Che."[30]

Carmichael's replacement as chairman of the SNCC, H. Rap Brown, was jailed in New York on charges of carrying a gun across state lines while under indictment.[31] Meanwhile, observers noticed that the SNCC was "growing smaller and financially weaker as its leaders talk of burning down towns and taking up arms against white society."[32]

King, while not defending them, said in Cleveland that the media and the public were missing the message from Carmichael and Brown. "Mr. Carmichael and Rap Brown are products of the problems," he said. "If we get rid of slums, poverty, and inadequate education, those who preach violence won't even get a hearing."[33]

In the first weeks of August, Sergeant John Ungvary was back in Washington urging Congress to pass legislation for federal aid to help fund new riot control equipment. "In urging broadening of the proposed antiriot law, Ungvary proposed the federal government subsidize the purchase of exotic weapons to fight riots, including nerve gas and laser beams," the *Plain Dealer* reported.[34]

King's one victory that summer in Cleveland arose out of his Operation Breadbasket, which sponsored a boycott of Sealtest Dairy. Sealtest eventually caved in early August, agreeing "to give 50 new and upgraded jobs to Negroes and other nonwhites."[35] Dr. King came to Cleveland to sign the agreement at Fellowship Baptist Church of Christ on the eastern border of Hough. No timetable for action was set.

Dr. King then turned his attention to voter registration drives as Carl Stokes and Ralph Locher hurtled toward a showdown in the Democratic primary on October 3.

King arranged a visit to Cleveland on August 23 to coincide with the close of voter registration for the mayor's race. He visited registration stations, telling black voters: "Today is just the beginning. Now you've got to get out and vote . . . for a better Cleveland." He found time to throw a football in the yard of a home in Shaker Heights with his two sons, Martin Luther III and Dexter Scott, whom he had brought with him.[36] Registration stations were swamped with record turnout. But the Locher forces showed strength as white ethnic voters edgy over the prospect of an African American mayor counterorganized. The *Plain Dealer* called it a wash. "The early guess: An even break for Stokes and Locher."[37]

Mayor Locher complained that "Negro voter registration drives" were unfair because they were underwritten by grants of money from national foundations. "Although not referencing them by name," the *Plain Dealer* observed, "the mayor obviously meant the voter registration drives by the Congress of Racial Equality, which got a $175,000 Ford Foundation grant, and the United Pastors Association and the Southern [Christian] Leadership Conference."[38]

In the end, it was no contest. Locher lugged around too much baggage; the aspiration for change was too great. Stokes more than carried the day on October 3. He won the Democratic primary by more than 18,000 votes—a stunning turnaround considering his close loss to Locher just two years earlier by 2,100 votes.[39]

Almost hidden away in the back pages of the *Call and Post*, columnist Bob Williams wrote of a hopeful sign for those in the black community concerned over black nationalism. Referring to Malcolm X's speech in 1964, he wrote, "Ballots, not bullets. If Cleveland has avoided a riot as you read this, written last Friday, it is because the inner-city campaign to use ballots—not bullets—for progress, has been successful in a city where the total uselessness and futility of rioting is already well known."

And then he wrote this:

Defeated Mayor Ralph Locher and his spouse, pledging support for Carl Stokes against Seth Taft, October 23, 1967. *Cleveland Public Library Collection/Photograph Collection*

> Fred (Ahmed) Evans, militant Black Nationalist and astrologer who has long and bitterly expressed his impatience with the plight of the Black Man has registered to vote!
>
> Ahmed's choice was personal, private; yet, it portrayed his wisdom in refusing to ignore this great tool of self-expression, the vote, which contains more hope than all the rioting of the past.[40]

Carl Stokes took credit for convincing Evans to register to vote.[41] With that, it was now up to Stokes to win in the general election. But he would face not a damaged and feckless mayor but the scion of a hugely popular political family in the person of Seth Taft. A closer contest was guaranteed.

19

"As Lambs
for the Slaughter"

Two days after Martin Luther King Jr. came to Cleveland to register voters, the FBI formalized its counterintelligence program against black nationalists. In a memo dated August 25, 1967, the director of the FBI issued a letter to twenty-three select field offices (including Cleveland) with instructions to establish a control file and assign responsibility for counter-intelligence to "an experienced and imaginative Special Agent well versed in investigations relating to black nationalists, hate-type organizations."

In Cleveland that man would be Special Agent John J. Sullivan, a longtime agent who was originally from New York. In FBI parlance, he "pulled the ticket."[1]

The COINTELPRO letter made the purpose of the endeavor entirely clear: it was to "expose, disrupt, misdirect, discredit, or otherwise neu-tralize the activities of black nationalists, hate-type organizations and groupings, their leadership, spokesmen, membership, and supporters, and to counter their propensity for violence and civil disorder." The dictate was to "follow on a continuous basis" black nationalist groups "so we will be in a position to promptly take advantage of all opportunities for counterintelligence and to inspire action in instances that warrant."

Special attention was to be paid to SNCC, SCLC, and RAM. By name, agents were directed to place emphasis on "extremists who direct the activities and policies of revolutionary or militant groups such as Stokely Carmichael, H. 'Rap' Brown, Elijah Muhammad, and Maxwell Stanford." Because of the nature of the program, agents were cautioned that "under no circumstances should the existence of the program be made known outside the Bureau."[2]

Part of this counterintelligence program was to locate and pay confidential informants. Within the FBI, the effort to identify sources to infiltrate black nationalist groups became known as the "Ghetto Informant Program," or the "Ghetto Listening Post." Thousands of sources or "assets" were employed over the next year across the United States.[3] In Cleveland at least five informants provided information on Fred Ahmed Evans and his group.

One informant, identified as T-5, gave a detailed report of a workshop that took place at the Karamu House in Cleveland (a multicultural theater and settlement house established in 1915) the weekend after Carl Stokes won his primary race against Ralph Locher. "CV T-5 advised on October 11, 1967, that over 200 people registered for the Black Unity Conference held at Karamu House, East 89th Street and Quincy Avenue, Cleveland Ohio, on October 6–8, 1967," the report read. "Source identified FRED EVANS as one of those in attendance."

The unity conference, calling on blacks from across Ohio, was chaired by Walter Beach, now out of football and working as an investigator for the Legal Aid Society of Cleveland, an organization to provide legal services to those unable to afford a lawyer. "I canvassed the neighborhoods, including the pool halls, to identify people who might be in trouble and in need of the assistance of Legal Aid," Beach recalled.

Beach was asked by Ahmed Evans, Harllel Jones, and other nationalists (Baxter Hill and DeForest Brown) to chair the unity event because of his celebrity as a former Browns player. The event was originally planned for a church in Hough in September, but when Carl Stokes found out about it, he called Beach and insisted that it be moved, at least until after the primary with Locher. When Beach initially resisted, Stokes threatened, "I'll have your fucking job." Matters were smoothed over and the event was moved to the weekend after the primary.[4]

The *Plain Dealer* noted that the conference was "closed to news media and to white participants." Beach told the *Plain Dealer* that the purpose of the confab was to "narrow the communications gap between the moderate and militant views in the Negro community."[5] The *Call and Post* reported that "234 delegates paid $2.50 per head to attend the orientation and work-shop sessions." Several observers came from Detroit and some from as far away as Ethiopia. The three-day affair ended with resolutions and action items, none of which were particularly controversial except perhaps reference to black youths being "sucked into the military machinery of 'Chuck' (slang for the US government)."[6]

An FBI report by T-5 provided summaries of the speeches of some of the participants, which oddly included Bertram Gardner, who was Ralph Locher's black director of community relations. The informant relayed that Don Freeman "spoke of the present Armageddon and the fact this group was the vanguard of the revolution and that plans must be made on the 'scientific division of labor.' Freeman stated that each man must be prepared to subvert his own ego to the needs of the revolution."

Martin Luther King Jr.'s local representative, Rev. Al Sampson, recommended that the group spend money on ads in the *Call and Post* so that they would be able to better control the content, which was considered Uncle Tom-ish.[7]

Carl Stokes had good reason to avoid public support for a black unity conference. The newspaper calculated that Stokes took only 14 percent of the white Democratic vote in the city in the primary, so now in the general campaign against Seth Taft, Stokes would have to meticulously guard those white votes and hopefully add some.

Stokes understood that his race would be the subject of vicious attacks. In the primary, the county Democratic Party chairman, Albert Porter, had circulated a flyer that warned that Dr. Martin Luther King Jr. would become "dictator" of Cleveland should Stokes become mayor. "Do you want Dr. Martin Luther King and his disciples running your lives?" the broadside asked.[8] The day after Stokes won the primary, he demanded that Porter step down as party chair, writing "it is crystal clear that you do not represent either basic decency or the great moderate majority of the Democratic Party."[9]

Doris O'Donnell warned white voters that there would be a shakeup in the police department should Stokes win. "Persons close to [Police Chief] Wagner believe the political nominee [Stokes] and the chief's views on police work are totally incompatible," O'Donnell wrote the day after Stokes won the primary. Stokes's likely replacement for chief, Inspector Michael J. Blackwell, she pointed out, was already sixty-seven and "has been eligible for retirement since 1952." She reported that "rank-and-file police personnel protected from dismissal by civil service status are apprehensive about transfers when a new mayor takes over."[10]

One political wag suggested that the most effective campaign strategy against Stokes would be to get "teams of Negro couples wearing Stokes buttons and send them through white neighborhoods, ringing doorbells and asking, 'Pardon me, is your house for sale?'" The operative dubbed the tactic "Operation Doorbell."[11]

But the Republican candidate Stokes faced was no racist. Seth Taft, forty-four, was the grandson of William Howard Taft, the only person ever to serve as both president and chief justice of the United States. His uncle, Robert Taft, had been a lion of the US Senate, known as "Mr. Republican." President Taft was a progressive Republican, all but hand-picked by Theodore Roosevelt as his successor. Seth Taft moved to Cleveland after graduating from Yale Law School (a family tradition) and left his home base of Cincinnati, a city where his father had been mayor. He joined the most prestigious law firm in Cleveland, Jones, Day, Coakley & Reavis, and was active in community and charitable affairs.

Taft was not from the ethnic neighborhoods as Locher had been. He lived in the tony suburb of Pepper Pike, a prickly problem that brought with it the dual charge that he was a "carpetbagger" and an aristocrat. He bought a second home in the city to meet the residency requirements.

The warmth of his personality did not come off at first. "He has a seemingly inflexible face that rarely breaks with humor ('there is no time for jokes in a political campaign')," the *Plain Dealer* wrote in profile.

"There is a certain gauntness to his face that projects him as being grim when it was not necessarily so and compared to the debonair Carl Stokes his clothes seemed to have a drip-dry hang on his slim frame."[12]

But Taft was smart, savvy, and a fighter. He campaigned resolutely, taking a small elephant imported from Wisconsin with him through neighborhoods as a stunt to bring out voters with whom he could shake hands. "Remember Taft in November," read a banner on the side of the elephant. In the short window from October 3 to November 7, he proved to be a surprisingly strong candidate.

Taft steadfastly refused to allow his campaign to make race the issue. He released a message to his backers early in October saying that he would not tolerate anyone working for him making race a topic in the election. "Every individual is entitled to his own beliefs," he wrote. "However, when working on behalf of a candidate for public office, individuals must present only the beliefs of the candidate. . . . I must rely on you to tell my story. It must be the real story and the SAME story all over the city." He was not unaware of the reality of the situation, but he deplored it. "Many people will vote for Carl Stokes because he is a Negro," he wrote. "Many people will vote for me because I am white. I regret this fact. I will personally work hard to convince people they should not vote on a racial basis."[13]

He courageously met with CORE and asked for black votes. When one man heckled him as he left, Taft stopped and walked over to the man, shook his hand, and said, "I know you're going to vote for Carl, but I hope you'll at least listen to me."[14]

While Stokes was in Washington attending a dinner at the White House—to emphasize his ability to bring HUD funding back to Cleveland—Taft made a speech before the Cleveland Real Estate Board calling for a fair housing law in Ohio. The group had vehemently opposed such legislation and sat in stone silence as Taft made his appeal.[15]

It was Stokes who got into trouble when he went after Taft over the race issue. In the second of four debates, Stokes complained that Taft and newspaper analysts projected Taft to win for one reason: "That reason is that he is white." Stokes made reference to a line written by James Naughton of the *Plain Dealer* to the effect that "a white Mickey Mouse could beat a black Carl Stokes" in Cleveland.[16] The crowd in a Stokes-friendly East Side high school booed as he went on. Taft rejoined, "Now it appears that if I say something on this subject, it's racism, and if Carl Stokes says something it's fair play." The crowd roared its approval. Stokes knew he made a grave, perhaps even fatal mistake.[17]

He finished strong, however. In the final debate at the Cleveland City Club, Stokes pulled off a masterstroke on the very last question, one about his poor attendance record in the state legislature. Taft had repeatedly jabbed Stokes during the campaign about his frequent absences. Stokes produced a letter from his coat pocket and began to read. "Dear Carl," Stokes started, "The reports I hear of your performance in Columbus are excellent and I congratulate you on the job." The letter was signed by Seth Taft.

The *Plain Dealer* editors observed, "And, as people partial to both candidates filed out of the Sheraton's Gold Room, they all knew one thing: Taft's chances to be mayor plummeted with one sentence, one letter he would wish he never had written. And it happened as the campaign ended."[18]

Martin Luther King Jr. continued to grope to find his approach to the multifaceted problems he confronted in the North, all as he waited anxiously to see if Stokes would be elected. He wanted to set a new course for himself and the SCLC. Out of debates with his inside circle in September and October, King began to see not the war or civil rights as the next-gen strategy. Convinced by the arguments of a young lawyer named Marian Wright, he decided that he would turn his full attention to "uplift the invisible poor."[19]

He would take as his model the actions of the Bonus Army from World War I—veterans who demanded cash-payment redemption of their service certificates and camped in large numbers in Washington, DC, over the summer of 1932. King conceived of the idea of leading "waves of the nation's poor and disinherited to Washington, DC, in the spring of 1968 to demand redress of their grievances and to secure at least jobs or income for all."[20]

Once the US Supreme Court announced in early October that it would not reconsider its decision in June to affirm King's criminal contempt conviction, King told everyone he was "willingly and in clear conscience" going back to jail in Birmingham to serve out the remainder of his five-day sentence.[21] Before doing so, King came to Cleveland for a concert to raise money for the SCLC. The headliners were supposed to be Aretha Franklin (whose father was a leading civil rights pastor in Detroit) and Harry Belafonte, but Franklin was a no-show, allegedly on doctor's orders. An angry crowd of four thousand gathered in Public Auditorium, many demanding their money back. Belafonte performed and King spoke and Peter, Paul and Mary, who happened to be in concert in the other half of the hall that night, came over to help out.[22]

The following Monday, Dr. King appeared in Washington on October 23 before the Kerner Commission on Civil Disorders. Afterward he told reporters of his idea for a poor people's "camp-in" in Washington for an indefinite period to pry action from the government. "We have to find a middle road between riots and timid supplication of justice, a program of escalating nonviolence to the dimensions of civil disobedience," he said. The time had come, he contended, and he vowed that if nothing was done about poverty in Washington, he would camp and "stay and stay till the Federal Government and Congress does something."[23]

On October 30 Martin Luther King Jr. surrendered to sheriffs in Birmingham to begin serving his sentence. King brought with him three books to read: the Bible, an economics text, and the *Confessions of Nat Turner*.[24]

He had the flu and was released one day early, on November 3.[25] He returned to Atlanta and delivered a sermon at Ebenezer Baptist Church on Sunday, November 5. "I say to you this morning, that if you have never found something so dear and so precious to you that you will die for it, then you aren't fit to live," he told his congregation.

The next day, Monday, King flew to Cleveland to assist in a last-minute get-out-the-vote effort, but Stokes again was unhappy with his presence and the potential negative publicity.[26] Dr. King and his associate Rev. Ralph Abernathy made the rounds on Cleveland's East Side and only narrowly escaped injury when their rented car was hit by a woman backing out of a driveway on Wade Park.[27] King spoke over the radio and appeared on television.

Martin Luther King Jr. shaking hands with Fred Ahmed Evans on November 6, 1967, the day before Stokes is elected. Likely FBI informant standing in between. *Western Reserve Historical Society*

One Democratic Party worker moaned, "If Stokes loses it will be because of Martin Luther King on television last night. Why did he have to come in here?"[28]

That day, Dr. King was photographed giving Fred Ahmed Evans a soul handshake in Glenville. A man standing in between them was later identified as an FBI informant.[29]

Carl Stokes and his brother Louis waited at campaign headquarters at the Rockefeller Building in downtown Cleveland for the election results on November 7. It would not be until the middle of the night, in the wee hours of November 8, that the result became clear. Dr. King and Ralph Abernathy joined Stokes sometime around two in the morning.[30]

When it was finally established that Stokes had won, he moved over to the Sheraton-Cleveland hotel to make a victory speech. Stokes had won a "wafer-thin" victory over Seth Taft—fewer than 2,500 votes, almost the same number by which Ralph Locher had defeated him in 1965.[31] King did not appear with Stokes at the victory party to share in the moment. He stayed at the Rockefeller with Louis Stokes. There was concern that King might hold a press conference to steal some of the thunder or take the credit.[32] Coretta Scott King would later say that her husband felt this was "one of the biggest snubs of his career."[33]

Stokes's first moves were to replace Police Chief Michael Wagner with the aging Michael Blackwell, and Safety Director John McCormick with a West Side Irishman who supported his candidacy, Joseph F. McManamon.[34]

As Carl Stokes was moving to take the reins of power, Martin Luther King Jr. turned incendiary, even apocalyptic. At the Fellowship Baptist Church in Hough on the day after the election, King spoke to newsmen and warned of winter riots in Cleveland unless the federal government and the business community came to the immediate aid of the poor. "I want you to understand," he said in a grim press conference, "I am not in favor of these riots. I will do everything in my power to help avert them. But, as a social analyst, I must speak honestly."

He said Cleveland needed federal aid against poverty. "To cut the poverty program would border on criminal responsibility," he declared, "and would be an open invitation to violence and social disorder in the streets of our ghettos." He seemed to take a jab at Stokes, perhaps a sign of pent-up resentment at being deliberately sidelined and ignored by Stokes during the campaign and then denied a chance to share publicly in the victory. "Carl Stokes may have friends in Washington," he growled, "but friends alone are not enough. He needs a strong poverty program and the support of Congress."

King threatened to cause massive disturbances in cities across America with crippling nonviolent civil disobedience demonstrations using a cadre of trained "disrupters." He said he would "not rule out Cleveland" as a target city. This is not what Carl Stokes wanted to hear at the moment of his triumph.

But King further forewarned that if assistance to the poor in the nation's ghettos was not immediately forthcoming, mayors like Carl Stokes would be set up "as lambs for the slaughter."[35]

His prophecy would come to pass.

20

"You Should Establish Their Unsavory Backgrounds"

CARL STOKES FLATLY ADMITTED THAT he was not prepared to govern. In Cleveland, the city charter called for the mayor-elect to be inaugurated on the Monday after the election, leaving almost no time to prepare a cabinet, let alone a working administration. Stokes, already exhausted by the intense campaigning, holed up with his advisers but discovered he had no clue about how the city actually worked.

"We went into those sessions with wild-eyed dreams of the reforms we would wreak on this corrupt machine, only to discover we didn't even know where the buttons were," he wrote in his autobiography. Stokes had never employed more than three people before in his life yet now "I found myself in charge of ten thousand."[1]

He needed support, and he needed it fast. One of his promising hires was a young white lawyer named John Little as his executive secretary. Little's father was one of the senior partners at Jones Day, Seth Taft's firm, and Little had taken a job with another prominent law firm after graduating from Yale and then Michigan Law School. He was, Stokes wrote, from an "old, established, Anglo-Saxon Protestant family." Little became in effect Stokes's chief of staff, tending to the administrative issues, leaving Stokes free to concentrate on political and ceremonial duties. "It took me some time to recognize how good he was because he was not flashy and aggressive," Stokes wrote. "John Little's loyalty was simply a gift."[2]

Stokes also hired Taft's wizardly public relations consultant, William Silverman, to help him with the white press. "It may seem at first glance curious that several of my most trusted advisers turned out to be white and engaged in either public relations or advertising," Stokes acknowledged. "But the fact was simply that my greatest need for advice was dealing with how public reactions to my conduct would be formed, since all my actions would reach the public through the interpretive structure of the white media."[3]

The stress proved too much. In January, Stokes said his health "broke down" for the first time in his adult life and he was forced to retreat to a two-week vacation in the Virgin Islands. He suffered a minor public relations setback when he fired a close aide over the phone after it was discovered she was tied to a "club that served as a cheat spot" in Hough. Stokes later called the move a "terrible blunder," but it was symptomatic of the initial chaos of his administration.

The black nationalists in town were unsure what to think of Stokes— was he a brother or a Tom? Right after the election, at a public meeting held on November 30 at the Hough Opportunity Center, black nationalists, led by Fred Ahmed Evans, spoke to an audience of 150 about their ambitions and goals, hoping in part to address division and mounting fears in the black community. "There is more concern for animals in the zoo than there is for little kids receiving $5 allotment for clothes in the ghetto," Evans said at the start of the meeting. "We have no desire to alienate our black brother against us. We are called all kinds of names for taking our stand. The reason for this is that we are not conformists."[4]

Columnist Bob Williams of the *Call and Post* was there and cynically described the meeting as a time for black nationalists to "redefine their beliefs and issue new tirades against 'the beast and his police force,' which, as they see it, is meant only to enforce 'oppressive' laws aimed at repressing individual expression of those who rebel against the 'rats and roaches and poverty of the ghetto.'"[5]

An FBI informant, T-1, also prepared a report of the meeting. "There were approximately 100 people present, including 30–35 Negro males wearing Afro-robes," a summary FBI memo recorded. "Sources stated FRED EVANS spoke on astrology. He declared that the stars and the heavens are foretelling the doom of the white man and the victory of the black man."[6]

This account corresponds with Bob Williams's report that one of the nationalists "avowed extreme personal reaction to the 'unlawful' police approach to him, personally, but charged the 'moment of truth' would come, not in local riots, but as a worldwide revolt against the 'beast of oppression.'"

A nationalist named Jay Arki commented on Stokes's election, calling it "a piece of bread thrown to the black people of Cleveland just to keep them in their place." He advised Stokes to avoid becoming an instrument of the establishment. "We say to Mayor Stokes," Arki declared, "if you choose to close your eyes to the oppression against black people in this city you then have the honor of being a good boy for the beast."

Twelve days later, one of the FBI informants, T-1, dropped by Ahmed Evans's astrology shop at East 111th Street and Superior Avenue in Glenville. "He advised that EVANS and approximately 10 other individuals were present," the FBI report noted. "He stated that a discussion took place involving the purchase of guns. Source stated he determined that some of the individuals present at this discussion did obtain weapons."[7]

The FBI stepped up its surveillance. On December 29, 1967, T-1 attended a meeting at a different storefront on Superior Avenue. "He stated that approximately 30 people were present, including the subject (Ahmed Evans)," the report stated. "There were instructions given on how to make Afro-art objects. The principal discussion concerned how to continue protests concerning the death sentence given Raymond Watson, a young Negro convicted of killing a Cleveland policeman." According to the informant, Ahmed Evans delivered "an unintelligible lecture on astrology."[8]

Raymond Watson had been sentenced to the electric chair on December 1, 1967, after being found guilty of shooting a policeman in the head following a late-night robbery. Watson, then eighteen, testified in his own defense that he had no intent to kill—that the incident took place after ten hours of partying with wine and marijuana.[9] The gun, he claimed, accidentally discharged. Lewis Robinson confirmed Watson had been a member of the JFK House.[10]

The Hoover COINTELPRO letter in August 1967 directed agents to uncover evidence of what he thought would be the seedy lifestyles of the black nationalists. "Many individuals currently active in black nationalist organizations have backgrounds of immorality, subversive activity, and criminal records," Hoover wrote. "Through your investigation of key agitators, you should endeavor to establish their unsavory backgrounds."

The informants in Cleveland followed the instructions to a tee. On New Year's Eve, T-1 attended a party at the storefront at 81st and Superior. "He estimated there were approximately 20 Negro males and nine or ten Negro females in attendance," the special agent wrote. "Source stated it was strictly a 'wild' party and no discussions of a serious nature were held. He stated that there was much beer and wine consumed and most of the individuals present smoked reefers. He stated that many of the individuals present engaged in sexual promiscuity during the course of the evening. Source advised that FRED EVANS was one of those in attendance."[11]

A summary report from Special Agent Sullivan repeats these themes—the locations where the black nationalists met were "indescribably filthy"; the members drank "wine and liquor to excess," "smoked pot," and engaged in "sexual promiscuity, frequently with girls 13–15 years of age." Sullivan was told that Evans preached total separation of the races and that "the white race must be destroyed and the black man must take over the United States." Evans, according to informants, maintained that "the stars and the heavens are foretelling the doom of the 'Beast' (white man) and the victory of the Black man." He told teenagers they did not need to attend public school and that black people did not have to obey "the white man's laws."

At some point—it is not entirely clear when—Evans began to call his group the Black Nationalists of New Libya, or the Republic of New Libya. By February 1968, informants reported that Evans and his New Libyans had taken over the Black Unity Conference started with Walter Beach's help in October 1967. None of the "liberation" or "freedom" schools recommended by the conference were ever established, nor were any of the other constructive proposals enacted.

Beach, while not losing touch with the nationalists, became more involved in mainstream politics. As chairman of the Negro Citizens' League scanning committee, he oversaw the endorsement of Louis Stokes as the candidate to run for the Twenty-First Congressional District.[12]

The other prominent black nationalist organization on the East Side was Harllel Jones's Afro Set, a "curio shop" organized after the JFK House had been permanently shut down. Jones and Evans were friendly rivals; both had their young followers. They circled each other like low forming storm clouds bearing down on Cleveland.

None of the FBI informants could identify any plans by Evans or the Republic of New Libya to overthrow the government by force or violence, let alone any coherent political philosophy. "CV T-1 advised that there is no deep seated philosophy motivating the organization," Sullivan wrote. Another informant, T-2, told Sullivan that the New Libyans "had no real purpose nor discipline." He said "their main topic of discussion is placing the blame on the white race for their own failures."

Nor were they able to connect Evans with black nationalists in different cities or establish the existence of some national conspiracy. One of the informants did overhear discussions of Evans visiting "brothers" in Detroit and Columbus. Another informant reported that Evans and "six or seven of his followers were in Detroit, Michigan, over the weekend of June 30–July 2, 1967, to attend the Black Power Conference. . . . He stated he learned the group traveled to Detroit in rental cars paid for by a representative of Reverend Martin Luther King." If this trip happened, it was just before the outbreak of rioting in Detroit.

As to funding, the FBI report states that T-1, the most prolific of the spies, "frequently heard remarks made by Ahmed to the effect that he receives funds from [comedian] Dick Gregory, Jim Brown, and other nationally known Negro personalities." T-1 conceded he had no way to know the truth of these statements or if they were just "fabrications on Ahmed's part to build up his ego."

Part of the effort to neutralize militant groups like the New Libyans and the Afro Set was to harass their leaders. By no later than the summer of 1967 the United States faced what amounted to an open insurgency by black Americans against the white ruling class. As two scholars put it, "The task thus presented in completing the federal counterinsurgency strategy was to destroy such community-based black leadership before it had the opportunity to consolidate itself and instill a vision of freedom among the great mass of blacks."[13]

Harllel Jones, who had been arrested on charges of vandalizing the Cleveland Cultural Gardens in the months after the Hough riots, finally went to trial in January 1968 with four other defendants. Louis Stokes was Jones's lawyer. The witnesses called by the prosecutors were of questionable trustworthiness. One young man, who confessed he was involved in the vandalism, admitted when cross-examined by Lou Stokes that he changed the story he told police after they told him he was "as good as convicted." He meekly said, "I changed my story because my mom told me to tell the truth." A second witness was brought in from the Ohio penitentiary to testify.

The jury was unimpressed. They sensed these witnesses had been promised leniency in some form in exchange for their testimony. After nineteen hours of deliberations, the jury could only agree on the guilt of the man from the penitentiary; they were hung on all the others. The prosecutors threw in the towel, dismissing all the cases, saying that there was a "reluctance of witnesses to testify again" because both were "frightened of possible reprisals."[14]

Similarly, Fred Ahmed Evans came to trial in February 1968 for his scuffle a year earlier with the black traffic cop, William Payne. Evans was represented by Stanley Tolliver in the aggravated assault case. This is the trial where Evans told the jury that he could have killed Payne with his bare hands if he had wanted to.

Tolliver, for reasons that are not apparent, decided to let Evans testify at length in his own defense. "My cult name, spiritual name, is Ahmed," Evans introduced himself to the jury. "My surname is Fred Allen Evans."

After relaying his military background, Evans was asked how he became acquainted with "this cult that is called Black Nationalism."

Evans started by describing his experience in Korea. "I had first-hand knowledge of, and I viewed this, and saw how cheap life could be," he said. "I saw people stacked like cordwood." The trauma of what he witnessed and his own injuries caused him to see the world differently. Then he returned to the ghetto.

He said he was curious to understand why racism existed and dominated his world. "I am born under the sign Gemini, the Twins, the third house of travel," he prattled. "This is a sign that is ruled by the Planet Mercury. It makes a person intuitive and wants to know why."

It is fairly obvious why the prosecutors were satisfied to let this irrelevant, rambling, and at times disconnected testimony continue. It is not so clear why the judge permitted it—but on it went.

At an early age, Evans explained, he wanted to know "why things had never changed." He knew he had a good mother and a good father and came from a supportive family, yet "conditions never changed." This, he said, is why he turned to the science of astrology. "Therein," he said, "I found a never-failing relationship of the cause and effect that teaches one lesson that man has to learn: that what ye sow must ye also reap." And as his vision of the true reality began to unfold before his eyes, he said, "I had an idea of how long it would last and what would happen in this eventuality."

Evans described the relentless surveillance of the police as a contributing factor to his radicalization. "As we sat on 81st Street and Hough in a very small apartment where we gathered, we were constantly observed by the police department," he testified. "That is to say, Sergeant John Ungvary of the Subversives Unit and just anybody. It was a fact that every day we were being observed, all of our motions, anything that we did, we were followed by the police department."[15]

Tolliver struggled to keep him on topic. "Black Nationalism is a very simple thing," Evans finally got to his point. "In fact, it is just like white nationalism. It is like any nationalism. It is like China or Cuba or like anything that is together, anything that is working, anything that is progressive." He elaborated in a way that had to have left the jury wondering about his lucidity:

I mean, it doesn't have to do with the murder of all white people in the world. That is something I would like you to understand. It hasn't anything to do with that at all.

It is built on the foundation that the Father of the Universe, this source, this power that made the universe and created all therein, is the father of nationalism, and the sun which carries all that is with it eastward in the heavens, or known as Michael as our leader, and we do not fight our brothers. These are the three laws of nationalism, nationalism that I am concerned with, the nationalism that I am part of.[16]

The jury convicted Evans and the judge sentenced him to six months in the Cleveland Workhouse in Warrensville Heights.[17] Special agent in charge, John Sullivan, sent an airtel (a letter typed and mailed the same day) to the director of the FBI on February 28, 1968, advising of Evans's conviction and sentence.[18] Evans, according to this message, was already listed on Hoover's "Rabble Rouser Index," a database made up of index cards to track individuals who had demonstrated "a potential for fomenting racial discord." Sullivan recommended that Evans also be placed on the established "Security Index."

During the same week that Ahmed Evans was on trial, the FBI expanded its counterintelligence program against black nationalists, moving from the original twenty-three field offices to forty-one nationwide. The FBI became increasingly paranoid that black nationalists in different cities would join forces that summer and was especially wary of the "rise of a leader who might unify and electrify those violence-prone elements."

The memo, dated February 23, 1968 (as amplified by Hoover's follow-on March 4 airtel), pointed to the FBI's activity in Philadelphia as a template for success, citing the arrest of RAM members:

The Revolutionary Action Movement (RAM), a pro-Chinese communist group, was active in Philadelphia, Pa., in the summer of 1967. The Philadelphia Office alerted local police, who then put RAM leaders under close scrutiny. They were arrested

on every possible charge until they could no longer make bail.
As a result, RAM leaders spent most of the summer in jail and
no violence traceable to RAM took place.[19]

Beyond the prevention of a coalition of black nationalist groups,
however, the FBI worried singularly about the "rise of a messiah" who
could unite and captivate the black nationalist movement. The specific
targets included Stokely Carmichael and Elijah Muhammad, but Hoover
now added Dr. Martin Luther King Jr. to the short list. King had not
been listed in the original COINTELPRO memo in August 1967 as a
black nationalist or a target of the program.

Perhaps FBI leadership worried about Dr. King's lean to the left
since Chicago and Cleveland. Perhaps they perceived his promotion of
many of the "black power" themes as a genuine threat. Maybe there
was deep concern over Dr. King's plan to paralyze or disrupt Washington, DC, and other large cities with his poor people's demonstrations
and camp-ins. Whatever the motive, Dr. King was added to the list of
potential "messiahs" that needed to be neutralized. "King could be a
very real contender for this position [of messiah] should he abandon
his supposed 'obedience' to 'white, liberal doctrines' (nonviolence) and
embrace black nationalism," Hoover wrote.

During this time, the Stokes administration finally seemed to be
settling down and finding its rhythm. In a lengthy article in the *New
York Times*, it was reported that Stokes had completed his first hundred days in office "on the upswing . . . after a slow start plagued by
disorganization, inexperience, and minor blunders." Stokes announced
on February 20 that he had chosen a dynamic young urban planner
from Boston to the post of urban renewal director. Seth Taft lauded
the move and the *Plain Dealer* labeled it as a "brilliant stroke." HUD
began to unfreeze funds for Cleveland. While the *Times* noted that black
nationalists grumbled about the largely white composition of Stokes's
cabinet, most were willing to give the new mayor a chance. He in fact
was rapidly moving to place blacks in city positions.

One black councilman was optimistic that the election of Stokes
had blunted the growth of militant dissent. "I don't expect any racial

upheavals this summer," Leo Jackson said, "simply because of the protective attitude of the great majority of Negroes here toward the Mayor."

Stokes also began to reorganize the police department. No longer would police wear the white riot helmets that had become standard issue after the Hough riots. Stokes also halted the nightly helicopter patrols with spotlights searching over the ghetto. His transfers of personnel to integrate patrols and elite units caused a sharp backlash from white officers, resulting in some police coming down with the "blue flu." In some black areas, enforcement stopped or slowed for a time—but the protest died down after a few weeks.

Still, there was enormous optimism that a black mayor could finally address problems that were afflicting America's big cities. "We are laying the groundwork with community support to show that Cleveland can alleviate and in some cases cure the ills that plague a city such as this," Stokes told reporters.[20]

Toward the end of March or in the first days of April, Ahmed Evans was released on bail from the Cleveland Workhouse after his lawyer, Stanley Tolliver, filed an appeal.[21] The FBI finally added him to the Security Index. He was described as a Negro with a three-inch scar at the end of his right eyebrow, "usually wears sun glasses; bebop type, fuzz under lower lip and beard."[22]

Events in Memphis were about to test Carl Stokes's leadership and the working hypothesis that a black mayor of a major city could control racial tensions and violence. A single bullet would change everything.

21

"The Voice of Madness"

LYNDON JOHNSON WAS IN TROUBLE. On the night of January 30, 1968, the beginning of the Vietnamese holiday celebrating the new year called Tet, the North Vietnamese and Vietcong launched one of the largest military campaigns of the war, attacking all across South Vietnam. The Americans and South Vietnamese were initially stunned and suffered heavy losses but soon regrouped and eventually repulsed the attack.

But the damage was done. The US Army looked unprepared and was embarrassed, even though they eventually defeated the North Vietnamese militarily and prevented the general uprising that had been the goal of the Communists. Johnson had to admit to himself that the war was not going to end any time soon.

On the home front, Johnson's commission on civil disorders issued its report on the last day of February. Known as the Kerner Commission, its report was direct, unflinching, and dire. "Our nation is moving towards two societies," the commission wrote, "one black, one white— separate but unequal." To the dismay of many Americans, the commission found that "white racism" was chiefly to blame for the riots that had torn apart northern cities like Chicago, Cleveland, Detroit, and Newark. Moreover, the report dispelled the notion that the riots were the consequence of any organized plan or "conspiracy."

"Segregation and poverty have created in the racial ghetto a destructive environment totally unknown to most white Americans," the

Commission wrote. "What white Americans have never fully under-stood—but what the Negro can never forget—is that the white society is deeply implicated in the ghetto. White institutions created it, white institutions maintain it, and white society condones it."

There was an unexpected heavy attack on the media. The commis-sion found that African Americans believed the media misrepresented what was going on in the ghetto and failed to fairly report from the perspective of black residents and leaders during times of rebellion. "Many people in the ghettos apparently believe that newsmen rely on the police for most of their information about what is happening during a disorder," the report noted, "and tend to report much more of what the officials are doing and saying than what Negro citizens or leaders in the city are doing and saying."[1]

The commission called for massive federal and local funding for law enforcement reforms, welfare, employment, education, and hous-ing, though it put no price tag on its sweeping recommendations. Its goal was to "mount programs on a scale equal to the dimensions of the problem." The *New York Times* opined that the programs "go far beyond social programs that are now in trouble in Congress because of a tight budget. They would cost many billions of dollars."[2]

"This deepening racial divide is not inevitable," the commission wrote. "The movement apart can be reversed. Choice is still possible. Our prin-cipal task is to define that choice and to press for a national resolution."

Reaction was as polarized as the nation. Representative Edward Herbert, a Democrat from Louisiana, called the report "propaganda ad nauseam."[3] Dr. King at home in his Ebenezer Baptist Church in Atlanta welcomed the honesty of the report and said the nation should be grateful for the wisdom of the commissioners. But he cautioned, "The commission report is a physician's warning of approaching death, with a prescription to life. The duty of every American is to administer the remedy without regard to the cost and without delay."[4]

Carl Stokes, a media sensation since winning the mayor's race (he appeared on the cover of *Time* magazine on November 17, 1967), was in Washington with six other mayors to appear on NBC's *Meet the Press* to discuss and endorse the Kerner Report. "Cleveland's Carl Stokes, the first

Negro Mayor of a large city in the United States," the *New York Times* reported, "complained that Congress consistently used Vietnam spending as an excuse for doing too little for urban slum-dwellers." Stokes said, "I would have to put my priorities at home; you have to take care of home first."[5]

Events quickly escalated. Martin Luther King Jr. darted across the country and started detailed planning of his Poor People's Campaign. He returned his focus to the South, from which all his victories had come. The march would start in the South, with more than three thousand volunteers trooping on foot or by mule train out of Mississippi, Alabama, Georgia, the Carolinas, and Virginia—all merging on the way to Washington, DC. Those who could not walk would come by bus or car. The campaigners would kick off on April 22, King announced on March 4.[6]

General Westmoreland requested an additional 206,000 troops for Vietnam just days later, on March 9. He asked for the 40 percent increase to "regain the initiative" from the enemy. There were already 510,000 American troops in Vietnam.[7]

The following Tuesday, March 12, a primary was held in New Hampshire. President Johnson and Republican Richard Nixon were "prohibitive favorites" to take most of the votes.[8] The nation was shocked when Minnesota Senator Eugene McCarthy harvested 42 percent of the Democratic votes—"Unforeseen Eugene" *Time* magazine dubbed him. McCarthy's platform centered on ending the Vietnam War. Though Johnson won the primary, McCarthy's strong showing spelled trouble for the incumbent president, even as pundits still believed McCarthy could not, as a practical matter, prevent Johnson's renomination.[9]

New York Senator Robert F. Kennedy finally decided to enter the race. McCarthy tried to delay his entry, saying, "Leave the primaries to me." McCarthy reasoned that he should carry the primary challenges to the president and that if he found he did not have the votes at Chicago in August, he would release his delegates to Kennedy.[10] Bobby Kennedy, though, had made up his mind.

On Saturday, March 16, Kennedy appeared with his wife and two of his young sons in the Senate Caucus Room of the Old Senate Office Building, the same room where his brother had launched his presidential campaign in 1960, to announce his candidacy for the presidency. "I run,"

Kennedy said, "to seek new policies—policies to end the bloodshed in Vietnam and in our cities, policies to close the gap between black and white, between rich and poor, between young and old, in this country and around the rest of the world."[11]

Columnist Scotty Reston of the New York Times entitled his article the next day: "Johnson Is the Issue."[12] He predicted a "vicious and arduous campaign."

In Congress, nervous legislators delayed a quick vote on the Fair Housing Act, a civil rights act that would require open housing. The measure was hotly contested by the real estate industry and southern senators threatened filibuster. Those opposed to delay worried that debate on the bill overlapped with "the time of the Rev. Dr. Martin Luther King Jr.'s 'poor people march' on Washington, scheduled to begin April 22, the day Congress returns from recess."[13]

King was diverted, momentarily it seemed, from his barnstorming recruitment for his poor people's march by events in Memphis. A pastor in Memphis, James Lawson, asked King to support striking sanitation workers who sought union recognition after two workers had been crushed to death by a compactor on a garbage truck. On March 28, King led a demonstration he had not organized in downtown Memphis that turned ugly. Riotous youths broke windows, and one of them was killed by police. King had to escape in a car that whisked him to a local hotel.

The disturbance sent tremors through a nation fearful of urban rioting. "The disorder in Memphis that left store windows on Beale Street smashed and one Negro youth dead exposes the danger in drawing large numbers of protesters into the streets for emotional demonstrations in this time of civic unrest," the New York Times editorialized. "Dr. King must by now realize that his descent on Washington is likely to prove even more counterproductive. . . . The whole incident underscores the general national edginess."[14]

Senator Robert Byrd of West Virginia told the Senate that "the nation was given a preview of what may be in store by the outrageous and despicable riot that King helped to bring about in Memphis."[15] President Johnson said that "mindless violence" would "never be tolerated in America."[16] Seth Taft's cousin, Robert Taft, a representative in the House, called on King to delay or call off his scheduled march, saying it would endanger the open housing bill.[17]

King doubled down. He promised to lead a "massive" civil rights demonstration in Memphis soon, "to show that protests can be conducted without violence."[18]

On Sunday, March 31, Dr. King spoke at the National Cathedral in Washington. He was the invited guest of the dean of the cathedral, Francis B. Sayre Jr., the grandson of Woodrow Wilson (whose remains are interred in the cathedral). Sayre, an antiwar critic, gave King the opportunity to calm fears in Washington with a sermon and a defense of his Poor People's Campaign.

The texts from scripture that he preached from that day came from the book of Revelations: "Behold I make all things new; former things are passed away." He spoke of the nation's debt to African Americans, held in slavery for 244 years. He preached of the man in a parable who Jesus said was cursed to hell not because he was rich, but because he passed a poor man every day and never saw him, never reached out to relieve his poverty.

"In a few weeks," he said, "some of us are coming to Washington to see if the will [to end poverty] is still alive in this nation. We are coming to Washington in a Poor People's Campaign. . . . We are not coming to tear up Washington. We are coming to demand that the government address itself to the problems of poverty."

He continued to assail President Johnson's war. "I am convinced that it is one of the most unjust wars that has ever been fought in the history of the world," he said. "It has played havoc with our domestic agenda. This day we are spending five hundred thousand dollars to kill every Vietcong soldier. Every time we kill one we spend about $500,000 while we spend only $53 a year for every person characterized as poverty-stricken in the so-called poverty program, which is not even a good skirmish against poverty."

"The judgment of God is upon us," he thundered.[19]

After his sermon, King told newsmen for the first time that he might be open to postponing or calling off the poor people's march if he was given "a positive commitment" that Congress would do something this summer to aid the nation's slums. Perhaps the sudden spark of violence in Memphis caused him to pause. In any event, he said he thought negotiations were unlikely to produce anything positive.[20]

That night, Lyndon Johnson went on national television to talk about efforts to end the Vietnam War and then astonished even his closest advisers by saying he would not run for reelection. "I shall not seek and I will not accept the nomination of my party as your President," he declared at the end of his talk. His decision, he said later, was "completely irrevocable." Instead of campaigning, he would concentrate all his time on the conduct of the war.[21]

On Wednesday of that week, Dr. King returned to Memphis. He spoke the night of April 3 to a crowd at the Mason Temple, a vast concrete structure capable of seating 7,500. King spoke in the midst of a terrific thunderstorm that brought lightning and killer tornados to the Memphis area. King delivered one of the most prophetic speeches in American history. He had been to the mountaintop, he said, and he was unafraid of the threats to his life.

"Like anybody I would like to live a long life; longevity has its place," he cried at the climax of the talk. "But I'm not concerned about that now. I just want to do God's will. And he's allowed me to go up the mountain. And I've looked over. And I have seen the Promised Land." He spoke almost as if in a trance.

"I may not get there with you," he said, "but I want you to know tonight that we as a people will get to the Promised Land. So I'm happy tonight. I'm not worried about anything. I'm not fearing any man. Mine *eyes* have seen the glory of the coming of the Lord!"

He all but fainted as he spoke these final words, having to be helped to a chair by fellow pastors on the podium. The audience in Mason Temple was in delirium, hardly grasping what they had just witnessed.

The next night, as he waited on the balcony of the Lorraine Motel to go to dinner, one bullet from a high-powered rifle shattered Martin Luther King's chin and drove through his neck "with a total transection of the lower cervical and upper thoracic spinal cord and other structures of the neck." Dr. Martin Luther King Jr. was thirty-nine years old—the exact age of Malcolm X when he was killed.

Across the nation, rioting, looting, and burning erupted. In Washington, President Johnson ordered five thousand army troops and National Guardsmen into the city as violence spread. It was the first time federal troops had been ordered into Washington since the summer of 1932, when President Hoover ordered a force under General Douglas MacArthur to disperse the Bonus Army that had encamped there to demand benefits—the very group that had inspired the "camp-in" idea behind Dr. King's Poor People's Campaign.

Stokely Carmichael, in Washington, bitterly advocated that African Americans "get guns" and "retaliate against white America." Severe violence broke out in Chicago where three black men were killed. Baltimore, Memphis, Denver, Oakland, Toledo, Trenton, Harlem, Raleigh, Boston, Brooklyn, Youngstown, Cincinnati, and Buffalo—all experienced rock throwing, looting, and arson.[22] Over the next few precarious days, news services counted racial outbursts in at least 120 cities, with a death toll of thirty-nine people.[23]

But not Cleveland. Carl Stokes took to the streets that night to walk Hough and Glenville and urge calm. He did the same on Friday night, April 5. He ordered white policemen to stay out of the black community, organizing black "peace patrols" to guard against hotheaded reaction to the assassination.[24] Early on Saturday morning—at a predawn meeting—Stokes huddled with a group of seventy-five black nationalists, including Fred Ahmed Evans, newly released from the Cleveland Workhouse, and Harllel Jones, and asked for their help in "quieting fears in the Negro neighborhoods."[25]

Evans later testified that Stokes "came out and he asked all of the organizations to lend their efforts in preventing any violence." He said they agreed to help, though they were not proponents of nonviolence. "We definitely don't believe in the principle of nonviolence," Evans said. "That is what he [Dr. King] believed in, and this was definitely not our thing. As a matter of fact, after the man was dead, it really didn't hurt me at all, because I knew this would happen to him, you know, eventually."[26] But Evans gave Stokes his word that he would not encourage any violence and would prevent it if he could. "In fact, we did," he testified. Bertram Gardner, retained by Mayor Stokes as his community relations director, "praised Black Nationalists for helping maintain calm."

It was Mayor Stokes's shining moment. Leaders in Cleveland were encouraged that the experiment in black leadership seemed to be working.

The morning after Dr. King's assassination, Bobby Kennedy arrived in Cleveland. He had been in Indianapolis the night before, where he announced Dr. King's death to a crowd. He was scheduled to speak to the City Club of Cleveland at a lunch at the Sheraton-Cleveland Hotel in its grand ballroom, an event that had been sold out, with standing room only. He and some of his aides, including Jeff Greenfield, were up most of the night composing a short address, recognizing it was no time for campaigning. Kennedy's talk, known as the "Mindless Menace of Violence" speech, was perhaps his greatest, though only ten minutes in length.

Robert and Ethel Kennedy at the City Club of Cleveland the day after the assassination of Dr. Martin Luther King Jr., April 5, 1967. Kennedy delivered his "Mindless Menace of Violence" speech. *Cleveland Public Library Collection/Photograph Collection*

"This is a time of shame and sorrow," he began. "It is not a time for politics. I have saved this one opportunity to speak briefly to you about the mindless menace of violence in America which again today stains our land and every one of our lives."

The audience was silent, over two thousand sitting quietly in sober reflection. Violence, Kennedy said, was not the concern of any one race. "The victims of violence are black and white, rich and poor, young and old, famous and unknown. They are, most important of all, human beings who other human beings loved and needed."

"Why?" he asked. "What has violence ever accomplished? What has it ever created? No martyr's cause has ever been stilled by an assassin's bullet. No wrongs have ever been righted by riots and civil disorders," he said.

"A sniper is only a coward, not a hero; and an uncontrolled, uncontrollable mob is only the voice of madness, not the voice of the people."

He told his listeners that the violent taking of a life, whether by police or mobs, damages all society. "Whenever any American's life is taken by another American unnecessarily—whether it is done in the name of the law or in defiance of the law, by one man or by a gang, in cold blood or in passion, in an attack of violence or in response to violence—whenever we tear at the fabric of a life which another man has painfully and clumsily woven for himself and his children, the whole nation is degraded."

He quoted Lincoln: "'Among free men,' said Abraham Lincoln, 'there can be no successful appeal from the ballot to the bullet; and those who take such appeal are sure to lose their case and pay the cost.'"

He said, "Some look for scapegoats, others look for conspiracies, but this much is clear: violence breeds violence, repression breeds retaliation, and only a cleansing of our whole society can remove this sickness from our soul."

In the end, violence was not the answer. Instead, he said, Americans needed to recognize all men and women as brothers and sisters, fellow citizens, not aliens to one another. His peroration was heartrending, particularly knowing of Kennedy's march toward his own fate two months hence:

> Our lives on this planet are too short and the work to be done
> too great to let this spirit [of violence] flourish any longer in

our land. Of course we cannot banish it with a program, or a resolution.

But we can perhaps remember—even if only for a time—that those who live with us are our brothers; that they share with us this same short moment of life; that they seek—as do we— nothing but the chance to live out their lives in purpose and happiness, winning what satisfaction and fulfillment they can.

Surely this bond of common fate, this bond of common goal, can begin to teach us something. Surely we can learn, at the least, to look at those around us as fellow men. And surely we can begin to work a little harder to bind up the wounds among us and to become in our hearts brothers and countrymen once again.[27]

Across the public square at the very time Kennedy was speaking, Carl Stokes sat weeping at a memorial service hastily assembled in Cleveland's venerable Old Stone Church. "I thank God we have been spared the trouble that has occurred in many localities as an aftermath of Dr. Martin Luther King's death," he told reporters.[28]

On Sunday evening, April 7, Carl Stokes attended a service at Cory Methodist Church in Glenville in honor of Dr. King, who had spoken there in 1963. Stokes's appearance at Cory coincided almost exactly with a date four years earlier—April 3, 1964—when Malcolm X first delivered his "Ballot or Bullet" speech there. The paper noted that a "scheduled silent memorial in memory of Rev. Bruce Klunder, killed in a Civil Rights demonstration here in 1964, was cancelled."

Before leaving to attend Dr. King's funeral in Atlanta, Stokes announced the formation of a Martin Luther King Memorial Action Fund. The purpose of the fund was to "gather together the necessary funds to provide progress in the areas of jobs, housing, welfare, and education."[29]

Over the next few weeks this idea for a memorial fund would expand and transform into a massive program, known—in homage to King's "Freedom Now!" civil rights slogan—as Cleveland: Now!

One of the groups who would receive initial funding from Cleveland: Now! was Ahmed Evans's black nationalists group. What they would do with those funds would have disastrous consequences for the Stokes administration and lethal consequences for Cleveland police and black nationalists alike.

22

Cleveland: Now!

IN THE WAKE OF DR. King's death and the rioting across the nation, Congress moved with alacrity to pass the Civil Rights Act of 1968, which outlawed discrimination in housing. President Johnson signed the bill on April 11. Events moved so quickly that the White House could not contact Coretta Scott King or Ralph Abernathy in time to allow them to attend the signing ceremony.[1]

But the bill also contained a stick—the antirioting legislation that Sergeant John Ungvary had requested in his appearance before a Senate subcommittee was made part of the package. The Anti-Riot Act was aimed at "outside agitators" and it made it a federal crime to travel in interstate commerce or use the facilities of interstate commerce with the "intent to do one of four things: (A) incite a riot; (B) organize, promote, encourage, participate in, or carry on a riot; (C) commit any act of violence in furtherance of a riot; or (D) aid or abet any person in inciting, participating in, or carrying on a riot, with an overt act for that purpose."[2] The law became known as the "H. Rap Brown Law," based on a widely held belief that he incited violence and rioting in cities around the country as the leader of the SNCC.

For his part, Brown called Stokes's election and those of other black politicians "a type of neo-colonialism." He said, "In other words, the man has set up puppet regimes. These black people are responsive to the needs and whims of the Democratic Party and not of the masses of black people."[3]

Scholars have long pointed out that antirioting laws present unique First Amendment issues because they implicate two protected freedoms: freedom of speech and freedom of assembly.

The day after President Johnson signed the Civil Rights Act of 1968, Carl Stokes met with his cabinet and business leaders in Cleveland to follow up on discussions they had started the day after Dr. King's assassination. Stokes's public relations guru, William Silverman, was summoned to the mayor's office at city hall on April 5. "Gathered around the conference table in the adjacent Tapestry Room were 20 or so of the city's most prominent executives," Silverman recalled. One of the executives, according to Silverman, said, "Mr. Mayor, we're completely behind you. Whatever you need to deal with the situation, you just call on us."

Silverman took the mayor aside and told him he just had been presented a golden opportunity to seek establishment funding for programs that would address jobs, housing, and police reforms. "So let's get the bastards back in here and tell them there is something they can do."[4]

Apocryphal or not, this was the start of Cleveland: Now! Stokes asked for plans to be drawn up to solicit federal, state, and local funding along with private money from the business community and individuals to underwrite an array of programs to address the problems of the ghetto. Though many of these programs already existed (especially on the federal side), packaging them all under the one banner of Cleveland: Now! was a marketing masterstroke, the kind for which Silverman was known. This would be Cleveland's miniature Great Society. And it would take many of its ideas from the Kerner Report.

"Cleveland: Now! is believed to be the first attempt by a major city to meet many of the challenges posed by the report of the National Advisory Commission on Civil Disorder," Robert McGruder of the *Plain Dealer* wrote. "The [Kerner] commission's report and the death of Rev. Dr. Martin Luther King Jr. provided the inspiration and impetus for the program, according to Mayor Carl B. Stokes."[5]

On Thursday, May 2, Stokes launched the Cleveland: Now! campaign in spectacular fashion with a carefully planned media assault. The front page of the *Plain Dealer* was devoted entirely to the story. "$1.5 Billion Is Asked to Rebuild Cleveland," the headline read, with a special editorial asking for public support of the plan.[6] "There is a challenge in the 10-year program to marshal the financial and business power of the city in a $1.5 billion reconstruction and development project," the editors wrote. "There is opportunity for cooperation never before proposed on such a magnificent scale involving the special talents of all facets of Cleveland's life."[7]

Over its first phase of eighteen months, the goal was to raise $177 million. The proposals during this phase included the creation of eleven thousand new jobs, 4,600 new and rehabilitated housing units, acceleration of existing urban renewal projects already on the books, creation of ten multiservice health centers and ten child-care centers, and money for youth resources, providing a wide variety of activities for young people "including neighborhood cleanups, work training, and cultural enrichment programs."

The "lion's share" of the money would come from federal grants. Of the initial phase goal of $177 million, only $34 million was to be raised from state, local, and private contributions. The Cleveland Growth Association was to begin a drive to raise $10.5 million from the city's business community. George Steinbrenner, then thirty-seven years old and CEO of the American Ship Building Company, was tasked with raising $1.25 million from his business friends and citizens in the community. Steinbrenner was the founder and chairman of Group 66, an organization of young entrepreneurs formed two years earlier to try to help improve Cleveland.[8]

Stokes appeared on television in a made-for-TV special to explain his program.[9] The *New York Times* carried the story on its front page. "Many crises which plague urban America are mirrored in Cleveland," Stokes told the *Times*. "That is why last November, the people voted for change."[10]

There was tremendous excitement generated by all the publicity, a lift after the depressing and frightful days after Dr. King's death. Stokes had a rock star quality about him and now, with the appearance of dynamic leadership, he caught the attention of all Cleveland and the nation. Vice President Humphrey, already a fan, began to consider Stokes for higher office as he started his own presidential campaign. Ralph Besse, chairman of the leading electrical utility and a frequent sparring partner with Mayor Ralph Locher, praised Stokes for "thinking big." Besse had not studied the plans but said, "Massive problems require massive solutions."[11]

Others were wary of the sheer scope of the undertaking. "Where will the money come from?" county prosecutor John T. Corrigan asked. Money aside, the real problem was that the plans were hatched in crisis, during all-day and late-night, caffeine-fueled emergency meetings, and little thought was given as to how the city would administratively oversee and manage the overabundance of programs and initiatives. The city hardly had the machinery in place to coherently organize it all with the required supervision.

Meanwhile, Fred Ahmed Evans poked back up on the radar screens of the Cleveland police and FBI, and they coordinated efforts to harass and neutralize him as an agitator, notwithstanding the assistance he had just lent to Mayor Stokes in keeping the peace in the days after the King assassination. The FBI and Cleveland police would take no chances as another summer approached.

On May 7, police padlocked his astrology store on Superior Avenue for "sanitary violations" on what seems to have been a pretext. FBI special agent Sullivan pasted a short article from the *Cleveland Press* into his file that describes the police action. "Lt. Michael Sirkot of the Police Sanitation Unit said a number of violations had been found, including inadequate lighting and ventilation, use of a hot plate and the absence of exit signs and toilet facilities," the *Press* reported. The reason for the inspection: firemen had complained that they were pelted by bottles and debris when summoned "to that area" by a false alarm.[12] No tie was made to Evans, yet his shop was raided.

The next week, seventeen buses carrying marchers on their way to the Poor People's Campaign in Washington pulled into Cleveland at 9:00 PM, later than expected because of police interference in Detroit when the buses stopped there to pick up recruits. The marchers were mainly from Milwaukee, led by a charismatic Catholic priest, Father

James Groppi, and Martin Luther King's brother, Rev. A. D. King. The buses were escorted by Cleveland police to Glenville High School, where seven hundred people, mainly teenagers, were served a dinner of stew, salad, bread, and milk. Most were carpooled off to the homes of generous Clevelanders for a night's sleep.[13]

The FBI had a spy mingling among the poor people's crowd. He reported that Ahmed Evans and Harllel Jones had approximately sixty of their followers present at the Glenville High School to provide protection ("they appear to be acting as security guards," Agent John Sullivan wrote). The source advised that these black nationalists "threatened members of the press and did not allow them to take many photographs." The spy also heard grumblings about Mayor Stokes—"that he refused to give the marchers any money."[14] In fact, Stokes met briefly with the marchers the next day before they left town after the marchers scrapped the plan for a parade in Cleveland because they were behind schedule.[15]

At this moment, Bobby Kennedy won the Nebraska primary, dealing a blow to Senator McCarthy's prospects. Vice President Humphrey was still the favorite for the nomination, with party regulars toeing the line, but he joined the contest too late to participate in the major primary contests. Kennedy and McCarthy spoke of potentially working together against Humphrey as they moved to the primaries in Oregon and California, but no deal was cut. McCarthy would in fact win the Oregon primary on May 28, making the California primary in early June mission critical for Kennedy. "For Kennedy, It's California or Bust," the *Times* wrote.[16]

On Friday, May 24, Ahmed Evans was physically evicted from his astrology shop on Superior Avenue, notorious as a black nationalist headquarters. A court had ordered Evans on April 18 to pay rent that was seven months overdue, and a second eviction notice was issued for eleven supposed sanitary and building code violations. Cleveland's sanitation unit, municipal bailiffs, and movers hired by the city stacked all the furniture and artwork from Evans's shop on the sidewalk in front of the building as a large crowd gathered.[17]

The FBI became paranoid about reprisals from the nationalists. An urgent teletype was sent to the director of the FBI from the special agent in charge of the Cleveland office on May 24. "Detective John Patton, Special Investigative Unit, Cleveland, PD, advised eighteen members of [the New Libya] organization, along with Ahmed, at scene of eviction, but no incidents or disturbances took place," the SAC wrote. The teletype also noted that a warrant for Evans's arrest was going to issue the following week for "bond default," presumably related to the bond that allowed Ahmed to go free pending his appeal on the assault and battery charge involving Officer Payne.

The FBI was told, in the strictest confidence, that the landlord of the astrology shop, Mrs. L. G. Steuer, paid Evans $125 to "move out and not cause any trouble." There was also a claim by the Cleveland police that Mayor Stokes had sent representatives to the eviction scene. Per the teletype to Hoover, "Detective Mahon also advised, again in the strictest confidence, that he heard from a source that two representatives from the office of Mayor Carl B. Stokes appeared at the scene of eviction and gave Ahmed an unknown sum of money saying that they understood his financial predicament."[18]

Another particularly well-placed source delivered a long report to the FBI, by phone only because of the "tense mood in the Negro community." He had been consulted on April 5, 7, 8, 18, 26, and 30 concerning the temper of the black nationalists following the slaying of Dr. King. Now, on May 14, the source described at length a significant conversation he had with one of the followers of Ahmed Evans:

> He stated this individual told him that AHMED is attempting to unify the several Afro-American stores in the Cleveland area under his leadership. Source advised he concluded from his conversation with this individual that there was some sort of black nationalist hierarchy in Cleveland. This hierarchy is composed of seven or eight leaders, such as LEWIS ROBINSON, FRED EVANS, ALBERT WARE, HARLLEL JONES, and others. Source emphasized that he has no definite information to prove this but he pointed out that he has associated with these people enough to conclude that decisions as to their activities are made by some higher echelon and then passed on to the other members of the various groups. As an example he pointed out that while other

cities had disturbances after KING's death, Cleveland was spared. Source stated that he heard on numerous occasions that there would be no riots in Cleveland. Source states that he does not attribute this lack of rioting to the activities of Mayor STOKES during the days following the death of KING. He said the fact that STOKES is a Negro was an important factor and also the fact that the black nationalists had decided not to embarrass STOKES was a major contribution to peace in Cleveland. He stated the black nationalists expect to gain recognition by the city administration for their activities.[19]

One of the persons who always suspected that he was hired by Carl Stokes as payback for the unheralded efforts of the black nationalists was Walter Beach, the former Browns football player. Beach, who was no militant, was, as Art Modell would put it, "a race man." His former neighbor and friend, Detroit lawyer Milton Henry (who had taken the name Gaidi Obadele), helped to found the provisional government of the Republic of New Africa (RNA) in Detroit on March 31, the same day Dr. King spoke in the National Cathedral and LBJ quit the race. Obadele was named the RNA's first vice president; Robert F. Williams was declared its president in exile. Max Stanford was on the ballot for several offices. Mae Mallory, Queen Mother Moore of New York, and Betty Shabazz, the widow of Malcolm X, were among the delegates to the convention.[20]

One of RNA's goals was to create an independent black nation out of portions of several southern states; another was to demand reparations for descendants of slaves from the US government in compensation for the horrors of slavery.[21] Detroit 1968 was their Philadelphia 1776. They referred to themselves as Malcomites.

On June 3, 1968, Stokes hired Walter Beach to become the staff coordinator of the Mayor's Council on Youth Opportunity. His first task was to organize summer youth programs funded by early contributions to the Cleveland: Now! project.[22]

The Mayor's Council on Youth Opportunity had been assembled at the end of 1967 at the suggestion of Dolph Norton, the head of the powerful Cleveland Community Foundation. Norton loaned an executive to set up the council, a person Beach would replace in June. The

Council consisted of fifty-three members, a cross section of Clevelanders, including some heavy hitters from the business arena. This group would review proposals for summer programs. The pool of funds available was "dramatically enlarged when the mayor awarded $344,436 in Cleveland: Now! funds to [the Mayor's Council] for the summer of 1968."[23]

On the evening of June 3, an FBI informant attended a meeting of black nationalists at the Second Tabernacle Baptist Church on East 119th Street. "Informant advised that approximately 35 people were present," including Fred Ahmed Evans, Harllel Jones, Walter Beach, and several members of the New Libya organization. Beach, the spy said, was the "Chairman," although he didn't specify whether Beach was chairman of the meeting or the Black Nationalists—likely the former.

He reported, "Beach stressed the need for Negro history being taught in predominantly Negro schools. Beach pointed out that in the past the white man has mistreated the black man and that all efforts by black men must be directed toward stopping this mistreatment. Beach instructed those present to obtain and store reserve food and other necessities so that in the event that a racial riot occurred there would be enough to keep them going."

The source further advised that Harllel Jones spoke briefly about "the possibility of rioting in Cleveland." Jones told the group, "If rioting starts the group must join in." The source was careful to qualify that Jones "gave no indication that the group was making plans to instigate a disturbance."

Evans spoke, too. "Source advised that Evans gave a brief talk on astrology which neither he nor anybody else could understand," Agent Sullivan recorded.[24]

The following night, a group of eighteen black nationalists marched down Wade Park Avenue in Hough around 9:00 PM, waving a black nationalist flag (red, black, and green). Their intent was to confront the crew filming the movie *Uptight*. The director was Jules Dassin, a known Hollywood success who had been run out of the United States during the McCarthy era. *Uptight* was a transposition of Liam O'Flaherty's novel, *The Informer*, about the Irish war of independence after the Great War.

The book had already been made into a movie of the same name in 1935 by John Ford.

Dassin chose to film his version in Hough. Instead of an Irish patriot who is betrayed by an informant, Dassin's hero is a charismatic revolutionary black nationalist who steals guns from a warehouse to prepare for coming violent racial conflict and in the process shoots a security cop. His informant is an African American friend who believed in nonviolence and was despairing over Dr. King's murder (the movie starts with actual footage from King's funeral). The film's eventual tagline: "Nonviolence is dead—it died in Memphis."

"I brought the story to Cleveland because I think Cleveland is more representative of a big American city than any other," Dassin told a Cleveland reporter. "New York's Harlem isn't really typical. Cleveland is." He elaborated about his idea for the screenplay, which he principally wrote (along with Cleveland's Ruby Dee, who starred in it): "I want to do this picture because I think we all must do something quickly about the black people before the whole bloody country blows up."[25]

A real FBI informant reported on the nationalists' clash with Dassin on the night of June 4. "The group approached the film crew and demanded that production be stopped on the picture or they would tear down the set," John Sullivan wrote in a memo to the special agent in charge. "They also demanded that Cleveland Police Officer (FNU) CHARACTER, who has a 'moonlight' job as a security officer for the film crew, be fired. Officer CHARACTER is a Negro traffic policeman and has been involved in several shootings in the past."[26]

Jules Dassin shut down the set for the night, vowing to see Mayor Stokes the next day about the interference.

The FBI source found it perplexing that the nationalists would make a show of it "inasmuch as Paramount Pictures has hired a large number of local Negroes to act as extras in their scenes." He said that those hired "include FRED EVANS and approximately 20 of the members of New Libya." Evans would continue to be employed throughout the filming, which wrapped at the end of June.[27] When it was finally edited, Evans, because of his unusual height and African garb, can be seen walking the streets of Hough in one early scene.

The California primary took place on Wednesday, June 5, two days after Beach assumed his new job. Kennedy won. He was shot in the back of the head that night as he walked through the kitchen area of the Ambassador Hotel in Los Angeles after a triumphant victory speech. He died the next morning.

It was not hyperbole to say that Kennedy's feared "voice of madness" seemed to be dooming the nation, robbing it of its future and its most promising young leaders.

At Robert Kennedy's funeral mass in St. Patrick's Cathedral in New York City, his brother Edward eulogized him. "My brother need not be idealized or enlarged in death beyond what he was in life," Teddy said, his voice intermittently cracking with emotion. "He should be remembered as a good and decent man, who saw wrong and tried to right it, saw suffering and tried to heal it, saw war and tried to stop it."[28] Carl Stokes was among the invited mourners.[29] Ralph Abernathy wore workmen's dungarees, symbol of the Poor People's Campaign. Thousands and thousands lined the tracks as Bobby Kennedy's body was borne by train cortege from New York to Washington on June 8, where he was buried in Arlington near his brother John.

David Crosby of Crosby, Stills & Nash wrote the protest anthem, "Long Time Gone," on the night Kennedy was shot, telling youth in America to "speak out against the madness."

On the night that Kennedy won the California primary, a portentous meeting took place in Cleveland in the basement of one of the homes where Ahmed Evans was living, on East 73rd near Hough Avenue.[30] An FBI source was present and noted that other black nationalists from Cleveland were in attendance, as well as a supposed representative from the US Office of Economic Opportunity; a nationalist leader from Barberton, Ohio; a female nationalist from Dayton, Ohio; and six "Black Stone Rangers," a violent street gang from Chicago.

"These individuals spoke on the theme that it was senseless for the 'brothers' to die foolishly and they want no trouble in Cleveland," the informant reported. "These individuals suggest that the Nationalists movement should be more unified. It was indicated by several that in the future some brothers might be sent to such cities as Chicago, Detroit, and Los Angeles to converse with the brothers in those cities."[31]

On the following Monday, June 10, the US Supreme Court handed down its ruling in *Terry v. Ohio*, recognizing the right of police to "stop and frisk" suspicious persons, even in the absence of probable cause. Louis Stokes had represented the black man arrested, John Terry.[32] Lou Stokes reacted in his trademark gentlemanly fashion: "I have no quarrel with the court. But I thought this was a dangerous precedent—to subject citizens to on-street searches in absence of any real reason."[33]

Carl Stokes left the Kennedy funeral and traveled up to Massachusetts to receive an honorary law degree from Tufts University. "It would be wrong to say we are a nation of assassins, although it is unquestionable that we have a nation with too many murderers in it," he told students. "I believe we are going to build a better society."[34]

Stokes would take advantage of his already established relationship with Vice President Hubert Humphrey, who, as a result of Kennedy's death, was the likely Democratic nominee for president. Stokes traveled to Chicago the weekend after his appearance at Tufts and took a leadership position with Mayor John Lindsey of New York City at the United States Conference of Mayors. Stokes proposed a resolution to form a committee to lobby Washington for a federally guaranteed annual income for poor Americans. The resolution passed.[35] On June 28 Stokes became one of nine big-city mayors to be named as cochairmen of a national Mayors for Humphrey Committee.[36]

Humphrey, in turn, made plans to visit Cleveland on July 1 to continue his pursuit of delegates for the Democratic National Convention.

At Harllel Jones's Afro Set shop on Superior Avenue on the northern border of Hough, some of his lieutenants, Omar Majid and Sababa Akili, found twelve boxes of ceramics shipped from California—costing $1,400—smashed when delivered on June 20. The boxes had obviously been opened and the contents destroyed. Jones blamed the Cleveland police. "This is just added harassment to the abuse we are taking from the police in this area," he said. "They probably thought we were shipping guns or something."

Jones told a reporter from the *Call and Post*, "The white police ride by our shop every week calling us niggers and threatening to close our shop like they did Lewis Robinson. Several times they have tried to break into the shop without warrant on the pretext of looking for suspicious persons."

Jones said the patience of the black nationalists with Carl Stokes was starting to run out. "We have been trying to go along with Carl Stokes to keep the peace," he declared, "but I don't know how much more of this kind of harassment we can take."[37]

Years later, writing in retrospect, Max Stanford quoted a "Brother A" who echoed these same sentiments, this time out of the mouth of Fred Ahmed Evans:

> Ahmed was constantly being harassed by police. He came to the council to seek guidance. He said he "couldn't take it any longer and the next time he would have to take action." Every unit within the council agreed that if the situation persisted, all units in the city would go into action opening up other fronts.[38]

In the ghetto, those in the know began to whisper about a future confrontation with police as "the pot," as in the pot is boiling or the pot is on.[39] They all waited for the signal, and Fred Ahmed Evans, who consulted the stars, began to talk about a guerilla uprising on July 24.

23

"The Good News in American Cities Is Coming Out of Cleveland"

AHMED EVANS NEEDED A SHOP. Having been evicted from his astrology store on Superior, he required facilities if he was going to apply for funds from Cleveland: Now! He began consulting with the Hough Area Development Corporation (HADC), both for assistance in locating a potential new venue and in preparing a formal proposal for a grant from Cleveland: Now! His point of contact was DeForest Brown, the director of HADC.

Brown had been an associate minister at Fellowship Baptist Church, the place where Martin Luther King Jr. delivered his bitter press conference after Carl Stokes's victory in the mayor's race in November 1967.[1] Brown also had experience working for Legal Aid as a tenant organizer. He was an unabashed black nationalist—the epitome of a local activist.[2]

The HADC was a community-based nonprofit corporation funded mainly by the federal government, but it also received loans, grants, and gifts from local government and private donors. The idea of a Community Development Corporation (CDC) had been born out of Lyndon Johnson's antipoverty programs. It was a vehicle originally conceived of by Senators Bobby Kennedy and Daniel Patrick Moynihan for use as a prototype in Brooklyn's Bedford–Stuyvesant neighborhood.[3] The CDC became the frontline organization for the war on poverty—a clearinghouse. It was used to identify opportunities and invest public and private money in projects to improve impoverished neighborhoods. As a grassroots organization, it was believed that people running a CDC would better understand the needs of their local residents.

DeForest Brown was formally hired as the director of HADC on July 1, 1968, though he had started his duties much earlier in the year.

With assistance from the HADC and Brown, a storefront was located for Evans's new operations at Hough Avenue and 66th, about half a mile west from the epicenter of the Hough rebellion. It was in the center of a row of attached single-story brick-and-frame structures. The place had been operated as a bar but had been abandoned for years. It was in shambles. The furnace and toilets had been removed or wrecked by vandals, and trash and debris were littered throughout.

A tentative agreement was struck for Evans to clean up the store and in return he would receive rent money from HADC, through a grant DeForest Brown would obtain from Cleveland: Now! Evans proposed to run the store as an African culture shop—one that would teach youngsters black history, Swahili, astrology, numerology, music, art, carving, sewing, and African culture. The shop would employ Evans and several of his young followers as instructors.[4]

The newspapers reported that the building at 6605 Hough Avenue was owned by an elderly widow who was seeking to sell it. According to her spokesman, "On June 16 or 17, there was an offer made to rent the store. The only agreement was verbal. And this agreement was only that the owner would be asked to approve the rental." The widow advised she did not wish to rent the store because she thought she had a buyer. The spokesman claimed that Evans was informed the next day, which would be in mid-June, that there was no interest in renting to him.

Nonetheless, Evans and several of his followers took possession and began to clean up the space, removing two truckloads of trash and making improvements, including painting the interior. The outside was also painted in the red, black, and green colors of the black nationalists, a fact

that assuredly did not help with an already-skittish landlord.[5] DeForest
Brown paid for the expenses.

Evans asserted that he made the improvements and only then was he
told he could not rent it. He believed police pressured the landlady to back
out of her agreement. He allegedly told his associates, "All I wanted was
a little piece of land—if I can't get it, looks like I'll have to go to war."[6]

Proposals for funding for youth programs for the summer of 1968
had been delivered to the Mayor's Council on Youth Opportunity and
they were considered in an open meeting on June 27. The large council
was presided over by the vice president and general counsel of Ohio Bell;
Walter Beach was the staff coordinator. The council followed guidelines set
down by the President's Council on Youth Opportunity out of the Office of
Economic Opportunity, which contained a directive to "place major stress
on utilizing local ghetto organizations and personnel for the programs."[7]

Among the thirty-seven summer programs that would be funded by
Cleveland: Now! was one sponsored by HADC called Project Afro. HADC
proposed to work as a facilitating agent that could receive and disburse
funds to the leaders of three programs under the umbrella of Project Afro:

- Harllel Jones's Afro Set in Hough
- The African Culture Center in Glenville, headed by a man named
  Boyd Roberts
- Ahmed Evans's African culture shop, which was supposed to be
  located in Hough[8]

A total of $31,000 was awarded to Project Afro for three separate
twelve-week summer programs: $10,000 to Evans, $10,000 to Boyd Roberts, and $10,400 to Harllel Jones.[9]

On July 1 Carl Stokes was in Minneapolis with eighty other Democratic
mayors to endorse Hubert Humphrey for president. "One of the most welcome figures at the meeting was Mayor Carl B. Stokes of Cleveland," the
New York Times reported, "whose support was expected to be influential
with Negro voters, the great majority of whom had backed Senator Kennedy during the Presidential primaries." After the luncheon Humphrey and
Stokes boarded a small jet and flew to Cleveland, arriving around 6:00 PM.[10]

Vice President Hubert Humphrey and Carl Stokes, both wearing
"Cleveland: Now!" buttons, on July 1, 1968. Humphrey delivered
a check to the Hough Development Corporation. *Cleveland Public
Library Collection/Photograph Collection*

This was supposed to be Humphrey's moment to animate and lock
up Ohio delegates. As a Cleveland paper noted, "Humphrey will apparently seek to impress the delegates by drawing large crowds especially
in the Negro neighborhoods and among youngsters."[11]

That did not happen. In fact, Humphrey's trip was an embarrass-
ment. He was still dogged by association with the increasingly unpopular
war in Vietnam, from which he would only break free too late in the
campaign.

In Cleveland, perhaps numb from the succession of assassinations,
Humphrey's reception was cool and underwhelming. "Hubert Humphrey's campaign for the Democratic Presidential nomination is long
on delegates but woefully short on excitement," the *Times* wrote. His
advance team hoped three thousand to five thousand would show up
at Burke Lakefront to greet him when he arrived in Cleveland with

Mayor Stokes, but less than five hundred were present, including a band, cheerleaders, and hostile picketers.

The following day, a coffee-and-cookies reception that Stokes had promised would draw two thousand to three thousand folks produced a crowd of less than five hundred, "an embarrassing number of whom drifted out the back while Mr. Humphrey was speaking," the *Times* noted.[12]

But Humphrey chose to deliver his major address on how he would solve the problems of America's cities in Cleveland. He saw Cleveland as a model for the nation. Humphrey spoke at the City Club in the same space where Robert F. Kennedy had delivered his "Mindless Menace of Violence" address after Dr. King's death, but the crowd was half the size that Kennedy drew and they failed to interrupt his forty-seven-minute speech even once with applause.[13] He proposed a $150–$300 billion "Marshall Plan" for the cities, financed over ten years by a national urban development bank, which would provide funds to pay "whatever it cost, not just of stopping the blight, but of perfecting our cities."

He said he chose Cleveland to make this major policy recommendation because of the "new spirit under Mayor Carl B. Stokes, whose Cleveland: Now! speaks for a nation, for America now!"[14] He made similar remarks the evening before at a special cabinet meeting he attended with Stokes and his directors. "The good news in American cities is coming out of Cleveland," Humphrey chirped.[15]

On the day he spoke at the City Club of Cleveland, Humphrey made a special visit to Hough with Stokes to announce the US Office of Economic Opportunity had awarded $1.6 million to HADC "to help develop Negro-owned business in the ghetto."[16] One antiwar protester wasn't pleased with the gift, holding up a sign that read, "I Will Not Trade the Blood of My Son for Cleveland Now Money."[17]

The *Cleveland Plain Dealer* concluded that the visit had been more of a boon to Stokes than Humphrey. "It was Stokes who kept getting the crowds excited and who profited from a unique vice presidential parley at City Hall with the mayor's cabinet," the paper wrote.[18]

Disaster, however, was brewing. On July 6 Ahmed Evans submitted a weekly payroll sheet to DeForest Brown of HADC, seeking payment for sixteen individuals who supposedly were working at Evans's African culture shop. Evans applied for $150 for himself; $125 for his lieutenant, a young man named Lathan Donald; and $100 each for seven male instructors, $75 for six female instructors, and $75 for James Taylor (Amir Rashidd), the poet who wrote and performed "The Beast." Evans also applied for a $300 check to reimburse him for "decorations" for the Hough shop and a $600 check for the purchase of a 1961 four-door Chevrolet station wagon for "transportation."[19]

The problem was there was no African culture shop. Evans had been told he could not occupy the Hough Avenue venue, though they continued to fix it up. He and his followers were now encamped in a two-story redbrick apartment building at 12312 Auburndale Avenue, just off Lakeview Road in Glenville. It had two apartments upstairs, one in the front and one in the back, and two apartments downstairs, one in front and the other in back. Oddly, the apartments had been rented to a sixteen-year-old male named Leslie Jackson, known to the New Libyans by the name of Osu Bey. The landlord claimed he thought Jackson appeared to be at least eighteen or twenty years old and that he was married.[20]

There was no program, no one instructing youngsters, no one carrying on a twelve-week summer camp as laid out in the HADC proposal. And no one from the mayor's office, the Mayor's Council on Youth Opportunity, HADC, or the federal government was monitoring what was being done with the money that was being distributed to Evans. There was no auditing function to see if those on the payroll were working or if supplies were being purchased or whether the automobile was titled in the name of Evans personally or his shop.[21]

Checks were given to Ahmed Evans from HADC on July 9. He and others from his group began cashing the checks on July 10, 11, and 15. With the cash, some of them began to buy rifles, first-aid kits, and ammunition pouches.

On Thursday, July 11, a man who identified himself as Ralph Smith entered the Atlantic Gun & Tackle Store on Northfield Road in the outer ring suburb of Bedford. He purchased a Winchester Model 190, a semiautomatic .22-caliber rifle that held between fifteen and sixteen bullets in a magazine tube. The man paid $44.90 cash for the rifle. He gave as his address 12312 Auburndale Avenue—the apartment building occupied by Evans and his followers. Three days later, on a Sunday, July 14, Fred Evans himself entered the store, buying a second .22-caliber Winchester rifle. He identified himself with a social security card and gave his address as 11105 Superior Avenue, the shop from which he had been evicted at the end of May.[22]

Earlier that same week, on July 10, Republican presidential candidate Richard Nixon visited Cleveland and spoke in Public Square. According to the *Plain Dealer*, Nixon came to Cleveland to open "his presidential campaign for widespread support in the nation's urban areas." His theme was that the Democrats were spending wildly on cities with negative results. "Democrats have spent the nation to the brink of economic crisis to solve our urban crisis," Nixon told a crowd of about 3,500 who gathered in Public Square. He didn't specify his solutions to the urban emergency, just that the Democrats were on the wrong track. In fact, the only thing he said for sure on this trip was that he would keep J. Edgar Hoover as the head of the FBI. (Eugene McCarthy pledged to remove Hoover if elected.)[23]

As he moved through the crowd to shake hands after his talk, he ran into a young man who held a shallow cardboard box with propped-up pictures of Martin Luther King Jr. He was soliciting contributions for the Poor People's Campaign. Nixon mistook the man as asking for an autograph and he started to sign the box. When he learned of his mistake, he gruffly turned to an aide and barked, "Give him something." The startled aide reached into his pocket and pulled out a penny and a nickel and threw them in the box. The *Plain Dealer* story the next day carried the headline, "Nixon Aide Gives 'Poor' 6 Cents."[24]

Over the weekend, according to FBI documents, Evans took some of his followers to a farm fifty miles east of Cleveland in rural Ashtabula County to practice shooting. The farm, owned by a black man named Lawrence Dozier, was known as a place that had been used by Lewis Robinson as a shooting range for his Medgar Evers Rifle Club.[25]

A neighbor of the Dozier farm told the FBI that on Sunday, July 14, he heard rifle fire coming from the Dozier property. "He advised that the firing was extremely concentrated and lasted for over an hour," the FBI report said. "He expressed the opinion that the weapons being used were probably of high velocity type." The sixteen-year-old who rented 12312 Auburndale Avenue, Leslie Jackson, known as Osu Bey, later told authorities that he had "been instructed by Ahmed and Sidney Taylor in the use of rifles at a farm in the country outside the City of Cleveland" just before the events on July 23.[26]

Sidney Taylor was the brother of James Taylor, the Muntu poet Amir Rashidd. Both were members of the New Libya organization. Sidney was known by the New Libyans as Malik Ali Bey.

On Monday, July 15, Evans submitted his second weekly payroll sheet to DeForest Brown at HADC. He also sought a check for $600 for unspecified "supplies and equipment."[27] All the checks were cashed the next day. At 7:30 PM on the night of July 16, Evans and two of his associates, James Dailey and James Mitchem, showed up at the sporting goods and tool department of an Uncle Bill's store in Mayfield Heights. Evans and Dailey each purchased two Marlin Glenfield Model 70 .22-caliber semiautomatic long rifles that were magazine fed (containing seven rounds), and a carton of five hundred rounds of .22 long rifle ammo. James Mitchem purchased a Stevens Savage slide-action shotgun, costing sixty-five dollars, and a box of ammunition. Evans bought several two-shot ammo belts and bandoliers to hold shotgun shells.[28]

The next evening, Evans appeared at the Sears Roebuck on Carnegie. It was nearly 9:00 PM, closing time. The salesman in the sporting division immediately recognized Evans from his photos in the newspapers. He came with at least four other young black men whom the salesman could not identify later. Evans purchased a .22 rifle and 150 rounds of ammunition, paying sixty dollars in cash.[29]

During these early weeks of July, a tall black man with a female companion, both wearing African garb, drove downtown to Adler's Sporting Goods on Prospect Avenue. They were met by one of the owners, Jim Newman, the first cousin of actor Paul Newman (the family was originally from Shaker Heights and owned several sporting goods stores). Newman served the black man who bought army surplus first-aid kits and pouches, pistol belts, and several fifteen-round carbine clips in two different visits to the store. The tall black man told a black salesman working with Newman that "there was going to be a big smash in Cleveland."[30]

At week's end, Friday evening, July 19, Evans traveled with two other men to the Northfield Road store of Forest City Materials Company in Bedford. Evans purchased a .22-caliber Marlin Carbine semiautomatic and five hundred rounds of ammunition. Evans used his driver's license for identification. His companions each bought a .22-caliber Marlin Carbine semiautomatic, with two hundred rounds of ammunition. One identified himself as Ralph Smith, living at 12312 Auburndale Avenue; the other James Mitchum of Ablewhite Road in Cleveland.

None of the salesmen for any of these sporting goods stores reported the heavy buying of guns and ammo to authorities, though they found the purchases, especially the amount of ammunition, alarming.

In nearby Akron, on Wednesday, July 17, race riots broke out between police and teenagers, and the mayor imposed a curfew. The disturbance continued for several days. One white tavern owner fired a shotgun at several black juveniles, wounding two with pellets. Almost 125 blacks were arrested, mainly for curfew violations. The National Guard was called in.[31] Ahmed Evans claimed that he went to Akron to support black nationalists there. According to his account, the police surrounded the Afro-American Liberation Society office in Akron, tossed tear gas inside, and then barricaded all the doors. "They blocked people inside for about 15 minutes," he told Dick Feagler of the *Cleveland Press*, "and then, when they were half-suffocated, they went inside and started hitting them with their Billy clubs. Women and kids too."

After the police left, Evans went in to help those who had been injured. "When we saw it, there was blood all over the floor," Evans remembered.[32]

On Saturday, July 20, Carl Stokes led hundreds of citizens in a long parade, commemorating the second anniversary of the Hough rebellion. The parade started off at the site of old League Park, where the Cleveland Indians and Cy Young once played—at Lexington and 66th—and marched down 66th to Hough Avenue, where it turned left to pass by the site where the Hough riots began. Then it continued east to Thurgood Marshall Playground at Hough and East 86th, where three thousand people greeted Stokes and his revelers.

The day was brilliant with the sun. Stokes walked in a tan summer business suit wearing a Cleveland: Now! button. A huge line of young men dressed in black, some with machetes, others with African drums, combat boots, and sunglasses, trooped not far behind Stokes in single file through the street in one continuous display of black power. The Cleveland Police Subversives Unit took photos and identified those they could: Sababa, Malik (Sidney Taylor), Omar, and Ronnie Pierce. When they finally reached Thurgood Marshall Playground, a group of teenage boys put on a machete ritual, twirling blades in the bright sun. Stokes stood at attention, looking uncomfortable, with Harllel Jones, goateed and wearing sunglasses, at his side.

One of the images from this parade that made it into the Cleveland newspapers the next day would haunt Stokes. A *Plain Dealer* photographer caught Stokes at Belvidere and 66th, shortly after the kickoff of the parade, with two of Harllel Jones's top lieutenants on each side of him: Omar Majid and Sababa Akili. Majid and Akili were dressed in dark paramilitary outfits with ammunition belts—with rifles slung over their shoulders.[33]

The police were horrified. They told the *Cleveland Press* that the rifles were "real," not ceremonial.[34] There they were: Negroes with guns—in Hough. And the mayor seemed to endorse them. The stars were about to turn blue.

24

"Having a Gun
Is No Crime"

Osu Bey (Leslie Jackson), the teenager who rented the Auburndale apartments, had been advised in mid-June that he was going to be evicted. Not only was the rent months overdue, but the owner was concerned that Osu Bey was running a flophouse. "There would be as many as eight to ten couples there," the owner complained to reporters from the *Plain Dealer*. "Only three months before, I was fined $40 in court for allowing a tenant in another building to turn his apartment into a rooming house. I didn't want any more trouble with the building department or court."[1]

On Monday, July 22, the eviction case came up in Cleveland Municipal Court and a red notice of eviction was authorized for service that day with a Wednesday eviction deadline.[2]

Time had run out. A "racial informant," whose identity remains obscured, provided the FBI with a running report of what was happening at 12312 Auburndale during the day and into the evening of July 22. The situation worsened as the day progressed.

The informant spent "most of the morning and afternoon of July 22, 1968, at 12312 Auburndale [Avenue], Cleveland, Ohio, which was the residence of Fred 'Ahmed' Evans and some of his followers in the New Libya organization," the FBI report stated. "Source relates that while no organized meetings were held during this period it was obvious from general conversation with Evans and others at the residence that they were planning to create trouble in the immediate future."[3] The informant saw several of the "brothers" bringing weapons and ammunition into the apartment house.

Carl Stokes started the day in Public Square, attending a small ceremony next to the statue of General Moses Cleaveland, founder of the city. A group sponsored by the Early Settlers' Association was celebrating the 172nd anniversary of the birth of the city of Cleveland. General Cleaveland arrived on July 22, 1796. The group presented a new bronze marker that recognized that the Settlers' Association had dedicated the statue of Moses Cleaveland on July 22, 1882. "Yesterday's observance may have been the only display of civic pride on the city's birthday," a reporter at the *Cleveland Press* lamented.[4]

The mayor was scheduled to speak the next day in Washington, DC, at a lunch seminar at the Sheraton Park Hotel, sponsored by the International Platform Association, an organization of public speakers. Stokes would appear with three other mayors—Kevin White of Boston, Joseph Alioto of San Francisco, and Walter E. Washington of Washington, DC. Their topic was "Is the Big City Dying?"[5]

Evans submitted his third payroll sheet to HADC on Monday, July 22. HADC made out checks that day, though it doesn't appear that they were picked up by Evans and his group until the next day.[6]

As the day wore on, heavy winds and rain pelted Cleveland. A half inch of rain fell in ninety minutes in the afternoon, and wind gusts of 60 mph tore off roofs and knocked down utility lines and trees. The line of thunderstorms sparked some tornados in Ohio, breaking an insufferable ninety-degree heat in Cleveland.[7]

By early evening, things had grown so tense at the Auburndale apartments that the FBI informant took a risk and left at 7:30 PM to call Special Agent John Sullivan by phone. He told him that violence was imminent. Sullivan instructed the informant to return to the apartments and "stay with the group to learn details of any plot." The informant agreed, even though he worked a night shift at his regular job.[8]

Sullivan in turn reported what he had learned to Sergeant John Ungvary of the Special Investigations Unit of the Cleveland Police Department as soon as he got off the phone with the informant.

The informant made his way back to the Auburndale apartments around 8:30 PM. He would later report that twelve of the "brothers" were present when he returned. He spoke with Ahmed Evans and learned that Evans was leaving for an odyssey that night—he planned to drive to Detroit, then back to Akron and then Pittsburgh before returning to Cleveland. "Ahmed told the source that the purpose of the trip was to contact the 'brothers' in those cities to make sure that they would be ready to 'start shooting' when Cleveland 'jumped off,'" the FBI report read.[9] It seemed an improbable trip (Detroit is 168 miles from Cleveland, Akron 191 miles from Detroit, and Pittsburgh 109 miles from Akron), but Evans asked the source to go with him.

Evans told the informant that a riot was supposed to kick off on the morning of July 24 when bailiffs came to enforce the eviction notice. He laid out a dark plan of riot and destruction—not just in Cleveland, but in other major cities in the country—which was faithfully relayed by the informant to the FBI and then the Cleveland Police:

> Source was also informed by Ahmed that when the eviction notice was served the "brothers" would start shooting any white people in the Auburndale [Avenue] vicinity. At the same time "brothers" in the East 66th Street and Hough Avenue area would start shooting, others would start in East 105th and Superior area. Ahmed alleged that they planned to move eastward from Auburndale Avenue to Hayden Avenue, located in East Cleveland, a bordering suburb. Ahmed indicated that Harllel Jones' group, the Afro-American Set, had agreed to participate and also some of the "brothers" from the Black Cellar at East 116th Street and St. Clair Avenue, Cleveland, Ohio.
>
> Ahmed also told the source that as soon as the shooting started in Cleveland, "brothers" in Chicago, Detroit, New York, and Pittsburgh would "jump off." No details as to who would take part in the disturbances in these cities or where they would be instigated were revealed by Ahmed.[10]

Evans, the informant, and three others loaded into the Chevrolet station wagon recently purchased with Cleveland: Now! money and set off for Detroit, arriving around midnight. "They drove to a Negro area in Detroit and stopped outside a two-story brick apartment building," the FBI report records. "Ahmed went into the building alone, remained about five or ten minutes and then exited carrying two rifles, which he placed in the back of the wagon." Ahmed told the men in the station wagon, "The brothers in Detroit are waiting on us."

The travelers headed for Akron—about a three-hour drive. The informant said they reached Akron around 3:30 AM on July 23. They proceeded to a private house in an old neighborhood. Ahmed and one other entered the house, remained inside for twenty minutes and returned without any weapons. The informant thought the purpose of the stop was to pick up checks.

The group drove to Pittsburgh, arriving around 6:00 AM. They went to a brick apartment building "in a Negro neighborhood." Ahmed entered and immediately returned, saying no one was there.

They finally drove back to Cleveland. They took the weapons they had picked up into the living room of one of the downstairs apartments, where at least fifteen rifles had already been set out on the floor in plain sight.

Ahmed and his group drove on enough interstate trips that night to trigger the federal Anti-Riot Act, and unquestionably with this information there was more than probable cause for search warrants, if not arrests, just as there had been with Max Stanford and his group in New York. Yet that did not happen.

Ahmed and his band arrived back in Cleveland around 10:30 or 11:00 AM. Evans, the informant, and at least two others drove to the PRIDE Inc.'s office on East 79th Street near Hough Avenue to pick up additional checks from Cleveland: Now! The regular payroll checks were ready, but one other Evans requested would not be prepared until 1:30 PM. So Evans and the others took ten of the payroll checks to Society bank downtown and cashed them. They had $900 in cash.

Evans and the group walked over to a downtown department store, Higbee's, and took escalators to the sporting goods department on the fifth floor to look for more guns. A security guard saw them enter and followed them. Evans inspected a high-powered deer rifle with a scope, but found it too expensive, and they all left.[11]

The group walked east to the Army-Navy Store and to Adler's store on Prospect. Evans purchased four black bandoliers, three brown ammunition belts, and four ammunition magazines at the Army-Navy Store. The clerk working with Jim Newman that day at the Adler's store nearby identified Bernard Donald as one of the men with Evans. Bernard was the brother of Lathan Donald; Bernard would be killed later that night. To the New Libyans, Bernard was known as Nondu Bey, and his brother Lathan as Nondu El.

Evans purchased six thirty-round ammo clips, four first-aid kits, and three pistol belts at Adler's.[12] Evans told his men he would not purchase too much equipment at any one store so as to avoid suspicion.[13]

In the middle of this shopping spree, the informant again slipped away and called his FBI contact. "He advised that he wanted to meet with a Negro Agent near 12312 Auburndale to discuss the situation," the report stated. "He pointed out that meeting with a white Agent would entail too great a risk." The FBI suggested he meet with John Smith, a black policeman who worked with Sergeant Ungvary in the Subversives Unit.

In the meantime, red flares were starting to go off at city hall. The problem was—and this would have huge implications for what would follow—Carl Stokes was out of town. His participation in the mayors' panel on whether big cities were dying that morning in Washington, DC, left the city without his leadership. He was supposed to return to Cleveland by 2:30 or 3:00 PM, but his plane had engine trouble and was delayed. He would not make it back until 7:00 PM.

Stokes delivered a memorable line at the symposium. When asked about women who had children just to obtain welfare ("babies for profit"), he said the charge was exaggerated. Given how little aid was available for dependent children, it was not a sensible business decision, Stokes said, to have babies to make money. He understood the racist overtone of the inquiry and jabbed back, "There is less fraud in the welfare system than in big business."[14]

With Stokes out of town, per the city charter, the law director became acting mayor. That meant that a thirty-four-year-old African American lawyer, Clarence "Buddy" James, was in charge. He was smart and hardworking but highly inexperienced. He had gone to night law school at Cleveland State and graduated in 1962, just six years earlier. He worked as an investigator for the Court of Common Pleas before joining Legal Aid in 1963. He had little criminal law or police experience. Buddy James was Carl Stokes's second law director—his first choice, Paul D. White, quit after just a few months, supposedly over health.[15] Without his mayor, Buddy James would now face one of the sharpest crises in Cleveland's history.

The other major actor that day was the safety director, Joseph F. McManamon. McManamon had been a cop and then received his law degree, but he was white and from Cleveland's West Side, and he worried about taking any provocative action involving the black community without the blessing of Stokes.

This was a perfect storm. The police, especially those who were subordinate to the police chief—the elderly and heavy-drinking Michael Blackwell—had hard feelings about Stokes and his promises of civil service reforms. The point man for gathering most of the information on July 23 was Captain George Sperber, the head of police intelligence. Sperber was a hard-liner who chafed at the restructurings Stokes spoke of implementing. He was unhappy, for example, that Stokes discontinued the flying of helicopters over Hough and Glenville with searchlights at night to look for criminals. He had been appointed to the Cleveland Police Department in 1942, about the same time as John Ungvary. He developed a reputation as a "gladiator in the department's war against vice."[16]

A black sergeant, Bosie Mack, who served as bodyguard to Mayor Stokes, thought that Captain Sperber was passive-aggressive in the face of the threat posed by Ahmed Evans and his black nationalists that day. He wrote that Sperber failed to act without consulting city hall. Bosie Mack was not pleased. "I asked Sperber why we should take this to City Hall?" he wrote. "Sperber said because the Chief said so. I argued that this was a police problem and that he, as the intelligence boss, and the Chief, should work out a plan to eliminate the problem. Sperber said, 'That's up to the Chief.'"[17]

The first warnings at city hall on July 23 came from Sergeant Ungvary, who obviously had been in touch with FBI special agent

Sullivan the night before. Bosie Mack, Ungvary, Sperber, and Detective John Smith all went to see Chief Blackwell around 10:30 or 11:00 AM, which was just the time Evans and his men were returning to Cleveland. They called John Little, the mayor's executive assistant, and requested an emergency meeting with Little and Buddy James. Little recalled the meeting at City Hall began around 2:00 or 2:30 PM.[18]

Evans and his crew left Adler's Sporting Goods around 12:30 PM and drove back to Hough, stopping at East 66th and Hough, the place Evans was supposed to rent for his African culture shop. "Ahmed indicated that he wanted to see some 'brothers' there to make sure they were ready to join in the disturbance but he was unable to locate anybody," the FBI informant told Sullivan. "They then drove back to 12312 Auburndale, picking up a six pack of beer en route. Upon their return they went upstairs where they divided the equipment, loaded the weapons and put shells in the ammunition belts."[19]

The informant left the apartments to meet up with Detective Smith. "He furnished Detective Smith with pertinent details, including the fact that an arsenal of weapons was in the house," the FBI report stated. Ungvary called the FBI to tell them what Smith had learned. Ungvary told Special Agent Sullivan that he was "taking immediate action to secure a search warrant." But that didn't happen.

At city hall, John Little and law director and acting mayor Buddy James met with the police contingent. Detective Smith told Little and James that "an informant with whom he had personal contact" told them that there was to be "a five-city uprising Wednesday morning at 8:00 AM, involving Cleveland, Detroit, Akron, New York, and Chicago." Smith said that the informant had spent the preceding evening with Ahmed Evans, where they had smoked a lot of pot. Captain Sperber remarked that he wasn't sure if it was the pot speaking or reliable information coming from the informant.

The group was perplexed. Smith described the all-night car ride. As Little told an investigator later: "You can figure out that they couldn't possibly have gone to both Pittsburgh and Detroit. They may have gone to one or the other, but not both." They all started to question the veracity of the informant.

To check, the police sent officers over to Higbee's and Adler's Sporting Goods to confirm what the informant had said. The officers took photos of suspects with them to show the salesmen who had interacted with Evans and his group, but the salesmen mistakenly identified Harllel Jones and his two lieutenants—who were in the photo with Stokes at the Hough parade— not Evans and his men. Suspicion about the informant's story grew. Little remembered being told that the informant "was not overly bright."

The group was also told that the informant had said there were six individuals marked for assassination—all African Americans: Mayor Carl Stokes, Councilman Leo Jackson, PRIDE Inc.'s executive Baxter Hill, *Call and Post* publisher William O. Walker, and Officer William Payne.[20]

The city officials were also told the informant said that the disturbance on Wednesday morning was not really supposed to be an uprising. "It was supposed to be some kind of spot demonstration with some display of force," Little recalled. "As far as the informant could advise, it was not to be open warfare or anything; it was to be sort of a display of muscle with shooting, presumably with guns and so on, but not a major outbreak or revolution."

There was also some indication that Evans intended to go back to Detroit or Pittsburgh that night to pick up more weapons.

In the midst of this jumble of information, safety director McManamon made a fatal call. As the only seasoned lawyer in the room with a law enforcement background, he told the group that the nationalists had a constitutional right to have guns and that there was no evidence they possessed automatic weapons (like machine guns), which were illegal in Ohio at the time.

He had totally missed that it was the threat of imminent violence that justified a search warrant at the least. He also took no heed of the Anti-Riot Act that Congress had just passed. He had access to state or federal judges for immediate relief.

McManamon later told an investigator, "Having a gun today is no crime, you can't do anything about that; I don't know of any judge that would have given you a search warrant."[21]

Sergeant Ungvary was beside himself. He told the FBI that "officials at City Hall were thwarting his efforts to obtain a search warrant on the grounds of insufficient evidence and lack of local violation." Ungvary, the FBI report noted, was "openly critical of this action, pointing out that lives were at stake and the only sensible course of action was to confiscate the weapons before anything broke out."

Around this time, Buddy James spoke to Mayor Stokes in Washington, who was waiting at the airport for his plane to be fixed. Stokes told James to get ahold of Walter Beach and George Forbes, the councilman for Glenville, and get them to city hall. They would know what was happening on the street. James called them, and they began to make their way downtown.

After his meeting with Detective John Smith, the informant returned to the Auburndale apartments around 1:30 PM. He found that Ahmed Evans had left. Seven or eight nationalists were downstairs "talking generally about the planned disturbance."

Evans had gone back to get a check from Cleveland: Now! and to shop for more guns and ammunition. He picked up and cashed a check for $600 from Cleveland: Now! Then he drove about four miles to Heckman Arms Company, a storefront in East Cleveland on Hayden Avenue. He was served by George Heckman, the owner of the shop, who billed himself as a master gunsmith. Heckman remembered Evans entering his store around 2:00 PM. He came in, he said, with about five other "colored" men. Evans said he was looking for an M-1 carbine, a lightweight, semiautomatic .30-caliber rifle, the kind Evans would have trained on and used in his days in Korea.

The M-1 cost eighty dollars. Evans also purchased two boxes of .30-caliber ammunition containing fifty rounds each and one thirty-shot banana clip for the M-1.[22] The gun came with a fifteen-shot magazine already attached. The bullets were all soft or hollow points, the kind that are meant to expand or mushroom once they hit their target to maximize damage. The total bill was $104.84, which Evans paid in cash.[23]

One of the men with Evans, James Dailey, who gave his address as 12312 Auburndale, purchased a World War I–vintage British Lee–Enfield Mk III rifle, costing thirty-two dollars. Heckman also sold Dailey ammunition for the British gun (eighty bullets) and .222 Remington bullets (twenty rounds).

These transactions took ten minutes, and then the men left.

Evans and Dailey returned about two hours later and purchased two Remington Model 760 .30-06 pump-action rifles, popular with big game hunters, costing $134.95 each. From army surplus, Evans bought a metal can of three hundred rounds of .30-06-caliber armor-piercing bullets for these rifles. The men also bought eighty rounds of British .303 bullets, fifty rounds of .30-caliber bullets, two hundred rounds of carbine ammunition, and three boxes of 410-gauge shotgun shells. Evans paid for it all with fifty- and twenty-dollar bills.

Heckman was virtually wiped out of ammunition in his store with these sales—yet he did nothing to notify authorities. The sales were all lawful.

The informant told the FBI that Evans returned to the Auburndale apartments around 4:00 PM with five or six rifles. Evans said a meeting in a park that night had been canceled but a planning meeting was to be held that night in the apartments. Several "brothers" showed up armed with weapons. "Source advised that there were approximately 15 brothers in the apartment and Ahmed began giving instructions to be carried out during the disturbance," the FBI report read. "Ahmed stated that his instructions were 'hit and fade.' He explained this tactic by saying that the 'brothers' should get out on the street, fire at the 'beast' from positions behind bushes, trees, or other type cover and then disappear from the location and reappear in some other spot to repeat firing at the 'beast.'"

Evans told the group that when the Cleveland shooting started, "brothers" in other cities would follow suit. He mentioned Chicago, Detroit, New York City, and Pittsburgh. "Ahmed also revealed that plans had been made to assassinate Carl B. Stokes, Negro mayor of Cleveland; Leo Jackson, Negro city councilman, and William O. Walker, Negro publisher of *Call and Post*, weekly Negro Cleveland newspaper," the FBI report noted. "He characterized these Negroes as Uncle Toms." Patrolman Payne was also identified for assassination, per the informant. There were rumors that gunmen from Detroit had arrived that day.

George Forbes and Walter Beach reached city hall in the mid-afternoon. Neither man could confirm what the informant was saying.

The group decided to establish surveillance around the Auburndale apartments and to possibly follow Evans should he drive to Detroit or Pittsburgh that night. There was heavy debate about the surveillance. Sergeant Ungvary "violently objected to the surveillance," per the FBI report, "because of the probability that it would be made and the lives of the men on the surveillance would be in extreme jeopardy."[24] Others worried the surveillance would be noticed and could provoke a show-down with heavily armed men.

The conclusion was to establish a "roving" surveillance, with cars driving through the neighborhood. But that is not what happened. Whether intentionally or not, the Cleveland Police set up two unmarked cars on street corners near the Auburndale apartments, each occupied with white men with binoculars and shotguns. Evans and his followers noticed, according to the informant. "Source advised that Ahmed then began to make plans to take action against these cars."[25] The fuse was lit.

Walter Beach and George Forbes were dispatched on a mission to try to calm the situation. Both remember the time as approximately 6:00 PM. They drove in Beach's 1965 Pontiac from city hall and stopped first at Harllel Jones's Afro Set store on 82nd and Superior. Jones was not there, but one of his lieutenants, Omar Majid (Elijah Irvin), was there and he agreed to accompany Forbes and Beach to Auburndale. Majid was aware that Evans was angry about the coming eviction.

When they pulled up to the Auburndale apartments, Ahmed Evans was standing outside next to the house holding a rifle with bandoliers strapped across his chest. Other nationalists were in the back, also armed with rifles. Beach and Forbes noticed the surveillance cars. "The beast is out there," Evans said to them. "They won't run me off the face of the earth no matter what."[26]

Speaking to Forbes, Evans said the cops were everywhere—even on rooftops. He said whites were intent on "pushing black folks off the face of the earth." He told Forbes, "We've got a right to live." Forbes later said to an investigator, "It boils down to the same damn thing, you know what I mean? He was trying to look out for his group." Evans discussed the eviction notice they had received and Forbes asked to see the red tag, which Evans brought out from the house. Forbes told him to keep things cool and he would try to get the eviction called off. He recognized that Evans was "caught in between" with nowhere to go, given his eviction from his astrology store and the fact the landlady reneged on the agreement on the Hough store.

But Forbes and Beach saw something else: Evans wanted out of the situation he was in. Evans told them of what he had witnessed in Akron just days earlier where police "had come in and ripped people's hair and beat the shit out of them," Forbes recalled. Evans felt he was being surrounded and about to be attacked by the police.

"Now pull out the beasts," Evans implored Forbes, looking for some face-saving act.

"I can't recall the exact words," Forbes would explain, "but as men talking to men, Ahmed was telling me that he wanted out of this shit, really, he really wanted out of it."[27]

Forbes, Beach, and Omar Majid walked back to Beach's car and Evans called out, "Tell the Big Brother downtown [Stokes] that everything is going to be all right." As they drove away, Forbes told Beach to stop for one moment as he thought of asking the cops in the surveillance cars to move out, but because they weren't regular beat cops he knew, he didn't do it. He noticed they were busy taking down the license plate number from Beach's car.

Forbes would always regret his decision not to at least try to get them to move out.

In the backyard of 12312 Auburndale, at least twenty to thirty nationalists dressed for guerrilla war with rifles and bandoliers became restless. A fifteen-year-old boy in an adjoining backyard talked with several of the nationalists over the fence. He asked why they had guns. One said they were "sick and tired of it." The other said, "It started 200 years ago."[28]

25

"Tow Truck in Trouble"

THE INFORMANT SENSED VIOLENCE WAS imminent. Around 7:45 PM ten to twelve nationalists were armed and ready to go in the Auburndale apartments; many were also in the backyard. Evans had sent five or six members out to get additional weapons and equipment fifteen minutes earlier. As Ahmed was giving final instructions on the action to be taken against the police surveillance cars, the informant quietly slipped out of the house, unobserved. He ran to a nearby telephone booth and called Detective Smith, giving a full report. "Detective Smith told him to get out of the area at once, which he did," the FBI report stated. "As he was running away, he heard shots."

The officers in Car 961 at the corner of 124th Street and Auburndale Avenue observed "a single colored male" come out of the Auburndale apartments carrying a carbine before any shooting began. He was dressed in an "Afro robe and dark pants." He stood on the sidewalk as if to take up an armed guard or sentry position. Car 961 radioed to headquarters.

Suddenly, within minutes, Evans emerged "followed by 16 to 18 colored males, some dressed in Afro robes," said Patrolman James O'Malley, one of three white officers in Car 961. "One in particular had a leopard-skin covering, I'd call it."[1] The man in the leopard-skin top was Lathan Donald, Evans's first lieutenant, known as Nondu El. He had just turned eighteen a month earlier. Like many in this group, including his brother Bernard, Lathan had injected himself with a heavy dose of heroin just before leaving the apartment building.[2]

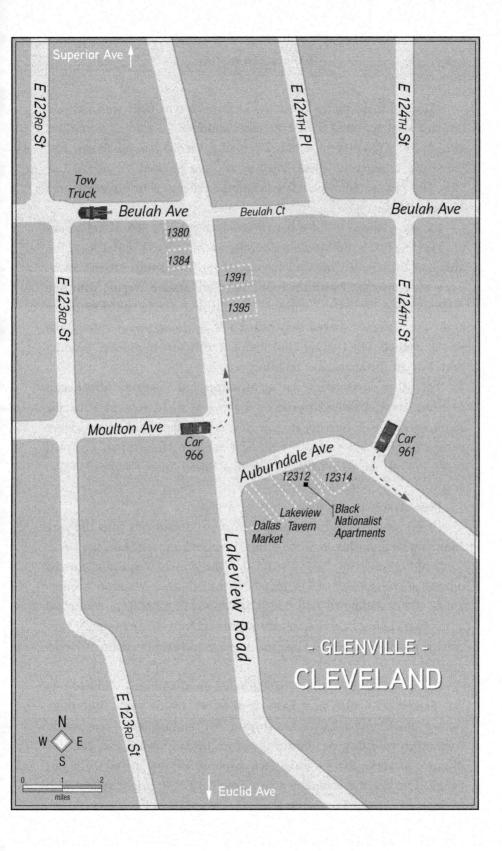

"Most of these males had army khaki web-type belts with first-aid kits and what appeared to be canteens, bandoleers of ammunition, shot-gun shells," O'Malley reported. They all gathered around Evans, and the sentry crossed the street, knelt down, and pointed his rifle at Car 961. The police radio hissed with another message to leave the area immediately.[3]

Car 961 radioed to the other surveillance car, Car 966, at the corner of Lakeview Road and Moulton Avenue, warning it to likewise leave the area and then pulled out and turned left up Auburndale to get away. They were pursued by a brown and tan Ford station wagon, with one male hanging out of the window brandishing a rifle. As they drove away, the officers believed they heard a shot, though their automobile was unscathed. The trailing Ford then abruptly turned around, heading back toward the apartment building.

The other surveillance car at Moulton and Lakeview also began to drive away, heading north on Lakeview Road toward Superior Avenue. The two officers in Car 966 reported that they also were being followed by a green Chevy and were being fired upon. "I heard shots, but our car didn't receive any hits," Patrolman Thomas Horgan reported.[4]

Both stake-out cars made clean getaways.

In the meantime, Evans and his group fanned out into the sur-rounding neighborhood. Some jumped fences and went into the back-yards of homes facing Lakeview Road. Others, including Evans, moved out to Lakeview Road, and he may have turned down Moulton Avenue, a side street leading to East 123rd Street. Or he may have continued with others down Lakeview Road toward Superior. In any event, Evans carried the M-1 carbine he had just purchased that afternoon at Heck-man's.

Earlier in the day, police had ticketed an abandoned Cadillac that was parked on Beulah near East 123rd Street, which was a little more than a block and a half away from 12312 Auburndale—one would walk north on Lakeview and turn west on Beulah toward East 123rd, a distance of about five hundred feet. Around 3:45 PM a tow truck was assigned to tow the abandoned car. Tow Truck 58, bright yellow with flashing red lights and "Cleveland Police Department" stenciled on the side, arrived around 8:15 PM, just as Evans and his followers had started to spread out into the neighborhood. The timing appears to have been purely coincidental.

Joseph Turpin, who worked as a special policeman at the Cleveland Workhouse where Ahmed Evans had spent time, lived on Lakeview Road, one house from the corner of Lakeview and Beulah Avenue. Sunset would not be until 8:52 PM that night. That evening, Turpin, who was black, was sitting on a slab in front of his house (in front of which he had built a little store) when he noticed two men trotting down Lakeview Road, dressed in black, and carrying rifles. Another nationalist, he recalled, was on the other side of the street, as if he came from the backyards of houses on Lakeview.[5]

A fifty-three-year-old white widow living next to Turpin on the corner of Beulah and Lakeview, Edithe B. Schepperd, happened to be sitting on her front porch reading a gospel magazine. She looked up and noticed a black male coming down Lakeview, who stopped right in front of her house, looking down Beulah, leaning against her front fence. Two other black males were across the street on the north side of Beulah, crouched near bushes. They all smiled at each other.

Edithe thought the black man was "fine featured," handsome. He was "colored with a beard about 3-4 inches long," she told the police, "with dark brown skin, and a black type uniform with red trim." At first she thought the man had an ornament around his neck. "I called it a belt," she said, "and I thought it was prettily decorated." When the man started pulling bullets or shells from the belt, she realized it was a bandolier.

The man then stiffened and shot three times in the direction of the tow truck. All three men proceeded to zig-zag their way down the street, as in a military operation. She told police, "They looked like expertly trained guerrillas."[6]

The tow truck operators, who were not policemen and carried no weapons, were nevertheless dressed in uniforms that made it appear they were policemen. They had pulled their tow truck next to the Cadillac, which was facing west toward East 123rd. The Cadillac had a car parked in front of it, so the tow truck pushed it back with its front fender to create space. The truck then turned around to back up to the Cadillac.

William McMillin was out of the truck standing next to the Cadillac with his back to Lakeview Road when he felt a blast strike him in the back. He had been hit by pellets from a shotgun. McMillin immediately started running toward the front of the tow truck, when he was hit two more times with shotgun pellets. He scrambled in front of the truck and crouched down to get out of the line of fire coming from Lakeview Road.

He yelled to his partner in the tow truck, Ray Bensley, to call for help, that he had been shot. At precisely 8:24 PM, Bensley radioed, "Tow truck in trouble, 123rd and Beulah, they're shooting!"

The dispatcher responded: "All cars, 508 go ahead, 507, 513, 508, 507, 505."

Bensley screamed, "Hurry up. Step on it!"

As McMillin hid in front of the tow truck, he was hit a fourth time by shotgun pellets from a shooter in bushes under a tree on the north side of Beulah. He looked up and saw a man he would later identify as Fred Ahmed Evans walking down the sidewalk on Beulah, coming from Lakeview toward him with a carbine in his hand (another version has him coming down 123rd). "There's one of those son-of-a-bitches who's stealing cars," the man growled, and shot at McMillin. McMillin pled with him, holding up his hands and saying he was not armed, but the man kept coming, firing his weapon.[7]

McMillin arose and started running down East 123rd when he was hit once on his right side by a bullet from a rifle. The man with the carbine fired four or five more times but all shots missed. McMillin ran down 123rd, where "an old colored woman" motioned him into her house.

Back in front of the Auburndale apartments, a twenty-five-year-old African American male named Charles Lee Teel was driving down Auburndale in his 1965 Chevrolet from East Cleveland, where he had just visited his grandmother. He drove northwest on Auburndale, passing in front of 12312 Auburndale, the apartment from which Fred Ahmed Evans and his nationalists had just dispersed into the neighborhood.

Teel encountered a small traffic jam—a 1961 green Chevy, presumably the car that had just chased stake-out Car 966 down Lakeview, had been slammed into reverse and backed onto Auburndale.[8] The green Chevy was being driven by a woman who was trying to turn the car around in the middle of Auburndale. She motioned for Charles Teel to move back toward East 124th, so she could turn around. Teel complied and then he proceeded to Lakeview and turned right, heading north toward Superior.

Teel immediately saw a line of young black men with rifles in what he took to be an army formation ahead of him on Lakeview. Teel had been in the army for three years and was a cadet at the East Cleveland police academy. "I noticed they were in a skirmish formation," he told police, "that is, a line across of at least five men. This was a military-type formation."[9]

Charles Teel saw the skirmishers start to fire at someone or something behind his car, though he didn't see whom. Teel worried he might be caught in cross fire, so he accelerated past them and took the first left he could—which happened to be right on Beulah Avenue where the tow truck had been under fire. He pulled up next to the tow truck and noticed its windshield was being riddled with bullets, coming from an area in front of the truck, which was facing west toward 123rd Street. This was the start of a firefight: the policemen in Car 966 were exchanging gunfire with nationalists taking cover behind the tow truck.

Stake-out Car 966, after leaving the area via Superior, circled back around when the patrolmen heard over the radio that the tow truck operators were in trouble. Patrolmen Thomas Horgan and Thomas Gerrity turned Car 966 east on Moulton, then sped north on 123rd toward Beulah. About three houses from the corner, they came under heavy fire and stopped. Patrolman Horgan got out of the car on the passenger side with a shotgun. Gerrity jumped from the driver's side with his .38 revolver. They arrived just in time to see the tow truck operator, William McMillin, raise his hands, begging "Don't shoot," after which he turned and began running north on 123rd—this is when McMillin was shot in his right side.

Horgan and Gerrity opened up at the same time that Charles Teel was pulling up next to the tow truck, shooting at nationalists who had taken refuge behind the tow truck. Car 966 was likewise riddled with return fire. After a quick exchange, the two officers ran out of ammunition and decided to get out fast and drove to the Beulah intersection and turned left away from the tow truck as their car continued to be struck with gunfire. They got to East 109th and Superior when their car broke down, its radiator pierced with bullets. At 8:28 PM, they radioed several messages, the last being, "966—the car is shot up, but we're OK."[10] This was just four minutes after the first distress call from the tow truck.

As Car 966 sped away, Teel jumped out of his car on the driver's side, using the door of his car as a shield. He ducked into the backyard of the house on the southwest corner of Beulah and 123rd. The yard was directly behind Edithe Schepperd's home and garage.

Teel crouched down and kept his eyes on his car and the tow truck to try to see what was going on when he heard an ominous sound— a jingling sound. To his trained military ear, it was the "noise loose cartridges would make." Teel turned around and standing right behind him was Fred Ahmed Evans, carbine in hand, loading a new magazine. He looked directly into Teel's eyes, and Teel was sure he was going to kill him.

But he didn't—he walked past him toward Teel's car and the tow truck from the back of the house on 123rd and Beulah. Teel quickly skirted around to the front of the corner house and knocked, but no one answered. He scrambled to the porch of the house next door on 123rd and frantically knocked. A man with two young daughters let him in.

Before he ducked in the house, he saw a large police paddy wagon— a GMC utility vehicle—driving up 123rd to the Beulah intersection. Vehicle 591 was being driven by Patrolman Joseph McManamon while Patrolman Chester Szukalski was riding in the passenger seat. They were responding to the call that the tow truck was in trouble. Just as Teel was entering the house, he heard a burst of gunfire. He dove inside and heard a crash outside. Vehicle 591 had been shot up, some of the fire coming from bullets later identified by a ballistics expert as having come from Evans's M-1 carbine rifle.[11]

In the wagon, Patrolman Szukalski was hit with a round that went through his door and into his right arm. He and his partner began to lay low in Vehicle 591, when Szukalski was hit a second time in the hip. In the commotion to escape the vehicle, Szukalski's service revolver was knocked off his belt and fell to the floor. Both men crawled out of the car on the driver's side as the vehicle continued, driverless, through the intersection, coming to rest on the other side of the Beulah at a dog-leg. Szukalski was left exposed in the street without a weapon where he took another bullet in his leg, shattering it. Charles Teel looked out and saw him in the street with rounds exploding around him. Szukalski was in agony, shouting for someone to assist him, bleeding profusely from his wounds, as he attempted to drag himself out of the intersection.[12]

Szukalski's partner, Joe McManamon, was grazed on his right hand with a bullet, but he ran behind a car on Beulah and fired at a shooter in the backyard of the house on the southwest corner—where Charles Teel had run into Ahmed Evans.[13] At this point, Evans claimed his M-1 jammed from all his firing, and he couldn't fix it. He jumped a fence and broke into Officer Turpin's side door at 1384 Lakeside, eventually making his way to the attic.[14]

Two policemen from Car 615, Robert Zagore and Richard Tanski, came on foot to the northeast corner of 123rd and Beulah, having parked their vehicle back near Superior on Lakeside. They saw Chester Szukalski prone in the street, screaming for help as the ground around him was "blowing up" from bullets being shot at him. Patrolman Zagore spied two to three black males standing at the corner of Lakeside and Beulah shooting with rifles in his direction. He and his partner, Patrolman Tanski, were pinned down behind a concrete curb, as bushes near them were being chopped away from the barrage of bullets from the national-ists. Zagore and Tanski fired back with their pistols and a shotgun they brought from their car.

The nationalists fled across the street up Beulah Court into the back-yards behind a three-story brick apartment building at 1391 Lakeview and a white frame house next door, 1395 Lakeview. Zagore and Tanski split up, with Zagore pursuing the nationalists across to Lakeview and Tanski moving south on 123rd toward Moulton. Before leaving, they helped load Szukalski and his partner in a police wagon that took them to a nearby hospital. They then relieved the tow truck driver hiding in the truck, who frantically scrambled out of the area.

Moments later, Harold Butler, who was responding on Motor Scooter 5S3, ditched his scooter a block west of 123rd on Beulah. Butler snuck up toward the intersection of 123rd and Beulah with his revolver. Somewhere along Beulah before reaching Lakeview, he beheld a nationalist with bandoliers who was spread-eagled on the north side of Beulah on the sidewalk or tree lawn with his gun under him; Butler assumed he was dead. This was Leroy Williams, known to the New Libyans as Amir ibn Khatib.[15] In all likelihood he was hit in the exchange with Car 966, the stake-out car that had returned in support and battled with nationalists who took cover behind the tow truck.[16]

Butler, an African American, continued east on Beulah to Lakeview, where he began to see tracer bullets coming from behind buildings across the street.[17] Evans must have fled by this time, as Butler did not confront him. After crossing Lakeview and running into the backyards of the buildings facing Lakeview, Butler discovered a nationalist who was firing one of the most fearsome weapons of the night—a Remington high-powered .30-06 pump-action rifle. Butler took cover behind the apartment building next door at 1391, as the nationalist shot at police in the street in front of the house.

Without yelling to the nationalist to drop his gun, Butler unloaded his .38 Smith & Wesson revolver, firing all six shots at the nationalist from thirty feet away. He did not know if he hit him. When later asked why he hadn't shouted a warning before shooting, Butler replied, "We weren't playing cowboys and Indians." Butler ran back in front of the apartment building to reload and joined other officers who were starting to assemble there.

Patrolman Zagore, after releasing the tow truck driver, crept through yards and over garage rooftops, following the path the nationalists took across Lakeview up Beulah Court, eventually emerging in front of the white frame house at 1395 Lakeview—the building from which sniper fire was now popping. On his way up Beulah, Zagore also had seen the body of Leroy Williams on the sidewalk on the northern side of Beulah.

Simultaneously, as all this was going on during a highly compressed period, two zone cars and one unmarked police car came screaming up Lakeview toward the intersection with Auburndale, arriving from the south. The first was Car 508, its appearance coinciding roughly with Charles Teel's turnoff onto Beulah.[18] Near the intersection of Auburndale and Lakeview, Car 508 was hit at least eighteen times with bullets coming from the nationalists in front of the car on Lakeview. One bullet pierced the roof of Car 508, apparently coming from Auburndale or the tower at the Lakeview Tavern.[19] The two officers "scooted down" in Car 508 and barreled through at a high speed north on Lakeview to the safety of Superior Avenue.[20]

Right behind Car 508 was a 1964 black-and-white police station wagon, Car 505, with Willard Wolff and Kenny Gibbons responding. Wolff was driving. Two car lengths behind Wolff and Gibbons was an unmarked 1966 Plymouth, Car 65E, with detectives Viola and Bennett in it.

Willie Wolff stopped Car 505 in the street at the intersection of Auburndale and Lakeview, near a tavern on the corner called the Lakeview Tavern. His partner Kenny Gibbons later testified, "As we were driving down Lakeview, I heard two shots go off; our car was slowing, and when we got to the corner of Auburndale, we stopped and my attention was grabbed by a plainclothesman making gestures to me."[21] Gibbons and Wolff exited Car 505 and Gibbons told Wolff, "Watch yourself, Willie."

The plainclothesman, who Gibbons assumed was a detective, was distinctive: tall—maybe six feet, four inches—blond hair, crew cut. He held a pistol on a black man who was on the ground in front of 12312 Auburndale. He told Gibbons to take his place so he could find a paddy wagon or police cruiser to take the prisoner. The tall man ran off.

As the man was running away, Gibbons felt a slight tap on his stomach. He reached with his free hand and found that he "was covered with blood." He turned and began to run back toward his car and Lakeview Tavern. He was hit six more times by rifle fire from the Auburndale apartments.[22]

Willie Wolff was hit with a rifle bullet right between his eyes and he dropped instantly, mortally wounded, in the fenced-in areas in front of the Auburndale apartments.[23]

At the same time that Wolff and Gibbons disappeared around the corner toward the Auburndale apartments, Jerry Viola and Bob Bennett

in Car 65E pulled up several car lengths behind. When they turned
a bend in Lakeview Road, they came under fire from tracer bullets,
which they thought were coming from the apartment buildings on their
right. Detective Bennett on the passenger side had already unlocked the
shotgun from its rack in the car and was shooting out of his window at
nationalists near the Lakeview Tavern. Viola stopped Car 65E near an
opening south of the intersection in between the Dallas Market (a store
that adjoined the Lakeview Tavern on the corner) and a three-story
apartment building on Lakeview. Bennett radioed, "Get some cars down
here, 65E, they're shooting carbines." The time was 8:27 PM, just three
minutes after the first call from the tow truck that they were in trouble.

Donald Simone, a civilian across the street visiting family, saw Car
65E come to an abrupt stop. He noticed three black males with rifles and
bandoliers in the middle of the intersection of Lakeview and Auburndale, who presumably arrived just after Wolff and Gibbons had run in
the direction of the Auburndale apartments. Simone said these black
men in the street began to "fire heavily" in the direction of Car 65E. He
saw the police jump out of their car, shout a warning to the nationalists,
and then return fire.[24]

Jerry Viola and his partner started to reload near the alley next to
the Dallas Market. Viola remembers seeing Willie Wolff in a crouched
position in the driveway between the Auburndale apartments and the
Lakeview Tavern, holding his pistol on several nationalists with long
rifles through his vantage point of the alley, moments before Wolff was
killed.[25] "Drop your guns," Wolff was shouting.

Viola returned to Car 65E to get more ammunition from the trunk
when Kenny Gibbons came staggering around the corner in front of
the Lakeview Tavern and Dallas Market. He was bleeding profusely,
hunched over with his revolver dangling from his right hand. "I am
shot, I am shot," Gibbons kept repeating. Viola, a champion wrestler
and weight lifter, threw Gibbons over his shoulder and placed him in
Car 65E. He and Bennett took Gibbons to a nearby hospital. At 8:31
PM, seven minutes after the first tow truck call for help, Bennett radioed: "We've got a policeman shot in the car and we're taking him to
Lakeside Hospital."[26]

Through the phalanx of police cars now gathering on Lakeview came Car 515, responding from an assignment near the Cleveland Clinic. Two officers, Joseph Torok and Louis Golonka, heard the call from the tow truck and drove east on Euclid before turning north onto Lakeview. As they navigated their way through the cars already there, they heard a call that a man with a machine gun was at East 109th and Superior, so Car 515 continued up to Superior and drove to East 109th. Turned out no shooter was there, so they reversed their course and drove back up Superior to Lakeview, where they got out of their car to walk on foot. Lakeview was now choked with police cars.

Golonka, who had been the passenger in Car 515, unlocked the shotgun from its rack in the car and took it with him. Car 508, the original car that raced past the shooters on Lakeview without stopping—and was hit eighteen times—had stopped near where Golonka and his partner, Joseph Torok, were on Lakeview. Car 508's radiator was steaming. Patrolman Simms from Car 508 and his partner exited and joined Golonka, Torok, and several other officers who had started to gather near Superior and Lakeview. They all started trotting toward Auburndale. As they reached Beulah, they experienced heavy firing and the officers scattered in different directions, taking cover where they could.[27]

Golonka ran back behind some of the houses on the eastern side of Lakeview. Directly behind him was Amos Floyd, who had joined the group that gathered on the north end of Lakeview. Floyd, an African American, was a special-duty vice squad cop who just happened to be in the area when he noticed a large number of police vehicles congregating near Superior and Lakeview. He parked his car and caught up with Patrolman Golonka on foot. He was three to four feet behind him when Golonka turned the corner at the rear of 1391 Lakeview, a brick apartment building.

Floyd heard shotgun blasts, as Golonka was hit at least twice from a shooter in the yard behind 1395. He fell back, landing in a sitting position against the corner of the building, his shotgun lying across his lap.

Golonka's partner, Joe Torok, was on Lakeview when he heard someone holler, "There is a policeman shot!" Torok ran behind 1391, near Floyd and other officers now bunched in the area, and shouted at a sitting Golonka, but got no answer. Torok asked other officers for cover and he and Floyd got down on their bellies and crawled to Golonka. Floyd described it as a "shooting gallery" with bullets flying in both directions between the backyards of 1391 and 1395.

Golonka was still breathing but with difficulty. The pellets had perforated his pericardial sac, both lungs, and his ascending aorta. He was experiencing massive internal hemorrhaging.[28] Torok took the shotgun in his lap and handed it back to officers behind him. He and Floyd then grabbed Golonka by his shoulders and feet and started dragging him to the front of the house amid a hail of bullets.

Amos Floyd was now joined by Patrolman Zagore, whom he had worked with before. Because of the intense fire from 1395, they decided to kick in the rear door of 1391 to see if they could find a better vantage point of what was going on in the backyard of 1395. They moved from the kitchen area to a dining room that had a large window with curtains. When they pulled back the curtains, they could see two nationalists in the backyard of 1395, one of them Lathan Donald, the other probably his brother Bernard.

At that moment, the nationalists fired, shattering the window and sending the officers diving for the floor. Slowly, they regrouped, and Zagore and Floyd shot at the nationalists with their revolvers. After this, Zagore saw the two nationalists still crouched next to 1395 with their weapons in hand.

Zagore then rose up with a semiautomatic shotgun and fired four times, hitting both nationalists, who fell to the ground. "I got them," he shouted to the officers outside 1391.

Around this time, Officer Peter Ventura arrived in Car 611, came up along the bushes between 1391 and 1395, and saw a nationalist with his rifle coming out of a back window, one leg in, one out, behind 1395. The nationalist fired at Ventura and Ventura shot back with one blast of his shotgun, causing, he believed, the nationalist to fall out of the window. He hollered for tear gas canisters, which were thrown to him. He then hugged the wall of 1395 and tried to lob tear gas in a window from close range. "As soon as I threw a tear gas," he later testified, "a hand stuck out and shot down at me." After firing multiple shots, a black male poked his head out and Ventura shot at him with a shotgun, causing the black male to fall back into the building.[29]

Slowly, a group of officers behind 1391 began to creep around to inspect the damage behind 1395 after Zagore yelled "I got them." They heard moaning and one person saying, "Ali, Ali, Ali," likely in reference to Sidney Taylor (Malik Ali Bey). As the officers got closer, one of the nationalists with a red shirt (Bernard Donald) raised his head and grabbed for his rifle. Several officers fired at him, including Officer Simms, who had been given Golonka's shotgun.[30]

Bernard Donald (Nondu Bey), Lathan Donald (Nondu El) and Sidney Taylor (Malik Ali Bey), all now lay behind 1395. Bernard was badly shot up, with a massive head wound. Sidney Taylor also had suffered multiple gunshots, including a fatal blast or blasts from a shotgun (six shotgun pellets were recovered from his brain) to the left side of his head. Officer Simms described him as having had "half his head shot off." There is some question of when the head shots were fired—some contend these shots came later, applied as a "coup de grace" by officers clearing out the backyard behind 1395.

Somehow, Lathan Donald was still alive, though he had been hit multiple times.[31]

Most of the action now began to shift to Auburndale. Dusk and darkness were fast approaching. As he was leaving the first-floor apartment at 1391, Amos Floyd, an African American policeman, heard what sounded like "small voices" coming from one of the rooms. He opened the door and found three young black children lying on the floor and he began to comfort them. He said to the kids, "Stay on your hands and knees and crawl with me," as he led them to the front door. Along the way, he ran into the terrified mother of the children, and she joined them. Policemen at the front of 1391 took them all to safety.

Across the street Ahmed Evans hid in the attic of the home owned by Joseph Turpin at 1384 Lakeview. At several points he came downstairs to ask Turpin through a locked door on the second floor to call the police so he could surrender.[32]

Next door, Edithe B. Schepperd read her Bible, said her prayers, and went to bed.

26

"This Is Only the Beginning"

AHMED EVANS HAD LEFT BEHIND two of his youngest followers to protect the women and children in 12312 Auburndale. Leslie Jackson (Osu Bey) and John Hardrick (Little Ahmed) were both minors. Osu Bey was just sixteen; John Hardrick was seventeen. Hardrick's sisters Linda and Sandra lived in the apartments. Sandra Hardrick, known as Simba, was "married" to Ahmed Evans and had a two-year-old, Kenya.

Osu Bey was perhaps the fiercest of the fighters. He also had the deadliest weapon of anyone that day—an automatic rifle (meaning it could be fired like a machine gun), a lethal .30-caliber M-2 carbine. An FBI investigation established that the gun had been stolen from the Twenty-Second Security Police Squadron, March Air Force Base, California, on December 3, 1967. No one definitively proved how the weapon made its way to Cleveland, but the FBI later checked someone in Philadelphia, where Max Stanford had lived.[1]

Little Ahmed (John Hardrick) was given one of the high-powered .30-06 rifles. Between the two, these teenagers would hold off dozens and dozens of police officers, as Osu Bey especially ran from window to window spraying bullets everywhere. He made it seem like the apartments were occupied by a small army of guerrillas.[2]

After Willie Wolff was shot and his partner Kenny Gibbons taken to a hospital, the intersection at Auburndale and Lakeview became clogged with police zone cars. The radio dispatcher started telling all units to stay out of the immediate areas and to park or circle on the periphery. Ignoring the directive, Car 513 arrived at Lakeview and Auburndale and its windshield was immediately shot out, with bullets striking on all flanks from fire coming from both sides of Lakeview. Like the zone car of Wolff and Gibbons, Car 513 was abandoned in the middle of the intersection.[3]

Car 553 with Sergeants Sam Levy and Thomas Moran stopped eight to ten houses south of Auburndale on Lakeview; both men got out. They tried to loop behind the Auburndale apartments through the backyards, but the fences were too high to scale without being exposed. So they moved back in front of the Lakeview Tavern, which was separated from 12312 Auburndale by a driveway with a carport that was used as a second-story porch.

As he leaned against the tavern, Levy heard someone say that the shooting was coming out of 12312 Auburndale, and he cautiously started walking up the driveway separating the apartment building and the tavern. Halfway up the drive, he was hit by bullets in his arm and chest, the bullets passing completely through his body. The force spun him around, and he was shot in his elbow and hip. He started to run out of the drive and then dove for cover in the street, trying to crawl under a car parked in front of the tavern. In the car was an African American male who lay on the floor, having been pinned down when he pulled up to the tavern to pick up a friend.

Levy was shot three more times (leg, thigh, ankle) as he lay partially exposed in the street under the front end of the parked vehicle. In an instant, he had taken a total of seven shots, but he was miraculously alive and conscious.[4]

At the same time, Lieutenant Elmer Joseph, who had come to the scene with two other policemen and Captain Herbert Dragalla in Car 551, followed Levy around the corner of the Lakeview Tavern. Lieutenant Joseph was also hit by a volley of shots, one a "through and through" bullet in his right thigh and another in his back, which traveled to his intestines. Joseph stumbled back toward the tavern, where he fainted. He was rescued by patrolmen and taken to Lakeside Hospital.[5]

Levy was in a no-man's land. He lay in the street, partly under the car, and would be the subject of multiple heroic rescue attempts over the next hour and a half, as complete darkness enveloped the scene. Levy testified that the car under which he sought shelter was hit over seventy times. Levy and Joseph were shot at 8:35 PM. The police radio crackled, "Lakeview and Auburndale, we've got a lieutenant and a sergeant shot here."

One of the officers who helped pull Lieutenant Joseph to safety was Patrolman Thomas Smith, a four-year veteran of the force. Smith was a motorcycle driver and came to the area on Motor Scooter 5S2, parking it near the Lakeview Tavern. He joined Captain Dragalla, who was huddled with several officers on the other side of the tavern. The tracers and bullets were hitting everywhere, and there was a great deal of confusion and yelling. They watched helplessly as Levy was struck several more times. "I seen him myself get hit twice," Smith recalled.

Smith decided to "reconnoiter" the area and circled back to Lakeview to the other side of Auburndale behind houses that faced the Lakeview Tavern. He was bit by a dog in one of the backyards. Kneeling in the bushes, he could see there was a shooter or shooters in an upper-story tower of the Lakeview Tavern and heavy fire coming from 12312 Auburndale. Smith then warily snaked his way back to Captain Dragalla in front of the tavern. His journey took almost half an hour or forty minutes.

Smith could take it no more. He impulsively jumped out into the street to rescue Sam Levy. Levy said, "What the hell are you doing? You will be killed." Smith fired at shooters in the upper story of the tavern and started to position Levy to drape him across his shoulder in a fireman's carry. "Leave me here," Levy said, "save yourself." Smith was hit in his left shoulder with two quick shots, the second of which traveled across his back and lodged in his right shoulder, shattering a piece of his spine along the way. He fell to the ground facedown, unable to move, and began to moan that he couldn't breathe. He was hit twice more on the ground.[6]

Seeing this disaster unfold, Patrolman Ernest Rowell, a black officer, ran into the street and dragged a paralyzed Smith to some cover behind the car. He removed Smith's gun belt to help him breathe and was hit in his backside and foot with a shotgun blast, falling on top of Smith. Levy tried to pull the men farther under the car. To make matters worse, tear gas that had been shot at the Auburndale apartments began to waft over all three men, who were already in distress. Rowell, after lying in the street for over forty minutes—able to move but fearing he would be shot again—began gagging from the tear gas and finally got up and darted to safety.[7]

Across Lakeview on the other side of Auburndale shortly after Sam Levy fell under the car, Patrolman Richard Hart, who had parked Car 541 at 123rd and Moulton, saw a black man "with an Afro style haircut" shooting at Levy from the Lakeview Tavern tower, a third-story Victorian structure over the Tavern that came to a conical point. Hart knelt down, took aim, and fired his revolver at the man in the tower, "quite a distance actually for a revolver."

Instantly, Hart was hit from behind on his right side by a high-velocity bullet that tore through him, exiting near his front armpit. Realizing he was being shot from behind, he stood up and ran out into Auburndale toward Captain Dragalla and the other officers in front of the tavern. He was hit several more times, the bullets all but severing his right arm from his body and knocking him to the street.

In a panic, he picked up his arm, which was only loosely attached, and ran back toward Moulton. "Then they really opened up," he said. "A barrage of shots was coming from [12312 Auburndale]. They were just popping like mad." Hart emptied his revolver at the tower with his left hand, still seeing the shooter in the window. He continued to be caught in a cross fire as he ran zigzag back down Moulton—shooters were everywhere in the neighborhood. He made it back to Car 541, where officers applied his gun belt as a tourniquet and he was driven to Mt. Sinai Hospital.[8]

On the other side of the Auburndale apartments—east toward East 124th Street and the almost ninety-degree angle of Auburndale Avenue that curves southeast toward Euclid Avenue—another drama was unfolding. Forty-seven-year-old Lieutenant Leroy Jones, the Sixth District supervisor, had teamed up with Sergeant Anthony Gentile and Patrolman Groynom.

They drove north on Auburndale, stopping a few houses from 124th, around the corner from 12312 Auburndale. Sergeant Gentile had retrieved a Thompson submachine gun issued by the Cleveland Police Department.

Lieutenant Jones, gripping a carbine he picked up at the Sixth District, walked ahead on the sidewalk in front of 12314 Auburndale, next to the house with the shooters. He was hit with a high-velocity bullet in his neck that caused him to stagger and drop in front of 12312 Auburndale, not far from where Willie Wolff lay dead. The time was 8:43 PM. It was now dusk.

Leroy Jones's wounds were grievous; and he took three bullets altogether. The first was a missile that entered the side of his neck on his left side and traveled across his neck, completely transecting his spine, leaving the vertebrae in little pieces. Two pieces of copper jacket, which surrounded the bullet's lead core, broke off and snagged in his neck muscles on the left and right side (the lead bullet mushroomed and exited out the other side of his neck, leaving behind its copper jacket pieces). The neck entrance wound was large, almost 2 inches round with rough, ragged edges.[9] Given the damage, this wound was likely caused by the high-powered .30-06 rifle. There was no evidence of fouling or stippling—powder burns—so the bullets were fired from some distance away.

Two other bullets entered and exited Jones's body. These entrance wounds showed evidence of a missile traveling at a lower velocity with smaller caliber bullets, probably a .22-caliber rifle from a shooter standing along the side of the 12312 apartment building.[10] One bullet entered over the left lower chest and exited through Jones's back; the other hit over the left side of his abdomen, exiting through the right side of his abdomen. He also suffered two graze-type gunshot wounds, one on his right forearm and the other over the back of his right shoulder.[11]

Behind him, Sergeant Gentile was driven back by withering fire coming out of 12312. In his retreat, he ran into Patrolman Angelo Santa Maria. Desperate to rescue Lieutenant Jones, Santa Maria came up with the idea of asking a civilian car to drive in front of 12312 so that Jones could be snatched up while officers laid down a protective fire from nearby. Santa Maria believed that a civilian car would not attract fire from the nationalists, especially if blacks were driving.

Santa Maria asked for volunteers and James Chapman and another African American male came forward (Santa Maria said other civilians, including a woman, also offered to help). Chapman retrieved his car—a two-door convertible—and picked up Santa Maria and another black male on Auburndale. Santa Maria gave the two men careful instructions. Once in front of Jones, the blacks were to lay low while Santa Maria, using the driver's side door as cover, would sneak out and recover Jones, pulling him into the backseat.

The plan went wrong from the start. Once in the middle of Auburndale near the downed lieutenant, Chapman's car attracted gunfire. Whether in panic or otherwise, all three men bailed from the car at the same time. Santa Maria recalled Chapman saying, "Let's go" or "Let's go get him," referring to Jones. The other male jumped out and ran away from the car, never to be identified.

Santa Maria dove behind some brick stairs near the apartment building. He yelled to Sergeant Gentile and others that he needed cover and a smoke grenade. Santa Maria threw the grenade while Gentile cut loose with his Thompson submachine guns. Santa Maria grabbed Lieutenant Jones by the feet and began to drag him. He was hit by one high-velocity bullet in his back near his armpit. The bullet tumbled internally and caused substantial damage—it fractured three ribs, injured his spleen and kidney, and nicked up his spine before exiting.

"Sarge, I'm shot," Santa Maria yelled to Gentile, and fell on top of Jones. He mumbled to Gentile, "Tell my wife I love her." Gentile and others provided more suppressive fire as yet another patrolman, Steven Merencky, risked his life and grabbed Santa Maria, throwing him over his shoulder to carry him out of harm's way. Lieutenant Jones remained down in front of 12312.

There is controversy as to what happened to twenty-three-year-old James Chapman. Some believe that he was killed, accidentally or intentionally, by police who shot him in the head at close range. Others think that he was killed by a high-velocity missile from the nationalists in the Auburndale apartments as he tried to rescue Willie Wolff. His body was found slumped over Wolff's in the front yard, though it was later moved to the sidewalk in front of the Lakeview Tavern.

The medical evidence is inconclusive. The Cuyahoga County Coroner opined that Chapman was hit from some distance by a high-velocity rifle shooting tracer bullets that contained phosphorous.[12] The coroner of Allegheny County (Pittsburgh), Pennsylvania, a former air force captain and experienced pathologist (a consultant on the autopsy of Robert F. Kennedy), thought Chapman was shot at close range.

One thing both pathologists agreed upon: Chapman was killed by "a gunshot wound to the head with massive destruction of the skull and brain."

Chapman's autopsy photos show "a large, gaping defect as opposed to a fairly small, circular kind of wound" on the right front of his head. The Allegheny County coroner identified "abundant" black-powder residue near Chapman's head wound on color photos of the autopsy, leading him to conclude Chapman had been shot at "very close range," which he characterized as "just a matter of a couple inches or so, certainly less than 6 inches."[13]

About this same time, Harllel Jones, George Forbes, and Walter Beach returned to the area hoping to stop the madness. An officer who had taken up a position on the other side of Lakeview near Moulton emerged from a house where he encountered the three men and others who had come with Forbes.

"Councilman Forbes, who knows me," Patrolman Richard Tanski testified, "he came up to me, shook my hand, and asked me how things were going."

"They're shooting at us," Tanski replied. "The situation isn't too good."

Walter Beach, who Tanski said was dressed in "iridescent green trousers and a green T-shirt," made a move to walk out in the front of the home. He was warned by a policeman not to walk into the line of fire. Beach purportedly responded, "They're not going to shoot at me; they're my brothers. They're after you white mothers." Before a fight could break out, Forbes intervened and said he was going to the Sixth District police headquarters to consult with Mayor Stokes.[14]

Darkness became the friend of the police. The sun set around 9:00 PM, and streetlights came up. One of the officers arriving to help, Robert Wood, had a high-powered rifle—a .30-06 Madsen. He began to shoot out the streetlights as he approached Auburndale and Lakeview. Others followed suit. With the cover of darkness, efforts were stepped up to rescue Sergeant Levy and Patrolman Smith. The tear gas fired into 12312 Auburndale had some effect. The incessant fire slowed down. A civilian who identified himself as "Brother Fields" asked Captain Dragalla near the Lakeview Tavern if he could try to talk the shooters into a cease-fire so the wounded could be evacuated. He asked the shooters to "fire one shot in the air" if they would allow the police to take the wounded men out. No shot was fired.

The Second District Mobile Wagon 291, which had been used as an ambulance that night, was pulled up to Auburndale. It was driven up on the sidewalk next to the tavern in front of the car under which Levy and Smith lay, providing a shield so other officers could scramble to finally recover Levy and Smith. One patrolman assisting at the time, Leonard Szalkiewicz, who had crossed Lakeview to try to see where bullets were coming from, was shot in the right arm.[15]

As Patrolman Wood was working to extricate the policemen under the car, he saw Lieutenant Jones sprawled in front of 12312. Wood organized several officers with a stretcher and ran to save him, this time without the protection of a vehicle, as the fire from the Auburndale apartments had slowed and all the streetlights were shot out.

Back near the tavern, Wood ran into Patrolman Peter Ventura, who had been in action at 1395 Lakeview battling with the nationalists inside the house and outside on the back lawn. Ventura made his way to Auburndale and had been told there was an officer down in front of the fenced-in area in front of the apartment complex on Auburndale. He declared his intention to recover him. Patrolman Wood had seen Willard Wolff lying motionless when he retrieved Lieutenant Jones, and he noticed a second body nearby—that of James Chapman. Woods and Ventura crawled on their stomachs to the fence, kicked in an iron gate, and pulled both Wolff and Chapman to the front of the Lakeview Tavern. Patrolman Wood recalled Willard Wolff had been astraddle Chapman who, Wood believed, was trying to lift him when he was mortally wounded in the head.[16]

Willard Wolff was taken to a hospital. James Chapman's body was left in front of the Lakeview Tavern, where it would remain for hours.

Peter Ventura next checked through the Lakeview Tavern for snipers and then reemerged to lead several officers into 12312 Auburndale. A dozen terrified customers of the Tavern had taken refuge in its basement, and they were now being pelted with tear-gas canisters. They were beginning to suffocate.

On the first floor of 12312 Auburndale, Patrolman Ventura and two officers threw tear gas up a staircase from a first-floor hallway, but the upstairs door was shut, and the canisters came rolling back down the steps. They left gagging from the fumes.

Ventura still heard shots coming from down the street at 1395 Lakeview, so he returned there. A shooter in the basement and at least one on the upper floor continued to bedevil police outside. Moans could be heard from whoever was in the basement. Several officers called for the shooters to come out and surrender. The person in the basement yelled back, "Go fuck yourself!"[17] At some point after the initial tear-gas assault, officers could hear women and children screaming. A police cease-fire was called as a woman and her children, the spouse and children of the owner of the house, Rev. Henry Perryman, emerged from the front door. They were whisked to shelter.

After that, the house caught fire. The police claim that curtains started burning from the tear-gas canisters; others claimed that the police shot in flares to deliberately burn the house to the ground. At this moment, Peter Ventura reappeared from the excitement at Auburndale, and he climbed through a window off the front porch of 1395 Lakeview. Others tentatively followed. The TV in the front room was on. In the back room, which Ventura thought was the kitchen, he saw a male lying with "blood about his head." He believed this was the black male who pointed the pistol out of the window at him.

Ventura went into the cellar and saw an automatic pistol but no person, though he didn't stay long. Back upstairs he and another officer found a door to the upstairs barricaded and impassable. By this time, the fire in the house drove them out.

All the policemen who guarded 1395 Lakeview as it burned swore no one emerged from the front or the back. They heard ammunition going off like fireworks as the blaze intensified.

In the backyard, a grisly scene was unfolding. The nationalists who had been shot behind the house apparently were still alive when the house caught fire. As the house began to burn, they were close enough that they began to be incinerated. The fact they were still alive was proven by the autopsies of Bernard Donald (Nondu Bey) and Sidney Taylor (Malik Ali Bey), both of whom had carbon monoxide in their blood—a sign they had inhaled smoke. Yet both had kill shots to their heads. One conclusion seems inescapable—these men were shot in the head after the fire in the house was well under way. The chief forensic pathologist from Allegheny County confirmed that neither would have survived their massive head wounds for even seconds and that carbon monoxide in the blood only happens if someone is still breathing. "The body does not take up carbon monoxide after death," he testified.[18]

Lathan Donald, who did survive, said that a policeman had a gun in his mouth when a photographer came around the corner, unintentionally saving his life. "I could never get the taste of that gun out of my mouth," he told a woman he later married.[19]

At this time, Bertrand Gardner, Stokes's community relations director, and a representative of the police, showed up with four black nationalists, including Harllel Jones, who had been cooperating in trying to stop the carnage. One of the nationalists, Albert Forrest, an army veteran and medic, made his way to the back of 1395. He witnessed the body of Sidney Taylor (Malik Ali Bey) engulfed in flames. He saw Lathan Donald (Nondu El) was still alive and asked a nearby fireman holding a stretcher to help move Donald out of the area to receive medical aid. The fireman stood unspeaking, refusing to assist. Forrest "snatched" the stretcher from him and began to place Lathan Donald onto it, when he was attacked by several policemen.[20]

"Let the nigger die," they said. One of the policemen stuck a shotgun in Forrest's stomach and told him he was going to "blow my guts out." Just then, another policeman hit Forrest in the face with the butt of his shotgun, knocking him down, where he was kicked and stomped. Forrest staggered back to the front of 1395 Lakeview, where he was taken to a hospital and treated for his injuries.[21]

Lathan Donald was eventually transported to a hospital.

At the Lakeview Tavern, the ten or so frightened customers who clustered in the basement were now terrorized by police. Earlier in the evening, two officers came in and took names and told the customers to hide in the basement, as bullets were piercing the walls of the tavern from all directions. But later that night, another set of officers became concerned that nationalists might be secreting themselves among the customers and shot multiple canisters of tear gas into the basement.

The man who had been a calming influence and the leader of the customers, John Pegues, was shot twice and severely wounded when police began shooting randomly into the basement. He and the others were eventually rousted from the basement and beaten as they were taken to a police wagon to be arrested. They all had to walk over the body of James Chapman, lying on the sidewalk in front of the tavern. "They beat me and stomped me," Pegues testified. "I lost two teeth that night. My face was puffed up. I was bleeding. My clothes were soaked in blood, and they took me and drug me and threw me in the wagon and I blacked out."

At the jail, Pegues was thrown in a cell with the others. His cellmates tried to tend to his bullet wounds and pleaded with the police to take Pegues to a hospital. Sometime later he was finally taken to Mt. Sinai Hospital and treated, but then taken to a prison hospital ward at Metro Hospital before being released once the police figured out he had nothing to do with the shoot-out.[22]

Others in the basement were badly beaten—one man had multiple broken ribs from being hit with shotgun butts and kicked.[23] The three women in the group testified their clothes were ripped as police roughly searched them, including their "private parts." All were required to sign "suspicious persons" waivers before being released.[24]

Across the street from 1395 Lakeview, Edithe B. Schepperd, who had fallen asleep during the madness around her home, woke up and looked out the window to see her neighbor's house on fire, casting, she said, "an eerie glow over everything."

"Nobody was trying to put it out," she recalled.

A fire burns out of control at 1395 Lakeview Road, the home where nationalists had barricaded themselves, July 23, 1968.
Western Reserve Historical Society

In the home next door, Ahmed Evans had come down to Joseph Turpin's second-floor apartment and pleaded for him to call the police to say he would surrender to black officers. Turpin had trouble communicating the message, though he called multiple times. Finally, at about 1:00 AM, Turpin came out on his second-story front porch and called to police watching the fire burn across the street and said he had Ahmed Evans in his house and that he wanted to give up.

Several heavily armed policemen gathered outside Turpin's side door. Evans, who had thrown his weapon out the front attic window (it landed in a flower garden), had also removed his shirt so the police could not claim he was concealing a weapon. He emerged from a side door, bare-chested, wearing only dark trousers and sandals, and was surrounded by white officers. He claims he was threatened and beaten about his body so as to leave no marks on his head or face.

One of the arresting officers testified that Evans asked him, "How many of my men died?" The officer responded that three or four were dead. Evans purportedly replied, "They died for a good cause."[25] He told them his weapon was in the bushes in front of the house. He said his gun jammed or he would still be shooting. The police found no expended shells in the attic when they searched it, though they did find banana clips, bullets for the M-1, and home-rolled marijuana cigarettes. They discovered one live round in the chamber of the gun, but it did not appear to have been jammed.

Evans was handcuffed and walked out to a shot-up zone car where Amos Floyd, the African American vice cop who had shepherded the children out of 1391, was sitting. Floyd and the arresting officers all testified that Evans was read his Miranda rights. "I know my rights better than you do," Evans told one of the officers.[26]

After the white officers left, Floyd turned around and asked Evans, "What are you accomplishing by this?"

"This is just the beginning," Evans replied, and then fell silent, watching the house burn across the street.[27]

27

"A Lot of People Are Going to Get Killed"

EVANS WAS TRANSFERRED TO ANOTHER cruiser to get him out of the area as quickly as possible. On the drive downtown, he sat in the backseat between two white officers while Patrolman Donald Kuchar, an eleven-year veteran, took the wheel. Kuchar recalled Evans "conversing freely" during the entire ride. Around them, Cleveland was again burning—fires and looting broke out on Superior Avenue; sniper fire was sporadic but seemingly coming from every rooftop. The National Guard was called up once more.

Per Kuchar, Evans rambled defensively about being called yellow. "The reason he gave up," Kuchar quoted Evans, "was because his carbine jammed, and if it hadn't jammed, he would still be shooting at police." Kuchar testified that Evans blamed the police for the evictions that sparked the uprising. "He said that the white man has pushed the colored man too far," Kuchar recalled, "and has caused them to live in bad conditions, something to this effect."[1] He kept telling everyone "this was just the beginning."

Ahmed Evans had a different recollection of the car ride to police headquarters. "We was going down Superior now," he testified in an evidence-suppression hearing, "and the whole side of the street is on blazes and a million people on the sidewalk, and this cop was saying, 'I hope they shoot you.'" The cop on his other side who held a shotgun to his head during the entire ride said, according to Evans, "If they don't, I will."[2]

When Evans finally was delivered to the criminal statement unit of the Detective Bureau on the third floor of the central police station located on 21st Street between Superior and Payne, he was met by his nemesis, Sergeant John Ungvary. The room was packed and buzzing at two in the morning, but Ungvary and Evans had a direct one-on-one exchange as others took notes. Still shirtless, Evans told Ungvary he would talk to him if he would remove the handcuffs that were biting into his flesh. Ungvary obliged and asked Evans if he wanted a lawyer. Evans said he did and the chief police prosecutor, James Carnes, sent that night by Mayor Stokes to oversee the interrogation, left the room to call Stanley Tolliver. Tolliver was sound asleep when the call came and he nodded back off. "I was pretty groggy," Tolliver testified.[3]

It was a mistake to continue with the examination, even though Evans had been counseled on his rights, because he had asked for a lawyer. The ultimate result was that his confession was ruled inadmissible at the time of his trial, but there is little reason to doubt the notes taken that night as they roughly comport with what is known from what the FBI informant had been relaying about the buildup to the shoot-out.

"I will say anything to you, John, that I would say to the newspapers," Evans began in his discourse with Ungvary, smoking a cigarette from a pack he had been given and drinking three glasses of water. "John," he continued, "it is no secret that I am a revolutionary. If you had been out there on the street tonight, I would have shot at you, too, even though you have always treated me right."[4] He again repeated the line that had his gun not jammed, he would still be shooting at policemen.

Evans told of his acquisition of weapons with money from the antipoverty federal programs and Cleveland: Now! He said he had purchased his M-1 at Heckman's the day before and that "he could have bought it with a library card." He regaled the police with his odyssey to Detroit, Pittsburgh, and Akron, though he said he had been in Detroit on Sunday, July 21. He said that the reason the shooting started was because "they heard they were going to be raided, and they were watching the streets, and had observed one or two police cars, unmarked, driving up and down Lakeview, and at this time they felt they were being surrounded, and at this time he stated that he called Mr. Beach and Mr. Forbes, and told them to get the police the hell out of there."[5]

Once the tow truck arrived, the nationalists took this as further evidence the police were about to attack them. Evans claimed he was asleep when he first heard shots and that he grabbed his M-1 and joined the fray. He told the police that the shooting was not planned for that night, but for "the following day at which time two other cities, Pittsburgh and Detroit, were to experience similar incidents."

Ungvary, of course, was laser focused on whether Evans had ties to Communists. Evans admitted that he was "soul brothers" with Ho Chi Minh and Chou En-lai and that his organization had connections to Robert F. Williams, "who went to Peking and Hanoi." The New Libyans regularly read Williams's newsletter, *The Crusader*, copies of which he picked up in his recent trip to Detroit.

Evans then explained his vision of urban guerrilla warfare. A transcriber wrote, "He stated that the country cannot fight two wars [referring to wars in Vietnam and at home in the streets], and that their supply lines are stretched out too thin, and that the police department is not organized and that today's action was more or less the beginning, and when coordinated nationwide, it will go off together, and this was their form of revolution."[6]

When asked who was shooting at police with him, Evans identified only those killed, wounded, or captured. "He stated that many of his followers are young, aged 14 to 16," he explained to his inquisitors, "who are questioning their ghetto status, and want to know why their sisters are prostitutes, and their mothers are unwed, and why they don't have any place outside the ghettos."

He acknowledged that the sole purpose for buying the weapons was to "shoot white policemen." He said, "As long as there are black and white, there will always be trouble."

By this time, several lawyers from Legal Aid had arrived but were not allowed to see Evans. Finally, one of the Legal Aid lawyers called

Stanley Tolliver and woke him up, saying, "Man, we are down here wait-ing on you. Ahmed wants to talk to you." Tolliver arrived just before dawn and told Evans to stop talking.

Meanwhile, back at the scene, police began to focus on the house next door to 12312 Auburndale—an identical brick apartment building with four suites, two up and two down—12314 Auburndale. Reports had been that a sniper might be on the roof.

Turns out, it was the place where Osu Bey (Leslie Jackson), John Hardrick (Little Ahmed), and Alfred "Unknown" Thomas had fled sometime after it got dark, when the tear gas began to permeate 12312 Auburndale. Osu Bey told investigators that he and Hardrick were left behind in the Auburndale apartments by Ahmed Evans with instructions to protect "the pad and the sisters." Hardrick's two sisters lived in downstairs apartments and Osu Bey lived upstairs in the rear apartment.

One of the families living next door in the 12314 Auburndale apart-ments was the Matthews family. John Matthews was a veteran of the army and an employee of Picker X-ray. On the night of July 23, Mat-thews's wife called him to come home from work (his shift started at 5:00 PM) because a fuse had blown in the apartment. By the time Mat-thews made it to Auburndale, the gun battle was in full swing. He ran into 12314 and upstairs to his rear suite, instructing his wife and four young children to lie on the floor.

After dark, Matthews and his wife heard what sounded like some-one with a crowbar trying to break into their apartment. They told the intruder to go away. Osu Bey, Hardrick, and Alfred Thomas hid in the basement of 12314 with the women and at least one child (Kenya, San-dra Hardrick's two-year-old son) after being driven from their apart-ments next door. Osu Bey would tell police that Omar Majid, one of the men who marched in the Hough commemoration parade next to Carl Stokes on Saturday, July 20, came into the basement at 12314 with a man named Ali—and both had rifles. "They told us there was still a lot of shooting going on next door and then they left," the police wrote in Osu Bey's statement. Majid was the chief lieutenant of Harllel Jones and a black nationalist affiliated with the Afro Set.

By sunrise on July 24 the three males knocked on the door of the Matthews apartment, each holding a different rifle. John Matthews let them in when they assured him they meant his family no harm. They hid their rifles in a back room used by the children, under some beds and in a closet, and asked Matthews if he had some clothes they could wear, changing out of the ones they were wearing. He agreed.[7]

At around 10:00 AM the National Guard surrounded the apartment complex. Two Cleveland policemen entered and arrested the three young men and found the stowed rifles in the back room and ammunition in the pockets of Osu Bey and John Hardrick. The deadly M-2, stolen from March Air Force Base, was one of the guns recovered. Osu Bey had ammunition for the M-2 gun in his pocket. The M-2 was eventually matched up with a bullet removed from Lieutenant Joseph.

Hardrick talked to police right away, confessing he shot the .30-06—but only four times—in response to what he thought was machine gun fire from a building behind the Lakeview Tavern. Hardrick said that he witnessed two unnamed nationalists fire at police in the street below from windows in the upper front apartment of 12312, but he could not remember their names.

Osu Bey wouldn't talk until his mother and father were brought to police headquarters, but then he gave a fairly accurate account of the lead-up to the shooting, though he denied ever shooting a rifle. He claimed, in fact, that he found the M-2 rifle in the basement of 12314. He admitted to going to a black nationalist headquarters in Detroit with Evans the day before, where Evans told "the brothers" that he had been served with an eviction notice and that this time he was not going to move out. "The Detroit brothers told Ahmed that they were with him whatever he did," he told investigators.[8]

Alfred Thomas had earned the nickname "Unknown." He was a bizarre character in Evans's group, and no one could figure him out. He told police he was handed a rifle, which he shot from the backyard of 12312 at no one in particular before his gun jammed and he fled to the basement of 12314. There was indeed a jammed rifle in 12312 that matched the description that Thomas gave. With the others, he would be charged with first-degree murder but eventually would be declared mentally incompetent to stand trial. He was committed to the Lima State Hospital for the Criminally Insane, "until reason is restored."[9]

Hardrick, seventeen, and Osu Bey, sixteen, were juveniles and after booking at the police headquarters were sent to the Juvenile Detention Home.

Mayor Stokes had returned the night before from Washington, DC, around 7:00 PM. He was met at the airport with extra security in light of the alleged assassination threats against him and other black leaders. He was driven to his home where word came that confirmed shooting had broken out in Glenville. Sergeant Bosie Mack, his African American bodyguard, drove him to city hall, where he stayed up all night trying to find out what was going on and issuing orders.

Stokes called a hundred black leaders to an emergency meeting the next morning at the hall to discuss what should be done. He knew from reports, including those of Walter Beach and his law director, Buddy James, that retribution was in the air. Beach and James had driven around Glenville and Hough the night before and they believed the police were in a temper for revenge. At the Sixth District, James had seen an officer call for officers to bring in personal automatic weapons. "I hope you don't mind," the officer said to the law director, "because I don't really give a shit." James said the officer said, "If these guys want war, they're going to get it."

While Beach and James were driving around the area, they arrived on the scene where a black watchman-custodian of an apartment building had been shot and killed in an alley off Superior and 82nd. Witnesses said police had murdered the man. The man's name was James Haynes, and he was a father of three girls. "I saw my first dead body outside of a funeral home, an undertaker parlor," James remembered. "This man had been shot up real bad, there was blood every place." James chased a police car that scurried away from the scene, eventually giving an order over the radio for the men in the car to stop. They denied knowing anything about the murder.[10] James concluded, "It was clear to me at that time that the police officer, the police, had shot this guy back here."

Some police also entered Harllel Jones's Afro Set with shotguns and fired a great number of rounds into the ceiling. The closed astrology shop Evans used to operate on Superior was burned to the ground. Beach noticed white gangs starting to enter the neighborhood, engaging in fighting with young blacks. Some of the whites were dragged from cars and severely beaten. It was, as one witness called it, "instant insanity."

James reported to Stokes, "It's rough out there. We have a war on our hands." James worried that once the initial shock of losing three policemen wore off, the police would go berserk. "This is nothing more than vindictiveness," he told the mayor. "A lot of people are going to get killed."

After meeting with black leaders early on Wednesday morning, July 24, Stokes mandated that white policemen stay out of a large area encompassing Hough and Glenville. "Mayor Carl B. Stokes ordered all National Guard troops and white policemen withdrawn yesterday from a six-square mile area of this city's troubled East Side," the New York Times reported.[11]

"I had to stop the small war going on in my city," Stokes wrote.

African Americans in the neighborhoods organized "Peace Patrols" to tour the streets and plead for calm. There was substantial looting and arson, but the violence stopped—no more lives were lost. One of the organizers of the peace crews was Lewis Robinson. "None of us who are concerned about people want this violence," he told a reporter.[12]

The police were furious. The order to stand down allowed nationalists to escape. Evans told Ungvary there were seventeen of his men involved in the shooting, yet only three were arrested. Just as bad, the police felt that they were not able to secure the crime scenes and recover crucial evidence, which now could be tampered with or destroyed. Stokes's order appeared to police to be a concession to black nationalists. "The feeling among several political sages was that Stokes was in good shape until his decision to pull guardsmen and police out of the trouble spot," James Naughton wrote for the Plain Dealer. "Until then, they reasoned, he was faced with a black nationalist insurrection, a plot, something different from race riots that have racked American cities."[13]

"Wanted" posters began to appear in police headquarters and districts with the photo of Stokes walking through Hough with the black nationalists who had rifles slung over their shoulders on Saturday, July 20. "These pictures show how to start a riot," the posters proclaimed, "which kills, wounds, and mains policemen, who are replaced by black power social workers."[14] Police radio in the days after the shoot-out recorded officers refusing to respond to calls, saying, "Let the nigger mayor take care of it." When Stokes demanded the tapes, police and the county prosecutor refused to turn them over, calling them "evidence" in a criminal proceeding.[15]

Word leaked from the police almost instantly that Ahmed Evans admitted in his interrogation that he bought guns with Cleveland: Now! funds.[16] Stokes suffered a stunning, irrevocable blow to his political image and reputation.[17] The *Call and Post* commented: "Now, Mayor Stokes has had his dreams and hopes shattered, not by white racists, but by his own people."[18]

Police officers threatened to quit and some did—a revolt was brewing. A police union was born the night of the shoot-out: the Cleveland Police Patrolmen's Association.[19] There were calls for safety director Joe McManamon's head.[20] A recall movement against Stokes was sparked. "Stokes gave the revolutionaries time to retreat and hide," a West Side group wrote. "Why else would he pull the law enforcement officials out one day and put them in the next."[21]

The toll had been appalling: three policemen (Golonka, Jones, and Wolff) dead; twelve officers and one tow truck driver (Gibbons, Szukalski, McManamon, Levy, Joseph, Smith, Rowell, Hart, Santa Maria, Szalkiewicz, Katonka, Sherbinski, and McMillin) wounded, some with life-threatening injuries. Most spent the night in emergency surgery, as doctors attempted to repair the catastrophic damage to muscle and bone caused by bullets shot from high-powered rifles. Three nationalists (Bernard Donald, Leroy Williams, and Sidney Taylor) were known dead. Lathan Donald survived seven bullet wounds. Two civilians caught in the melee were killed: James Chapman and James Haynes. At least two others were killed that night under suspicious circumstances. One black man in the car in front of the Lakeview Tavern, Henry Orange, was also wounded.

No one can be sure that the nationalist snipers trapped in 1395 Lakeview were not killed. Within days, Mayor Stokes had the site bulldozed before any remains could be searched for and recovered.[22]

The FBI was on high alert. William Sullivan, the legendary assistant director to J. Edgar Hoover and manager of the FBI's COINTELPRO operations, called the Cleveland office on Friday, July 26, asking questions and demanding answers. "He stated he wanted us to vigorously press our investigation to develop all evidence to show that this outbreak was or was not a previously planned conspiracy," one of the Cleveland agents recorded. "He also stated he hopes we can develop information why the demonstrations did not go off in the other cities that the informant originally reported on."[23] Another senior agent from FBI headquarters called Cleveland later that day to say he was working on a "summary for the White House Sunday afternoon covering the entire Cleveland incident" and asked his own questions. The White House was especially concerned about the allegation that federal funds were used to buy weapons—which is why later there was continued emphasis on the funds originating exclusively from Cleveland: Now![24]

The FBI's working theory as to why demonstrations in other cities did not "go off" was because of the premature start of the hostilities in Cleveland. It became clear, sources told the FBI, that the cover of the operation had been blown with FBI informants telling authorities of the nationwide plan at the same time they ratted out Evans, and militants in the other cities therefore backed down. "Source advised that he learned [a militant in Cleveland] had made statements to the effect that the disorder in Cleveland was to signal similar disorders in other cities," an FBI summary report noted. "He advised that [the militant] stated that because of the advance information, which caused Evans to prematurely attack the Cleveland Police Department, the disorders in the other cities did not take place."[25]

The FBI informant who had infiltrated Ahmed Evans's inner circle continued to provide information after the shoot-out. He worried that he might be suspected of being a source of the information—in a press conference, Stokes talked about information from the FBI tipping them off—but he went out of his way to tell nationalists and New Libyans he encountered on the street that "when the shooting started he followed Ahmed's instructions, ran out of the apartments and shot at police officers from behind bushes." This seemed to quell any doubts about his loyalty to Evans and the nationalist cause.

The informant said that the weapons that had been stockpiled were being dispersed to individual homes and apartments. He reported on the congregation of members of New Libya who had engaged in the battle at the Esquire Hotel, including some wounded, but by the time Sergeant Ungvary and his people raided the hotel, they had slipped away—though Ungvary did discover "blood stains on the walls and floor of one of the rooms."

The FBI took the informant to Detroit on August 8 to try to locate the nationalists' house Evans had visited the night before the shoot-out, but not being from Detroit the informant was unable to identify the house with certainty.

From all accounts, the most likely persons to have been this informant were either James Daly (sometimes spelled Dailey), known as Jamil (an FBI document refers to him as Jamal) or James Mitchem (sometimes written as Mitchell).[26] By process of elimination, it had to be one of these two—they were the only two in the inner circle who were not arrested or killed on July 23. Both helped purchase rifles with Evans and both were on the payroll for the African culture shop.

The only other candidate is Amir Rashidd, but he was at a workshop with the Muntu Poets on the night of the outbreak. He would be a highly unlikely candidate in any event, given that his brother Sidney Taylor (Malik Ali Bey) was one of the most militant of the New Libyans and was killed on July 23.

By all accounts, Jamil was a junkie, who, if he became an informant, probably did so for the money to support his habit. According to black nationalists still living, Jamil faded away into obscurity, eventually leaving Cleveland in the years after the shoot-out. If he was the informant, there is some poignancy in a photograph taken of him standing in between Ahmed Evans and Martin Luther King Jr. on November 6, 1967, the day before Stokes was elected.

The five nationalists arrested were charged with first-degree murder of the three police officers killed and James Chapman. On August 8, Evans and Lathan Donald were bound over to the grand jury.[27] A week later, the two juveniles, Osu Bey and John Hardrick, were also bound over to be tried as adults if indicted by the grand jury.[28] Alfred Thomas was also put before the grand jury, though his mental stability was suspect. The grand jury listened to over thirty witnesses in one day on August 23 and returned indictments against all five for first-degree murder the following Monday, August 26, 1968.[29]

Louis Stokes was one of the lawyers assigned as counsel for Lathan Donald on account of his indigence, but he resigned in November when he was elected to Congress, eventually winning the first of what would turn out to be fifteen terms. He was the first black congressman elected from the state of Ohio.

The prosecutors had a problem. The main target, Ahmed Evans, hadn't been near any of the policemen killed or James Chapman. He undoubtedly shot at the tow truck driver and Chester Szukalski, but it seemed abundantly clear he hid in James Turpin's attic during most of the gun battle. None of the people killed was shot with his M-1 carbine. Stanley Tolliver foreshadowed the main defense theme in a bond hearing when he told the judge that the case against Evans was "circumstantial."[30]

If he was going to be convicted, it would have to be as a conspirator—and for that the prosecution would need witnesses.

Carl Stokes was asked by Hubert Humphrey to second his nomination at the violence-scarred Democratic National Convention in Chicago on August 28, two days after the grand jury handed down its indictments. Stokes delivered a stem-winder, but his star had fallen precipitously. Glenville had ruined his national political prospects. He was no longer whispered for vice president or a cabinet position.

Stokes's famous luck had run out. Even his seconding speech for Humphrey, which he believed would be watched by twenty million people, was overshadowed by the antiwar protesters who battled with Mayor Richard Daley's police in the streets outside the convention hall. "When it was over and I got back into my car," he wrote, "they told me that as soon as I had got to the podium, the cameras had switched to the street action outside the arena."[31]

28

"The Case Against Fred Ahmed Evans Is Weak"

THE TRIAL OF AHMED EVANS was scheduled to begin March 24, 1969.[1] He would be tried on his own. The prosecutors decided Evans was the ringleader and that if he were tried together with the others indicted there may be sympathy for his young followers, whose minds, they believed, had been twisted by Evans's charismatic and eccentric leadership. The case was assigned to George McMonagle, a conservative and fair judge.

On Saturday, March 1, Judge McMonagle heard several motions, ruling on some and deferring on others. Depositions, an unusual thing in criminal cases, were ordered for March 7.

The day before the depositions were to take place, in the early morning hours of March 6, the bloody body of Ahmed Evans's brother—William R. "Bootsie" Evans—was dumped on the doorstep in front of the offices of Stanley Tolliver, Ahmed's lead lawyer.[2]

Tolliver confided to a close friend that he received a telephone call the same night warning that he would be killed "in the same manner as 'Bootsie' within the near future." "You're next, nigger," Tolliver said the man on the phone menaced before hanging up.[3]

An official investigation found that Bootsie was engaged in criminal activity when he was killed. He allegedly tried to hold up a bus with a shotgun but was rebuffed by the bus driver, who told him they only accepted exact fares in the fare box and no longer carried cash. Bootsie supposedly got off the bus and tried to rob several other people, one of whom was in a car and had a pistol and shot him in the chest and head before speeding away. The man later turned himself in—and was never charged, the police declaring the shooting was in self-defense.[4]

Still, the timing and the location of where the body was found were peculiar. There was already deep concern about violence during Evans's trial and now black nationalists were even more on edge. A determined group of them, many in full African regalia and with drums, stood vigil outside the Criminal Courts Building, flying the red, black, and green nationalist flag. Whenever Evans entered or left the courtroom in pre-trial proceedings, a chorus of "salaam" was shouted—until McMonagle instituted stringent security rules of decorum.[5]

Evans heard in jail "through the grapevine" that his brother had been assassinated by the police. Judge McMonagle refused to allow Evans to visit the funeral home, worried about resulting mayhem, and instead ordered that Bootsie's remains be brought to the basement of the county jail for Evans to view and pay his respects. Evans refused to leave his cell.[6]

The FBI meticulously mounted press clippings about the murder in its file. An urgent teletype was sent to the director from the special agent in charge in Cleveland, expressing concern about violence during Bootsie's funeral.[7] According to an FBI memo, "500 brothers" attended the funeral on March 13 without incident.[8] The *Call and Post* painted a somewhat different picture. "On the streets of Cleveland," the paper reported, "throngs of angered Blacks followed the funeral procession of Ahmed Evans' younger brother to the grave. Their silence did nothing to hide the rage in their eyes."[9]

The trial of Ahmed Evans commenced with the start of jury selection on Monday, March 24. FBI Director J. Edgar Hoover was provided regular briefings by FBI agents in Cleveland. An informant told the FBI that Evans's supporters decided to avoid violence during the trial. "These supporters feel any violence would hurt Evans's chances of acquittal," the FBI report to Director Hoover read. "Source stated feeling in the streets is that the state cannot convict Evans of first-degree murder with the evidence that they have at hand."[10]

This was indeed a huge concern for the prosecutors—they had skimpy evidence of conspiracy to murder. Without doubt Evans assembled an arsenal leading up to the events—but in America arsenals are constitutionally protected. And it seems clear a plot was hatched to kill white policemen and others on July 24, the day of the scheduled eviction. But the defense could argue the shootings on the 23rd were provoked by the police surveillance and that the massacre started spontaneously in reaction to fear generated by the prospect of an imminent police attack, perhaps reinforced with the arrival of the yellow tow truck with its flashing lights and the Cleveland Police insignia on its doors.

Prosecutors dropped charges of shooting to kill or wound and possession of narcotics, recognizing the real possibility that a jury could default to these more provable, lesser crimes, allowing Evans to walk on the murder charges. It was all or nothing.

The stakes were high on both sides. One of the FBI sources told of a meeting in Cleveland of seventy members and sympathizers of the Republic of New Africa who sent a delegation to Detroit to try to convince Milton Henry (Gaidi Obadele) to come to Cleveland to assist the defense team in Ahmed Evans's murder trial. The Yale-educated lawyer declined.[11]

It took three weeks, until April 10, to finally seat a jury: seven women, five men, all white, and three alternates, also white.[12] Judge McMonagle had to threaten prospective jurors with contempt because so many of them were refusing to sit on the jury, expressing a fear of retribution.

Behind the scenes, a quiet but desperate drama was unfolding for the prosecutors. On March 21, just days before the trial was to begin, Special Agents John Sullivan and Thomas Corbett of the Cleveland office of the FBI received a panicked call from their main informant, saying he needed to meet with them "on a matter of great importance." The informant told the special agents over the phone that he was sitting with Detective John Smith at the Cleveland Police Department and he was being pressured to testify.

Sullivan and Corbett immediately drove over to police headquarters.

There they met with the informant, Detective Smith, and Sergeant John Ungvary. Detective Smith told the FBI agents that earlier that morning, the chief of police, Patrick Gerity (Stokes had replaced Chief Blackwell) met with Assistant County Prosecutor Charles Laurie, Ungvary, and himself. "The Prosecutor pointed out that the case against Fred Ahmed Evans was weak and that unless they came up with a witness who could establish a conspiracy to commit murder on the part of Evans, there was a good chance he will walk away from the trial as a free man," the FBI recorded in a memo sent to Director Hoover.

Charlie Laurie was almost frantic, according to the memo. "Pros. Laurie also stated that he was aware of the existence of the informant who could testify to the existence of the conspiracy," they wrote. "Pros. Laurie added the testimony of the informant at this time had become essential to the successful prosecution of Evans."

Detective Smith told the agents he refused to provide Laurie with the name of the informant, but the chief was putting pressure on him. (Smith, because he was black, was the only Cleveland policeman to meet in person with the informant.) Smith said he would take contempt rather than divulge the name.

The FBI agents vehemently opposed the use of the informant. They said they had told the informant that the possibility existed of him being called to testify, but the prospect was remote. Sullivan said he would not pressure the informant to testify "in view of the danger involved." He pointed out "that the informant had become involved with the Black Extremists and had lived up to his part of the bargain by furnishing information re activities of these individuals including advanced plans to start the Glenville riot of 1968."

They turned to the informant and advised him that by testifying he would "put himself in extreme peril and possibly lose his life as a retaliatory measure at the hands of the Black Nationalists."

The agents warned Smith and Ungvary that if they allowed Laurie to put the informant on the stand, "whatever happens to him at the hands of the Black Nationalists will be their responsibility."

A week later, as jury selection was still under way, the FBI contacted the informant, who "had steadfastly indicated he would not testify for fear of reprisal, however, on today's date informant referred to the Evans's trial, which is now going on, and stated he did not have the fear of testifying he once had, stating he realized he had not done anything wrong, therefore he would not be afraid to testify."

While the agents thought the informant now might be "persuaded or cajoled into accepting the role of the prosecution witness," they worried that his relationship with the FBI would surface, "possibly resulting in the subpoena of Agent personnel."[13] The idea of FBI agents testifying, risking disclosure of the FBI's COINTELPRO operation, likely did not sit well with Director Hoover. If Hoover applied pressure on the Cleveland Police Department, it worked.

On April 2, the chief of police assured the special agent in charge of the Cleveland FBI office, Charles Cusick, that the prosecutors would only call the informant if it became "absolutely necessary." The chief understood it took years to develop any source and that this informant provided "extremely valuable information concerning the extremists." Chief Gerity confided that the prosecutors were hard at work trying to cultivate conspiracy witnesses. "He indicated that members of his department who are conducting the investigation in regard to Evans have developed witnesses, or at least are attempting to develop witnesses, who could be in a position to furnish worthwhile information, and, therefore, it would not be necessary to utilize the informant," Cusick wrote in a memo to his file.[14]

The "witnesses being developed" were Walter Washington and Thomas Lanier. They were two young men in serious trouble. On September 11, 1968, Washington (who went by various aliases, including Walter Brown), Lanier, Roy Ogletree, and Darryl Payne fire-bombed St. Mark's Presbyterian Church and two nearby storefronts on the East Side, causing over $10,000 in damage. That day or the next, a man named Willie T. Davis, an elderly man believed to have been a witness to the arson, was stabbed to death. Washington, Lanier, and Ogletree—who all considered themselves Black Panthers—were arrested in December 1968 and charged with arson and other crimes. On January 23, 1969,

Washington and Darryl Payne were charged with first-degree murder in the Willie Davis stabbing.[15] Washington was found in possession of the long knife used in the attack.

At some point, Washington, in custody, was visited by John Smith of the Subversives Unit. Washington remembered it was when he was in the Cleveland Workhouse before being charged with first-degree murder. Charlie Laurie also came to see him two or three times—Washington's testimony was unclear as to when.

What is known is that on February 20, 1969, the grand jury—over whom prosecutors exert influence in secret—refused to indict Walter Washington on the first-degree murder charge. They issued a "no bill." Washington's remaining charges, including arson, were transferred to the juvenile court, as the prosecutors say they discovered that Washington's true age was seventeen when he committed the acts.[16]

The juvenile court took Washington's plea of guilty and found him "delinquent" in connection with the arson and other charges on March 25, 1969—just days after the frantic meeting between the FBI, its informant, Smith, and Ungvary. Two days after committing Washington to the Ohio Youth Commission, the juvenile court stayed its order and Washington was not transferred, staying in a Cleveland jail so he could testify against Ahmed Evans.

Washington appeared on April 12 as the sole conspiracy witness in the Ahmed Evans case. He told the court that three days after he testified he expected to be inducted into the army, leaving Ohio. On April 28, after Washington successfully testified, the juvenile court dismissed all remaining charges against him.[17]

Washington's testimony appears to have been entirely fabricated. He testified that Evans called a meeting of the Black Panthers and the nationalists on the morning of July 23. He placed fourteen Panthers and twenty-eight nationalists at a meeting that supposedly started around 9:00 AM. Evans, per Washington, showed up an hour later. The timeline is off (Evans, the FBI informant had reported, returned closer to noon) and, more important, the FBI informant said nothing about a gathering of over forty-two militants at the Auburndale apartments that morning, let alone any call to Black Panthers to join the nationalists.

Washington said Evans told everyone the "pop was going to jump off" that day (meaning there would be revolution) and instructed the group on how to use rifles. He said he had received $600 that day "from the suckers," and that "we was supposed to have a shootout with police." Evans left to buy more guns and Washington left to see his aunt. He testified that he did not take part in the shoot-out.[18]

Thomas Lanier, his codefendant in the arson case, was called next, and he confirmed that he was at Evans's apartment on July 23 with Washington, but he refused to say anything more than that they discussed "black history, that's all." Frustrated, the prosecutors quickly got him off the stand. Lanier also was inducted into the army shortly thereafter and charges against him were dropped.[19]

A third witness, Curtis Martin, an inmate of the Ohio State Reformatory in Mansfield, was brought up to testify about meetings with Evans and Harllel Jones where they demonstrated how to handle rifles, but he did not claim to have been anywhere near Auburndale on the day of the shootings.[20]

The defense spent considerable time attacking Washington's credibility, but to no avail. After eighty-seven witnesses testified for the prosecution and thirty-seven for the defense, the jury convicted Evans. Judge McMonagle sentenced him to death in the electric chair. The sentence was to be carried out on September 22, 1969, between the hours of 12:00 and 6:00 PM.[21]

The trial had been brutal. Police had to relive nightmarish moments. Judge McMonagle's front porch was bombed just before the trial started.[22] Jurors worked six-day weeks and were sequestered in a hotel. Two jurors and one witness reported being threatened.[23] Someone slipped a collection of disparaging *Plain Dealer* articles about Stanley Tolliver containing charges of professional misconduct into the evidence packet sent back with the jury when they retired for deliberations, almost triggering a mistrial.[24]

The families of the three police officers killed had to listen to or read about how drunk two of the policemen were at the time of their deaths and that the third had been drinking at some point that day, though he was sober when he was shot. It is true that Patrolmen Golonka and

Wolff were substantially impaired, having ingested the equivalent of thirteen to fifteen ounces of hard liquor or an equal number of beers, but given when and how they were killed, their drinking probably slowed their response to the threats they faced, but it had little to do with how they died. Speculation that they were shot by other drunk policemen is far-fetched as both were killed in daylight and were among the first responders.

But it is troubling that the three killed all had some alcohol in their system. One could speculate that a great number of police may have been intoxicated that night. Clearly, there was an acceptance, if not culture, of drinking on the job—a dangerous practice for authorities sanctioned to carry and use deadly weapons.

James Chapman's family had to wonder if he was killed by angry police officers. There is an especially sad note in John Little's file in the Stokes Papers recording a call from Chapman's father on July 26, 1968. It reads: "Son killed the other night. Son left home and got two policemen to escort him home; got home, turned on light, firing into house; started to get in car; got shot getting into car. Powder burns. Was shot by policemen. Twin brother says he knows who the people are."[25]

While the existence of substantial powder near Chapman's wounds raises the possibility he was shot at close range, the problem is that the autopsy X-rays showed no bullet or pellets shot directly into his brain— the shot was a gutter-type wound across the top front quadrant of his head. He would have had to be at an odd angle to receive such a close shot that grazed across his head. Still, questions remain.

Charlie Laurie, the hard-charging assistant prosecutor who worked himself to exhaustion, had trouble at times controlling his emotions. His almost day-long closing argument was filled with near-hysterical arguments, waving of bloody shirts, and even attacks against the mayor and his safety director for not doing more to warn police about the weaponry they faced. He put Carl Stokes on trial with Ahmed Evans. Laurie's racism was never far from the surface. He frequently referred to his opposing counsel as "boys" and he viciously laid into a poor woman who had been maltreated by police as she was taken from the basement of the Lakeview Tavern.[26] A single example suffices:

> Mr. Laurie: You hate white people, don't you?
>
> Ms. Brown: No.
>
> Mr. Laurie: You hate white people, don't you?
>
> Ms. Brown: No, I don't hate white people.
>
> Mr. Laurie: This country was good to you, wasn't it? You received training from the government, didn't you, in various fields of your endeavors? Didn't you?
>
> Ms. Brown: I told you it doesn't make no difference to me in no way.
>
> Mr. Laurie: Wasn't it my color of people that put up the money for these programs?
>
> Ms. Brown: You don't need to holler at me.[27]

After Ahmed Evans was sentenced to die, he became a symbol of oppression to many African Americans. H. Rap Brown called Evans a "political prisoner." The chairman of the Student Nonviolent Coordinating Committee called for "retaliatory violence in the black community."[28] A minister in Cleveland labeled the verdict a "legal lynching."[29] National magazines carried articles with titles like "The Frame-Up of Ahmed Evans."[30] A group of prominent citizens from Guyana appealed to President Nixon to pardon Evans.[31]

Seven weeks after the Evans was convicted, the trial was reprised against Lathan Donald (Nondu El), but conspicuously without the conspiracy witnesses. Pellets from Patrolman Golonka's body were matched to the type of shotgun found on Donald as he lay wounded behind 1395 Lakeview.[32] Donald testified in his own defense, suggesting a fairly preposterous story that he had gone to a drugstore just before the shooting started; came back in the middle of the gun battle only to find his brother dead in the yard behind 1395 Lakeview; and took his brother's gun, gun belt, and bandolier, strapped them on himself, and engaged in self-defense.[33]

Ahmed Evans came from death row to testify. He did Donald no favors as his rambling testimony was mostly about himself and his view of black nationalism—a defense of the revolution. Yet Evans refused, on his attorneys' advice, to talk about his own actions once the shooting started (even though he expressly waived his Fifth Amendment privilege against self-incrimination at the outset of his testimony).[34] His demeanor was off-putting. Lathan Donald's lawyer had to ask him to take off his sunglasses when his testimony started, and he had to be reminded regularly to sit up and speak into a microphone so the jury might hear him.

However, in one spirited exchange with Charlie Laurie, he did make the case that he heard shooting before leaving the Auburndale apartments. His testimony fit with the theme that the police shot first.[35]

Lathan Donald was convicted of three counts of first-degree murder and four counts of second-degree murder in the four deaths, but the jury recommended mercy, so he was sentenced to serve a minimum of one hundred years on all counts. Under Ohio law, twenty years must be served on a first-degree murder charge and ten years on a second-degree murder charge before eligibility for parole. Lathan reacted calmly to his conviction but delivered a short, defiant speech. "When I incarnated into this world," he said, "I was subjugated and indoctrinated. I submitted to your will and did obeisance at your feet. Then I decided to stand up and become a man, not a Negro and not a slave, but a man." He concluded, "Let it be known that I killed no man. I never have and never will."[36]

A reporter wrote that the "story of Lathan Donald is an American dream turned sour. A tragedy." He referred to his "reticent but polite" demeanor, his intelligence, his voracious reading habits of black authors like Richard Wright, Langston Hughes, and Ralph Ellison. His high school teacher described him as shy but creative. "I called him Donald Lathan for a semester before I learned his real name," she said. "He just never bothered to correct me."[37] He had a brother who was serving as a Green Beret in Vietnam, another who graduated from Oberlin College, a sister who worked for TWA. Bernard, his brother who was killed, was described by his mother as her troubled child, "a slow learner."[38]

But Lathan also read Robert F. Williams. He joined the JFK House. He rioted during Hough with Osu Bey and met Ahmed Evans. "Evans exploited Donald's talents and intelligence," the reporter for the *Plain*

Dealer wrote. "He made him his first lieutenant in the Republic of New Libya, a black cultural organization."

Lathan was paroled in 1994. He married his high school girlfriend, a woman who had gone to Cornell, received her PhD, and taught sociology and wrote about African dance at Rutgers University. He died in 2010.

Osu Bey (Leslie Jackson) and John Hardrick, after long legal battles over whether they could be tried as adults, finally were sent to juvenile court in 1970, where they were found delinquent and sentenced to the Mansfield Youth Center. "Juvenile Judge Walter G. Whitlatch said Hardrick and Jackson must serve until they are 21—at the maximum," the *Plain Dealer* reported.[39] They both died of cancer in 2014.

Ahmed Evans was granted a stay of execution pending his appeal just days before he was to be electrocuted in September 1969. Because the Supreme Court's 1972 ruling in *Furman v. Georgia* struck down all death penalty schemes in the United States, Evans had his sentence commuted from death to life imprisonment by the Eighth District Court of Appeals, effective August 17, 1972.[40]

Harllel Jones, who became known as Harllel X, was arrested the night after the shoot-out for carrying brass knuckles in his car. His life was one of continuous run-ins with the law. He was arrested for kidnapping and gun battles and never found guilty, but in 1972 he was convicted of second-degree murder for allegedly ordering the random killing of a man in retaliation for the slaying of an Afro Set member by a security guard at a restaurant. Jones purportedly ordered lieutenants to shoot any policeman or security guard as vengeance. One man driving on the expressway shortly thereafter was shot dead in his car and another wounded.[41] Jones was sentenced to life in prison.

Five years later, a federal judge ordered Jones released from prison and directed the state to retry him or set him free because prosecutors working for John T. Corrigan, the lead in the Ahmed Evans case, had failed to disclose that one of the juvenile witnesses involved in the shooting had given a statement to prosecutors that disclosed nothing about Jones ordering the hit. The key witness against Jones admitted during the trial that he became an FBI informant after the shooting.[42] In 1978

Corrigan reluctantly dismissed the case when the former FBI informant and chief prosecution witness "could not be found."[43]

The law professor who represented Jones said that FBI files showed that "Jones was under constant surveillance because of his ability to get young blacks to follow him and was considered a threat."[44] One reader of the *Plain Dealer* wrote that Jones was the "victim of the FBI's COIN-TELPRO, a local political prisoner, the target of harassment because he was a black leader confronting the inequities of the 60's."[45]

A white male reader from Parma wrote, "To add insult to outrage, not only is Harllel Jones a free man, but is being transformed into a folk hero by well-wishers." The Parma man ranted that the "only injustice in this case is the failure of the original court to impose the execution sentence that this thug imposed on his victims."[46]

At the same time that Jones was being exonerated, Prosecutor Corrigan indicted eight city council members (all black except one), including George Forbes, for supposedly taking kickbacks from local carnival operators. Forbes was acquitted by a visiting judge from another county in July 1979.[47] "The eyes of justice are still blindfolded in this community and this land," Forbes said.[48]

Carl Stokes was never the same after Glenville. He won reelection in 1969, but he was effectively through as a politician. He began fighting with white city councilmen, and the local businessmen who once supported him fell away. Stokes burned through a series of safety directors, all spectacular failures or quitters. Cleveland: Now! died a slow death along with its lofty plans to transform the ghetto. Cleveland remains one of the nation's poorest cities.

Stokes found himself back in his recurring dream—a young boy outdoors in the piercing cold wearing a thin jacket and looking through the big picture window at a white family sitting in a living room, the father throwing a baby in the air. "A fireplace is going," he wrote, "the family is warm, happy, alive. There is a fence in front of the house. I am outside."[49]

Lewis Robinson gave up and returned to his hometown in the South, having divorced his wife, Beth. His two sons, Medgar Bruce and Malcolm Ari, moved to California with their mother. "The New South is a lot like the old Cleveland," he told a reporter in 1979. "We have a weak mayor and an entrenched police chief, the same as in Cleveland in 1965."[50] Robinson eventually returned to Cleveland in the 1990s and ran unsuccessfully for city council in Shaker Heights. He died at the Cleveland Clinic in 2013. He was eighty-four.[51]

The policemen who were wounded on July 23, 1968, continued to suffer from their injuries. Patrolman Thomas Smith, who was shot attempting to rescue Sergeant Levy, was paralyzed from his waist down and confined to the VA hospital. Chester Szukalski had nine operations on his leg, eventually suffering an amputation. Sam Levy, who was shot seven times, slowly recovered but carried bullets in him the rest of his life. Patrolman Sherbinski, who was shot on the porch of the Lakeview Tavern, had six operations to repair his shattered elbow. Richard Hart, whose arm was nearly severed, had three operations to save his arm, but retained limited use of it. Kenny Gibbons returned to work after a lengthy hospitalization.[52]

All the officers had a common reaction: "Somebody should have told us all those rifles were there." Eight of the policemen and the tow truck operator sued the city and Stokes in 1977 for $8.8 million, blaming the tragedy on the use of Cleveland: Now! money that funded the nationalists' arsenal. Stokes, the policemen's attorney Milt Shulman contended, was trying to keep peace by paying off black militants. "It failed," he shouted in court. "They took a calculated risk and my clients got shot up."[53] A judge did not let it go to the jury, finding that criminal acts, not official negligence, caused the shoot-out. The judge blamed the dismissal in part on the erratic behavior of the lawyer for the policemen. "If the plaintiffs have any action at all, it should be against Mr. Shulman for malpractice," the judge said at case end. "I'm sure each of you jurors would volunteer as a witness."[54]

Mae Mallory returned to Cleveland to protest the arrests of Evans and his followers. After his conviction, she led protesters to the Criminal Courts Building in violation of an injunction banning a sit-in. A scuffle with police ended with Mae Mallory and a deputy sheriff tumbling down an entire flight of stairs.[55] She was charged with contempt and sentenced by Judge McMonagle to a year in the Cleveland Workhouse and a $1,000 fine.[56]

Her codefendant from the Freedom Riders days in Monroe, North Carolina, Robert F. Williams, was finally persuaded to return to the United States. He was met at the Detroit airport by his lawyer, Milton Henry (Gaidi Obadele), on September 12, 1969. After winning acquittal on the kidnapping charges, Williams returned to Michigan where he died in relative obscurity in 1996, believing he had never been given his proper due in the black power movement. He did consult with the Nixon administration before the opening of China.[57]

Milton Henry's Republic of New Africa fell apart from internal bickering and FBI nudging.[58] So did Maxwell Stanford's Revolutionary Action Movement. Stanford (later known as Muhammad Ahmad) spent considerable time in Cleveland on the run from his arrest in 1967 for criminal anarchy. He eventually pled guilty to bail jumping and received three years' probation in 1974. Stanford did write in his 1986 thesis that Evans was part of RAM and that the police attacked his house on July 23. "Ahmed's unit fought back in the battle and later that night other units moved into action for backing as the rebellion continued."[59]

And what to make of the mystery man who Patrolmen Kenny Gibbons saw in front of the Auburndale apartments just before he was hit with gunshots? Ahmed Evans testified the police shot first and this is what caused him to leave the apartment, thinking he was being attacked.[60] Could this man have fired the first shots—perhaps even after Evans and his group had dispersed into the neighborhood but before the tow truck came under fire?

Lathan Donald later told his spouse that he wasn't going to let the FBI and the police do to him what later was done in the case of Black Panther leader Fred Hampton in Chicago. (Hampton was double-crossed by an FBI informant who was in his inner circle, allowing the Chicago police to raid his home and shoot him to death in 1969.)[61]

"Lathan swore that either the police shot first or there is the possibility that the first shot came from yet a third unknown source," his widow wrote in 2017.[62]

29

"To Strive, to Seek, to Find, and Not to Yield"

SIXTEEN DAYS AFTER THE GLENVILLE shoot-out, on August 8, 1968, Richard Nixon addressed the Republican National Convention in Miami Beach, Florida, accepting his party's nomination to run for president of the United States. He painted a bleak picture.

"As we look at America, we see cities enveloped in smoke and flames," he warned. "We hear sirens in the night. We see Americans dying on distant battlefields abroad. We see Americans hating each other; fighting each other; killing each other at home."

Nixon promised a solution to the chaos at home. He pledged to be the law-and-order president. "And to those who say that law and order is the code word for racism," he challenged, "there is a reply: Our goal is justice for every American."

Nixon spoke against Johnson's Great Society and its war on poverty. "For the past five years," he said, "we have been deluged by government programs for the unemployed; programs for cities; programs for the poor. And we have reaped from these programs an ugly harvest of frustration, violence and failure across the land." It was time, he said, "to quit pouring billions of dollars into programs that have failed in the United States of America."[1]

Almost exactly forty-eight years later, on July 7, 2016, a heavily armed sniper ambushed police in Dallas during a Black Lives Matter protest over the fatal police shootings of two black men: Philando Castile in Minnesota and Alton Sterling in Louisiana. Both brutal killings were caught on tapes that were widely circulated on social media and on television. Like Ahmed Evans, the sniper in Dallas was an army veteran. Like Evans, he targeted white policemen in retaliatory violence. "The heavily armed sniper who gunned down police officers in downtown Dallas, leaving five of them dead, specifically set out to kill as many white officers as he could, officials said Friday," the *New York Times* reported.[2]

Fourteen days later, Donald Trump addressed the Republican National Convention in Cleveland, Ohio—five miles from where the Glenville shoot-out took place almost half a century earlier—accepting his party's nomination to run for president of the United States. Like Nixon, he painted a desolate picture.

"Our Convention occurs at a moment of crisis in our nation," Trump warned. "The attacks on our police, and the terrorism in our cities, threaten our very way of life. Any politician who does not grasp this danger is not fit to lead our country."

Trump promised a solution to the chaos at home. "I am the law and order candidate," he proclaimed. "I have a message to every last person threatening the peace on our streets and the safety of our police: when I take office next year, I will restore law and order to our country."

Like Nixon, Trump decried the sitting president's record in addressing poverty and racism. "This Administration," Trump said of the Obama White House, "has failed America's inner cities. It's failed them on education. It's failed them on jobs. It's failed them on crime. It's failed them on every level."[3]

If Trump's acceptance speech sounded a lot like Richard Nixon's in 1968, it is because it was designed to do so. "In a startling disclosure on the first day of the convention, Mr. Trump's campaign chairman, Paul Manafort, declared that the candidate was using, as the template for his own prime-time speech accepting the Republican nomination,

Nixon's convention address 48 years ago in Miami Beach," the *New York Times* wrote. "'If you go back and read,' Mr. Manafort said at a *Bloomberg News* breakfast, 'that speech is pretty much in line with a lot of the issues that are going on today.'"[4]

And so, the question is why? Why after the passage of fifty years was a black man leveling high-powered rifles at white police? Why are African Americans—boys, men, and some women—dying at the hands of the police? Why is it that few of the police face any consequence for the taking of a black life and that black men now crowd our nation's prisons such that there are more African Americans incarcerated today than there were slaves in 1850? Why are our inner cities blighted beyond recognition—most in worse shape than in 1968?

In Cleveland, twelve-year-old Tamir Rice was shot and killed in a park in 2014. His weapon was a toy gun. A grand jury declined to indict the patrolman who fatally shot Rice.[5] Eric Garner, Michael Brown, Laquan McDonald, Walter Scott, Freddie Gray, Sandra Bland, Alton Sterling, Philando Castile—the list is long and tragic. Justice Department investigations in Baltimore, Chicago, Cleveland, and Ferguson, Missouri, found widespread evidence of officers regularly violating the rights of black citizens, though many of the consent decrees are in jeopardy under the Trump administration.[6] "We are not evolving as a civilization," Philando Castile's mother said after a jury failed to convict the policeman who shot him. "We are devolving. We're going back to 1969."[7]

There are glib responses but no easy answers.

One answer, oddly, seems to lie in the Cleveland experience. Carl Stokes was elected in an apparent triumph of the ballot over the bullet. But even his election could not turn back the generations of frustration, anger, and neglect—as one of the nationalists in the backyard of 12312 Auburndale said to young Ricky Hogue, "It goes back 200 years." And there probably should be no illusion here. Evans and his group did not riot and murder only in retaliation for police brutality—though there was an astounding record of cruelty in Cleveland, as elsewhere. It was neglect that created the atmosphere of desperation and eventually the murderous suicide mission on July 23.

African Americans, owned as property for hundreds of years on this continent, have been seen as subhuman, as animals, as people without rights—and to whites their suffering is invisible. In the North, they were thrown together in festering ghettos, rats eating their babies' faces, and there was no way out—no jobs, no opportunities to advance or to move into nice neighborhoods, no chance to receive a quality education, or to live the American dream. African Americans weren't like other American immigrants who could, by dint of work, assimilate and bootstrap themselves into American society—the color of their skin and the legacy of slavery branded them as "other."

This is why Martin Luther King Jr. spoke to the students at Glenville High School about developing a sense of "somebodiness." This is why Lathan Donald after his conviction spoke of becoming a man and leaving behind all that it meant to be a "Negro."

Racism in America has its own peculiar pathology. We are all sick with this mental disease. How could we be otherwise? It has permeated our culture and our national, state, and local politics. It is a wedge issue that still carries incredible power to turn and twist people's minds. It is a cancer that metastasizes and, as its victims, we are all in denial; hundreds of years later, we are only beginning to understand the full extent of the diagnosis.

But the situation, while ugly, is not irredeemable.

The heartbreak is that in 1968 we had made a start; we had taken a first step in honestly acknowledging our nation's racial sickness, and we at least groped for solutions. President Johnson's war on poverty was the right path. The Kerner Commission gave the right diagnosis. Carl Stokes had the right instinct in developing Cleveland: Now! What was needed was a Kerner Commission–like recognition that white racism lay at the root of the problem, not black depravity. What was needed was the kind of massive infusion of money that could actually address the needs of housing, education, jobs, recreation centers, and health facilities.

Tragedy, though, intervened. In the case of the Great Society, the Vietnam War drained national resources, but more important it created the internal chaos—see Kent State—that Nixon fed on. Add to it the disruption of the civil rights movement and the riots in almost all major cities, and this toxic brew cooked up a spectacular counterrevolution—a backlash that became the Reagan Revolution.[8] The philosophy became that the government should stay out of it; the poor should lift themselves out of their own poverty. "We will help those who help themselves," Nixon said in his second inaugural. No fact better exemplifies what happened to the war on poverty than Nixon's appointment of Donald Rumsfeld as the Director of the Office of Economic Opportunity—the engine of Johnson's antipoverty programs. While many Great Society programs—Medicaid, Medicare, food stamps, Head Start, Job Corps—remain, the Nixon administration dismantled the Office of Economic Opportunity.[9]

Tragedy likewise intervened to crush Cleveland: Now! It had no chance after Ahmed Evans used its funds to buy rifles to shoot white policemen. The backlash in Cleveland brought Ralph Perk, the mayor who set his hair on fire and was a bad rerun of Ralph Locher. Cleveland: Now! never got off the ground. Glenville and Hough, though the beneficiaries of important housing upgrades thanks to government financing and city leadership, have been decimated in population and poverty is rampant. Cleveland's schools are still troubled.

Carl Stokes called Ahmed Evans a "punk" for what he did to Cleveland and his mayoralty. "He did not intend that there would be a shooting," Stokes bitterly wrote. "He just wanted to keep his hustle going."[10] Evans died of cancer in prison in 1978.[11] Mutawaf Shaheed, one of the Muntu poets who became an imam of a local mosque, washed his body and wrapped him in shrouds, in the Islamic tradition, only to have family members show up, tear off the shrouds, and dress him in African garb. One of his brothers jumped on his corpse, beating his chest and sobbing, "Fred, Fred, Fred . . ."[12]

Two things are necessary to again restart the mission of 1968. First, the nation needs to massively invest in our inner cities and in antipoverty programs. Imagine if the trillions wasted on military blunders over the past decade alone went to education, job training, housing, and health care. The Kerner Commission put it this way when talking about the "two Americas" and the challenge for change:

Ahmed Evans, with sunglasses, in a religious meeting with other Muslims in the Ohio Penitentiary and Imam Mutawaf Shaheed (white collar). The inmates were all on death row. *Mutawaf Shaheed Personal Collection*

This deepening racial division is not inevitable. The movement apart can be reversed. Choice is still possible. Our principal task is to define that choice and to press for a national resolution.

To pursue our present course will involve the continuing polarization of the American community and, ultimately, the destruction of basic democratic values.

The alternative is not blind repression or capitulation to lawlessness. It is the realization of common opportunities for all within a single society.

This alternative will require a commitment to national action—compassionate, massive, and sustained, backed by the resources of the most powerful nation on this earth. From every American it will require new attitudes, new understandings, and, above all, new will.[13]

Second, we must enforce our nation's gun laws and further regulate gun ownership. Ahmed Evans taunted his captors that he could have purchased his rifles with "a library card." Safety director McManamon claimed that he was powerless to intervene in the arms buildup at the Auburndale apartments because there was nothing illegal about owning high-powered rifles—so long as they weren't machine guns.

In the end, there has to be a way forward where we all recognize our fellow citizens as brothers and sisters.

Before President Obama traveled to Dallas to memorialize the fallen officers in July 2016, he wrote an open letter to law enforcement—praising the courage and heroism of our police forces. He could have been writing about the bravery demonstrated by those Cleveland police officers killed and wounded on July 23:

> Every day, you accept this responsibility and you see your colleagues do their difficult, dangerous jobs with equal valor. I want you to know that the American people see it, too. We recognize it, we respect it, we appreciate it, and we depend on you. And just as your tight-knit law enforcement family feels the recent losses to your core, our nation grieves alongside you. Any attack on police is an unjustified attack on all of us.

But President Obama also made reference to Bobby Kennedy's "Mindless Menace of Violence" speech—the one delivered in Cleveland at the City Club on April 5, 1968, the day after Martin Luther King was assassinated. "Robert Kennedy," he wrote, "once our nation's highest-ranking law enforcement official, lamented in the wake of unjust violence a country in which we look at our neighbors as people 'with whom we share a city, but not a community.'" He went on, "This is a time for us to reaffirm that what makes us special is that we are not only a country, but also a community. That is true whether you are black or white, whether you are rich or poor, whether you are a police officer or someone they protect and serve."[14]

We cannot expect our police to solve the problems of poverty and racism. That is a job for all Americans. Nor can we deny that rebels like Ahmed Evans and Lathan Donald, though twisted and wrong, were fighting a political battle—one that, in their desperation, they believed was being waged for their people and their own sense of self-respect.

There is no excuse for violence, ever—by black nationalists or police. As Bobby Kennedy said, "No wrongs have ever been righted by riots or civil disorder. A sniper is only a coward, not a hero; and an uncontrolled, uncontrollable mob is only the voice of madness, not the voice of reason."

But violence like that seen on July 23 is a symptom of a greater disease—and unless we start treating that disease, it is destined to recur in a divided nation that is armed to the teeth.

Bobby Kennedy would ask us, as he did at the end of his speech at the City Club of Cleveland, to follow Tennyson's advice from his poem *Ulysses*.

It is not a time to give up, Kennedy would say, it is a time for action: "To strive, to seek, to find, and not to yield."

Afterword

THE STORY OF FIFTY YEARS ago feels oddly immediate today as we have witnessed the rise of hatred politics in America. Violence against Jews and African Americans, often conflating the two groups, has spiked under Donald Trump. It requires us think anew of how these two minorities have suffered a common plight, one that in the past brought them together, however jagged and flawed the relationship.

The Jews in Glenville followed the pattern established nationally when they moved up in society and out of their old neighborhoods in urban areas, breaking apart what had been an empathetic relationship with African Americans. The two groups became disconnected in the late 1960s over calls for militant "black power" and a divergence over upward social and economic mobility. As one author put it, "America's cities had worked for Jews," facilitating their arrival into the elite circles of society, whereas African Americans "remained trapped in ghettos, unable to break through to prosperity."[1]

But have the renewed, frequently lethal attacks of white supremacists on both groups opened an opportunity for the rebuilding of a coalition, tempered by a conflicted past but perhaps informed by a more distant but encouraging history of alliance and support?

***

On October 28, 2018, three months after the publication of *Ballots and Bullets*, a forty-six-year-old, heavily armed gunman entered the Tree of Life Synagogue in Pittsburgh, Cleveland's nearby sister city, and began a killing spree. The shooting during Shabbat morning services in the Squirrel Hill neighborhood resulted in the deaths of eleven Jewish worshippers, with six more injured. It was the deadliest attack on the Jewish community in the history of the United States. The violence took place almost a half century after the Glenville shootout.

The bearded, heavy-set white male rampaged through the building with an assault rifle and Glock pistols for twenty terrifying minutes, shouting, "All Jews must die!" A native of the greater Pittsburgh metropolitan area, the shooter was a white nationalist, a neo-Nazi who trafficked in anti-Semitic conspiracy theories. He posted content online favorable to groups that took part in the Unite the Right rally in Charlottesville, Virginia, in 2017, and in the weeks prior to the shooting, he obsessed about a caravan of Central American migrants trekking through Mexico toward the US border. President Trump had hyped the caravan as "an invasion of our country," a bogeyman designed to alarm and energize his base prior to the 2018 midterm elections—a ploy that ultimately failed.

Nonetheless, the attacker was convinced that the Hebrew Immigrant Aid Society (HIAS), a humanitarian organization that supported international refugees, was aiding the caravan. He called the migrants "invaders" and believed that Jews were deliberately undermining "white" America. "HIAS likes to bring invaders in that kill our people," he wrote online in a paranoid post just before the attack. "I can't stand by and watch my people get slaughtered. Screw your optics. I'm going in." Most of his victims were quite elderly; Rose Mallinger was the oldest at 97.

What the Unite the Right rally in Charlottesville exposed was the modern-day mixing of racism and anti-Semitic hatred, all spewing from a group of primarily white males who fear their majority status is slipping away, along with their sense of entitlement, power, and privilege. Like the Tree of Life terrorist, the alt-right, neo-fascist, white-nationalist marchers in Charlottesville chanted slurs like "the Jews will not replace us" and the Nazi slogan "Blood and Soil" as they protested the removal of a statue of Robert E. Lee from Charlottesville's Lee Park. These twisted Americans think the "white race" is doomed to extinction by the "rising tide of color" being coordinated and directed by Jews. On Friday, August 11, 2017, tiki torch–carrying demonstrators clashed with counterprotestors who had locked arms around a statue of Thomas Jefferson in front of the University of Virginia campus. The next day, violence resulted in injuries and the death of Heather Heyer when a car plowed into a group peacefully assembling in the alleyway off a pedestrian mall. It was one of the ugliest days in American history—yet President Trump found "very fine people on both sides."

The mingling of hatred against Jews and African Americans made me think of Cory Methodist Church in Cleveland. Built as a Jewish Center on East 105th in Cleveland's Glenville neighborhood in 1920, this sacred space would change hands after World War II when the Jewish population had largely migrated east to Cleveland Heights, Shaker Heights, and beyond. The congregation Anshe Emeth Beth Tefilo sold the Cleveland Jewish Center in 1947 to Cory Methodist Church, making it the largest black-owned church in Cleveland and one of the biggest in the United States. It can seat up to 2,400 in its sanctuary, and its size is what attracted Dr. Martin Luther King Jr. and Malcolm X to the pulpit within a year of one another in 1963 and 1964. But more, this one space was triply blessed, the embodiment of the three Abrahamic traditions: conceived as a Jewish synagogue, Christian Martin Luther King Jr. and Muslim Malcolm X found it a welcoming forum to examine and debate the most important questions in the black freedom movement in the 1960s. It says much about the Methodists of that church that Malcolm X felt the freedom to deliver his incendiary "Ballot or Bullet" speech there for the first time.

The Jewish community built a new campus in Cleveland Heights. Named in honor of Park School, it is located in a wooded and bucolic tract of land situated within the suburban city limits. Members of Park Synagogue commissioned Erich Mendelsohn, a German-born architect who had escaped Nazi Germany in 1933 and was world renowned for his expressionist-style buildings (including the ingenious Einstein Tower in Potsdam), to design the new worship space. The centerpiece of Mendelsohn's design for Park was a vast hemispheric temple dome, weighing over 680 tons. Large clear glass windows in the interior sanctuary provide an inspiring sense of nature as the surrounding wooded landscape seems to blend into the core worship space. A bubbling creek runs between structures on the property.

At a time when the attack against the Pittsburgh synagogue laid bare the destructive forces released in the nation by the 2016 election, members of Cory Methodist Church and Park Synagogue quietly began to meet to talk of their common roots as sketched out in this book and to survey the larger, troubling questions of the rise of hatred and violence in our nation as a form of political expression. Neither group was new to this conversation. Jews and blacks have been the consistent targets of violence from majority white populations, often sponsored, or at the very least inspired, by the government.

This is not to say, however, that the dialogue between Jews and blacks is an easy one. A short digression into the complex history between these two groups is in order.

**

Cultural historians have long noted the sympathies that have existed between American Jews and African Americans. When great numbers of Jews began arriving in America from Eastern Europe after 1880, they saw the predicament of blacks through ethical lenses that reminded them of their own struggles. Poor and embattled, the ideology of socialism predominated among many of the Jewish immigrants, making them leaders in union organizing and crusaders in public life. Side by side with their political philosophy of egalitarianism was a pronounced concern about American racism. In their adopted country, these Jewish reformers perceived a bundle of evils, all related, that they sought to combat and eliminate. One writer put it this way: "The catechism of socialism impelled an alliance with Blacks: The brotherhood of the workers would overthrow the bosses and banish racism, anti-Semitism, war, and exploitation."[2]

Black people and Jews faced similar existential battles in the modern world. Jews in Europe were plagued by pogroms and state-sponsored murder, while African Americans were demeaned and terrorized by repressive Jim Crow laws and the sanctioned practice of lynching. African American citizens saw the Biblical story of the Jews' triumph over slavery in Egypt as inspirational, not just in the religious context of spiritual music ("Go Down, Moses"), but also as a direct historical analogue to their own experiences of woe and the hoped-for victory over powerful oppressors.

Jews and Africans in America are exilic peoples, groups who have been separated from their land. Both have espoused ethnocentric nationalism: Zionism for Jews, Pan-Africanism and black nationalism for African Americans. Where the diasporic Jews produced Theordor Herzl, African Americans brought forth Marcus Garvey, W. E. B. Du Bois, Malcolm X, and Stokely Carmichael. One early Black Zionist, Edward Blyden, wrote in 1903: "The Jewish question, in some respects, is similar to that which at this moment agitates thousands of descendants of Africa in America, anxious to return to the land of their fathers."[3]

Over time, Jews could be found in the front lines supporting African Americans in such battles as the legal representation of the defendants in the Scottsboro Boys trial in Alabama in 1931, a case involving nine young men falsely accused of rape. Jewish leaders like Rabbi Stephen Wise of New York and Rabbi Emil Hirsh of Chicago joined W. E. B. Du Bois in helping to organize, finance, and support the formation of the National Association for the Advancement of Colored People (NAACP) in the first decades of the twentieth century. Other Jews were instrumental in the founding of the National Urban League in 1912 and later the funding of local chapters of the Congress on Racial Equality. Large numbers of Jewish college students joined the ranks of the Freedom Riders in 1961. Two of the three civil rights activists killed in Mississippi in the Freedom Summer of 1964 during a voter registration drive were Jewish: Andrew Goodman and Michael Schwerner.

But this kinship had an underlying tension. Jews could be quite racist, using the racial slur *schwartze*, Yiddish for "black," behind closed doors. African Americans could just as easily slip into stereotypical invectives about Jewish merchants as predatory and moneygrubbing.

Things began to shift in a material way in the 1960s. Just as many Jews joined Dr. King and his followers in the civil rights movement, open hostility began to creep into the relationship between Jews and blacks in large part because of the transition of Jewish neighborhoods to predominantly African American enclaves. As Jews moved out, they continued to own the majority of the businesses, properties, shops, apartment complexes, and many of the housing units in their former neighborhoods. As was the case in Hough and Glenville, slumlords took advantage of the immobility of blacks, who still dealt with severe housing restrictions. Likewise many Jewish business owners overpriced their goods knowing that they had a captive clientele with few transportation options. Because the Jews and African Americans had started off together—poor and discriminated against in housing—a consequence was that many of the landlords and business owners in the ghetto were Jewish.

The Hough rebellion started outside a Jewish tavern. Looters and firebombers targeted mainly Jewish establishments. Ahmed Evans's landlords were Jewish. The rise of black nationalism and black Muslims added fuel to the fire, leaving both groups feeling estranged and bitter toward one another. Statements uttered by the Nation of Islam leaders over the years, for example, have been among the most rank and malign anti-Semitic invectives ever spoken.

***

When Ahmed Evans started his war against the Cleveland Police in 1968, the Holocaust was as fresh in the collective consciousness as 9/11 is to us today. A mere generation—twenty-five years—separated the people of that time from the horrors of Auschwitz, Treblinka, and other Nazi extermination camps. Jews who escaped the genocide in Europe had heightened reason to understand the black freedom struggle in life-and-death terms.

In Cleveland, Paul Zilsel, a professor of physics at Case Western Reserve University, joined students and members of the July 23rd Defense Committee (Mae Mallory was one of the founders), established to support Ahmed Evans and Lathan Donald in their trials. Zilsel was the son of renowned Austrian science philosopher Edgar Zilsel, a Jewish Marxist who had been a member of the famed Vienna Circle. Edgar Zilsel and his family escaped during Hitler's annexation of Austria, known as the *Anschluss*, in 1938 when son Paul was fifteen. Paul attended Yale University where he received his doctorate in theoretical physics. He was called before the House Un-American Activities

Committee for involvement with the American Communist Party in 1953 and was blacklisted at universities for several years.

He told friends in the late 1960s that, having fled Nazi persecution, he identified with the black minority in the United States. He put it in a peculiar but provocative way: "I came from a situation where I was the nigger into one where somebody else was the kike." To another friend he confessed, "If I were black, I'm sure I would be a Panther."[4]

Events at Case Western Reserve University turned riotous following Ahmed Evans's conviction on May 12, 1969, and Zilsel was in the middle of it. In the immediate aftermath of Glenville, another professor at Case Western Reserve, Louis Masotti, had been asked by the National Commission on the Causes and Prevention of Violence, an organization created by President Johnson after the King and Kennedy assassinations in 1968, to write a report on the causes of the shootout. Masotti, along with a graduate assistant named Jerome Corsi (more on him later) and a team working out of the CWRU Civil Violence Research Center, began intensive work just weeks following the shootout. As Masotti wrote in a preface to his report, "hundreds of man-hours were invested in interviewing, researching, writing, and safeguarding the accuracy and completeness as we rushed to deadline." The deadline set by the Commission was November 15, 1968.[5]

Masotti and his team conducted taped interviews of Walter Beach, George Forbes, Safety Director Joe McManamon, Stokes assistant John Little, and others, transcriptions of which (now in the Carl Stokes papers in the archives of the Western Reserve Historical Society) allowed me to provide a fairly reliable firsthand account of events that led up to the start of the battle.

But the issuance of Masotti's report, though it had been finalized, was delayed. According to Masotti, the Commission thought twice about releasing the report before Ahmed Evans was put on trial; they wished to avoid any potential pretrial prejudice to either the prosecution or defense. This postponement, however, created a cross-current of conspiracy theorists who believed both that Masotti and his researchers had uncovered evidence that would exonerate Evans at trial and that the Commission had been pressured by the FBI or local authorities to keep it under wraps until after the trial. The calls for the release of the report mounted in the days following Evans's conviction in May 1969.

The night after the jury returned its verdict, Professor Masotti was kidnapped by black nationalists who were furious that the report had not been released. An internal FBI airtel from the special-agent-in-charge in Cleveland to the Director of the FBI confirmed what happened:

> On the evening of 5/13/69 Masotti telephonically contacted Colonel William G. MacDonald of the Commission in Washington, DC, and related that while making a speech on that date at Western Reserve University, he, his wife, and mother were held captive for two hours by a Negro militant group, New Libya, who demanded that the report be furnished to the defense attorney of Fred Evans, who had been sentenced to death for the slaying of three police officers. Masotti and his family were released and he was fearful that harm would come to them if he does not furnish the report to Evans' defense attorney. Masotti was reluctant to advise the Cleveland police of this matter as his report, although not yet made public, was generally regarded as being highly critical of the Cleveland Police Department.

The FBI responded that they could not provide Masotti with security.[6] Meanwhile, Professor Zilsel got out in front of protestors on the campus and organized mass meetings at Haydn Hall where a list of demands for the university was created. During the chaos, someone broke into Masotti's Civil Violence Research Center and stole files showing the university had helped fund the Center, despite previous public denials from the president.

An injunction was issued against Zilsel for instigating violence. A sit-in at the administration offices turned into a slugfest outside the provost's office. (Ernie Green, who had just retired as a Cleveland Browns running back, was the vice provost and can been seen in a photo trying to stop the scuffle.) Professor Zilsel held a press conference days later where he predicted that the university may go up in flames if the Masotti report was not published. He charged that the university was "an accomplice in the legal lynching of Ahmed Evans." He was eventually arrested with Mae Mallory when they attempted to disrupt a hearing at the Cuyahoga Common Pleas Court with a demonstration demanding an investigation into the alleged police abuse of patrons of the Lakeview Tavern during the night of the shoot-out.

Nothing came of the protests. Masotti's work, *Shoot-Out in Cleveland: Black Militants and the Police, A Report to the National Commission on the Causes and Prevention of Violence,* was published shortly thereafter, and the public discovered that Professor Masotti took issue with the police, the nationalists, and society in general. He warned that it could all happen again because "America itself has not changed in ways that matter."

Sadly, that statement remains true today in so many respects.

Masotti's graduate assistant and coauthor of the report, Jerome Corsi, went on to Harvard University where he received his PhD in political science in 1972. Corsi would become a leading conspiracy theorist for the far right, writing dozens of bestselling books about such things as John Kerry's swift boats and President Obama's birth certificate, as well as eccentric notions about 9/11, Hitler escaping Germany, and JFK's assassination. He worked for a time for Alex Jones and InfoWars before suing Jones for defamation. In August 2018, Corsi was subpoenaed by Robert Mueller and the special prosecutor's office as a result of his dealings with his friend and associate Roger Stone. Trump campaign aide Rick Gates testified in Stone's 2019 federal trial that he thought of Stone as the campaign's intermediary to WikiLeaks, the outfit that released damaging Clinton campaign e-mails in the 2016 election. According to news accounts from the Stone trial, Corsi played a key role: "In late July and early August 2016, Stone tasked conservative conspiracy theorist Jerome Corsi to try to reach [Julian] Assange and find out what files he had, and when he planned to release them."[7]

"Word is friend in Embassy [referring to Assange who was holed up in the Ecuadorian embassy in London] plans 2 more dumps," Corsi e-mailed Stone on August 2, 2016. "Impact planned to be very damaging." Stone was convicted by a jury on all counts of witness intimidation, lying to investigators, and lying to Congress. Corsi somehow skated. He did not even testify in Stone's trial, with commentators surmising that both sides "viewed him as an unreliable narrator."[8]

Corsi's evolution in one lifetime from a serious graduate student interested the causes of racial injustice and abuses of police authority to a purveyor of racist "birtherism" attacks on Barack Obama and paranoid assaults on the "deep state" is mind-blowing. It speaks to how far off track the nation has lurched. Corsi grew up in a blue-collar home in East Cleveland, his father a railroad union official and Democrat who helped to organize the United Transportation Union and was a loyal follower of JFK and Lyndon Johnson. Corsi graduated from St. Ignatius, a progressive Jesuit high school in Cleveland, and while he worried that President Johnson's "Great Society" would lead to socialism and he did not trust Carl Stokes as a candidate, there is a wide gulf between such embryonic anxieties and a full-blown distrust of the American system of government.

In Donald Trump, Corsi and Stone found a leader who revels in their irrational theories, whether he actually believes them or not. By his provocative speech about "invaders" and "infestations" in our urban areas—exacerbating the sense of "otherness" of people of color and Jews—he encourages and activates deranged loners like the shooter in Pittsburgh or the twenty-one-year-old white man in Texas who, hunting for Mexican immigrants, traveled eleven hours to shoot up the Walmart in El Paso in October 2019, killing twenty-two people and injuring twenty-six others.

And in this time of extreme danger and incitement, a small political minority continues to refuse to take guns away from lunatics and blocks even the most sensible gun regulation. Locked and loaded describes the true state of our nation.

It is hard to fathom how these people—whose parents and grandparents fought Nazis and fascists, joined in the creation of the New Deal with its vital social security protections, and elected leaders who passed bold civil rights legislation in the 1960s—could somehow, half a century later, descend so easily into America's darkest past of hatred and bigotry.

***

During the disturbed times in Cleveland in the aftermath of the summer of 1968, Mayor Carl Stokes tried to convince militant blacks that violence was not the answer. In one recording of a public meeting (date unknown), Stokes went further and counseled that a violent white backlash could turn catastrophic for the black community just as it had for the Jews in Europe. His dire warning of genocide is chilling precisely because, to Stokes and perhaps many in his audience, the prospect did not seem far-fetched. Stokes said:

> This country is, I'd have to admit to you, teetering on the brink of whether or not it is going to observe at least the modicums of the protections of a democratic system, as opposed to evidencing some of the signs of going into a totalitarian system. But I can say to you without equivocation, and in a sense of preservation of both you and myself, that you can't beat the system by violence. And if you just think about it for a minute, you're talking about a country that's got the antiballistic missiles systems, it's got the Polaris submarines, it's got the army, the navy, the Coast Guard, the CIA—why do you know what would happen if they turned, as they can turn, on an identifiable minority group in this country? Why, they'd wipe you out tomorrow morning, and, as horrendous as it would be to me and you, it would not be inconsistent with history. [Applause] It was just twenty-five years ago that the Germans exterminated six million Jews. That wasn't back in the times of the Romans, the times of the Greeks; that's just in the last twenty-five, twenty-seven years that they did that.

Fast forward to November 16, 2019, when I heard a similar warning at the memorial service for Norma Jean Freeman, Don Freeman's spouse, held in Cory Methodist Church. Don Freeman, the reader will recall, was the junior high school teacher who was fired by the Cleveland Board of Education in 1964 for his work in forming the Revolutionary Action Movement, or RAM. Norma Freeman, who Don always introduced as his "soul mate," grew up in Cleveland and was a graduate of Fisk University in Nashville. She once told me that she remembered meeting W. E. B. Du Bois on the Fisk campus. She and Don stayed in

Glenville, even as it deteriorated around them, working as educators and volunteers for all manner of social justice causes. They had three children, one of whom grew up to become a Cleveland policeman.

Norma Freeman's memorial was like none I have ever witnessed. Black nationalist flags adorned the sanctuary. In the African tradition, the elders were consulted before the service could begin. The black national anthem, "Lift Every Voice and Sing," filled the space, with many fists raised in salute. African American Cleveland politicians spoke while Muslims, Christians, and African spiritualists circulated together in peace and solidarity. It was as much political pageantry as religious service.

One eulogist, a pastor from a Christian church, said that Norma, knowing she was in her last illness, called a lifelong friend to her death-bed to take down a sort of final testament. She had many thoughts, but this pastor said her most urgent message was to shake black folks into the reality of the times. "We're in trouble," the pastor quoted Norma. "We have a fascist in the White House who is taking care of the Mexicans and is coming for the niggers next."

I was shocked to hear the n-word in a church setting but even more amazed by how this message seemed to be instantly accepted by the people in attendance, who released a collective, audible affirmation. Like Mayor Stokes fifty years ago, African Americans in 2019 had no trouble believing that annihilation for their people could be right around the corner. The eulogist asked the audience to think of what Jews in Germany in the 1930s must have sensed was coming but had acted too late to stop. His message—Norma's message, really—was to get ready, to be prepared. It was as much a call to arms as the one expressed more directly by Malcolm X in that same space over fifty years earlier.

***

There is only one answer, of course, and that is for people of goodwill, like the current members of Cory Methodist Church and Park Synagogue, to continue to see the human struggle as one struggle and to engage in dialogue, however uncomfortable that may be. Bobby Kennedy still speaks to us. When he came to Cleveland two months before his death, at a time when the nation was reeling from Dr. King's murder the day before, Bobby found the right words. He said:

> Yet we know what we must do. It is to achieve true justice among our fellow citizens. The question is not what programs we should seek to enact. The question is whether we can find in our own midst and in our own hearts that leadership of human purpose that will recognize the terrible truths of our existence.
>
> We must admit the vanity of our false distinctions among men and learn to find our own advancement in the search for the advancement of all. We must admit in ourselves that our own children's future cannot be built on the misfortunes of others. We must recognize that this short life can neither be ennobled or enriched by hatred or revenge.
>
> Our lives on this planet are too short and the work to be done too great to let this spirit flourish any longer in our land.

Key Figures

Cleveland Mayor's Office

James Carnes—chief police prosecutor
Bertrand Gardner—community relations director
Clarence "Buddy" James—city law director, acting mayor
John C. Little—mayor's executive secretary
Sergeant Bosie Mack—mayor's security
Carl B. Stokes—mayor, 1967–1971
Louis Stokes—lawyer, congressman

Cleveland Police Department

Daniel Balogh—patrolman, Car 341
Robert Bennett—patrolman, Car 65E
Ray Bensley—Tow Truck 58
Michael Blackwell—police chief, Stokes
Earl Brown—patrolman, Car 508
Harold Butler—patrolman, Scooter 5S3
Kenneth Childers—patrolman, Car 507
Herbert Dregalla—captain, Car 551
Amos Floyd—patrolman, special-duty vice squad
Michael Franko—patrolman, Car 507
John Gallagher—patrolman, surveillance Car 961

Anthony Gentile—sergeant, Car 653, Thompson submachine gun
Thomas Gerrity—patrolman, surveillance Car 966
Kenny Gibbons—patrolman, wounded
Louis Golonka—patrolman, Car 515, killed
Walter Granger—detective, Car 64H
Richard Hart—patrolman, Car 541, wounded
Lawrence Hernandez—patrolman, Car 414
Thomas Horgan—patrolman, surveillance Car 966
Leroy Jones—lieutenant, Car 653, killed
Elmer Joseph—lieutenant, Car 551, wounded
Joseph Katonka—patrolman, wounded
Donald Kuchar—patrolman, Car 341
Sam Levy—sergeant, Car 553, wounded
Joseph McManamon—patrolman, Car 591, wounded
Joseph P. McManamon—city safety director
Steven Merencky—patrolman
Donald Milla—patrolman, Car 211
William McMillin—Tow Truck 58, wounded
Thomas Moran—sergeant, Car 553
James O'Malley—patrolman, surveillance Car 961
Walter Phillips—patrolman, Car 506
Ernest Rowell—patrolman, Car 506, wounded
Angelo Santa Maria—patrolman, Car 417, wounded
George Sekerak—patrolman, Car 541
Robert Shankland—detective, Car 64H
Anthony Sherbinski—patrolman, wounded
Leonard Simms—patrolman, Car 508
Thomas Smith—patrolman, Scooter 5S2, wounded
Steve Sopko—patrolman, Car 417
George Sperber—captain, chief of intelligence
Jack Starr—patrolman, off duty
John Sweeney—patrolman, surveillance Car 961
Leonard Szalkiewicz—patrolman, Car 414, wounded
Chester Szukalski—patrolman, Car 591, wounded
Richard Tanski—patrolman, Car 615

Joseph Torok—patrolman, Car 515
Joseph Tuft—patrolman, Car 513
Peter Ventura—patrolman, Car 611
Gerald Viola—patrolman, Car 65E
Richard R. Wagner—police chief, Locher
Richard Wilson—patrolman, Car 513
Willard Wolff—patrolman, Car 505, killed
Robert Woods—patrolman, Car 211
Robert Zagore—patrolman, Car 615

Subversives Unit

John Smith—detective
John J. Ungvary—sergeant

Post-Investigation

Louis Garcia—detective
Ralph Joyce—sergeant
Victor Kovacic—sergeant
Richard Reiss—detective

Black Nationalists

Sababa Akili—Afro Set
Russell Atkins—Muntu poet
Walter Beach—Browns defensive back, Mayor's Council on Youth
    Opportunity
DeForest Brown—executive director, Hough Area Development Cor-
    poration
James Dailey—New Libya
Bernard Donald [Johnson]—Little Nondu, New Libya, killed
Lathan Donald—Nondu El, New Libya, wounded and arrested
Fred Ahmed Evans—Republic of New Libya leader, arrested
Don Freeman—Cleveland school teacher, cofounder of RAM
John Hardrick—Little Ahmed, New Libya, 17, arrested
Linda Hardrick—New Libya

Sandra Hardrick—Simba, New Libya, Evans's spouse
Leslie Jackson—Osu Bey, New Libya, 16, arrested
Harllel Jones—Harllel X, leader, Afro Set
Norman Jordan—Muntu poet
Omar Majid—Afro Set
Mae Mallory—New York City nationalist
James Mitchem—New Libya
Sharon Moore—New Libya
Sandra Parks—New Libya
Lewis G. Robinson—civil rights activist, lawyer, city housing inspector
Jean Samuels—New Libya
Anita Scott—New Libya
Mutawaf Shaheed—Clyde Shy, Muntu poet
Max Stanford—Philadelphia, leader of RAM
James Taylor—Amir Rashidd, Muntu poet, "The Beast"
Sidney Taylor—Malik Ali Bey, New Libya, killed
Alfred Thomas—"Unknown," New Libya, arrested
Leroy Williams—Amir ibn Khatib, New Libya, killed
Robert F. Williams—North Carolina activist, RAM president-in-exile

FBI

Thomas A. Corbett—special agent, Cleveland office
Charles Cusick—special agent in charge, Cleveland office
John J. Sullivan—special agent, Cleveland office

Other

James Chapman—volunteer, killed
Charles Fleming—Evans's lawyer
George Forbes—city councilman for Glenville, lawyer
James Haynes—civilian, killed
Milton Henry—Gaidi Obadele, Detroit lawyer, founder Republic of New
    Africa
Charles Laurie—prosecutor
Ralph McAlister—school board president

George McMonagle—trial judge

Doris O'Donnell—*Cleveland Plain Dealer*

Henry Orange—civilian, car in front of Lakeview Tavern, wounded

Edithe Schepperd—widow, key witness

Charles L. Teel—police academy, key witness

Stanley Tolliver—Evans's lawyer

Joseph Turpin—city workhouse, Evans hid in his attic

William O. Walker—editor, *Call and Post*

Notes

Chapter 1: "Watch Yourself, Willie"

1. Transcript, *State of Ohio v. Fred (Ahmed) Evans*, Case No. 90257, Court of Common Pleas, Criminal Branch, Cuyahoga County, Ohio, Vol. 13, Cuyahoga County Archives, Cleveland, Ohio (Kenneth Gibbons), 4980.

2. Transcript, *State of Ohio v. Fred (Ahmed) Evans*, 4990.

3. Transcript, *State of Ohio v. Fred (Ahmed) Evans*, 4990–95.

4. Transcript, *State of Ohio v. Fred (Ahmed) Evans*, 2881–84 (Adelson).

5. Transcript, *State of Ohio v. Fred (Ahmed) Evans*, 5018.

6. Kenneth Gibbons, interview, April 24, 2017.

Chapter 2: "We Will Meet Violence with Violence and Lynching with Lynching"

1. "DiSalle Weighs Dixie 'Justice' for a Negro," *Cleveland Plain Dealer*, February 4, 1962.

2. Interview with Robert F. Williams, YouTube video, 27:59, posted by Anthony Johnson, September 4, 2015, http://youtu.be/_NuxaMYYGJY.

3. "NAACP Leader Urges 'Violence,'" *New York Times*, May 7, 1959.

4. "Jail Fails to Damp Mrs. Mallory's Spirit," *Cleveland Plain Dealer*, August 25, 1962.

5. Ibid.

6. "Mallory Jailing Ends 2-Year Fight," *Cleveland Plain Dealer*, January 10, 1964.

7. "Civil Rights Battle of 1964 Launched," *Cleveland Plain Dealer*, January 10, 1964.

8. "Testimony Due in Mallory Trial," *Cleveland Plain Dealer*, February 23, 1964.

9. "Mae Mallory Found Guilty," *Cleveland Plain Dealer*, February 28, 1964; "Willie Mae Appeals Conviction," *Cleveland Plain Dealer*, February 29, 1964.

Chapter 3: "We Will Meet Physical Force with Soul Force"

1. "Glenville Fights Blight," *Cleveland Plain Dealer*, March 12, 1961.

2. Todd Michney, *Surrogate Suburbs: Black Mobility and Neighborhood Change in Cleveland, 1900–1980* (Chapel Hill: University of North Carolina Press, 2017), 11.

3. "Glenville Fights Blight," *Cleveland Plain Dealer*, March 12, 1961.

4. "We Shall Overcome . . . Someday!" *Cleveland Call and Post*, May 18, 1963.

5. "King Inspired Many to Give Bushels of Money for Cause," *Cleveland Call and Post*, January 16, 1986. Bob Williams likewise referred to King as "the 20th Century Moses." "Throngs Cheer Dixie Leaders' Attack on Bias," *Cleveland Call and Post*, May 18, 1963.

6. "Throngs Cheer Dixie Leaders' Attack on Bias," *Cleveland Call and Post*, May 18, 1963.

7. "Kennedy Reacts," *New York Times*, May 9, 1963.

8. "Sanity in Birmingham," *New York Times*, May 11, 1963.

9. "Dr. Martin King and Aides at Cory Tuesday," *Cleveland Call and Post*, May 11, 1963.

10. David M. Swiderski, "Approaches to Black Power: African American Grassroots Political Struggle in Cleveland, Ohio, 1960–1966" (Dissertations, Paper 844, University of Massachusetts Amherst, 2013), 98.

11. "Negroes End Alabama Truce," *Cleveland Plain Dealer*, May 9, 1963.

12. Ibid.

13. "Seeking US Dream, King Tells Throngs," *Cleveland Plain Dealer*, May 15, 1963; "Enthusiastic Reception 'Deeply Moves' King," *Cleveland Call and Post*, May 18, 1963.

14. "Throngs Cheer Dixie Leaders' Attack on Bias," *Cleveland Call and Post*, May 18, 1963.

15. "Seeking US Dream, King Tells Throngs," *Cleveland Plain Dealer*, May 15, 1963.

16. "$12,000 Donated at King Talks," *Cleveland Plain Dealer*, May 16, 1963.

17. "Dr. King Was Frequent Ohio, Cleveland Visitor," *Cleveland Plain Dealer*, April 13, 1963.

18. Leonard Moore, *Carl B. Stokes and the Rise of Black Political Power* (Urbana: University of Illinois Press, 2002), 4.

19. "Birmingham Bomb Kills 4 Negro Girls in Church; Riots Flare; 2 Boys Slain," *New York Times*, September 16, 1963.

20. "House Unit Votes Civil Rights Bill," *New York Times*, October 30, 1963.

21. "Malcolm X Scores U.S. and Kennedy," *New York Times*, December 2, 1963.

Chapter 4: "The Hate That Hate Produced"

1. "Malcolm X Silenced for Remarks on Assassination of Kennedy," *New York Times*, December 5, 1963.

2. Ibid.

3. Karl Evanzz, *The Messenger: The Rise and Fall of Elijah Muhammad* (New York: Random House, 1999), 23–25.

4. Evanzz, *Messenger*, 133–156.

5. Elijah Muhammad, *Message to the Blackman in America* (Chicago: Muhammad's Temple No. 2, 1965), 31–32.

6. Muhammad, *Message to the Blackman in America*, 290–93.

7. Randy Roberts and Johnny Smith, *Blood Brothers: The Fatal Friendship Between Muhammad Ali and Malcolm X* (New York: Basic Books, 2016), 75–81; Louis Lomax, *When the Word Is Given: A Report on Elijah Muhammad, Malcolm X and the Black Muslim World* (Westport, CT: Greenwood, 1963), 27–29.

8. Lomax, *When the Word Is Given*, 15–16.

9. Mike Wallace and Louis Lomax, "The Hate That Hate Produced," *News Beat*, July 13–17, 1959, YouTube video, 1:34:42, posted by Richmond Ekiye, May 2, 2014, http://youtu.be/GsOR6wGcG9M.

10. "Louis Lomax, 47, Dies in Car Crash," *New York Times*, August 7, 1970.

11. Lomax, *When the Word Is Given*, 15.

12. Ibid., 11.

13. "Malcolm X: Interviewed by Mike Wallace and Others," YouTube video 23:04, posted by Steven Nur Ahmed, November 19, 2015, http://youtu.be /RK3h7kuL9Ns.

14. Roberts and Smith, *Blood Brothers*, 217.

15. Ibid., 218.

16. "Malcolm X's Role Dividing Muslims," *New York Times*, February 25, 1964.

17. "Clay Discusses His Future, Liston and Black Muslims," *New York Times*, February 26, 1964.

18. Ibid.

19. Transcript, *State of Ohio v. Lathan Donald*, Case No. 90257, Court of Common Pleas, Criminal Branch, Cuyahoga County, Ohio, Vol. 13, Cuyahoga County Archives, Cleveland, Ohio (Fred Ahmed Evans), 1751.

20. "Bail Denied: Ahmed Calm as Murder Trial Looms," *Cleveland Call and Post*, September 28, 1968.

21. Mutawaf Shaheen, interview, May 17, 2017.

Chapter 5: "You Little Nigger Pickaninnies, Stay Out of Our Schools, This Is Our Neighborhood!"

1. Cleveland City Planning Commission, *Report on the Glenville Community Plan* (March 1964), City of Cleveland Archives, 7.

2. Ibid., 8.

3. Daniel Kerr, *Derelict Paradise: Homelessness and Urban Development in Cleveland, Ohio* (Amherst: University of Massachusetts Press, 2011), 138.

4. Ibid., 155.

5. "Rap Locher, Lister but Plans Approved," *Cleveland Call and Post*, December 18, 1965.

6. *Report on the Glenville Community Plan*, 11–12.

7. Ibid., 8–9.

8. Ibid., 9.

9. "Buslift Eliminates Half-Day Sessions in Schools Jan. 29," *Cleveland Plain Dealer*, January 16, 1962.

10. Lewis G. Robinson, *The Making of a Man* (Cleveland: Green & Sons, 1970), 64–65; David M. Swiderski, "Approaches to Black Power: African American Grassroots Political Struggle in Cleveland Ohio, 1960–1966" (Dissertations, Paper 844, University of Massachusetts Amherst, 2013), 130–32; "Civil Rights Groups to Unveil Plan," *Cleveland Call and Post*, June 22, 1963.

11. "Schools, UFM Settle Dispute," *Cleveland Plain Dealer*, October 1, 1963.

12. "Board Picks McAllister, Gallagher," *Cleveland Plain Dealer*, January 7, 1964; "Plot Drive to Oust McAllister," *Cleveland Call and Post*, February 1, 1964.

13. Ibid.

14. Robinson, *Making of a Man*, 70.

15. "School Board Won't Yield, Restates Stand on Mixing Pupils, Parents Picket," *Cleveland Plain Dealer*, January 30, 1964.

16. Ibid.

17. "In Little Italy: Violence Shatters Long Peace," *Cleveland Plain Dealer*, January 31, 1964.

18. "Italo-American Offers to Help Police Disperse School Rioters," *Cleveland Plain Dealer*, January 31, 1964.

19. Ibid.

20. "Board Faces Picketing, Sit-Ins," *Cleveland Plain Dealer*, January 31, 1964.

21. "Urgent Pleas Kept Negroes from Walking into Mob," *Cleveland Plain Dealer*, January 31, 1964.

22. Robinson, *Making of a Man*, 75.

23. "Locher Says He'll Sit Out School Row," *Cleveland Plain Dealer*, January 30, 1964.

24. "Cops Batter Negro Pickets, Two Hospitalized," *Cleveland Call and Post*, February 8, 1964.

25. Carl B. Stokes, *Promises of Power, A Political Autobiography* (New York: Simon & Schuster, 1973), 62.

26. Swiderski, "Approaches to Black Power," 135–36.

27. "It Was a Pity the Way Cops Beat That Boy," *Cleveland Call and Post*, July 27, 1963.

28. "Cleared Victim of Cop Abuse Charged Again," *Cleveland Call and Post*, October 19, 1963.

29. Mutawaf Shaheed and Isa Yusef, interview, July 1, 2017.

30. Walter Beach, *Consider This* (New York: New World Media, 2014), 102–10.

Chapter 6: "The Ballot or the Bullet"

1. Malcolm X, "The Ballot or the Bullet," Cleveland, OH, April 3, 1964, transcript, www.edchange.org/multicultural/speeches/malcolm_x_ballot.html.

2. "Malcolm X, Louis Lomax to Debate Here," *Cleveland Plain Dealer*, April 2, 1964.

3. "3 Schools Given Planning Speedup," *Cleveland Plain Dealer*, February 5, 1964.

4. "Picket Line Planned for School Site," *Cleveland Plain Dealer*, March 20, 1964; "Campus-Type Schools Backed at Panel Session," *Cleveland Plain Dealer*, March 22, 1964.

5. "UFM Puts Ultimatum to Schools," *Cleveland Plain Dealer*, February 28, 1964.

6. "Clay Talks with Malcolm X Here," *New York Times*, March 2, 1964.

7. "Clay, on 2-Hour Tour of UN, Tells of Plans to Visit Mecca," *New York Times*, March 5, 1964.

8. "Clay Puts Black Muslim X in His Name," *New York Times*, March 7, 1964.

9. Louis Lomax, *When the Word Is Given: A Report on Elijah Muhammad, Malcolm X and the Black Muslim World* (Westport, CT: Greenwood, 1963), 26.

10. Ibid.

11. Lomax, *When the Word Is Given*, 26

12. "Clay, on 2-Hour Tour of UN, Tells of Plans to Visit Mecca," *New York Times*, March 5, 1964.

13. "Malcolm X Splits with Muhammad," *New York Times*, March 9, 1964.

14. Ibid.

15. "Malcolm X Sees Rise in Violence," *New York Times*, March 13, 1964.

16. "Clay Calmly Accepts Decision That Will Keep Him from Military Service," *New York Times*, March 21, 1964.

17. "1,000 in Harlem Cheer Malcolm X," *New York Times*, March 23, 1964.

18. "It's Ballot or Bullet, Answers Malcolm X," *Cleveland Plain Dealer*, April 4, 1964.

19. Malcolm X, "Ballot or Bullet," April 3, 1964.

20. "Top 100 American Speeches of the 20th Century," University of Wisconsin–Madison, December 15, 1999, http://news.wisc.edu/archive/misc/speeches. The "Ballot or the Bullet" is ranked number seven among the top one hundred speeches of the twentieth century.

Chapter 7: "There's No Room for a Rifle Club Named After Medgar Evers"

1. "Rifle Club Forming Here 'to Protect' Rights Drive, Police Acting; Locher Alarmed," *Cleveland Plain Dealer*, April 5, 1964.

2. Ibid.

3. Lewis G. Robinson, *The Making of a Man* (Cleveland: Green & Sons, 1970), 84.

4. Ibid., 84.

5. Ibid., 14–56.

6. Ibid., 69.

7. Ibid., 76.

8. Ibid., 77.

9. "Talks Rejected by McAllister," *Cleveland Plain Dealer*, April 4, 1964; "School Site Pickets Set, CORE Says," *Cleveland Plain Dealer*, April 5, 1964.

10. "School Site Pickets Set, CORE Says," *Cleveland Plain Dealer*, April 5, 1964.

11. Joanne Klunder, "My Husband Died for Democracy," *Ebony*, June 1964, 30.

12. "City's Worst Rights Violence Erupts After Minister's Death," *Cleveland Plain Dealer*, April 8, 1964.

13. Klunder, "My Husband Died for Democracy," 32.

14. "A Time for Sober Reflection," *Cleveland Plain Dealer*, April 8, 1964.

15. "McAllister Has Long, Hard Day," *Cleveland Plain Dealer*, April 10, 1964.

16. "Silent March Is Tribute to Rev. Klunder," *Cleveland Plain Dealer*, April 8, 1964; "CORE Chief Is Due Here," *Cleveland Plain Dealer*, April 9, 1964.

17. "UFM Plans to Picket Board Today," *Cleveland Plain Dealer*, April 13, 1964.

18. "Bulls-Eye," *Cleveland Plain Dealer*, April 9, 1964.

19. Robinson, *Making of a Man*, 87.

20. Ibid., 99–100.

21. Ibid., 103.

22. Christian Davenport, *How Social Movements Die: Repression and Demobilization of the Republic of New Africa* (New York: Cambridge University Press, 2015), 119–20.

23. Walter Beach, *Consider This* (New York: New World Media, 2014), 116–23.

24. Robinson, *Making of a Man*, 112.

25. Ibid., 115; "2 Youth Tell of Terror in City Jail," *Cleveland Call and Post*, June 6, 1964.

26. "Youths Tell Jury About Nightmare in City Jail," *Cleveland Call and Post*, October 17, 1964; "'Barking Dog Jury' Is Hung," *Cleveland Call and Post*, October 24, 1964.

Chapter 8: "I Am on the Outside"

1. Randy Roberts and Johnny Smith, *Blood Brothers: The Fatal Friendship Between Muhammad Ali and Malcolm X* (New York: Basic Books, 2016), 325–26.

2. "Mystery of Malcolm X," *Ebony*, September 1964.

3. "Malcolm X Repeats Call for Negro Unity on Rights," *New York Times*, June 29, 1964.

4. Brian Behnken and Simon Wendt, eds., *Crossing Boundaries: Ethnicity, Race, and National Belonging in a Transnational World* (Lanham, MD: Lexington Books, 2013), 129.

5. Angela D. Dillard, *Faith in the City, Preaching Radical Social Change in Detroit* (Ann Arbor: University of Michigan Press, 2007), 162–65.

6. Don Freeman, interview, July 20, 2017; David M. Swiderski, "Approaches to Black Power: African American Grassroots Political Struggle in Cleveland, Ohio, 1960–1966" (Dissertations, Paper 844, University of Massachusetts Amherst, 2013), 121–26. Freeman spoke just before Malcolm X on the final day of the Grass Roots Conference in Detroit in November 1963. Malcolm X invited Freeman to speak at the Audubon Ballroom in New York City on Sunday, March 29, 1964 (Easter Sunday). When Malcolm X came to Cleveland to speak at Cory Methodist Church (on the following Friday, April 3), Freeman was still in New York on spring break. He did travel up to Detroit, though, to see Malcolm X deliver the "Ballot or Bullet" speech at King Solomon Baptist Church on Sunday, April 12. Freeman then had to drive back to Cleveland that night so he could teach school the next day.

7. Robin D. G. Kelley, *Freedom Dreams: The Black Radical Imagination* (Boston: Beacon, 2002), 72–74. Freeman said in a 2017 interview that he melded the Cruse article with V. I. Lenin's *What Is to Be Done* book to develop his core philosophy.

8. Harold Cruse, "Revolutionary Nationalism and the Afro-American," in *Rebellion or Revolution* (Minneapolis: University of Minnesota Press, 2009), 74–96.

9. Maxwell C. Stanford, "Revolutionary Action Movement (RAM): A Case Study of an Urban Revolutionary Movement in Western Capitalist Society" (master's thesis, Atlanta University, May 1986), 63.

10. Ibid.

11. Ibid., 60.

12. Don Freeman, interview, July 20, 2017.

13. Lewis G. Robinson, *The Making of a Man* (Cleveland: Green & Sons, 1970), 122–27.

14. "'Rifleman's Youth Center Wins Praise from Parents and Police," *Cleveland Call and Post*, December 12, 1964.

15. Ibid.

16. Carl B. Stokes, *Promises of Power, A Political Biography* (New York: Simon & Schuster, 1973), 23.

17. Ibid.

18. Ibid., 26.

19. Ibid., 22.

Chapter 9: "The Black Stalin"

1. "William Worthy, A Reporter Drawn to Forbidden Datelines, Dies at 92," *New York Times*, May 17, 2014. Worthy traveled to Cuba in July 1961 and was arrested upon his return and convicted in a federal court in Miami. His conviction was overturned in 1964 by a three-judge panel of the US Court of Appeals for the Fifth Circuit (one of the judges being future attorney general Griffin Bell). "Cuba-Travel Ban Upheld by Court," *New York Times*, February 21, 1964.

2. William Worthy, "The Red Chinese American Negro," *Esquire*, October 1964.

3. Freeman also wrote an essay entitled "Nationalist Student Conference" published in the *Liberator*, July 1964, 18.

4. National Archives, Federal Bureau of Investigation Files, Fred Allen Evans, File 157-897, RAM memo is attached as an Appendix to Memo by Special Agent John J. Sullivan, Cleveland Office, March 7, 1968.

5. Ward Churchill and Jim Vander Wall, *The COINTELPRO Papers, Documents from the FBI's Secret Wars Against Domestic Dissent* (Boston: South End, 1990), 92–93 (August 25, 1967, Counterintelligence Program, Black Nationalist–Hate Groups, Internal Security, SAC, Albany, to Director, FBI), https://www.krusch.com/books/kennedy/Cointelpro_Papers.pdf.

6. "4 Held in Plot to Blast Statue of Liberty, Liberty Bell and Washington Monument," *New York Times*, February 17, 1965.

7. "Malcolm X, Back in the U.S., Accuses Johnson in Congo," *New York Times*, November 25, 1964.

8. Randy Roberts and Johnny Smith, *Blood Brothers: The Fatal Friendship Between Muhammad Ali and Malcolm X* (New York: Basic Books, 2016), 362.

9. "Speed Negro Vote, Alabama Is Told," *New York Times*, February 5, 1965.

10. Roberts and Smith, *Blood Brothers*, 369–70.

11. Jackie Shearer, interview with Coretta Scott King, conducted by Blackside Inc., November 21, 1988, Washington University Libraries, Film and Media Archive, Henry Hampton Collection. http://digital.wustl.edu/e/eii/eiiweb/kin5427.0224.089corettascottking.html.

12. "1965: France Bars Malcolm X," *New York Times*, February 9, 1965.

13. "Malcolm X Flees Firebomb Attack," *New York Times*, February 15, 1965.

14. Malcom X, "Speech at Ford Auditorium," February 14, 1965, BlackPast.org, www.blackpast.org/1965-malcolm-x-speech-ford-auditorium.

15. "Malcolm Accuses Muslims of Blaze; They Point to Him," *New York Times*, February 16, 1965.

16. Roberts and Smith, *Blood Brothers*, 373. "In 1964, officials from the NYPD's intelligence agencies, the Bureau of Special Services (BOSS), had directed [Gene] Roberts, a twenty-five-year-old detective, to infiltrate Malcolm's organization and get as close to the minister as possible."

17. "Malcolm X Dies; Shot 4 Times at New York Rally," *New York Herald Tribune*, February 22, 1965.

18. "Teacher Tied to Negro Rebels," *Cleveland Plain Dealer*, February 27, 1965.

19. This is the theme of Karl Evanzz, *The Judas Factor: The Plot to Kill Malcolm X* (New York: Thunder's Mouth, 1992).

20. "Freeman Explains: Writer at Variance with Extreme Views," *Cleveland Plain Dealer*, February 27, 1965.

21. "RAM Probe Is Begun by Schools," *Cleveland Plain Dealer*, February 28, 1965.

22. "CORE Leader Hits PD Article," *Cleveland Plain Dealer*, February 28, 1965.

23. "RAM Probe Is Begun by Schools," *Cleveland Plain Dealer*, February 28, 1965.

24. "A Violent Man Leaves in Peace," *Cleveland Plain Dealer*, February 28, 1965.

25. "School Board Fires Teacher Freeman," *Cleveland Plain Dealer*, March 17, 1965.

26. "School Board Fires Freeman," *Cleveland Plain Dealer*, March 17, 1965; "NAACP Says Freeman Had Right to Talk," *Cleveland Plain Dealer*, April 4, 1965.

27. "All Lies Not Perjury, Jury Told by Freeman's Lawyer," *Cleveland Plain Dealer*, January 19, 1967; "Freeman Acquitted on Perjury Charges," *Cleveland Plain Dealer*, January 23, 1967.

Chapter 10: "Whatever You Fear Is What You Worship"

1. Maxwell C. Stanford, "Revolutionary Action Movement (RAM): A Case Study of an Urban Revolutionary Movement in Western Capitalist Society" (master's thesis, Atlanta University, May 1986), 67–68. Dr. Katrina Hazzard, widow of Lathan Donald, one of the July 23 shooters, also said that Ahmed

and his group were part of a "loosely organized RAM cell." Katrina Hazzard, interview, April 18, 2017.

2. National Archives, Federal Bureau of Investigation Files, Fred Allen Evans (a.k.a. Ahmed, Maulana Ahmed), Bureau File 157-897, Background Memo on Fred Allen Evans by Special Agent John J. Sullivan, Cleveland Office, March 7, 1968, 2. Other sources place Evans's birthdate in 1931.

3. Louis H. Masotti and Jerome R. Corsi, *Shoot-Out in Cleveland: A Report Submitted to the National Commission on the Causes and Prevention of Violence* (Washington, DC: Government Printing Office, 1969), 20; "Calm as Murder Trial Looms," *Cleveland Call and Post*, September 28, 1968 (Dick Peery interview of Evans in jail; hereafter Peery Interview).

4. Transcript, *State of Ohio v. Fred (Ahmed) Evans*, Case No. 90257, Court of Common Pleas, Criminal Branch, Cuyahoga County, Ohio, Vol. 13, Cuyahoga County Archives, Cleveland, Ohio (Kenneth Gibbons), 4980.

5. Evans FBI File 157-897, 2.

6. Masotti and Corsi, *Shoot-Out in Cleveland*, 20.

7. Peery Interview.

8. Transcript, *State of Ohio v. Lathan Donald*, Case No. 90257, Court of Common Pleas, Criminal Branch, Cuyahoga County, Ohio, Vol. 13, Cuyahoga County Archives, Cleveland, Ohio (Fred Ahmed Evans), 1723–26.

9. Transcript, 1967 Criminal Case, *State of Ohio v. Evans*, Case No. 86596, Parrino, J., excerpt of testimony of Fred A. Evans in Prosecutors File. Found at the Cleveland Police Museum, Louis Garcia Collection. The transcript excerpt was made only of Evans's testimony for use in his 1969 trial.

10. Peery Interview.

11. Transcript, 1967 Criminal Case, 6.

12. Evans FBI File 157-897, Sullivan Memo, March 7, 1968, 6.

13. Transcript, 1967 Criminal Case, 29–30.

14. Evans FBI File 157-897, Sullivan Memo, March 7, 1968, 5.

15. Ibid., 6.

16. Bill Russell, interview, July 5, 2017.

17. Transcript, *Ohio v. Lathan Donald*, 1917–19.

18. Ibid., 1730–31.

19. "Harvey and the Phenomenals," heavyweightfunk45s, February 19, 2017, www .heavyweightfunk45s.com/2017/02/04/harvey-the-phenomenals-not-ready.

20. Frank L. Keegan, *Blacktown, U.S.A.* (New York: Little, Brown, 1971), 322.

21. Transcript, *Ohio v. Lathan Donald*, 1822.

22. Transcript, *Ohio v. Lathan Donald*, 1734–38.

23. Keegan, *Blacktown*, 323.

24. Carl B. Stokes, *Promises of Power, A Political Autobiography* (New York: Simon & Schuster, 1973), 80.

25. Ibid., 82.

26. "Perk Enters Torrid Mayor Race," *Cleveland Plain Dealer*, June 22, 1965.

27. "Ace Administrator, Wagner, Now Chief," *Cleveland Plain Dealer*, April 9, 1963.

28. "Wankowski Admits He Got 'Hot' Money," *Cleveland Plain Dealer*, September 14, 1963; "Police Had Tough Job—Catching Crook on Force," *Cleveland Plain Dealer*, April 9, 1963.

29. "New Police Chief Talks to *Call & Post*," *Cleveland Call and Post*, January 12, 1963.

30. Ibid.

31. "Police Rap Racist Plot Here, Wagner Defends Death Penalty to Deter Killers," *Cleveland Plain Dealer*, May 21, 1965.

32. "Racial Integration Condemned by RAM," *Cleveland Plain Dealer*, May 21, 1965.

33. "Pity Our Frightened Police Chief," *Cleveland Call and Post*, May 29, 1965.

34. "RAM Witch Hunt," *Cleveland Plain Dealer*, May 24, 1965.

35. "Pity Our Frightened Police Chief," *Cleveland Call and Post*, May 29, 1965.

36. "'No One Is Going to Coerce Me,' Locher says of UFM," *Cleveland Plain Dealer*, October 2, 1965.

37. "UFM Wait-In Ends in 'Beat Locher' Cry," *Cleveland Plain Dealer*, June 16, 1965.

38. "Freedom Fighters Endorse Carl Stokes," *Cleveland Call and Post*, June 12, 1965.

Chapter 11: "Their Fight Is for Dignity and Work"

1. "Alabama Police Use Gas and Clubs to Rout Negroes," *New York Times*, March 8, 1965.

2. "Johnson Pressed for a Voting Law," *New York Times*, March 9, 1965.

3. "Johnson Urges Congress at Joint Session to Pass Law Insuring Negro Vote," *New York Times*, March 16, 1965.

4. Ronald Williams, "Another Summer Comes," *Negro Digest* 15, no. 8 (June 1966), 5.

5. Robin D. G. Kelley, *Freedom Dreams: The Black Radical Imagination* (Boston: Beacon, 2002), 78.

6. "Rena Price Is Dead at 97; Catalyst for the Watts Riots," *New York Times*, June 29, 2013.

7. "Report on Watts—and Now What Action?" *New York Times*, December 12, 1965; "Negroes Critical of Watts Report," *New York Times*, December 8, 1965.

8. "Watts Riot Panel Warns on Danger of New Violence," *New York Times*, December 7, 1965.

9. "In Cleveland Visit: Dr. King to Emphasize the Power of the Ballot," *Cleveland Call and Post*, July 24, 1965.

10. Dr. Martin Luther King Jr., "Statement to the Press," August 20, 1965, Los Angeles, CA, www.thekingcenter.org/archive/document/mlk-press-statement-regarding-riots-los-angeles.

11. Ibid.

12. "Rhetoric? Bah, Great Debate Has Fireworks," *Cleveland Plain Dealer*, October 31, 1965.

13. "Locher Barely Edges Stokes," *Cleveland Plain Dealer*, November 3, 1965.

14. "Locher the Politician Shuns Razzle-Dazzle," *Cleveland Plain Dealer*, November 3, 1965.

15. "Quaker Torches Self in Pentagon Protest," *Cleveland Plain Dealer*, November 3, 1965.

16. Robert F. Williams, *The Crusader* 6, no. 3 (published in Cuba, March 1966), https://freedomarchives.org/Documents/Finder/DOC513_scans/Robert_F_Williams/513.Crusader.Vol.6.3.March.1965.pdf.

17. Timothy B. Tyson, *Radio Free Dixie: Robert F. Williams and the Roots of Black Power* (Chapel Hill: University of North Carolina Press, 1999), 293.

18. Kelley, *Freedom Dreams*, 71–72.

19. Transcript, *State of Ohio v. Lathan Donald*, Case No. 90257, Court of Common Pleas, Criminal Branch, Cuyahoga County, Ohio, Vol. 13, Cuyahoga County Archives, Cleveland, Ohio (Fred Ahmed Evans), 1899–900.

Chapter 12: "A Daily Battle Against Depression and Hopelessness"

1. Beth Robinson, "Laments Closing of JFK House" (letter to the editor), *Cleveland Call and Post*, January 15, 1966.

2. Lewis G. Robinson, *The Making of a Man* (Cleveland: Green & Sons, 1970), 141–43.

3. Leonard Moore, *Carl B. Stokes and the Rise of Black Political Power* (Urbana: University of Illinois Press, 2002), 44.

4. "Gang Traced to JFK House," *Cleveland Plain Dealer*, January 23, 1966.

5. "Dr. King to Rent Slum Apartment," *New York Times*, January 21, 1966.

6. Martin Luther King Jr., "The North: Myth of the Promised Land," *Cleveland Call and Post*, December 11, 1965.

7. Martin Luther King Jr., *The Autobiography of Martin Luther King Jr.*, ed. Clayborne Carson (New York: Warner, 1998), 299–300.

8. Robinson, *Making of a Man*, 144–48.

9. "Rights Quiz Will Her Rhodes," *Cleveland Plain Dealer*, April 2, 1966.

10. *Cleveland's Unfinished Business in Its Inner City*, US Commission on Civil Rights, Ohio State Advisory Committee, Cleveland Sub-Committee, June 30, 1966, Cleveland Public Library.

11. Robinson, *Making of a Man*, 145–46.

12. Cleveland was the first presbytery to establish an office of religion and race in cooperation with the Interchurch Commission on Religion and Race in June 1963 with Rev. Charles W. Rawlings as director, www.preswesres.org/index .php/about-us/history.

13. "Church Official Asks Aid for JFK House," *Cleveland Plain Dealer*, April 22, 1966.

14. "JFK House Should Stay Closed," *Cleveland Plain Dealer*, April 23, 1966.

15. "More Comment on JFK House," *Cleveland Plain Dealer*, April 28, 1966.

16. "JFK House Is Needed," *Cleveland Plain Dealer*, April 25, 1966.

17. "Some Plain Talk About the Kennedy-Kenyatta House," *Cleveland Call and Post*, May 7, 1966.

18. "Boy, 9, Shot in East Side Rowdyism," *Cleveland Plain Dealer*, June 24, 1966.

19. "Police Lift Hough Blockade After Violence," *Cleveland Plain Dealer*, June 25, 1966.

20. Robinson, *Making of a Man*, 151.

21. Ibid., 151–53.

22. "Locher Gets Plan on Racial Tension," *Cleveland Plain Dealer*, July 6, 1966; "Locher, Community Leaders Pledge 8-Point Peace Pact," *Cleveland Call and Post*, July 9, 1966.

23. "Dr. King Declares Rights Movement Is 'Close' to a Split," *New York Times*, July 9, 1966.

24. "41 Seized in Outbreaks After Hydrants Used in Heat Are Shut," *New York Times*, July 13, 1966.

25. "Armed Negroes Fight the Police in Chicago Riots," *New York Times*, July 15, 1966; "4,000 Called Up, National Guard Units Patrol Streets After Three Days of Strife," *New York Times*, July 16, 1966.

26. "Chicago Negro Area Calm as Guard Is Reduced," *New York Times*, July 19, 1966.

27. Ibid.

28. "Time for Plain Talk," *Cleveland Call and Post*, July 23, 1966.

Chapter 13: Hough

1. "Funeral Fund Helped Spark a Riot," *Cleveland Plain Dealer*, July 23, 1966.

2. "Victim Had Gun, Didn't Use It," *Cleveland Plain Dealer*, February 11, 1965. The shooting appears to have been related to union hooliganism. A member of Local 17 of the Bridge, Structural, and Ornamental Iron Workers Union,

Alan Walch, was arrested and tried for murder in 1965. He was acquitted by the jury. Feigenbaum had the name of another ironworker in his pocket when he was killed. "Walch, in Jail Seven Months in Slaying, Files 'Alibi,'" *Cleveland Plain Dealer*, September 12, 1965. Abe Feigenbaum testified at Walch's trial about a rift between his uncle and brother-in-law, William Maltz (they were "enemies") and Ben Feigenbaum thought Maltz was cheating him on the $1,000 weekly gross income from the bar. The Feigenbaum brothers bought out Maltz after their uncle was killed. Prosecution witnesses testified that the Seventy-Niner's Café was "a hangout for drug addicts, prostitutes, and thieves." "Walch Lawyer Digs into Victim's Habits," *Cleveland Plain Dealer*, September 29, 1965. Two of the Walch alibi witnesses were charged with perjury after Walch was acquitted. "Key Walch Witness Indicted," *Cleveland Plain Dealer*, November 20, 1965.

3. "Bar Owner Shot at Wheel of Car," *Cleveland Plain Dealer*, February 11, 1965.

4. "Owners Deny Ice-Water Story; Charge Police Refused to Help," *Cleveland Plain Dealer*, July 23, 1966; "Bar Owner's Death Probe Is Pushed," *Cleveland Plain Dealer*, February 12, 1965. "Detectives want to learn why the victim, 53-year-old Benjamin Feigenbaum, had parked his car on E. 101st near where he was shot to death, almost every morning for the last few months. Feigenbaum was shot five times in the head and chest as he sat in his car in front of 1820 E. 101st. He was the owner of the Seventy-Niner's Café at 7800 Hough Avenue N. E."

5. "Funeral Fund Helped Start Riot"; "Owners Deny Ice-Water Story"; Marc E. Lackritz, "The Hough Riots of 1966," Regional Church Planning Office, report no. 43, July 1968, City Hall file, Cleveland Public Library, 7.

6. "'Like Western,' Says Policeman," *Cleveland Plain Dealer*, July 20, 1966.

7. "I Ran Scared with Hough Area Looters," *Cleveland Call and Post*, July 23, 1966.

8. Ibid.

9. Maxwell C. Stanford, "Revolutionary Action Movement (RAM): A Case Study of an Urban Revolutionary Movement in Western Capitalist Society" (master's thesis, Atlanta University, May 1986), 67. Stanford wrote that his information came from first-person interviews or "reliable sources." He wrote, "The following are interviews of those who were active participants

in the 60's rebellion. Due to the nature of the subject, the real names of the respondents will not be used."

10. Lewis G. Robinson, *The Making of a Man* (Cleveland: Green & Sons, 1970), 155–58.

11. Ibid., 166.

12. Photo on p. 11 of the *Cleveland Plain Dealer*, July 23, 1966. "The police returned fire using pistols, shotguns and tear gas. Chief of Police Richard B. Wagner patrolled the riot area with his personal hunting rifle." "Negro Killed in Cleveland; Guard Called in New Riots," *New York Times*, July 20, 1966.

13. "Woman Killed in Hough Violence," *Cleveland Plain Dealer*, July 19, 1966. 1704 East 73rd Street was the address.

14. "Shooting Described by Victim's Cousin," *Cleveland Plain Dealer*, July 19, 1966.

15. "Tenants Charge Unnecessary Vandalism, Roughness," *Cleveland Call and Post*, July 23, 1966.

16. David M. Swiderski, "Approaches to Black Power: African American Grassroots Political Struggle in Cleveland, Ohio, 1960–1966" (Dissertations, Paper 844, University of Massachusetts Amherst, 2013), 165–73.

17. "Wounded Citizens Cry Out . . . Were Police the Snipers," *Cleveland Call and Post*, August 13, 1966.

18. "Wagner Led Hough Forces, Sure of Police Ability in Riot," *Cleveland Plain Dealer*, July 20, 1966.

19. Robinson, *Making of a Man*, 164.

20. Ibid., 168.

21. Ibid., 167.

22. "'Tragic Day in Our City,' Locher Says," *Cleveland Plain Dealer*, July 20, 1966.

23. Ibid., 169–70.

24. Swiderski, "Approaches to Black Power," 199–203.

25. "Shooting Ends Hough Calm," *Cleveland Plain Dealer*, July 23, 1966; "Sniper Rumors Rampant in Little Italy, Trial Is Told," *Cleveland Plain Dealer*, February 16, 1967.

26. "All-White Jury Hung in Hough Riot Death," *Cleveland Plain Dealer*, February 22, 1967.

27. Ibid.

28. "LaRiche Acquitted in Riot Killing," *Cleveland Plain Dealer*, December 9, 1967.

29. Swiderski, "Approaches to Black Power," 214–18. The Townes lived near 107th Street and Cedar Avenue, about two miles south and east from the Seventy-Niner's Café. The building that was burned was a roller rink, which many believed was torched by the opportunistic owners to obtain insurance proceeds.

30. Ibid., 209–10.

31. Robinson, *Making of a Man*, 170.

32. "Guard Brings Relative Order to Hough," *Cleveland Plain Dealer*, July 21, 1966.

33. Ibid.

34. "President Warns Negroes of Peril to Their Advance," *New York Times*, July 21, 1966.

35. "Rioters Follow Pattern: Burn, Run," *Cleveland Plain Dealer*, July 22, 1966.

36. Ibid. In a limited sense, the structure of welfare did exacerbate the conditions in the ghetto. As Dr. King wrote in his autobiography,

    My neighbors [in Chicago] paid more rent in the substandard slums of Lawndale than the whites paid for modern apartments in the suburbs. The situation was much the same with consumer goods, purchase prices of homes, and a variety of services. This exploitation was possible because so many of the residents of the ghetto had no personal means of transportation. It was a vicious circle. You could not get a job because you were poorly educated, and you had to depend on welfare to feed your children; but if you received public aid in Chicago, you could not own property, not even an automobile, so you were condemned to the jobs and shops closest to your home. Once confined to this isolated community, one no longer participated in a free economy, but was subject to price fixing and wholesale robbery by many of the merchants in the area.

    The Autobiography of Martin Luther King Jr., ed. Clayborne Carson (New York: Warner, 1998), ch. 28. None of this excuses O'Donnell's vile racist remarks—in fact, it makes them all the more deplorable, given she was blaming the victims.

37. "Guard Brings Order to Hough," *Cleveland Plain Dealer*, July 21, 1966.

38. "President Warns Negroes of Peril to Their Advance," *New York Times*, July 21, 1966.

39. "Hating Police Is a Way of Life in Hough Area of Cleveland," *New York Times*, July 23, 1966.

40. "Chief Calls JFK House School for Arsonists," *Cleveland Plain Dealer*, July 23, 1966.

41. "Trouble Persists in Hough Section," *New York Times*, July 21, 1966.

42. Don Freeman, interview, July 20, 2017.

Chapter 14: "Reliability and Discretion Assured"

1. Martin Luther King Jr., "Chicago Campaign," in *The Autobiography of Martin Luther King Jr.*, ed. Clayborne Carson (New York: Warner, 1998), ch. 28.

2. "Rock Hits Dr. King as Whites Attack March in Chicago," *New York Times*, August 6, 1966.

3. Ibid.

4. Ibid.

5. "New March Is Due in Chicago Today," *New York Times*, August 7, 1966.

6. "JFK House Shut as Health Peril," *Cleveland Plain Dealer*, July 27, 1966.

7. "JFK House Leader Vows It Will Reopen," *Cleveland Plain Dealer*, July 28, 1966.

8. "Cleveland Riots Linked to Reds," *New York Times*, August 10, 1966.

9. Lewis G. Robinson, *The Making of a Man* (Cleveland: Green & Sons, 1970), 100; "PR Man Sues Press," *Cleveland Plain Dealer*, April 9, 1965.

10. "Should Indict Mayor, Robinson Says," *Cleveland Plain Dealer*, August 11, 1966.

11. Frank L. Keegan, *Blacktown, U.S.A.* (New York: Little, Brown, 1971), 118.

12. Ibid., 120–21.

13. Ibid., 123.

14. David M. Swiderski, "Approaches to Black Power: African American Grass-roots Political Struggle in Cleveland, Ohio, 1960–1966" (Dissertations, Paper 844, University of Massachusetts Amherst, 2013), 223–36. The FBI document is attached to Swinderski's dissertation as Figure C.1, Appendix C.

15. "Harllel Jones: His Hatred Is White Hot," *Cleveland Plain Dealer*, July 28, 1966.

16. Ibid.

17. "City to Give Married Poor Free Birth Control Aids," *Cleveland Plain Dealer*, July 28, 1966.

18. "Jury Blames Hough Riot on Professionals, Reds," *Cleveland Plain Dealer*, August 10, 1966.

19. Ibid.

20. Swiderski, "Approaches to Black Power," 237, citing the Report of Special Agent Thomas J. O'Hara Jr., Cleveland, September 26, 1966, Medgar Evers Rifle Club, Bureau File 157-1624.

21. "Red Says Party Hit as Riot 'Scapegoat,'" *Cleveland Plain Dealer*, August 11, 1966.

22. Joanna Connors, "Harvey Pekar, Cleveland Comic-Book Legend, Dies at Age 70," *Cleveland Plain Dealer*, July 12, 2010.

23. "Indifference to Slums," *Cleveland Plain Dealer*, August 17, 1966.

24. "Grand Jury in Awkward Position," *Cleveland Plain Dealer*, August 12, 1966.

25. "Should Indict Mayor, Robinson Says," *Cleveland Plain Dealer*, August 11, 1966.

26. "Civil Rights Group Hold Own Hough Riot Hearings Tonight," *Cleveland Plain Dealer*, August 25, 1966.

27. "Housing Pact Set, Dr. King Calls Off Chicago Marches," *New York Times*, August 27, 1966.

28. "Chicago Civil Rights Dissidents Postpone Open-Housing Demonstration in Cicero to Next Sunday," *New York Times*, August 28, 1966.

29. "Guards Bayonet Hecklers in Cicero's Rights March," *New York Times*, September 5, 1966.

30. "Carmichael Plans Black Unity Talks with Muslims," *New York Times*, July 29, 1966.

31. "Riot-Linked City Worker Suspended," *Cleveland Plain Dealer*, August 17, 1966.

32. Doris O'Donnell, "Riot Figure Has Head Start Job," *Cleveland Plain Dealer*, December 9, 1966.

33. "Stupid Punks," *Cleveland Plain Dealer*, September 9, 1966. "Some 24 monuments in the gardens were defaced. They were smeared with black paint and racist slogans such as 'Black Power' and 'Get Whitey.'" "Undivided World Grows in Gardens, Says Vail," *Cleveland Plain Dealer*, September 12, 1966.

34. "Jury Indicts Jones, 7 Others in Rampage," *Cleveland Plain Dealer*, November 17, 1966. With some irony, the Jones indictment was on the day that Dr. Sam Sheppard won acquittal in his second trial—the trial caused by Louis Seltzer's antics in the *Cleveland Press*. It was this case that helped cement F. Lee Bailey's national reputation as a lawyer.

35. "Manhunt Turns Up Nest of Delinquents," *Cleveland Plain Dealer*, December 24, 1966.

36. "Harllel Jones Defended by W. Side Cleric," *Cleveland Plain Dealer*, December 11, 1966.

37. "Pollster Finds Backlash Grows," *New York Times*, September 28, 1966.

Chapter 15: "Blood Will Flow in the Streets"

1. "Queen Aide Cites 'Black War' Plan," *New York Times*, April 2, 1968. The case involving Stanford and the New York defendants made its way to the US Supreme Court when the defendants filed a separate federal case seeking to have New York's antianarchy statute declared unconstitutional. *Samuels v. Mackell*, 401 U.S. 66 (1971). During the first oral argument in the case on April 1, 1970, the attorney for the state of New York provided further detail as to the infiltration, the planning, the training, and the possession of weapons and ammunition. "Samuels v. Mackell," Oyez, accessed August 25, 2017, https://www.oyez.org/cases/1970/7.

2. Bill Russell, interview, July 5, 2017.

3. "'Could Have Killed Him,' Ahmed Tells Assault Jury," *Call and Post*, February 24, 1968.

4. Special Agent John J. Sullivan, Report, Cleveland, March 7, 1968, Fred Allen Evans, Bureau File 157-897, 2.

5. "Inquiry Is Begun on Negro Rioting," *New York Times*, May 3, 1967. Bill Russell remembers being threatened by dozens of nationalists in a makeshift trial in Harlem during one of their trips to New York over a dispute about someone from Cleveland taking the title of prime minister. This recollection corresponds with Ungvary's Senate testimony that Evans had declared himself prime minister of the Harlem's People Parliament in 1967.

6. "'Could Have Killed Him,' Ahmed Tells Assault Jury," *Call and Post*, February 24, 1968.

7. "Charge Police Beating, Wrecked Astrology Store," *Call and Post*, March 18, 1967.

8. Ibid.

9. *The Confessions of Nat Turner: The Leader of the Late Insurrection in Southampton, Va.*, electronic edition, University of North Carolina at Chapel Hill, 1999, accessed November 4, 2017, http://docsouth.unc.edu/neh/turner/turner.html.

10. "Astrologer Charged in Policeman's Beating," *Cleveland Plain Dealer*, March 11, 1967.

11. "Racial Powder Keg," *Wall Street Journal*, March 14, 1967.

12. "HUD Axes City Renewal Funds," *Cleveland Plain Dealer*, January 19, 1967; "City Broke Vow; Weaver Rejects Visit," *Cleveland Plain Dealer*, February 9, 1967.

13. "City's Renewal Lag Bombed," *Cleveland Plain Dealer*, January 19, 1967.

14. "Racial Powder Keg," *Wall Street Journal*, March 14, 1967.

15. Carl B. Stokes, *Promises of Power, A Political Autobiography* (New York: Simon & Schuster, 1973), 93.

16. "Cleveland Study Laments Ghettos," *New York Times*, March 19, 1967.

17. "Cleveland Scans Hate Group Funds," *New York Times*, March 29, 1967.

18. Taylor Branch's compilation of his three Pulitzer Prize–winning books on King, *The King Years, Historic Moments in the Civil Rights Movement* (New York: Simon & Shuster, 2013), 152.

19. "Dr. King Proposes a Boycott of War," *New York Times*, April 5, 1967.

20. Benjamin Hedin, "Martin Luther King Jr.'s Searing Antiwar Speech, Fifty Years Later," *New Yorker*, April 3, 2017.

21. "N.A.A.C.P. Decries Stand of Dr. King on Vietnam," *New York Times*, April 11, 1967.

22. "Dr. King and the War," *New York Times*, April 14, 1967.

23. "The FBI's War on King," American RadioWorks, American Public Media, accessed November 5, 2017, http://americanradioworks.publicradio.org /features/king/d2a.html.

24. Martin Luther King Jr., *The Autobiography of Martin Luther King Jr.*, ed. Clayborne Carson (New York: Warner, 1998), 342.

Chapter 16: "Life for Me Ain't Been No Crystal Stair"

1. "Racial Fuse Sputtering Again in Cleveland," *Cleveland Plain Dealer*, April 6, 1967.

2. "Black Nationalist Claims to Be New Ghetto Leader," *Cleveland Plain Dealer*, April 7, 1967.

3. "Violence Flares in Hough Section," *New York Times*, April 17, 1967.

4. "Ahmed Sent to Workhouse for Store Disorder," *Cleveland Call and Post*, April 22, 1967.

5. "Store Looted on E. 105th for Second Night Straight," *Cleveland Plain Dealer*, April 18, 1967.

6. Ibid.

7. "Astrology, Hippie Stores Officials Close E. Side," *Cleveland Plain Dealer*, April 22, 1967.

8. "Iron-Fisted Hoodlum Stand Rings in Council," *Cleveland Plain Dealer*, April 19, 1967.

9. "Few Leaders Object to Orders to Police to End Vandalism and Arson," *New York Times*, April 24, 1967.

10. "King Vows to Help Cure Ghetto Ills," *Cleveland Plain Dealer*, April 26, 1967.

11. "Martin Luther King Jr.'s 1967 Glenville High School Speech to Be Played at 50th Anniversary Event," *Cleveland Plain Dealer*, April 19, 2016.

12. Carl B. Stokes, *Promises of Power, A Political Autobiography* (New York: Simon & Schuster, 1973), 97.

13. "Inquiry Is Begun on Negro Rioting," *New York Times*, May 3, 1967.

14. "Ungvary Urges Senators to Curb Black Nationalists," *Cleveland Plain Dealer*, May 3, 1967.

15. "Racial Tensions in City Eased," *Cleveland Plain Dealer*, May 4, 1967.

16. "New Conspiracy Law Opposed by ACLU," *Cleveland Plain Dealer*, May 5, 1967.

17. "Ungvary Criticized," *Cleveland Plain Dealer*, May 9, 1967; "Stop All Extremists," *Cleveland Plain Dealer*, May 8, 1967.

18. "Astrology Shop Arrest Cases Are Continued," *Cleveland Plain Dealer*, May 11, 1967; "'Cool' CORE Aide Hot on City Police," *Cleveland Plain Dealer*, May 11, 1967.

Chapter 17: "He Speaks My Views"

1. "Robinson Denies Hough Riot Role," *Cleveland Plain Dealer*, May 11, 1967.

2. "Cleveland Fears New Outbreaks as It Awaits 'Nonviolent Action' by Dr. King," *New York Times*, May 21, 1967.

3. "King to Launch Rights Push Here June 1," *Cleveland Plain Dealer*, May 17, 1967.

4. "Organize Negro Ghettos, Back Stokes, King Urges," *Cleveland Call and Post*, May 20, 1967.

5. "Cleveland Fears New Outbreaks as It Awaits 'Nonviolent Action' by Dr. King," *New York Times*, May 21, 1967.

6. Ibid.

7. "Hoover Links Carmichael to Negro Leftist Group," *New York Times*, May 17, 1967.

8. "Cleveland Democrats Urging Mayor Locher Not to Run Again," *New York Times*, May 24, 1967.

9. "Bar Group Attacks Cleveland's Mayor," *Cleveland Plain Dealer*, May 30, 1967.

10. Ryan Cortes, "Jim Brown Retires While on the Set of *The Dirty Dozen*," *The Undefeated*, July 13, 2016, https://theundefeated.com/features/jim -brown-retires-while-on-the-set-of-the-dirty-dozen.

11. "Help for Browns," *Cleveland Plain Dealer*, July 31, 1967.

12. "Beach Sues Browns, Charges NFL Bias," *Cleveland Plain Dealer*, June 11, 1971.

13. "Negro Economic Union Charters California Unit," *Cleveland Plain Dealer*, June 16, 1966.

14. "Remembering Cleveland's Muhammad Ali Summit, 45 Years Later," *Cleveland Plain Dealer*, June 3, 2012.

15. Walter Beach, interview, December 25, 2016.

16. Chuck Heaton, "Cassius Still Won't Go," *Cleveland Plain Dealer*, June 5, 1967.

17. "Stokes Sees Racial Peace in Campaign," *Cleveland Plain Dealer*, June 17, 1967.

18. "Negro to Bid for Mayor," *New York Times*, June 17, 1967.

19. "Locher Announces Candidacy," *Cleveland Plain Dealer*, June 14, 1967.

20. "16 Negroes Seized; Plot to Kill Wilkins and Young Charged," *New York Times*, June 22, 1967.

21. "Pioneer Black Militant," *New York Times*, September 13, 1968. In China, through his newsletter, *The Crusader*, Robert F. Williams responded to the allegations that RAM was involved in an assassination plot to kill other blacks, writing in part,

    > This vicious plot against RAM and other black militants was supposed to serve as a brake on America's headlong plunge into the long hot summer. RAM had been informed months ago by sympathetic police sources that a frame-up was in the making. This is why some brothers moved out of the New York area. This is why they had become deliberately inactive. All revolutionary acts of violence now taking place in America, according to police logic, are done under the direction of members of RAM. This is not true. RAM has long advocated a policy of self-defense and revolutionary resistance to tyrannical oppression. We are anti-imperialist, anti-racist and all black, and for this we offer no apologies. The police vultures dared not contrive a plot around an alleged murder plan against Whitey because they knew that this would project RAM as the greatest saviors of Black America. This would make RAM the toast of the ghetto, for every black child now knows that black men who kill white oppressors are great heroes worthy of emulation.

The Crusader, 9, no. 1 (July 1967), www.freedomarchives.org/Documents /Finder/Black%20Liberation%20Disk/Black%20Power%21/SugahData /Journals/Crusader.S.pdf.

22. "Raids Foil Plot on Negro Lives," *Cleveland Plain Dealer*, June 22, 1967. The stories that appeared in both the *Times* and the *Plain Dealer* are nearly identical, referencing the exact same facts about Robert F. Williams. Unless the indictments themselves contained these details (which had nothing to do with the arrests), this suggests that both papers were given advance information by the FBI.

23. "3 Names Added as Plot Targets," *New York Times*, June 23, 1967.

24. "Queens Aide Cites 'Black War' Plan, Tells High Court Militants Trained as Guerrillas," *New York Times*, April 2, 1969.

25. The New York antianarchy law in question had actually been repealed and replaced with a new version of the law by the time the case involving Max Stanford and others made it to the Supreme Court. See *Samuels v. Mackell*, 401 U.S. 66 (1971), n. 1. Therefore, the statute in question was the same one that had been upheld by the US Supreme Court in 1925 in *Gitlow v. New York*, 268 U.S. 652 (1925), which was later discredited by the Supreme Court's ruling in *Brandenburg v. Ohio*, 395 U.S. 444 (1969), which found Ohio's criminal syndicalism statute unconstitutional.

26. Maxwell C. Stanford, "Revolutionary Action Movement (RAM): A Case Study of an Urban Revolutionary Movement in Western Capitalist Society" (master's thesis, Atlanta University, May 1986), 67–68.

27. Max Stanford, now known as Muhammad Ahmad, refused multiple entreaties for an interview, so it is difficult to test the reliability of what he wrote about Ahmed Evans and Cleveland in his thesis.

28. See n. 20 of ch. 18.

29. "'War on White Man' Urged at Jersey City Negro Rally," *New York Times*, July 18, 1967.

Chapter 18: "He Desperately Needed a Victory"

1. "Negro Pastor Urges King to Leave Town," *Cleveland Plain Dealer*, April 20, 1967.

2. "Martin Luther King's Mistake," *Cleveland Plain Dealer*, April 19, 1967.

3. "King Could Sway Negro from LBJ," *Cleveland Plain Dealer*, May 22, 1967; "Dr. King Considers Kennedy and Percy Best '68 Candidates," *New York Times*, April 27, 1967.

4. *Walker v. City of Birmingham*, 388 U.S. 307 (1967).

5. ". . . And Dr. King to Jail," *New York Times*, June 14, 1967.

6. "High Court Refuses Cincinnati NAACP Suit; Turns Down King; Ponders Open Housing," *Cleveland Call and Post*, October 14, 1967.

7. "Martin Luther King Defines 'Black Power,'" *New York Times*, June 11, 1967.

8. Carl B. Stokes, *Promises of Power, A Political Autobiography* (New York: Simon & Schuster, 1973), 100.

9. Ibid., 101–3.

10. "Area Clergymen Invited to Meet Dr. King Here," *Cleveland Plain Dealer*, June 15, 1967.

11. "King Marks Bakeries Top Target," *Cleveland Plain Dealer*, June 16, 1967.

12. Ibid.

13. "Locher Likely to Meet King Despite 'Extremist' Label," *Cleveland Plain Dealer*, June 16, 1967.

14. "King Backers Plan Meeting," *Cleveland Plain Dealer*, June 20, 1967.

15. Special Agent John J. Sullivan, Report, March 7, 1968, Fred Allen Evans, Bureau File 157-897, Cleveland, 14.

16. "Dr. King Raps Ghetto Wall at Freedom Assembly Here," *Cleveland Plain Dealer*, June 22, 1967. Dr. King attended the convention of the National Newspaper Publishers Association, hosted by the *Call and Post* in Cleveland, on Wednesday, June 21, and was the keynote speaker at a dinner the night before where he delivered his "invisible wall" speech. "*Call and Post* Hosts NNPA," *Cleveland Call and Post*, June 24, 1967. Stokes spoke to the group at lunch on Saturday, June 24.

17. "'Ghetto Jury' Convicts City of Trampling Negro Rights," *Cleveland Plain Dealer*, June 29, 1967.

18. "Handcuffed Prisoner Beaten in Police Car," *Cleveland Call and Post*, June 17, 1967.

19. "Sidelights on Hough's 'Ghetto Grand Jury,'" *Cleveland Plain Dealer*, June 30, 1967; "Ghetto Jury Judges City," *Cleveland Call and Post*, July 8, 1967.

20. Sullivan, Report, BF 157-897, 14.

21. C. E. Shy, et al, *Straight Up!* (compilation), vol. 1 (Cleveland: Uptown Media Joint Venture Publishing, 2017), 23. Muntu is derived from a word from African Zulu culture that means "a human being," sometimes used to mean "a Black person." Sadly, John Coltrane died on July 17, 1967, just forty years old. "Jazz Great John Coltrane Is Dead at 40," *Cleveland Plain Dealer,* July 18, 1967.

22. "Locher OK's Hough Parade," *Cleveland Plain Dealer*, July 18, 1967.

23. "1,000 Take Part in Hough Parade," *Cleveland Plain Dealer*, July 21, 1967.

24. "Hough Remembers '66 with Mammoth Parade," *Cleveland Call and Post*, July 29, 1967.

25. "Riot Group, LBJ Meet Today; Tough-Line Course Expected," *Cleveland Plain Dealer*, July 29, 1967.

26. "LBJ Popularity Slips to 39%," *Cleveland Plain Dealer*, August 11, 1967.

27. "U.S. Will Not Inherit Kingdom of Heaven, Dr. King Says Here," *Cleveland Plain Dealer*, July 29, 1967.

28. "King Taking Militant's Rights Views," *Cleveland Plain Dealer*, August 20, 1967.

29. "Carmichael Is Quoted as Saying Negroes Form Guerrilla Bands," *New York Times*, July 26, 1967.

30. "Carmichael Pledges Aid for Reds," *Cleveland Plain Dealer*, August 3, 1967.

31. "H. Rap Brown Jailed on Gun Charges," *Cleveland Plain Dealer*, August 20, 1967.

32. "Militancy of Leaders Saps SNCC Strength," *Cleveland Plain Dealer*, August 20, 1967.

33. "King Warns Landlord in Rent Strike," *Cleveland Plain Dealer*, August 31, 1967.

34. "Hough Dwellers' Testimony Asked," *Cleveland Plain Dealer*, August 11, 1967.

35. "Sealtest Is First Target of Dr. King," *Cleveland Plain Dealer*, July 8, 1967; "Sealtest Boycott Lifted; 50 New Jobs Promised," *Cleveland Plain Dealer*, August 9, 1967.

36. "King Visits, Calls Voter Signup 'a Start,'" *Cleveland Plain Dealer*, August 24, 1967.

37. "Voter Stations Swamped by Record Turnout," *Cleveland Plain Dealer*, August 24, 1967.

38. "Locher Calls Negro Voter Drives Unfair," *Cleveland Plain Dealer*, August 11, 1967.

39. "Stokes Defeats Locher by 18,000 in Record Vote," *Cleveland Plain Dealer*, October 4, 1967.

40. "Bobbing Along," *Cleveland Call and Post*, August 5, 1967.

41. "Cleveland: 'I Must Prove Their Fears Are Groundless'—Stokes," *New York Times*, December 5, 1967.

Chapter 19: "As Lambs for the Slaughter"

1. Thomas A. Corbett (former FBI agent in the Cleveland Field Office), interview, September 7, 2017.

2. Memorandum, Hoover to the SAC, Albany, August 25, 1967; reproduced in full in *Hearings on Intelligence Activities*, vol. 6, p. 383. See Ward Churchill and Jim Vander Wall, *The COINTELPRO Papers: Documents from the FBI's Secret Wars Against Domestic Dissent* (Boston: South End, 1990), 91–164 (and accompanying footnotes).

3. Churchill and Wall, *COINTELPRO Papers*, 354. "The Ghetto Informant Program, also called 'Ghetto Listening Post,' was launched [in 1967] and, by the summer of 1968, employed some 3,248 snitches, in addition to an 'unknown number' of such 'assets' already in place under TOPLEV [top level black community leadership program] and BLACKPRO [black program]. Hoover described this small army of contract spies 'inadequate,' and demanded a major expansion of its ranks during the fall of 1968."

4. Walter Beach, interview, December 25, 2016.

5. "Negroes to Meet on 'Black Unity,'" *Cleveland Plain Dealer*, October 6, 1967.

6. "Demands Black Classes, Afro-American History," *Cleveland Call and Post*, October 14, 1967.

7. Special Agent John J. Sullivan, Report, March 7, 1968, Fred Allen Evans, Bureau File 157-897, Cleveland, 14–19.

8. "Open Appeal to Bigotry," *Cleveland Plain Dealer*, October 1, 1967.

9. "Stokes Spurns Porter Aid, Urges He Quit," *Cleveland Plain Dealer*, October 5, 1967.

10. "If Stokes Becomes Mayor, Police Shakeup Certain," *Cleveland Plain Dealer*, October 5, 1967.

11. "Bare Knuckle Politics in City," *Cleveland Plain Dealer*, September 24, 1967.

12. "The Making of a Mayor," *Cleveland Plain Dealer*, December 10, 1967.

13. "Avoid Race Issue in Campaign—Taft," *Cleveland Plain Dealer*, October 10, 1967.

14. "Taft Stresses Equality Plank for CORE Vote," *Cleveland Plain Dealer*, October 18, 1967.

15. "Taft Tells Realtors Group He Favors Fair Housing," *Cleveland Plain Dealer*, October 27, 1967.

16. Carl B. Stokes, *Promises of Power, A Political Autobiography* (New York: Simon & Schuster, 1973), 104–5.

17. "Stokes Booed in 2d Debate," *Cleveland Plain Dealer*, October 19, 1967.

18. "The Making of a Mayor," *Cleveland Plain Dealer*, December 10, 1967.

19. Taylor Branch, *The King Years, Historic Moments in the Civil Rights Movement* (New York: Simon & Shuster, 2013), 165.

20. Martin Luther King Jr., *The Autobiography of Martin Luther King Jr.*, ed. Clayborne Carson (New York: Warner, 1998), 346.

21. "Dr. King Plans to Go to Jail 'Willingly,'" *New York Times*, October 11, 1967.

22. "Belafonte Adds Lustre to Benefit," *Cleveland Plain Dealer*, October 22, 1967.

23. "Dr. King Suggests 'Camp-In' in Cities," *New York Times*, October 24, 1967.

24. "Dr. King Gives Up in Alabama to Start 5-Day Jail Sentence," *New York Times*, October 31, 1967.

25. "Dr. King, Released from Alabama Jail, Plans Soviet Visit," *New York Times*, November 4, 1967.

26. "M. L. King in Cleveland Tomorrow," *Cleveland Plain Dealer*, November 5, 1967.

27. "Dr. King Escapes Car Crash Injury on Vote Tour Here," *Cleveland Plain Dealer*, November 7, 1967.

28. "Amateurs All Abuzz as Political Pros Hide," *Cleveland Plain Dealer*, November 8, 1967.

29. Mutawaf Shaheed, interview, May 17, 2017.

30. Stokes, *Promises of Power*, 106.

31. "Stokes Is Elected Mayor," *Cleveland Plain Dealer*, November 8, 1967.

32. Stokes, *Promises of Power*, 106.

33. "Coretta Is Wrong About Stokes," *Cleveland Call and Post*, November 14, 1970; "Finally, I've Begun to Live Again: An Intimate, Revealing Interview with Mrs. Martin Luther King, Jr.," *Ebony*, November 1970, 173–74. The author, Charles Sanders, had once written for the *Call and Post*. Coretta King made her remarks at the Olivet Baptist Church in 1970 at a Women's Day event. William O. Walker, in responding to the *Ebony* story, says King was at the Sheraton-Cleveland hotel with the Stokes supporters in a suite upstairs. Stokes has King at the Rockefeller Building headquarters. In either event, King was not invited to the victory speech.

34. "Stokes Begins Naming His Cabinet," *Cleveland Plain Dealer*, November 9, 1967.

35. "King Warns of Riots if Aid Meets Delay," *Cleveland Plain Dealer*, November 9, 1967. The church was Fellowship Baptist Church, 1754 East 55th Street. The reporter of the story was Joe Eszterhas, a future screenplay writer (e.g., *Basic Instinct* and *Flashdance*) and one of the journalists to expose the My Lai massacre.

Chapter 20: "You Should Establish Their Unsavory Backgrounds"

1. Carl B. Stokes, *Promises of Power, A Political Autobiography* (New York: Simon & Schuster, 1973), 108–9.

2. Ibid., 111.

3. Ibid., 112.

4. "Black Nationalist Panel Are Heard," *Cleveland Call and Post*, December 9, 1967.

5. "Bobbing Along," *Cleveland Call and Post*, December 9, 1967.

6. Special Agent John J. Sullivan, Report, March 7, 1968, Fred Allen Evans, Bureau File 157-897, Cleveland, 19.

7. Ibid., 19.

8. Ibid., 19.

9. "Police Killer Weeps at Verdict," *Cleveland Plain Dealer*, December 1, 1967.

10. "Watson Called JFK Member," *Cleveland Plain Dealer*, May 12, 1967.

11. Sullivan, Report, BF 157-897, 20.

12. "Backing Due Today for Stokes," *Cleveland Plain Dealer*, February 17, 1968; "20 Dems File for Congress," *Cleveland Call and Post*, February 24, 1968. Bizarrely, white nationalist Robert Annable threw his hat in the ring for the congressional seat, saying that the "black nationalist ought to be for me. We stand for the same thing, separation of the races. They should be more inclined to vote for someone who represents the same thing, even though he is white, than for some politician who speaks out of both sides of his mouth." "10 White Democrats File in Negro 21st," *Cleveland Plain Dealer*, February 20, 1968.

13. Ward Churchill and Jim Vander Wall, *The COINTELPRO Papers: Documents from the FBI's Secret Wars Against Domestic Dissent* (Boston: South End, 1990), 106, www.freedomarchives.org/Documents/Finder /Black%20Liberation%20Disk/Black%20Power!/SugahData/Government /COINTELPRO.S.pdf.

14. "Jones Led Gang, Vandal Jury Told," *Cleveland Plain Dealer*, January 10, 1968; "Park Vandal Trial Awaits Bench Rule," *Cleveland Plain Dealer*, January 11, 1968; "Pen Inmate Identifies 5 as Vandals," *Cleveland Plain Dealer*, January 12, 1968; "Jones Freed in Gardens' Vandalism," *Cleveland Plain Dealer*, January 31, 1968.

15. Transcript of Excerpts of Testimony of Fred A. Evans, *State of Ohio v. Fred A. Evans*, Case No. 86596, Cleveland Police Museum, 11–12. These excerpts were provided by a court reporter to the prosecutor for use in the shootout trials. The transcript is in the prosecutor's file.

16. Ibid.

17. "Ahmed Jailed, Gets 6 Months," *Cleveland Call and Post*, March 2, 1968.

18. SAC, Cleveland, to Director, FBI, February 28, 1968, Fred Allen Evans, Bureau File 157-897-11.

19. Churchill and Wall, *COINTELPRO Papers*, 109.

20. "Stokes Program Gains Momentum," *New York Times*, February 23, 1968.

21. "Ahmed Freed," *Cleveland Call and Post*, April 6, 1968.

22. SAC, Cleveland, to Director, FBI, Security Index card, April 10, 1968, Fred Allen Evans, Bureau File 157-897.

Chapter 21: "The Voice of Madness"

1. Philip Meranto, ed., *The Kerner Report Revisited* (Urbana: Institute of Government and Public Affairs, University of Illinois, June 1970), https://archive.org/details/kernerreportrevi00asse.

2. "Panel on Civil Disorders Calls for Drastic Action to Avoid 2-Society Nation," *New York Times*, March 1, 1968.

3. "Massive Spending Plea in Riot Report Met with Alarm," *Cleveland Plain Dealer*, March 3, 1968.

4. "Dr. King to Start March on the Capital April 22," *New York Times*, March 5, 1968.

5. "7 Mayors Uphold Report; Seek More Funds," *New York Times*, March 4, 1968.

6. "Dr. King to Start March on the Capital April 22," *New York Times*, March 5, 1968.

7. "Westmoreland Requests 206,000 More Men, Stirring Debate in Administration," *New York Times*, March 10, 1968.

8. "Johnson and Nixon Given Big New Hampshire Edge," *New York Times*, March 10, 1968.

9. "New Hampshire Primary," *New York Times*, March 13, 1968.

10. "McCarthy Favors Delay by Kennedy," *New York Times*, March 15, 1968.

11. "Kennedy's Statement and Excerpts from News Conference," *New York Times*, March 17, 1967.

12. "Washington: Johnson Is the Issue," *New York Times*, March 17, 1968.

13. "House Panel Bars Quick Rights Vote Asked by Johnson," *New York Times*, March 20, 1968.

14. "Mini-Riot in Memphis," *New York Times*, March 30, 1968.

15. "Senator Urges Ban on Dr. King," *Cleveland Plain Dealer*, March 30, 1968.

16. "President Offers U.S. Aid to Cities in Curbing Riots," *New York Times*, March 30, 1968.

17. "Delay by Dr. King Urged," *New York Times*, March 31, 1968.

18. "Dr. King to March in Memphis Again," *New York Times*, March 30, 1968.

19. "Dr. King Hints He'd Cancel March If Aid Is Offered," *New York Times*, April 1, 1968.

20. Ibid.

21. "Johnson Says He Won't Run; Halts North Vietnam Raids; Bids Hanoi Join Peace Moves," *New York Times*, April 1, 1968.

22. "Troops Ordered into U.S. Capital," *Cleveland Plain Dealer*, April 6, 1968.

23. "Manpower, Not Firepower, Kept Lid on Riots After King Slaying," *Cleveland Plain Dealer,* April 13, 1968.

24. Leonard Moore, *Carl B. Stokes and the Rise of Black Political Power* (Urbana: University of Illinois Press, 2002), 71.

25. "New Job Program Slated Here," *Cleveland Plain Dealer*, April 7, 1968.

26. Transcript, *State of Ohio v. Lathan Donald*, Case No. 90257, Court of Common Pleas, Criminal Branch, Cuyahoga County, Ohio, Vol. 13, Cuyahoga County Archives, Cleveland, Ohio (Fred Ahmed Evans), 1763–64.

27. "Text of Kennedy's Speech Here," *Cleveland Plain Dealer*, April 6, 1968.

28. "Stokes Works Around Clock for Peace in City," *Cleveland Call and Post*, April 13, 1968.

29. Ibid.; "King Fund Announced by Stokes," *Cleveland Plain Dealer*, April 7, 1968.

Chapter 22: Cleveland: Now!

1. "President Signs Civil Rights Bill; Pleads for Calm," *New York Times*, April 12, 1968.

2. Margot Kaminski, "Incitement to Riot in the Age of Flash Mobs," *University of Cincinnati Law Review* 81, no. 1 (2013): 27, http://scholarship.law.uc.edu /cgi/viewcontent.cgi?article=1103&context=uclr.

3. Gil Noble, presenter, "H. Rap Brown Breaks Down Politics of America," *Like It Is*, 1968, YouTube video, 20:20, posted by Donnie Mossberg, February 21, 2013, https://youtu.be/ izKmQgNmYao.

4. Diane Tittle, *Rebuilding Cleveland: The Cleveland Foundation and Its Evolving Urban Strategy* (Columbus: Ohio State University Press, 1992), 169–73.

5. "Riot-Panel Report Sparked the Idea," *Cleveland Plain Dealer*, May 2, 1968.

6. "$1.5 Billion Is Asked to Rebuild Cleveland," *Cleveland Plain Dealer*, May 2, 1968.

7. "An Editorial: Support Stokes' Plan," *Cleveland Plain Dealer*, May 2, 1968.

8. "Ex-Coach Is Out to Score a Million," *Cleveland Plain Dealer*, May 2, 1968.

9. "Special Gets 'Rush' Action," *Cleveland Plain Dealer*, May 2, 1968.

10. "$1.5–Billion Cleveland Renewal Planned by Stokes Over a Decade," *New York Times*, May 2, 1968.

11. "'Thinking Big,' Says Besse; Some React with Caution," *Cleveland Plain Dealer*, May 2, 1968.

12. Mounted clipping, May 8, 1968, Fred Allen Evans, Bureau File 157-897.

13. "Poor Marchers Cheerful, Weary on Arrival Here," *Cleveland Plain Dealer*, May 15, 1968.

14. Special Agent John J. Sullivan to SAC, Cleveland, May 20, 1968, Fred Allen Evans, Bureau File 157-897.

15. "Marchers Meet Mayor, Call City 'Fine Town,'" *Cleveland Plain Dealer*, May 16, 1968.

16. "For Kennedy, It's California or Bust," *New York Times*, June 2, 1968.

17. "City Evicts Group of Black Nationalists," *Cleveland Press*, May 24, 1968; "Evict Black Nationalists," *Cleveland Call and Post*, June 1, 1968.

18. SAC, Cleveland, to Director, FBI, teletype, May 24, 1968, Fred Allen Evans, Bureau File 157-897.

19. John J. Sullivan to SAC, Cleveland, re New Libya, May 27, 1968, Fred Allen Evans, Bureau File 157-897.

20. "Negro Group Asks End of Ties to US," *New York Times*, March 31, 1968; "Nation of Negroes Proposed at Detroit," *Cleveland Plain Dealer*, April 1, 1968.

21. Christian Davenport, *How Social Movements Die: Repression and Demobilization of the Republic of New Africa* (New York: Cambridge University Press, 2015), 162–73.

22. Transcript, *State of Ohio v. Fred (Ahmed) Evans*, Case No. 90257, Court of Common Pleas, Criminal Branch, Cuyahoga County, Ohio, Vol. 13, Cuyahoga County Archives, Cleveland, Ohio (Walter Beach), 3414; "Ex-Brown Gets City Youth Post," *Cleveland Plain Dealer*, June 12, 1968.

23. Tittle, *Rebuilding Cleveland*, 171.

24. Special Agent John J. Sullivan to SAC, Cleveland, June 24, 1968, Fred Allen Evans, Bureau File 157-897, June 24, 1968.

25. "Dassin Makes His 'Honest' Film in Hough," *Cleveland Plain Dealer*, August 18, 1968.

26. Character's first name was Carl. He would later become a judge of the Court of Common Pleas in Cleveland.

27. Special Agent John J. Sullivan to SAC, Cleveland, June 25, 1968, Fred Allen Evans, Bureau File 157-897.

28. "Text of Edward Kennedy's Tribute to His Brother in Cathedral," *New York Times*, June 9, 1968.

29. "Former Kennedy Aides and Adversaries Among 2,300 at St. Patrick's Rites," *New York Times*, June 9, 1968.

30. Special Agent John J. Sullivan to SAC, Cleveland, June 24, 1968, Fred Allen Evans, Bureau File 157-897.

31. Lawrence T. Sweeney to SAC, Cleveland, June 10, 1968, Fred Allen Evans, Bureau File 157-897. The address was 1652 East 73rd Street, blocks from where the Hough riots started in 1966.

32. "High Court Backs Stop-Frisk Actions," *New York Times*, June 11, 1968.

33. "Court Upholds Friskings Here," *Cleveland Plain Dealer*, June 11, 1968.

34. "Nation Not Sick, Stokes Tells Tufts," *Cleveland Plain Dealer*, June 10, 1968.

35. "Mayors Will Ask Assured Income," *Cleveland Plain Dealer*, June 16, 1968.

36. "Stokes to Join National HHH Unit," *Cleveland Plain Dealer*, June 24, 1968.

37. "Afro Art Shop Hints Sabotage," *Cleveland Call and Post*, June 22, 1968.

38. Maxwell C. Stanford, "Revolutionary Action Movement (RAM): A Case Study of an Urban Revolutionary Movement in Western Capitalist Society" (master's thesis, Atlanta University, May 1986), 68.

39. Mutawaf Shaheed, interview, July 1, 2017.

Chapter 23: "The Good News in American Cities Is Coming Out of Cleveland"

1. "DeForest Brown to Head Model Cities," *Cleveland Plain Dealer*, July 17, 1971.

2. DeForest Brown testimony, Evans Trial, 3833–951.

3. Alexander von Hoffman, "The Past, Present and Future of Community Development in the United States," *Investing in What Works for America's Communities: Essays on People, Place & Purpose*, ed. Nancy O. Andrews David J. Erickson (San Francisco: Federal Reserve Bank of San Francisco and Low Income Investment Fund, 2012), 10–54, www.jchs.harvard.edu/sites/jchs .harvard.edu/files/w12-6_von_hoffman.pdf.

4. It appears that the original proposals for youth summer programs prepared by HADC go back to early 1968 under the auspices of the President's Council on Youth Opportunity, which was part of the Office of Economic Opportunity. See Executive Order 11330 (March 5, 1967). The Mayor's Council on Youth Opportunity had been established in Cleveland at the end of 1967, the brainchild of Seymour Slavin, who worked for a major Cleveland foundation. Slavin thought that planning for summers should be more institutionalized and not determined each year on a new basis without city guidelines. Diane Tittle, *Rebuilding Cleveland: The Cleveland Foundation and Its Evolving Urban Strategy* (Columbus: Ohio State University Press, 1992), 170–72. The proposal for Evans's African culture shop is in the Carl Stokes Papers at the Western Reserve Historical Society, and it references the shop on Superior Avenue as the place where Evans would carry out the summer program. One newspaper article refers to a decision in February 1968 to cut the original funding request from Project Afro from some number to $30,000. "Jones' Afro Set Allocated $10,400," *Cleveland Plain Dealer*, July 28, 1968. Thus, the original proposal was drafted before Cleveland: Now! existed and became the funding vehicle.

5. "Tangled Trail Behind Evans' Eviction Account," *Cleveland Plain Dealer*, August 2, 1968; "Suspect 'Upset' by Clash on Lease," *New York Times*, July 29, 1968.

6. "Suspect 'Upset' by Clash on Lease," *New York Times*, July 29, 1968.

7. "Jones' Afro Set Allocated $10,400," *Cleveland Plain Dealer*, July 28, 1968. The President's Council on Youth Opportunity was created by Executive Order

in March 1967. Lyndon B. Johnson, "Executive Order 11330—Providing for the Coordination of Youth Opportunity by Programs," March 5, 1967, The American Presidency Project, www.presidency.ucsb.edu/ws/?pid=106074.

8. "Project Afro $10,000 Grant Made at Meeting of Council," *Cleveland Plain Dealer*, July 30, 1968.

9. DeForest Brown testimony, Evans Trial, 3864.

10. "136 Mayors Back Humphrey Drive," *New York Times*, July 2, 1968.

11. "HHH Takes Aim at Ohio's Public in 2 Days Here," *Cleveland Plain Dealer*, June 29, 1968.

12. "Humphrey's Campaign," *New York Times*, July 4, 1968.

13. "Humphrey Bars Pre-convention Debate with Rival," *New York Times*, July 3, 1968.

14. "Give Negotiators Time, HHH Tells War Critics," *Cleveland Plain Dealer*, July 3, 1968.

15. "Stokes Cabinet Meeting Joined by Vice President," *Cleveland Plain Dealer*, July 2, 1968.

16. "Give Negotiators Time," *Cleveland Plain Dealer*, July 3, 1968. The federal grant was not used to fund Evans or the Project Afro proposals. The FBI interviewed Ralph Findley, the head of the Office of Economic Opportunity, who acknowledged the grant but said it had not been funded as of the time of the shoot-out. Report of Special Agent Paul V. Daly, August 30, 1968, Fred Allen Evans, Bureau File 157-897.

17. "Humphrey's Campaign," *New York Times*, July 4, 1968.

18. "Stokes Appears Gainer in HHH's Visit Here," *Cleveland Plain Dealer*, July 3, 1968.

19. State's Exhibit No. 77, Evans Trial, Cleveland Police Museum collection; DeForest Brown testimony, Evans Trial, 3872–90.

20. "Tangled Trail Behind Evans' Eviction Account," *Cleveland Plain Dealer*, August 2, 1968.

21. DeForest Brown testimony, Evans Trial, 3876–904.

22. Testimony of Salvatore Borsellino and George Kurk, Evans Trial, 3351–67. These rifles were found at 12312 Auburndale the day after the shoot-out by police. Louis Garcia, *Preemptive Strike* (self-pub., Cleveland Police Museum, 2015).

23. "Nixon Aims at Cities," *Cleveland Plain Dealer*, July 11, 1968.

24. "Nixon Aide Gives 'Poor' 6 Cents," *Cleveland Plain Dealer*, July 11, 1968.

25. "Rifle Range Set Up on Farm," *Cleveland Plain Dealer*, July 29, 1966. A copy of this article was attached to the FBI report.

26. Report of Special Agent Paul V. Daly, August 30, 1968, Fred Allen Evans, Bureau File 157-897. This file also shows the creation of a file under the "Anti-Riot Laws" (FBI No. 176) after the shoot-out. The first three numbers of an FBI file show the offense being investigated when the file was opened—176 is for the Anti-Riot Laws.

27. State's Ex. No. 82, Evans Trial.

28. Anthony Adams testimony, Evans Trial, 3368–95.

29. William Talley testimony, Evans Trial, 3322–40.

30. Otis Lewis testimony, Evans Trial, 3241–59.

31. "Akron Curfew Off; Snipings Reported," *New York Times*, July 19, 1968; "99 Akron Curfew Violators Seized After Riots Erupt," *Cleveland Plain Dealer*, July 19, 1968; "Akron Lifts Curfew Despite More Shooting and Fires," *Cleveland Press*, July 20, 1968.

32. "Ahmed Tells How the Riots Started," *Cleveland Press*, August 2, 1968.

33. "Parade Marks Riots in Hough," *Cleveland Plain Dealer*, July 21, 1968.

34. "Just Two Years Ago," *Cleveland Press*, July 22, 1968.

Chapter 24: "Having a Gun Is No Crime"

1. "Tangled Trail Behind Evans' Eviction Account," *Cleveland Plain Dealer*, August 2, 1968.

2. Ibid. The *Plain Dealer* article was attached to Special Agent Paul Daly's report of August 30, 1968, referenced in earlier notes.

3. Special Agent Arthur G. Pote to SAC, Cleveland, September 9, 1968, Fred Allen Evans, Bureau File 157-897. This file also shows it was under the FBI code 176, Anti-Riot Laws.

4. "Happy Birthday," *Cleveland Press*, July 23, 1968.

5. "4 Mayors Discuss Cities Problems," *New York Times*, July 24, 1968.

6. DeForest Brown testimony, Evans Trial, State Exhibits 77–84.

7. "Wind and Rain Sweep Greater Cleveland," *Cleveland Plain Dealer,* July 23, 1968.

8. Special Agent Arthur G. Pote to SAC, Cleveland, September 9, 1968, Fred Allen Evans, Bureau File 157-897.

9. Ibid.

10. Ibid.

11. Ibid.; Roger Heimberger, Evans Trial, 3341–50. His testimony synchs exactly with the informant's report to the FBI, both as to timing and the number of people who entered the store with Evans and the fact he inspected but did not purchase an expensive rifle.

12. Otis Lewis Jr. testimony, Evans Trial, 3254, State's Exhibit 43. Again, Lewis's testimony matches exactly the report from the FBI informant.

13. Special Agent Arthur G. Pote to SAC, Cleveland, September 9, 1968, Fred Allen Evans, Bureau File 157-897.

14. "Stokes Says ADC 'Baby' Plans Fail," *Cleveland Plain Dealer*, July 24, 1968; Stokes Hits Criticism of Welfare," *Cleveland Press*, July 23, 1968; "4 Mayors Discuss Cities Problems," *New York Times*, July 24, 1968.

15. "Stokes Picks James for No. 2 Post," *Cleveland Plain Dealer*, April 18, 1968; "James Pegged as Hard Worker," *Cleveland Plain Dealer*, April 18, 1968.

16. "Police Promote 6 Men, Transfer 14; One Retires," *Cleveland Plain Dealer*, August 1, 1962; "Sperber Optimistic as Safety Chief," *Cleveland Plain Dealer*, January 12, 1972.

17. Carl B. Stokes, *Promises of Power, A Political Autobiography* (New York: Simon & Schuster, 1973), 209.

18. John Little, interview by L. H. Masotti, August 20, 1968, Carl B. Stokes Papers, Western Reserve Historical Society, MS 4370, container 84, folders 1654, 1655 and 1656 (hereafter cited as Stokes Papers).

19. Special Agent Arthur G. Pote to SAC, Cleveland, September 9, 1968, FRED ALLEN EVANS, Bureau File 157-897.

20. Clarence James, interview by Masotti, August 27, 1968, Stokes Papers.

21. Joseph McManamon, interview, Stokes Papers.

22. Heckman could not sell the M-1 with the thirty-shot banana clip attached to the gun because under the law at the time that made the weapon an illegal "machine gun."

23. Heckman testimony, Evans Trial, 3168–240.

24. Special Agent Arthur G. Pote to SAC, Cleveland, September 9, 1968, Fred Allen Evans, Bureau File 157-897.

25. Ibid.

26. Walter Beach, interview by Masotti, September 16, 1968, Stokes Papers.

27. George Forbes interview by Masotti, September 12, 1968, Stokes Papers. Forbes said the exact same thing to the FBI when interviewed on September 6, 1968. Special Agent Arthur G. Pote to SAC, Cleveland, September 10, 1968, Fred Allen Evans, Bureau File 157-897. "Forbes advised that from his conversation with Ahmed he felt that Ahmed would not start shooting as he felt Ahmed was actually looking for a way out of the situation without losing face."

28. Ricky Hogue, statement to Cleveland Police Department, April 7, 1969, Cleveland Police Museum.

Chapter 25: "Tow Truck in Trouble"

1. James O'Malley testimony, Evans Trial, 4709–43.

2. Katrina Hazzard (widow of Lathan Donald), interview, April 18, 2017.

3. James O'Malley testimony, Evans Trial, 4709–42.

4. Thomas Horgan testimony, Evans Trial, 4817–918.

5. Joseph Turpin Jr., statement to Cleveland Police Department, July 25, 1968, Cleveland Police Museum; Joseph Turpin Jr. testimony, Evans Trial, 6694–765.

6. Edithe B. Schepperd, statement to Cleveland Police Department, August 8, 1968, Cleveland Police Museum.

7. William H. McMillin, statement to Cleveland Police Department, July 25, 1968, Cleveland Police Museum.

8. Louis Garcia does not believe this is the same car that gave chase, which he said had a black nationalist flag flying from it. He also doubts a woman was driving the green car.

9. Charles Lee Teel, statement to Cleveland Police Department, July 30, 1968, Cleveland Police Museum; Charles Lee Teel testimony, Evans Trial, 4032–91.

10. Thomas Horgan testimony, Evans Trial, 4817–918.

11. Victor Kovacic testimony, Evans Trial, 4613–708; Louis Garcia testimony, Evans Trial, 4538–612.

12. Chester Szukalski, statement to Cleveland Police Department, July 27, 1968, Cleveland Police Museum; Chester Szukalski testimony, Evans Trial, 5019–39.

13. Joseph McManamon testimony, Evans Trial, 6192–221; Joseph McManamon, statement to Cleveland Police Department, August 2, 1968, Cleveland Police Museum.

14. Per an interview with Louis Garcia, October 1, 2017, the M-1 was not jammed—it was operable and police used it to fire test shots to compare ballistics with copper bits recovered from Vehicle 591.

15. Harold Butler testimony, Evans Trial, 5437–81.

16. Louis Garcia thinks Patrolman Zagore shot Leroy Williams (Amir ibn Khatib) and he staggered back to where he fell closer to Lakeview on Beulah. There is conflicting testimony about exactly where his body ended up. Charles Teel said when he walked past the body on Beulah and 123rd, "a crowd of people gathered around and they were trying to get him up." He said further, "Someone in the crowd was calling him by name, but I don't remember what they were calling him." He elaborated, "One of the crowd kept shaking him to get up, and calling him by name." One witness saw a black woman, seemingly a nationalist, performing some sort of CPR on Williams near 123rd and Beulah. We do know that his body was picked up and taken to an area near Superior Avenue by people in the neighborhood, where an angry mob gathered around it. Sandra Lee Parks testimony, Evans Trial, 7004–100; Albert Forrest testimony, Evans Trial, 6883–953. Forrest testified that Williams was still alive when he first saw him at 123rd and Beulah. Police told him and a young boy to stop assisting and fired warning shots and tear gas, which drove the two away.

17. The fact that Butler could continue to Lakeview up Beulah unmolested may coincide with Evans's claim he had experienced the jammed gun. Evans clearly was firing from the yard behind the corner house on the west side of Beulah and East 123rd. Butler would have walked right past him if he had still been there.

18. Teel testified that the nationalists in front of him on Lakeview were shooting at a car behind him, which probably was Car 508. Car 505 (Gibbons and Wolff) and Car 65E (Viola and Bennett) came moments or minutes later when the nationalists were closer to Auburndale and Lakeview. Patrolman Simms

of Car 508 and his partner did not stop at Auburndale, but instead powered through, past the people shooting at them to Superior Avenue.

19. Simms also testified that one bullet pierced the top of their car, suggesting a sniper, perhaps in the Lakeview Tavern tower, who fired at them as they drove by.

20. Leonard Simms testimony, Evans Trial, 5248–92.

21. Kenneth Gibbons testimony, Evans Trial, 4986.

22. Kenneth Gibbons testimony, Evans Trial, 4973–5019.

23. Wolff was either hit by (1) a shooter inside 12312 Auburndale, (2) a nationalist who Jerry Viola saw running back toward Auburndale from Moulton carrying a rifle right after Gibbons and Wolff had run in the direction of 12312, or (3) one of the two nationalists in the driveway next to 12312. Viola saw Wolff crouched holding a pistol on the two nationalists, who had been firing at Viola and Bennett, telling them to drop their guns. He fell inside the iron fenced-in area in front of the apartment complex.

24. Donald F. Simone testimony, Evans Trial, 3952–76.

25. Gerald Viola, interview, July 20, 2017.

26. Gerald Viola testimony, Evans Trial, 5482–512.

27. Joseph Torok testimony, Evans Trial, 5150–98; Robert Zagore testimony, Evans Trial, 5040–98; Amos Floyd testimony, Evans Trial, 5059–149; Richard Tanski testimony, Evans Trial, 5199–226; Leonard Simms testimony, Evans Trial 5248–292; Peter Ventura testimony, Evans Trial, 5293–359.

28. Dr. William Hoffman testimony, Evans Trial, 2751–873.

29. Peter Ventura testimony, Evans Testimony, 5300–1.

30. Officer Simms, who was African American, said he unloaded three or four shots into the head of the nationalist who raised his head and grabbed for his gun. He described him as wearing a red shirt. Bernard Donald had on a red shirt. Simms also said there was one nationalist still alive—Lathan Donald. And the third nationalist had "half his head shot off," likely Sidney Taylor (who could have been shot by Peter Ventura at close range coming out of the window in the back of 1395). Officer Torok also testified that the man who raised his head was "this man in red."

31. The policeman who recovered the guns of the nationalists identified Lathan Donald as the one who had the 410-gauge "Savage" pump shotgun made by Springfield that likely killed Patrolman Louis Golonka. Lathan was easy to

identify as he was the only one with a leopard-skin top and thick dark-rimmed glasses. Testimony of Patrolman Jack T. Starr, Evans Trial, 5538–86. Starr testified he found the .30-06 Remington next to Bernard Donald and the .222 Remington rifle next to Sidney Taylor.

32. Statement of Joseph Turpin, Cleveland Police Department, July 25, 1968, Cleveland Police Museum; Joseph Turpin testimony, Evans Trial, 6698–701.

Chapter 26: "This Is Only the Beginning"

1. Report of Special Agent Lanford L. Blanton, Riverside, California, Los Angeles FBI Office, August 7, 1968, attached to Report of Special Agent Paul V. Daly, August 29, 1968, Cleveland FBI Office, FBI Bureau File 176-1.

2. Katrina Hazzard, interview, April 18, 2017. Dr. Hazzard knew Osu Bey until his death in 2010 and heard the story directly from him and her husband, Lathan Donald. She said Osu "held off police all by himself." He had "brass balls" and was a "wild man."

3. Statements of Joseph Tuft and Richard Wilson, Cleveland Police Museum.

4. Sam Levy testimony, Evans Trial, 5775–804.

5. Elmer Joseph testimony, Evans Trial, 5513–27.

6. Thomas Smith testimony, Evans Trial, 5805–26.

7. Ernest Rowell testimony, Evans Trial, 5414–36.

8. Richard Hart testimony, Evans Trial, 5614–34.

9. Dr. Hoffman originally called this wound a shotgun wound but later changed his mind. Given all the evidence, it is unlikely this was a shotgun wound.

10. Sergeant Gentile testified he saw spent .22 cartridges along the side of 12312 when he tried to flank the house, again driven back after a shooter in the house aimed at him—Gentile "opened up" the Thompson submachine gun to cover himself as he retreated. Anthony Gentile testimony, Evans Trial, 5528–73.

11. Dr. William Hoffman testimony, Evans Trial, 2751–873.

12. Dr. Lester Adelson testimony, Evans Trial, 2874–921.

13. Dr. Cyril Wecht testimony, Evans Trial, 7137–245.

14. Richard Tanski testimony, Evans Trial, 5197–223.

15. Leonard Szalkiewicz testimony, Evans Trial, 5752–59.

16. Robert Wood testimony, Evans Trial, 5635–92; Peter Ventura testimony, Evans Trial, 5293–359.

17. Leonard Sims testimony, Evans Trial, 5260–63; Steve Sopko testimony, Evans Trial, 5227–47; Joseph Torok testimony, Evans Trial, 5150–93.

18. Dr. Cyril Wecht testimony, Evans Trial, 7165–76.

19. Katrina Hazzard, interview, April 18, 2017.

20. Albert Forrest also got into a tussle with Rev. Perryman, who stood behind his burning house in great distress. When Forrest asked Perryman to help lift Lathan Donald, Perryman said, "Fuck the brother, my house is burning." Forrest hit Perryman in the face, knocking him to the ground. The police had to break up the fight.

21. Albert Forrest testimony, Evans Trial, 6883–953.

22. John Pegues testimony, Evans Trial, 6614–65.

23. Patricia Walker testimony, Evans Trial, 6567–80 (medical records); Donald Brown testimony (broken ribs), Evans Trial, 6783–89. Trenton Ervin testimony, Evans Trial, 6598–613; Arthur Reden testimony, Evans Trial, 6513–66.

24. Mary Louise Brown testimony, Evans Trial, 6280–406; Peggy Finley testimony, Evans Trial, 6581–97; Mary Jean Grisby testimony, Evans Trial, 6429–512.

25. Frank Stroiker testimony, Evans Trial, 5839–43; Donald Kuchar testimony, Evans Trial, 5947–90.

26. Robert Shankland testimony, Evans Trial, 5875–990.

27. Amos Floyd testimony, Evans Trial, 5123.

Chapter 27: "A Lot of People Are Going to Get Killed"

1. Donald Kuchar testimony, Evans Trial, 5947–90.

2. Suppression Hearing, Ahmed Evans testimony, Evans Trial, 141–53.

3. Suppression Hearing, Stanley E. Tolliver testimony, Evans Trial, 355–61; James Carnes testimony, Evans Trial, 219–62.

4. Suppression hearing, Carl Roberts testimony, Evans Trial, 289–316. Roberts was the main note taker that night.

5. Carl Roberts, statement to Cleveland Police Department, July 25, 1968, Cleveland Police Museum.

6. Carl Roberts put it this way when he testified at the suppression hearing: "This country is fighting a war on two fronts, here at home and in Vietnam. Their lines are stretched too thin. . . . The police department don't know what they are doing, but we know what we are doing; and as long as there are black and white, there will be trouble." Carl Roberts testimony, Evans Trial, 314.

7. John Edward Matthews, statement to Cleveland Police Department, August 1, 1968, Cleveland Police Museum; Mary Ann Matthews, statement to Cleveland Police Department, August 1, 1968, Cleveland Police Museum.

8. Leslie Jackson, statement to Cleveland Police Department, July 26, 1968, Cleveland Police Museum; John Hardrick, statement to Cleveland Police Department, July 25, 1968, Cleveland Police Museum; Alfred Thomas, statement to Cleveland Police Department, July 26, 1968, Cleveland Police Museum; Louis Garcia, statement to Cleveland Police Department, July 25, 1968; Louis Garcia, supplementary report, Cleveland Police Department, July 29, 1968, Cleveland Police Museum.

9. "Ahmed Aide Ruled Insane," *Cleveland Plain Dealer*, July 10, 1969. See also "Sanity Test Is Sought for Thomas," *Cleveland Plain Dealer*, June 11, 1969.

10. Clarence "Buddy" James, interview by L. H. Masotti, August 27, 1968, Stokes Papers, Western Reserve Historical Society. "Negro Slain Defending Building," *Cleveland Plain Dealer*, July 25, 1968. Haynes had battled earlier with black youths who threatened his apartment complex, shooting at them with a pistol. He retrieved his shotgun from his home shortly before he was killed.

11. "Area Where 10 Died Is Calm After Guardsman Withdrawn," *New York Times*, July 25, 1968.

12. "Leaders Say Area Negroes Averted Spread of Violence," *Cleveland Press*, July 24, 1968.

13. "Stokes Political Image Takes Blow," *Cleveland Plain Dealer*, July 26, 1968.

14. "Police Withdrawal Focal Point of Split," *Cleveland Plain Dealer*, August 31, 1968. A copy of the "Wanted" poster is in the Stokes Papers.

15. Carl B. Stokes, *Promises of Power, A Political Autobiography* (New York: Simon & Schuster, 1973), 218.

16. "City Admits Ahmed Got $10,000," *Cleveland Plain Dealer*, July 26, 1968.

17. "Stokes Political Image Takes Blow," *Cleveland Plain Dealer*, July 26, 1968.

18. "Racial Tensions, Terror in Cleveland," *New York Times*, July 28, 1968.

19. The CPPA website states, "Like much of the progress obtained in policing America, the Cleveland Police Patrolmen's Association was born out of the most tragic day in the history of the Cleveland Police Department. On July 23, 1968, in the Glenville Section of the city, rioting militants murdered three of our own and a fourth officer died years later as a result of his injuries inflicted that day." "History of the CPAA," Cleveland Police Patrolmen's Association, www.cppa.org/about-us.html.

20. "600 Policemen Demand McManamon Quit Post," *Cleveland Plain Dealer*, August 2, 1968; "McManamon Backed by Stokes," *Cleveland Plain Dealer*, August 3, 1968.

21. "Old NAAWP Establish Committee to Recall Stokes," *Cleveland Call and Post*, August 31, 1968. This was Robert Annable's group—the National Association for the Advancement of White People, which changed its name to the United Citizens Council.

22. "Cleveland Negroes Recall Gun Battle," *New York Times*, July 27, 1968. The house was bulldozed on July 26, three days after the shoot-out: "Negro residents of the East Side and helmeted policemen stood beneath shade trees with brown, fire-scorched leaves today and watched a yellow bulldozer flatten what had been the home of Rev. and Mrs. Henry L. Perryman."

23. ASAC James L. Startzell to SAC, Cleveland Office, July 26, 1968, Fred Allen Evans, Bureau File 157-897-145.

24. ASAC James L. Startzell to SAC, Cleveland Office, July 26, 1968, Fred Allen Evans, Bureau File 157-897.

25. FBI Memo, August 30, 1968, Fred Allen Evans, Bureau File 157-897-174. Another FBI report confirms this theory. A summary memo states, "Source advised that it is his opinion that the premature outbreak also was the reason for the failure of the other groups in Cleveland and other cities to join in the disturbance. Apparently they were caught unaware by the premature outbreak and then decided not to go ahead with the plans for violence on 7/24/68 since they realized that authorities were aware of the plot." Special Agent Arthur G. Pote to SAC, Cleveland, September 9, 1968, Bureau File 176-1, copies to Bureau File 157-897.

26. Special Agent John J. Sullivan to SAC, Cleveland, November 11, 1968, Fred Allen Evans, Bureau File 157-897-205 (contains a list of New Libyan and

African names). Mutawaf Shaheed (Muntu poet; formerly Clyde Shy), interviews, June–October 2017.

27. "Accused Police Killers Bound to Grand Jury," *Cleveland Plain Dealer*, August 8, 1968.

28. "Rifle Obtained from Ahmed, Police Quote Sniper Suspect," *Cleveland Plain Dealer,* August 16, 1968.

29. "Fred (Ahmed) Evans, militant black nationalist leader, and four Negro teenagers were indicted yesterday on 39 charges, including seven counts each of first-degree murder, in the July 23 sniper slayings of three white policemen and a Negro civilian." "Evans, 4 Others Indicted by Jury," *Cleveland Plain Dealer*, August 27, 1968. See also "3 Plead Not Guilty in 4 Sniper Murders," *Cleveland Plain Dealer*, September 12, 1968.

30. "Ahmed Evans Denied Bail in Sniper Slayings," *Cleveland Plain Dealer*, September 21, 1968.

31. Stokes, *Promises of Power*, 257.

Chapter 28: "The Case Against Fred Ahmed Evans Is Weak"

1. "Ahmed Evans Trial Is Scheduled for Mar. 24," *Cleveland Call and Post*, February 22, 1969.

2. "Bloody Murder Haunts Trial of Ahmed Evans in Cleveland," *Cleveland Call and Post*, April 11, 1969.

3. Ibid.

4. "Suspect Found Slain After Bus Holdup Fails," *Cleveland Plain Dealer*, March 7, 1969; "City Worker Cleared in Slaying," *Cleveland Call and Post*, March 15, 1968.

5. "Tight Security for Ahmed's Trial," *Cleveland Call and Post*, March 15, 1969; "Judge Gives Rules for Evans Trial," *Cleveland Plain Dealer*, March 12, 1969. Both articles were carefully pasted into the FBI file. See also "Ahmed Tells of Police Threats," *Cleveland Call and Post*, March 22, 1969.

6. "Body Goes to Jail, but Evans Balks," *Cleveland Press*, March 12, 1969.

7. Teletype, SAC, Cleveland, to Director, FBI, March 12, 1969, Fred Allen Evans, Bureau File 157-897-224.

8. Thomas A. Corbett to SAC, Cleveland, March 26, 1969, Fred Allen Evans, Bureau File 157-897-247.

9. "Bloody Murder Haunts Trial of Ahmed Evans in Cleveland," *Cleveland Call and Post*, April 11, 1969.

10. Teletype to Director from Cleveland, March 24, 1969, Fred Allen Evans, Bureau File 157-897-245.

11. Teletype to Director and Detroit from Cleveland Office, March 26, 1968, Fred Allen Evans, Bureau File 157-897-246.

12. "One Alternate Is Needed to Complete Evans Jury," *Cleveland Plain Dealer*, April 9, 1969; "12 Jurors, 2 Alternates Selected in Evans Trial," *Cleveland Call and Post*, April 12, 1969.

13. Airtel to Director, FBI, from SAC, Cleveland, March 28, 1969, Fred Allen Evans, Bureau File 157-897-255.

14. SAC Charles G. Cusick to File, April 2, 1969, Fred Allen Evans, Bureau File 157-897-262.

15. "Youth Charged in Murder Following Fire Bombings," *Cleveland Plain Dealer*, January 24, 1968. A third young man, Charles Jordan, was also charged with the murder and Washington testified at a proceeding against Jordan in juvenile court. This was not known until after the Evans verdict and was made the basis of a motion for new trial. Proceedings, Evans Trial, 8002–52. The motion was denied.

16. "Murder Case Is Tagged 'No Bill,'" *Cleveland Plain Dealer*, February 21, 1969.

17. Lottie Polinsky, Leo G. Chimo, John J. Vondruska, Jr., Joseph Mengel, Rodulphus Butler, Joseph Toohig, Nathan Singer, and Louis Kulis testimonies, Evans Trial, 6222–66.

18. Walter Washington testimony, Evans Trial, 2968–3064.

19. Thomas Lanier testimony, Evans Trial, 3065–92.

20. Curtis Martin testimony, Evans Trial, 3093–167. Curtis Martin was granted shock probation after testifying. Proceedings, Evans Trial, 8002–52.

21. Teletype to Director, From Cleveland, May 13, 1969, Fred Allen Evans, Bureau File 157-897-347; "Evans Trial Long and Costly," *Cleveland Plain Dealer*, May 13, 1969; "Evans Joins 30 Men on Death Row," *Cleveland Plain Dealer*, May 13, 1969.

22. Judge Richard McMonagle, Judge George McMonagle's son and his bailiff for the Evans trial, confirmed the bombing, interview, May 4, 2016.

23. "Report Threats in Evans Trial," *Cleveland Press*, April 19, 1968.

24. Proceedings, Evans Trial, 7977–78, Court's Exhibit 1. Evidence was uncovered that Tolliver himself ordered a collection of the news clippings from the *Plain Dealer*. Perhaps worried that Evans was going to be convicted, he threw the stink bomb into the evidence package—though no definitive ruling was ever made.

25. John Little file, Stokes Papers, Western Reserve Historical Society.

26. Dick Peery, "White Racism Comes to Surface at Evans' Trial," *Cleveland Call and Post*, May 10, 1968.

27. Mary Louise Brown testimony, Evans Trial, 6380–82.

28. "Brown Sees Retaliation by Blacks If Evans Dies," *New York Times*, May 16, 1969.

29. "Evans Trial Is Called a 'Legal Lynching,'" *Cleveland Press*, May 14, 1968.

30. "The Frame-Up of Ahmed Evans," *World Magazine*, October 11, 1969.

31. "Guyana Group Demands Ahmed Evans' Pardon," *Muhammad Speaks*, June 20, 1969.

32. Victor Kovacic testimony, Donald Trial, 1619–700; "Donald List of Witnesses Is Secret," *Cleveland Plain Dealer*, July 26, 1969.

33. Lathan Donald testimony, Donald Trial, 2884–3211.

34. Dick Peery of the *Call and Post* wondered if all the talk about black nationalism was overshadowing the case against Lathan Donald. "Are local black nationalists—summoned by the defense—so anxious to broadcast their philosophy that they may unintentionally send 20–year-old Donald to the electric chair?" "Black Nationalism: Unseen Defendant in Donald Trial," *Cleveland Call and Post*, August 9, 1969.

35. Ahmed Evans testimony, Donald Trial, 2026–73.

36. "Donald Gets Life Terms in Slayings," *Cleveland Plain Dealer*, August 19, 1969.

37. "'Reticent . . . Polite,' Teacher Remembers Lathan Donald," *Cleveland Plain Dealer*, August 19, 1969.

38. Frank L. Keegan, *Blacktown, U.S.A.* (New York: Little, Brown, 1971), 333–64.

39. "2 in Glenville Case Sent to Youth Center," *Cleveland Plain Dealer*, May 26, 1970. Osu Bey was eighteen at the time, Hardrick nineteen. They both had been in the Cuyahoga County Jail since July 1968.

40. Memo, SAC, Cincinnati to SAC, Cleveland, September 14, 1972, Fred Allen Evans, Bureau File 157-897. *Furman v. Georgia*, 408 U.S. 238 (1972).

41. "'Gentle Man' Found Shot, Dead in Car," *Cleveland Plain Dealer*, August 8, 1970.

42. "Harllel Jones Is Given Life Term in Slaying," *Cleveland Plain Dealer*, October 19, 1978.

43. "Harllel Jones' Murder Charge Dismissed," *Cleveland Plain Dealer*, October 19, 1978.

44. "Lawyers for Harllel X Say FBI Harassed Him," *Cleveland Plain Dealer*, December 9, 1978.

45. "Freedom, at Last," *Cleveland Plain Dealer*, November 15, 1978.

46. "Society the Victim," *Cleveland Plain Dealer*, November 23, 1978.

47. "Cleveland City Council President Freed in Carnival Kickback Case," *New York Times*, July 19, 1979.

48. "Throng Cheers for Indicted 8," *Cleveland Plain Dealer*, October 31, 1978.

49. Carl B. Stokes, *Promises of Power, A Political Autobiography* (New York: Simon & Schuster, 1973), 22.

50. "Activist Finding New South Is Like the Old Cleveland," *Cleveland Plain Dealer*, June 10, 1979.

51. "Lewis G. Robinson, 84, Civil Rights Activist," *Cleveland Plain Dealer*, January 26, 2013.

52. "6 Policemen Still Healing," *Cleveland Plain Dealer*, July 23, 1970.

53. "Payoff to Militants Alleged in Glenville Riot Suit," *Cleveland Plain Dealer*, April 29, 1977.

54. "NOW! Case Dismissed; Appeal Due," *Cleveland Plain Dealer*, May 19, 1977.

55. "Violence on Court Steps," *Cleveland Plain Dealer*, May 29, 1969.

56. "Willie Mae, Followers Post Bail," *Cleveland Plain Dealer*, June 25, 1969.

57. "Robert F. Williams, 71, Civil Rights Leader and Revolutionary," *New York Times*, October 19, 1996.

58. Christian Davenport, *How Social Movements Die, Repression and Demobilization of the Republic of New Africa* (New York: Cambridge University Press, 2015), 272–95.

59. Maxwell C. Stanford, "Revolutionary Action Movement (RAM): A Case Study of an Urban Revolutionary Movement in Western Capitalist Society" (master's thesis, Atlanta University, May 1986), 68.

60. Ahmed Evans testimony, Donald Trial, 2025–80.

61. "Chicago Divided Over Proposal to Honor a Slain Black Panther," *New York Times*, March 5, 2006.

62. Katrina Hazzard, personal communication, April 18, 2017.

Chapter 29: "To Strive, to Seek, to Find, and Not to Yield"

1. Richard Nixon, "Richard Nixon Address Accepting the Presidential Nomination at the Republican National Convention in Miami Beach, Florida,"August 8, 1968, The American Presidency Project, www.presidency.ucsb.edu/ws/?pid=25968.

2. "Five Dallas Officers Were Killed as Payback, Police Chief Says," *New York Times*, July 8, 2016.

3. "Donald Trump 2016 RNC Draft Speech Transcript," *Politico*, July 21, 2016, www.politico.com/story/2016/07/full-transcript-donald-trump-nomination-acceptance-speech-at-rnc-225974.

4. "It's Donald Trump's Convention. But the Inspiration? Nixon," *New York Times*, July 18, 2016.

5. "Cleveland Officer Will Not Face Charges in Tamir Rice Shooting Death," *New York Times*, December 28, 2015.

6. "Attorney General Jeff Sessions ordered Justice Department officials to review reform agreements with troubled police forces nationwide, saying it was necessary to ensure these pacts do not work against the Trump administration's goals of promoting officer safety and morale while fighting violent crime," the *Washington Post* reported on April 3, 2017 ("Sessions Orders Justice Department to Review All Police Reform Agreements").

7. "There Is No Justice in America for Black People Killed by Cops," *Huffington Post*, June 16, 2017.

8. James Robenalt, *January 1973: Watergate, Roe v. Wade, Vietnam, and the Month That Changed America Forever* (Chicago: Chicago Review Press, 2015), 299–308.

9. "Everything You Need to Know About the War on Poverty," *Washington Post*, January 8, 2014.

10. Carl B. Stokes, *Promises of Power, A Political Autobiography* (New York: Simon & Schuster, 1973), 223.

11. "Ahmed Evans Dies," *Cleveland Plain Dealer*, February 27, 1978.

12. Mutawaf Shaheed, interview, May 17, 2017.

13. Report of the National Advisory Commission on Civil Disorders, Summary Report.

14. "Read President Obama's Open Letter to America's Police Officers," *Fortune*, July 19, 2016.

Afterword

1. Salzman and West, eds., *Struggles in the Promised Land: Towards a History of Black–Jewish Relations in the United States* (New York, Oxford University Press, 1997), 117.

2. Ibid., 108.

3. Shaul Magid, "Zionism, Pan-Africanism, and White Nationalism," *Tablet*, December 12, 2018.

4. "Zilsel Identifies with Minority," *Cleveland Plain Dealer*, June 10, 1969.

5. Louis Masotti and Jerome R. Corsi, *Shoot-Out in Cleveland: A Report Submitted to the National Commission on the Causes and Prevention of Violence* (Washington, D. C., Government Printing Office, 1969), xxv.

6. National Archives, Federal Bureau of Investigation Files, Fred Allen Evans, Bureau File 157–897, Fred Ahmed Evans, Racial Matter, Memo from SAC, Cleveland, to Director, FBI, May 15, 1969.

7. "Roger Stone trial evidence reveals fresh detail about Trump campaign's interest in WikiLeaks," *Washington Post*, November 14, 2019.

8. Ibid.

Index

Page numbers in *italics* refer to photographs and captions.